GW01402980

NOBLE
GOVERNMENT

Victor L. Stater

Noble Government

The Stuart Lord Lieutenancy

and the Transformation

of English Politics

The University of Georgia Press
ATHENS AND LONDON

© 1994 by the University of Georgia Press
Athens, Georgia 30602
All rights reserved
Designed by Louise OFarrell
Set in 11/13 Garamond #3 by Tseng Information Systems, Inc.
Printed and bound by Thomson-Shore, Inc.
The paper in this book meets the guidelines for permanence
and durability of the Committee on Production
Guidelines for Book Longevity of the Council on
Library Resources.

Printed in the United States of America

98 97 96 95 94   C   5 4 3 2 1

Library of Congress Cataloging in Publication Data
Stater, Victor Louis, 1959–
Noble government : the Stuart lord lieutenancy and the
transformation of English politics / Victor L. Stater.
        p.   cm.
Includes bibliographical references and index.
ISBN 0–8203–1613–X (alk. paper)
1. Great Britain—Politics and government—1603–1714.
2. Central-local relations—Great Britain—History
—17th century.   I. Title.
JN191.S73   1994
942.06—dc20
93–28208
CIP

British Library Cataloging in Publication data available

For Sue

CONTENTS

PREFACE
ix

INTRODUCTION
1

CHAPTER I
The Early Stuart Lieutenancy
8

CHAPTER II
War and the End of the Old Regime
32

CHAPTER III
Restoration, 1660–1663
66

CHAPTER IV
Internal Security, 1660–1674
95

CHAPTER V
Politics and Rebellion, 1660–1685
122

CHAPTER VI
Revolution: The Deposition of James II
161

CONTENTS

CONCLUSION
183

NOTES
193

BIBLIOGRAPHY
233

INDEX
255

PREFACE

THIS BOOK BEGAN its wayward career longer ago than I care to think, stimulated by an offhand comment made by Mark Kishlansky. "What about deputy lieutenants?" he asked, and thus unknowingly launched a project that demanded far more of his time and energies than he could have dreamed possible from such a casual statement. My own time has likewise been spent in the pursuit of those far-off gentlemen, and despite the inevitable trials of research and writing, it has all been worth it.

Writing a book is an individual experience, but it is by no means lonely work. This project has offered the excuse for countless convivial evenings and been the agency of a series of lasting friendships. Friends and colleagues on both sides of the Atlantic have allowed me to ramble on about lords lieutenant most unpardonably; this manuscript is the better for their forbearance. Thanks for their hospitality and goodwill are due to many: Sabrina Alcorn Baron, Tom Cogswell, Patricia Croot, Peter Earle, John Fielding, Anne Hyde, David Hebb, Chris Kimball, Peter Lake, John Morrill, Ed Muir, Paul Paskoff, Meredith Veldman, and Tim Wales, to name only a few. As a mentor, Mark Kishlansky went well beyond the call of duty and has been a model of the species.

The archivists and staffs of many libraries deserve a great deal of credit for their assistance and toleration for an inexperienced researcher—the British Library, Public Record Office, Institute of Historical Research, Bodleian Library, and the county and city record offices in Norfolk, Northampton, Derbyshire, Cheshire, Lancashire, and Lincolnshire. I would like to express special thanks to the Marquis Townshend for allowing me to inspect documents in his possession.

Above all, I thank my family, who despite endless provocations, have put up with my apparently obscure and obsessive historical interests for years now. An author could hardly wish for more. No words can express my debt to my wife, Sue, who has always been my best editor and critic. The infelicities of style and errors of fact that remain owe everything to my own pig-headedness and so much of what is worthy in this book to her good sense that settling accounts between us would be impossible.

Writing in the mid-seventeenth century, Anne Bradstreet, well aware of her own deficiencies as a writer, wrote a poem, "The Author to Her Book," to accompany a collection of her own verse, a "rambling brat" for whose ultimate fate she was more than a little concerned. I share her diffidence but am secure in the knowledge that the experience of researching and writing this book, and the friendships that have grown around it, have made the risk one worth taking.

Introduction

THE POLITICAL HISTORY of Stuart England has always been dominated by the dramatic events of the mid-century: political turmoil, civil wars, regicide. Yet riveting though these years of crisis are, they have often made a thorough understanding of English political evolution impossible. Dazzled by the sight of Roundhead and Royalist armies as they joined battle, or carried away by the rhetoric of a Cromwell or Winstanley, many historians have allowed broader patterns of change to escape their view.

No one would assert that the civil wars and interregnum were experiences unworthy of study, yet our preoccupation with locating origins and assessing results has allowed us to overlook larger processes of political change occurring over the course of the seventeenth century. Symptomatic of a political and social world under enormous pressure, the civil wars did not provide a clear solution to England's political problems, nor did they permanently sweep away an older sociopolitical structure imbued with the values and convictions of the old regime.

Looking across the divide that separates Charles I and Charles II, then, may make it easier to understand the passing of a traditional political order and the creation of a new one. The old order in fact survived the Restoration; championed by an older generation of statesmen such as the earl of Clarendon and Lord Treasurer Southampton, it staggered on, battered but still animate. The pressures that had overwhelmed it in the 1640s were still present—indeed, they had grown more intense. Avoiding another bout of chaos seemed less and less likely as Charles II aged, but without realizing it a younger generation found a cure for the old illness: the single-party state.

The Restoration, bawdy and colorful though it may have been, has until recently often been treated as a mere curiosity. The bedroom antics of Samuel Pepys and Nell Gwynn loom far larger than the serious business of a political system in the throes of a radical transformation.[1] That is, to some degree, as it should be; the marvelously detailed pictures left by Pepys, John Evelyn, Celia Fiennes, and others are part of the fascination of the age.[2] The images of Peter the Great and his "right nasty" entourage merrily demolishing Evelyn's beloved Sayes Court, or of Pepys racing through a flaming London with a coachload of the perquisites of office capture the popular imagination in a way that political and institutional histories will never equal.[3]

Though impressive in their force, however, popular images of the Restoration have perhaps obscured the deeper, transformative significance of the period. The civil wars and interregnum unleashed political and social forces that transformed England, but the settlement that followed the return of the Stuart dynasty did nothing to resolve the problems posed by the mid-century conflict. Most important, the ambiguity surrounding the power of the crown and the treatment of religious and political dissent continued. Unnoticed by most historians until quite recently, the Restoration stands out as the period in which a new constitution was fashioned. Stuart historians such as Mark Kishlansky have shown how the essentially medieval political system that stressed stability and consensus in the early seventeenth century was replaced by something else during this era: a system dominated by political choice and a grudging acceptance of ideological divisions.[4] Other historians, even those who question Kishlansky's conclusions, have added substance to the view that the Restoration, so long in the shadows, marks an important turning point in English history. Recent biographers of Charles II have rescued that most interesting of kings from his former characterization as the most frivolous, and detailed studies of the Restoration and its makers reveal a process of fundamental change.[5]

The history of the Stuart lord lieutenancy illustrates the striking political changes that occurred under the dynasty. Chapters 1 and 2 of this book will provide a brief overview of the prewar lieutenancy, in an attempt to illuminate the social and political changes wrought by the war. Beginning the seventeenth century as an institution of remarkably old-fashioned ways, it became a vital component of the new order.[6] Lords lieutenant were first appointed by Edward VI to ensure the loyalty of the provinces, but by 1603 the lords lieutenant and their deputies had become an integral part of the constitution.[7] The lieutenant's responsibilities were wide: the militia, some tax collection, formal and informal mediation between center and locality, all fell within his purview. Lords lieutenant were chosen by virtue of their rank and standing within their shires, and they in turn chose their deputies (without interference from the crown) by the same criteria. A lieutenancy provided its holder with immense prestige and social power within his own community. These socially determined criteria persisted down to the outbreak of the civil wars, when, like the rest of the political system of which it was a part, the lieutenancy collapsed, unable to cope with the passions engendered by the divisions of the age. Though the extent of consensus in the prewar period remains controversial among historians, the destruction of the early Stuart lieutenancy offers an object lesson in the consequences of irreconcilable differences in the early modern political world.[8] The lieutenancy's fall came only after direct association with Charles I's unpopular policies undermined the gentry's support for the institution, both within and without.

Like the monarchy itself, the lieutenancy endured a long, humiliating spell in the wilderness. Most of its members were Royalists, and the institution was abolished in the wake of Charles I's execution. Yet, like the quasi-monarchy created for Oliver Cromwell in the Protectorate, the lieutenancy too had its analogue in the interregnum: the major generals.[9] The replication proved to be unpopular: outsiders imposed upon local communities could not function in the same manner as had their noble predecessors. Unlike the old lieutenancy, which had always enjoyed a certain popularity, the major generals were execrated from the beginning. Their creation, however, illustrates the continuing need for an institution that combined the central and the local.

Charles II's triumphant return to England was accompanied by a restored lieutenancy, and the 1660s and 1670s saw the slow elaboration of an entirely new spirit in government.[10] Although the old forms were recreated—lords lieutenant were quickly appointed, with the same powers their predecessors enjoyed—the substance of the institution had changed. New men, with new ideas about politics and very different life experience, arrived on the scene. Consensus, social obligation, and provincialism persisted into the 1660s but could not withstand the increasing pressures for political change. Provincialism waned as the importance of Westminster grew, and reward for political fidelity became more important than mere social standing.[11] The decisive shift came as a result of the Exclusion Crisis, when the lieutenancy was not only transformed but also played a vital transformative role in English politics. Jonathan Scott has argued that the Exclusion Crisis has received too much attention from historians determined to explain the eighteenth-century constitution and puts it firmly within a wider context, the "Restoration Crisis." The continuing political instability of the Stuart regime from 1603 to 1688 is self-evident, and Scott is correct to link the events of 1679–81 to earlier crises. This should not, however, obscure the point that the struggle over Exclusion was a catalyst for dramatic political change.[12] Lieutenants devised political tactics, employed propaganda, and enforced the hegemony of the anti-Exclusionists. Not merely one institution among many, the lieutenancy encapsulated the great political sea change of the Restoration.[13]

The subject of the relationship between central authority and local communities has long been the focus of tremendous historiographical energy. Yet if numerous county studies of the Restoration era have provided many details of central-local relations, few historians have attempted broader syntheses that treat the issue as a whole.[14] The later seventeenth century saw a shift in the political and social center of gravity from the provincial to the cosmopolitan; Squire Western had become an anachronism even before Henry Fielding invented him. The new importance of metropolitan concerns and the decline of provincialism stand out with great clarity in the lieutenancy, which, unique among English political institutions, represented both central authority and local community. By the 1670s and 1680s the time when a lord lieutenant could be counted on to defend the interests of his country neighbors against an intrusive central government was long past. Militia obligations were enforced with increased rigor, political conformity enforced with more zeal, and religious dissent persecuted with little regard for local social standing. Although this growing sensitivity to the center's demands is evident in other areas—the bench, for example—nowhere was it more evident than in the lieutenancy.[15] Indeed, lieutenants played a key role in selecting and purging magistrates after 1679. This altered center of gravity pulled the entire political nation inexorably toward London and Westminster. The lieutenancy, as the only institution that still straddled the line between capital and province, offers dramatic confirmation of this changed balance.

The Restoration was a critical period in English history, and the lieutenancy reflects—and created, in some respects—a new world. Changing political values and a new balance between central and local authority are obvious changes that many historians have noted.[16] One area, however, to which few historians have devoted much attention is the phenomenon of loyalism in the later Stuart period. Sir Keith Feiling's *History of the Tory Party* (Oxford, 1924) provides an overview of the strong attachment Englishmen felt for their church and king following the civil wars, but the lion's share of the attention has gone to those on the other end of the spectrum: radicals who espoused Exclusion, republicanism, religious upheaval, or all three. Christopher Hill's memorable description of "a world turned upside down" and his studies of radicals after the Restoration have kept the historical spotlight upon these fascinating characters.[17] The lives of visionaries and nonconformists who struggled against monarchy and prelacy have been examined in some detail, and their ability to capture the imagination of their contemporaries has also exerted effects on modern historians.[18] Often underrepresented in these accounts of the forces of nonconformity is the amazing power and resilience of loyalism, as well as its paradoxical existence independent of the crown.[19] I hope in this study of the lieutenancy to begin to redress the balance.

Loyalism was not manifested merely through devotion to the person of the monarch; both Charles II and James II earned more than their share of opprobrium from the most "loyal" gentlemen. "Loyalism" was a constellation of beliefs in which the monarchy and the Church of England were the fixed stars. It combined elements of prewar divine right theory with a horror of religious dissent and social disorder born of the civil wars.[20] The principles of loyalism demanded rigid adherence, but it was a set of beliefs with enormous potential power. Charles II, the shrewdest of the Stuart kings, recognized the latent force of loyalism and used it with devastating effect against the threat of Exclusion. Loyalism provided the foundation for what became in the 1670s and 1680s J. C. D. Clark's celebrated "ancien régime"; it is no accident that Robert Filmer's *Patriarcha* was first published in 1681.[21] And yet loyalism cannot simply be equated with the standard Whig/Tory divide. James II's overthrow—in which the lieutenancy, that supposed Tory bastion, played a key role—came not as a triumph of the Whigs but as the ultimate assertion of loyalist principles: a defense of church and king against the monarch himself. Recent studies of the politics of this period have shown that much of the pressure for an Anglican monopoly originated in the provinces, and a study of the lieutenancy during the Restoration supports this argument.[22] As will be seen in Chapters 4 and 5, Charles II, initially reluctant to pursue the loyalist hard line, came to adopt it. James II's principal error, Chapter 6 will argue, was his failure to understand the power of loyalism and its unshakable Anglicanism.[23]

The lieutenancy was at the center of loyalist thought and action, and its part in the Glorious Revolution belies the common historiographical reliance upon the categories of party ideology. Lords lieutenant were Tories, but they assisted in the overthrow of James II. "Whig" and "Tory" were indeed terms in common use among contemporaries, and yet their continued use in later reigns has endowed them with a freight of baggage that obscures as much as it illuminates. The widespread support William of Orange enjoyed in 1688–89 came because, whatever his true intentions, he appealed to the strongest political forces in the kingdom: supporters of church and king. James II, ironically, had proven himself no friend to either, and, no less than Shaftesbury and Monmouth, he had to be removed.[24]

The political role of aristocratic lords lieutenant changed dramatically after the Restoration, and so did their social role. The lieutenancy, with its great prestige and political power, was an engine of aristocratic revival.[25] Before the civil wars, social standing was the chief prerequisite for political power: a noble became a lieutenant because of his ancestry. After the Restoration, however, the possession of political interest often created social standing. A lieutenant, appointed for straightforwardly political reasons, might lack some of the traditional attributes of his prewar predecessors: high rank, ancient lineage, close local connections. But such deficiencies were mitigated by the fact that the lord lieutenant controlled the most coveted marks of royal favor at the local level: he was permitted to appoint deputy lieutenants and magistrates. Political hegemony now conveyed social dominance rather than the reverse, as was the case before the 1640s; gentlemen courted the favor of their lieutenants for a share of honors which in earlier times would have been conferred as a matter of course. The nature of social relations in the provinces had changed, and the foundation of elite status was being recreated; the aristocratic oligarchy of the eighteenth century was fabricated through the skilled use of just such political tools as the lieutenancy.[26]

The Stuart lord lieutenancy assisted at the birth of a new political order in which dissent and interest outweighed consensus and social standing. Lieutenants personified the loyalist ancien régime that dominated English politics for generations to come; they helped to elaborate a new social order in which a cosmopolitan aristocracy, centered in the luxurious new squares in London's west end, exercised a profound social influence on provincial society.

Today lords lieutenant have been shorn of nearly every substantive power wielded by their predecessors; greeting royals at airports and sponsoring charity events are now their main duties. Yet though the glory days of the institution have passed, the work of long-dead lords lieutenant—aristocrats whose memory often survives only in the titles of their descendants—was vital in England's passage from the medieval past to the modern world.

CHAPTER I

The Early
Stuart Lieutenancy

ON APRIL 24, 1607, HENRY HASTINGS, fifth earl of Huntingdon, came of age. Less than two weeks later he was commissioned lord lieutenant of Leicestershire, the third successive Hastings to hold the office. Such quasi-hereditary descent was common in the pre–civil war lieutenancy, the most prestigious and potentially the most powerful local office in the crown's gift, and Huntingdon probably accepted the post as his due. It was crucial to his social and political position in his community. But even if he felt entitled to the lieutenancy, his appointment must have been a relief, for the post was vital to his standing in the county.

Raised in the stern Puritanism of his forebears, Huntingdon was a formidable presence. He combined the vigor of youth with the self-assurance of ancient lineage, though his haughty behavior created enemies.[1] The earl headed Leicestershire's most noble and respected family, resident in the county since at least the reign of Edward I. In the 1460s the first Lord Hastings dominated the county from Ashby-de-la-Zouche, one of the strongest castles in the midlands. The fortress symbolized the power wielded by the Hastings family for generations to come.[2] Although the dramatic death of the first Lord Hastings at the hands of Richard III threatened the family's high standing, the family flourished in the sixteenth century. Henry VIII rewarded them with an earldom in 1529, and the third earl served as Elizabeth I's president in the north for over twenty years. By the time of the fifth earl's succession to the title in 1604, the leadership of the county had rested securely in the hands of the Hastings family for 140 years.[3]

Despite the long predominance of the Huntingdons in Leicestershire, the fifth earl faced extremely difficult circumstances and had to struggle to maintain his position. Inflation, poor management, and royal service had ravaged the earl's estate. The worst damage had been done by the third earl: from the 1560s until his death in 1597 he sold no less than £100,000 worth of land and saddled what remained with heavy debts. Settling those debts was not easy, and many of the third earl's obligations were still being met in the 1630s through the enforced sale of family property.[4]

By the early seventeenth century the house of Hastings was in serious trouble, and Huntingdon was forced to use any means available to forestall the decline of his family's fortunes. His salvage operation depended heavily on the unsalaried position he received at age twenty-one. Unlike one of the many lucrative monopolies routinely distributed to others at court, Huntingdon's lord lieutenancy was to recompense its holder in a coin more valuable than mere gold: he received "worship."[5] Lords lieutenant possessed the king's particular favor; they were the peers whom the monarch trusted above all others during periods of civil or military disorder. A lieutenancy ratified a noble's position as leader of the local community, and for a peer like Huntingdon, besieged by debt and doubt, this status was invaluable. The lieutenancy was especially important to the fifth earl for, unlike many of his predecessors, who had been loaded down with offices and grants from the crown, the lieutenancy was his only tangible connection to the court.[6]

Huntingdon used the one position he had skillfully, manipulating the wide patronage inherent in the office and maximizing its potential as a setting for political and social theater, always with the aim of bolstering the standing of his house. The interests of the crown were assigned a secondary role in the earl's calculations. From the start of his tenure, Huntingdon made his priorities clear. In June 1607, after less than a month in office, widespread antienclosure riots flared throughout the midlands. The Privy Council frantically demanded exemplary executions, but instead of hanging the rioters his troopers captured, the earl publicly demonstrated his mercy. He had "two or three" of the rioters brought before him with halters about their necks and, "finding them penitent for their fault . . . I thought it fit to spare their execution for that time."[7] Huntingdon's act of mercy was obviously calculated to burnish his own image, and he was quite prepared to ignore the demands of king and council if they threatened his popularity.

Such moments of high drama were rare before the civil wars; Huntingdon usually had to make do with less exciting demonstrations of his power. Nevertheless, the earl showed a considerable talent for social stagecraft. He transformed the ordinary annual musters of the Leicestershire trained bands into a colorful event that reaffirmed his preeminence in the local community. The musters brought together about a thousand citizen-soldiers representing every hundred and parish and every social group in the shire, from the laborers who served as infantrymen to the gentlemen enrolled in the cavalry.[8] Huntingdon presided at the muster as lord lieutenant—the only time a regular assembly of the entire county took place apart from the assizes. Unlike the assizes, however, in which the king's judges from Westminster sat on a dais and judged the local community, the musters were all-provincial affairs. Led by local gentlemen, militiamen served with their neighbors; above them all, the focus of the occasion's attention, was the lord lieutenant.

Huntingdon knew the importance of the event for his own standing and spared no effort to direct the county's attention to himself. The ceremonial of the muster began when the earl emerged from his tent, a gorgeous silk affair adorned with the royal arms. From there, under the banners of the county waving in the late summer breeze, Huntingdon watched as his soldiers passed before him in review. It was a moment laden with political and social symbolism, when the county paid obeisance to its chief, the leader of the shire. The troops practiced with their weapons and drilled for the lieutenant's inspection, and even this most practical and often tedious of the soldier's duties confirmed Huntingdon's standing. He publicly awarded colors, prizes for marksmanship, and ribbons to his men, illustrating the care and benevolence of his leadership. The most important gentlemen of the shire, the militia officers and deputy lieutenants, assisted as the earl's acolytes. They too were rewarded with signs of the lieutenant's favor: they dined in state with him in his tent and received other tokens of his esteem. The Leicestershire militia accounts for 1626, for example, note the expenditure of more than five pounds for hats, gloves, feathers, and "silver little things" that probably went to the deputy lieutenants.[9]

After two or three days of military showmanship, the lieutenant's tent was stored away, the banners furled, and the trained bands sent home for another year. His moment of glory over for the moment and his status as the county's leading figure reaffirmed, Huntingdon returned home to face the bleak reality of unpaid debts and falling rents. But Huntingdon had demonstrated his power and worth by adroitly exploiting the symbolic potential, not to mention the public funds, available to the lord lieutenant. Huntingdon had not needed to dip into his own depleted coffers; the trappings with which the lieutenant magnified his role were all paid for with rates provided by militiamen. From the earl's tent down to the ribbons given to common soldiers, all of the money came from the county treasury.[10]

Huntingdon's lieutenancy supported the Hastings's interest in early Stuart Leicestershire. The office put Huntingdon at the center of local politics and enabled him to use his influence to seat his clients—many of whom were deputy lieutenants—in the Commons and make himself indispensable as a mediator in local affairs.[11] He intervened in quarrels among the Leicestershire gentry and used his office as his warrant to maintain the peace—"in regard his majesty hath placed me his lieutenant of this county."[12] Moreover, while all of these activities worked to confirm Huntingdon as the linchpin of local political and social life, they also served the interests of the central state, which was anxious to maintain order and stability in the county but lacked direct control in provincial affairs. The two were in fact mutually supportive—a stable local community was also in the interests of the monarchy.

THE EARL OF HUNTINGDON might be considered an exemplar of the lord lieutenant of the early Stuart period. His official duties were laid out by the crown: to defend public order, to represent the crown's interests in the provinces, and to carry out the orders of the Privy Council. The lieutenancy, however, was much less bound to the center than to the provinces. Lieutenants were primarily concerned with the perpetuation of their families' influence, the maintenance of stability within the shire, and the pursuit of local interests at court. The lieutenancy formed part of a distinctly local power structure in which a provincial hierarchy, headed by the lord lieutenant himself, worked to preserve a traditional system of political and social values that emphasized autonomy and stability.

The institution of the lord lieutenancy was founded by the Tudors, and by the early seventeenth century noble lords lieutenant were firmly established in every county.[13] The crown relied on the peerage to serve as lords lieutenant, reflecting the aristocracy's preeminent position in the local community. Commoners had sometimes been appointed lieutenants in the sixteenth century, but under the Stuarts the lieutenancy became an exclusively aristocratic preserve.[14] According to James I, the peers were "yet over far first in greatness and power, either to do good or evil, as they are inclined." A wise king took advantage of the influence of local aristocrats: "They must," wrote James, "be your arms and the executors of your laws."[15] The king's theoretical freedom of choice when appointing lieutenants was in fact quite limited. As was true for officeholders throughout the realm, the commissions of lieutenancy issued by King James were void upon his demise, but Charles I made no attempt to alter the new commissions at his accession. He confirmed all incumbent lieutenants in their places and added two peers to joint lieutenancies—the earl of Warwick in Essex and Lord Wentworth in Bedfordshire. The king named one other, Lord Conway, to the vacant lieutenancy of Hampshire. The heavily aristocratic and politically untouchable lieutenancy was a royal acknowledgment of the peerage's continued dominance in early Stuart provincial society.

By the time of James I's death in April 1625, the lieutenancy had become fully integrated into the fabric of society. James's reign had been peaceful, and lieutenants and deputy lieutenants had been accorded exceptional authority and prestige for very little effort. Musters were held only sporadically, and except for the campaign of 1624, no large armies were raised in England.[16] James's determination to remain at peace allowed him to avoid the problems that came with the provisioning of troops, and in the absence of commands from the center, the lieutenancy's provincial orientation grew more pronounced. By the 1620s, the lieutenancy was a profoundly localist institution. Lords lieutenant and, even more, their deputies, saw themselves as part of a locally oriented political and social order. The crown's benign neglect allowed the lieutenancy to flourish as a legitimate and respected part of provincial society.

Every English county, singly or joined with a neighbor, had its lieutenant.[17] Who, then, were these lord lieutenants? An examination of the lieutenants who served under Charles I illuminates the nature of the office. Of the men confirmed in their places in 1625, the great majority were appointed by James I. Only two Elizabethan lieutenants survived: Viscount Wallingford, the dean of the lieutenancy, had served as lieutenant of Berkshire and Oxfordshire since 1596; following him in seniority was the earl of Worcester, lieutenant of the Welsh marches since 1602.[18] The frailty of human life accounted for the rarity of such long tenures; an appointment as a lord lieutenant was generally held for life. Age or ability usually mattered less than lineage and local standing; Wallingford and the earl of

Sussex in Essex, for example, were old and rarely active in their offices, yet they remained in place. Lieutenants were appointed as soon as they reached their majority (as was Huntingdon), and, at times, "place holders" were commissioned to warm the seat of a young noble not yet of age.[19]

One factor in Charles's failure to make many new appointments in 1625 was the limited number of appropriate candidates; the pool of possible lieutenants was small, and the grip of the peerage—and more specifically certain powerful noble families—on the lieutenancy had become very tight. Despite the relatively brief history of the institution, lieutenancies already ran in families. In the case of Lancashire, for instance, Stanley had followed Stanley for three generations; the same held true for the Greys in Bedfordshire and the Hastingses in Leicestershire. Three successive earls of Devonshire served in Derbyshire, as did three earls of Suffolk in Suffolk. Competition for lieutenancies was virtually unheard-of; candidates acceded to their office as they did to their titles as a matter of course. Fathers and sons were commonly named joint lieutenants, as for example the earls of Derby and Arundel with their heirs, Lords Strange and Maltravers. Though the principle was never explicitly acknowledged by the crown, the tendency toward a hereditary lieutenancy was very strong. In practice, when a family had clear dominance within a shire the custom was rarely broken—the Stanleys, for instance, continued to hold the lieutenancy of Cheshire despite the presence of other, more influential candidates even after the Restoration, when competition for the office was fierce.[20]

The crown determined a candidate's suitability using standards defined by social position and lineage: in this era there were no ideological tests for the candidates, as there would be after 1660. Lieutenants had to be the leaders of their shires, for their utility depended on their ability to retain the respect and deference of the gentry; the lieutenants needed to be of sufficient standing to bring together all local factions. Thus the most important quality a lord lieutenant could possess was his membership in a powerful local family. As in the case of Henry Hastings, scions of old and respectable noble houses were often selected on the basis of their lineage alone.

The overwhelming majority of the king's lieutenants were not merely peers but were descendants of England's most venerable noble stock. All but five of the sixty-four men who served as lords lieutenant from 1625 to 1642 were secular peers. Three of those five were successive bishops of Durham, who represented the last of the ancient tradition of the warrior-bishops in England. Another, the first Viscount Savile, was an Irish peer who held his lieutenancy in Yorkshire for a mere two and a half months in

1641. The only unadulterated commoner to hold the office was Sir Thomas Jermyn, the joint lieutenant of Suffolk during the crisis of 1641–42. Older noble families dominated the lieutenancy; a relatively high proportion of them possessed titles that dated back to before the Stuart accession. About one-third of the lieutenants came from such families, and among those elevated after 1603 (like the Cecil earls of Salisbury and the Knollys earls of Banbury), many had been very prominent in the previous reign. This trend persisted despite the huge growth in the peerage initiated by the openhandedness of James I.[21]

Lords lieutenant were not only from ancient noble families; they were most often from the upper reaches of the peerage. Excluding the bishops and two commoners, during King Charles's reign there were two ducal lieutenants (Buckingham and Lennox), one marquess (Hertford), and no less than forty-nine earls. Of the rest, there were two viscounts (not including Savile) and five barons. Interestingly, nearly all of the men of lesser rank to be appointed received their commissions between 1640 and 1642, when the lieutenancy faced its greatest challenge and the king searched frantically for political support among the peerage.[22]

The high rank of lords lieutenant reflects an important social aspect of the office. Buckingham, Lennox, and Hertford were the highest-ranking members of the English nobility, and they all held lieutenancies in two or more counties. Buckingham held four, Lennox two, and Hertford two. The lieutenancy was a hierarchical institution in a hierarchical society, and the rank of a lord lieutenant was immensely important. He stood at the head of county society and presided over a chain of subordinates ranging from deputy lieutenants with baronetcies and thousands of pounds a year to drummer boys for whom £100 was an unimaginable fortune. He represented the crown in his shire, and the institution he headed was an elaborate and very concrete reconstruction of the social order. The social hierarchy demanded that appointment to high office correspond with the possession of noble rank.[23]

Along with lineage and rank came wealth. Eight of the ten noble families in England with annual rentals of more than about £9,000 provided lords lieutenant. The two families of this group excluded from the lieutenancy were the lords Arundell of Wardour and Craven, who though immensely rich were nevertheless mere barons. A lord lieutenancy required rank as well as wealth, and though both commanded ample fortunes, their baronies were a significant handicap. The Arundells were also staunch Roman Catholics, making them even less attractive candidates. The qualifications of the Cravens were equally suspect: the first lord was a city merchant who secured his title at a cost of £7,000. Commerce and the lieutenancy did not mix. Only twelve of the sixty-four (excluding the bishops of Durham and Sir Thomas Jermyn) had rentals of under £2,199—and four of those, Conway, Cottington, the Westons, and the Richs (earls of Holland), enjoyed substantial income from court office or connections.[24] The rest all had rent rolls assuring them an income of over £2,200 per annum, raising them head and shoulders above most of their gentry neighbors.

In addition to their wealth and high rank, many lieutenants combined their local post with high office at court. Twenty-nine of the sixty-four were privy councillors, and thirty-four held one or more important places at court. Twenty-five were created knights of the garter, a special mark of the king's esteem, and virtually all were knights of the Bath. Relatively few—fourteen—held only minor office (or none) in addition to their lieutenancy.[25] A privy councillor or court official had easy access to the king and could put forth his own or his countrymen's case when necessary. Thus lords lieutenant were well placed to play an informal role as mediator between center and locality; the onerous tasks they sometimes executed on behalf of central government were compensated by convenient proximity to the court. This was an important factor during much of the early Stuart period, when recourse to Parliament was relatively rare and the lieutenancy was the local institution with the closest connections to the Privy Council.[26]

Most of the fourteen peers with no offices belonged to families that were declining in interest and prosperity, such as the Grey earls of Kent, Howard earls of Nottingham, and Ramsay earls of Holderness, or to families who were only beginning their rise. These included the Cavendish earls (and later dukes) of Devonshire, St. Johns, and Mordaunts. The grant of a lieutenancy could be the first solid proof of a noble house's arrival, just as it might be the last refuge of a declining race. For some peers, a lieutenancy was a political apprenticeship, initiating a family into the mysteries of aristocratic governance. The third earl of Devonshire, for example, was appointed lieutenant of Derbyshire on his twenty-first birthday in 1638, marking the beginning of a new political dynasty. The office was the first of Devonshire's real responsibilities and was followed by an active political career after the Restoration.

Qualified by their birth and social standing, the lieutenants needed no formal training. In spite of the martial character of the lieutenancy, the lords lieutenant were not, on the whole, military men. Only thirteen had seen military service. Typically, what passed for soldiering even among this minority was a short stint as a gentleman volunteer for the Protestant cause in the 1610s or 1620s. The first earl of Holland, lieutenant of Middlesex and Berkshire, was typical: he served as a volunteer at the siege of Juliers in 1610 but saw no other action. One of Holland's fellow volunteers at Juliers was Theophilus, second earl of Suffolk. This was Suffolk's first and only campaign. Clearly, neither of these men could bring much soldierly expertise to the lieutenancy.[27] There were, however, at least a few lieutenants with considerable military experience. Lords Conway, Wimbledon, and the first earl of Lindsey had all fought in many Continental engagements.[28] Nevertheless, a lieutenancy required no military experience, and many lieutenants with no campaigning behind them were very interested in military affairs. William Compton, first earl of Northampton, established an artillery ground in Coventry to train the burghers of that city in the arts of war that he himself had never practiced. Few lieutenants failed to appear at musters at least occasionally to review their men; the fashionability of military affairs in the era of the Thirty Years' War ensured this if nothing else did.

Despite the practical limits on the king's powers to choose his lieutenants, he was not wholly impotent. He could, and sometimes did, overturn traditional standards, demonstrating his sometimes careless disregard for old customs—a tendency that wreaked incomparable harm to his image and success as a monarch. Charles I deprived sixteen peers of their office over the course of his reign. All but one was removed in the crisis years between 1627–29 and 1639–41. Four lieutenants incurred the king's wrath in 1626–27 when they obstructed the forced loan.[29] These four, the earls of Kent, Bolingbroke, Warwick, and Essex, forfeited the king's good opinion through their recalcitrance and were dismissed. Charles reinstated all four in 1629 in an attempt to appease an obstreperous Parliament. The king sacrificed five others at the same time—victims of the popular outcry against papists. Even those only suspected of Catholicism suffered. The earls of Worcester, Rutland, Monmouth, and Sunderland were all accused of harboring Catholic opinions, and one other lieutenant, the earl of Sussex, lost his joint lieutenancy of Essex because he quarreled with his newly returned colleague, Warwick.

Another round of dismissals came in the years 1638–41. Three lieutenants, the earls of Suffolk, Pembroke, and Newcastle, were removed from the lieutenancies of Cumberland and Westmorland, Somerset, and Derbyshire. These changes came not as a snub to the lieutenants involved but rather as a reward to the new appointees. All three were already lieutenants in more than one county. In the north, the earl of Arundel and his vigorous heir, Lord Maltravers, replaced Suffolk, while Somerset fell to the earl of Hertford, an immensely rich peer whose support the king needed very badly. Likewise, the earl of Newcastle, already lieutenant of Nottinghamshire, made way in Derbyshire for his cousin the earl of Devonshire, who came of age in 1638. The earl of Strafford, lieutenant of Yorkshire, was one obvious loser in the political struggle of 1641, and two others, Lords Cottington and Savile, were also sacrificed to political exigency.

The changes of 1627–29 were overtly political. The lieutenants who displeased the king over the forced loan temporarily lost their places, and the Catholics in office were abandoned when Charles placated a strongly antipapist Parliament. In both periods of instability, 1627–29 and 1640–42, the king used his control of appointments to the lieutenancy to reward his friends and punish the recalcitrant; such dismissals were unusual and the outcome of political crisis. They represented a failure of the traditional politics of inclusion, provoked uneasiness and outrage in the kingdom at large, and seriously damaged the lieutenancy by undermining its credibility and efficacy. Charles's unprecedented actions pointed the way toward a political style that would flourish a generation later; in the 1620s and 1630s, though, such momentous changes proved counterproductive and typify Charles's tendency to disregard traditional forms when it suited him. The lieutenants sacked for questioning the loan were all taken back, and the desperate alterations of 1641 failed to prevent the ultimate collapse of the king's government. The precedent was not forgotten, however, when the post-Restoration lieutenancy later became as much a political vehicle as a guardian of local interests.

The loss of face inherent in dismissal was keenly felt; such a mark of royal disfavor was extremely damaging, both socially and politically. The earl of Worcester, dismissed from his lieutenancy by Charles in 1629 to satisfy parliamentary demands, was still smarting from the blow seven years later. His heir, Lord Herbert, pleaded with the king for his father's restoration as a sign of royal favor. Worcester, who had served with distinction since 1602, had been humiliated by his loss, which had left him at the mercy of his inferiors: "Many of the country do put daily affronts upon him and his, he being now as they term him, Jack Out of Office."[30]

The reverberations from Worcester's displacement, continuing years after the fact, illustrate how important appointments to lord lieutenancies could be. Similarly, the sacking of Francis Manners, sixth earl of Rutland, as lieutenant of Lincolnshire heralded the rise of the Bertie family there and might also help explain the adherence of the Manners family to Parliament during the civil wars.[31] The replacements of Worcester by Lord Bridgewater and Rutland by the Bertie family were destabilizing, and as the king would discover, the lieutenancy could not function effectively when the local political equilibrium was upset. The removal of these men, popular though it might have been in Westminster, was a blow to the traditional political system that had awarded them their places. The effects would be felt in later years.

The lords who made up the lieutenancy, then, had reached the pinnacle of local society. They were the richest, most powerful, and most respected men in their counties. The places they filled were greatly esteemed as marks of honor. Lords lieutenant attempted to perpetuate their families' hold on their county by including their sons in their office, and their deputies did the same when they could.[32] The lieutenancy reflected the provincial social order: the lords lieutenant presided over an institution that embodied the hierarchy and localism of early Stuart government. Like the king himself, they headed an intricate system of patronage and mutual responsibility that was at the heart of county society.

Every lord lieutenant was enmeshed in the complex web of patronage relationships that characterized English society. Above him stood the king, to whom he was bound by ties of custom, tradition, and law. The peerage's relationship with the crown had evolved from an almost exclusive dependence on military service in the early Middle Ages to an all-encompassing set of duties and obligations, civil and military, by the seventeenth century. In exchange for his privileged status, an aristocrat provided the king with advice, political support, and military and administrative service. Below the lieutenant, his social inferiors—deputy lieutenants, trained band captains, and other official functionaries—were all bound to their patrons through kinship, service, tradition, and self-interest. The exploitation of these ties was symbiotic; patron and client pursued their own interests by advancing those of their allies.

The key to the successful operation of this system of patronage was exchange.[33] Every act of patronage required some return, and every favor performed necessitated further patronage. A patron's act might be a minor one—the award of a trophy for superior marksmanship to a trained band musketeer, for example—or as significant as the appointment of a client as a colonel of foot, a post that carried enormous prestige. Each act required a response, which was to be gauged by the nature of the favor bestowed and the standing of the client. The response of a yeoman to a lord lieutenant's patronage differed greatly from that expected of a deputy lieutenant. Equally, a courtesy such as the gift of a buck from a gentleman's deer park to his lieutenant commanded a different response than some special service such as support in a lawsuit or local feud.

The patronage enjoyed by lords lieutenant was extensive and the exercise of it within their shires of crucial importance. The appointment of deputy lieutenants and officers in the militia was an opportunity for the lieutenant to confer status and confirm his primacy among his neighbors. Though by no means honorific, these places were sought for the prestige and authority they provided their occupants. A deputy lieutenancy or captaincy of a local company of militia was a special sign of the lord lieutenant's favor and, by extension, carried the royal imprimatur.

By far the most important offices at the disposal of a lieutenant were deputy lieutenancies. They were avidly pursued and offered the greatest prestige of all the places in a lord lieutenant's gift. The office evolved during Elizabeth's reign when it became clear that the administrative burdens assigned to the lieutenant were too much for one man (who was sometimes an absentee courtier) to bear.[34] Deputies were initially vetted by the crown, but as time passed, lieutenants gained the authority to name their deputies without interference from Whitehall. James I granted this authority piecemeal and as a special favor to select lieutenants; he never acknowledged the principle that lieutenants should have sole power of appointment. In one of Charles I's very first Privy Council meetings, however, the king conceded to the lords lieutenant the right to appoint their own deputies.[35] This step bolstered the independence of lieutenants, freeing them from the scrutiny of central government and allowing them to use the power of appointment for their own purposes.

Hamon Lestrange, a new Norfolk deputy, illustrated the patron-client relationship when he acknowledged his appointment in 1625, writing the earl of Arundel, "I return to your lordship the due recognition of your honorable affections to have esteemed me worthy of the love and labors you have formerly bestowed to have added me to the number of deputy lieutenants in Norfolk."[36] Although he was no stylist, Lestrange's letter acknowledged a relationship of dependent and patron; in bestowing his commission, Arundel had harnessed the new deputy's interest in his own behalf. The lieutenants in turn could rely on the deputy lieutenant's support in their pursuit of their own interests as well as the king's business. Directly subordinate to the lord lieutenant, the deputies were transformed from potential rivals in the county to dependents.

Social and political alliances with deputies were of importance because of their high standing. Like their masters, deputy lieutenants were most often men of distinguished pedigree. They were also among the wealthiest of local gentlemen. The income of the twelve Worcestershire deputy lieutenants whose 1620s assessments are known average over £1,100 per annum.[37] Deputy lieutenants were eminent men—nearly always justices of the peace and invariably of the quorum. All of the eight Norfolk deputy lieutenants in 1626 were justices of the quorum, and most held very high places on the commission of the peace.[38] Deputy lieutenants belonged to the innermost circle of the provincial gentry; the Cheshire deputies, for example, were drawn from among the same twenty-five families throughout the reigns of James I and Charles I, as were the deputies in Warwickshire.[39]

Typical of the four-hundred-odd deputy lieutenants in office during Charles I's reign was the Lancashire gentleman Sir Cecil Trafford. Born in 1599 and knighted in 1617, Sir Cecil was the scion of one of Lancashire's most important families. The Traffords claimed to have been resident at Trafford, in Salford hundred near Manchester, since the time of King Canute, and the family was certainly present in the area by the early fourteenth century.[40] Generation by generation the Traffords had prospered and built an estate that was second to none in the hundred. Their seat, Trafford Hall, was the largest in Salford with twenty-four hearths, and in his prime Sir Cecil owned some seventeen manors and messuages and "lands in various places."[41] In the subsidy of 1622 (for which he was named a collector), Trafford was charged twice as much as his nearest competitor.[42]

The Traffords had long taken a prominent part in local affairs, appearing as sheriffs of Lancashire eight times from 1557 to 1642.[43] Sir Cecil's father, Sir Edmund, had been high on the quorum of justices, and the son succeeded his father upon his death in 1620. Throughout the 1620s and 1630s Sir Cecil was one of the county's most active magistrates as well as a busy deputy lieutenant. The records of Manchester quarter sessions show that he was a regular attendant on the bench, and those of the lieutenancy reveal a man who fulfilled his responsibilities with vigor.[44]

Typical of his fellow deputy lieutenants in standing and experience, Trafford also offers an illuminating example of the wide connections of the deputies. Deputy lieutenants were not mere country gentlemen. Like the lords lieutenant, they had interests beyond the bounds of their shire— Trafford, for instance, owned land in counties outside of Lancashire (principally in Cheshire). A deputy lieutenancy was one of the means by which a gentleman preserved his interest, cultivated relations with his lieutenant, and maintained contact with the court. Trafford, like many others, could claim extensive connections with the world outside; he was the maternal grandson of Thomas Cecil, first earl of Exeter, after whom he was named, and he married the daughter of Sir Humphrey Davenport, lord chief baron of the exchequer. Combined with the connection to the earl of Derby that a deputy lieutenancy represented, these ties made Trafford a man to be reckoned with, even beyond the local level.[45]

The growing number of such prosperous gentlemen and the desire to confirm their standing through the possession of office led to an important trend over the course of the seventeenth century—the gradual increase in the size of the lieutenancy. Under Elizabeth and in the early years of King James's reign, there were relatively few deputy lieutenants. Their numbers generally ranged from two to five per shire. In 1607 Herefordshire and Shropshire had three deputies each; only a year later, the Shropshire commission contained five.[46] A Book of the Peace made in 1608 lists the deputies of fifteen counties, for a total of sixty-eight.[47] Norfolk also illustrates this tendency. The county made do with three deputies in 1588, but their number grew steadily until there were five in 1605, six in 1615, and eight in 1626.[48] The commission in Somerset expanded from two or three deputy lieutenants in the late sixteenth century to an average of ten by the 1620s and 1630s, and it did the same in Cheshire from 1603 to 1630.[49] This pattern was repeated all over the country, and by 1630 most counties had between five and fifteen deputies.[50]

The burgeoning lieutenancy offers an illustration of social pressures at the local level. Lords lieutenant had an interest in expanding the scope of their patronage, and local gentlemen craved the status conferred by a deputy lieutenancy. A lieutenant could strengthen his house by appointing deputies, and a gentleman with a commission was instantly raised to the inner circle of provincial society. Lieutenants, however, could not devalue their commissions by indiscriminately creating deputies, despite intense pressure from their neighbors to do so. In 1623 the earl of Huntingdon was earnestly petitioned to appoint Lord Grey of Groby to a deputy's post. Aged about twenty-four in 1623, Grey had acquired a reputation as an arrogant and haughty man and was frequently at odds with his neighbors.[51] Despite this, or perhaps because of his local difficulties, Grey wanted to be a deputy lieutenant. Huntingdon resisted Grey's blandishments, but in January 1623 he received a letter from Sir Robert Spencer of neighboring Northamptonshire putting forth Grey's case. Having a noble deputy, Spencer argued, would be an honor. But he then implied a threat: "Next my

good lord consider how justly he may hold himself disgraced to be repudi-
ated and what . . . heart burning disgraces and crossings and . . . factions
raised in the country." If Huntingdon failed to meet Grey's expectations,
Spencer suggested, he would create an enemy who might challenge the
lieutenant's dominance in the shire. Although the lieutenant's patronage
was extensive, it had to be exercised with care.[52]

Deputies occupied the top of the social pyramid, but the lieutenant's
list of clients stretched far beyond this small group of the county's leaders.
Dependent on them were a wide range of officers, mostly connected with
the militia, and a few supernumeraries such as provost marshals. In many
counties, moreover, lords lieutenant exercised an informal role in the selection of justices of the peace and members of Parliament.[53] Though this
authority was not formalized until after the Restoration, the lord lieutenant's position in his county made reference to him in the appointment and
selection of these men natural.[54] Lieutenants were in a position to know
more about the local context of these affairs than were strangers at court.

The foundation upon which the lieutenancy and its patronage rested was
its role in supervising and training the militia. When the kingdom was
at peace, the exercise and upkeep of the trained bands formed a principal
duty of the lieutenancy. The lieutenancy provided the crown's only available military force in case of emergency, and with the collapse of European
peace in 1618, the government felt obliged to maintain at least a minimum level of readiness.[55] The perilous European situation required a more
elaborate infrastructure, and the need for clerks, officers, contractors, and
the like offered a broad scope for patronage. Whatever the quality of this
militia, its increasing size widened the compass of the lieutenancy's already
considerable influence. By 1638, the English trained bands totaled 73,116
foot and 4,835 horse.[56] By administering the trained bands on behalf of the
monarchy, the lord lieutenant and his deputies bolstered their importance
among their neighbors. The sheer size of the militia made it a significant
part of local society.

After the deputy lieutenants, the lieutenants selected captains and colonels of the militia regiments. These appointments were of considerable
importance in the shires, and the ability to name gentlemen to them gave
the lieutenants (and their deputies, who frequently chose the inferior officers) a wide network of semiofficial patronage. The lieutenants had many
places to fill. Even in small counties like Huntingdonshire there were eight
trained band captains to appoint, and as the size of the county grew, so
did the number of officers. Each of Somerset's six regiments had a colonel

and eight company commanders; the lord lieutenant of Norfolk disposed of twenty-nine captaincies, while the lieutenant of Devon had forty-four. Each of these companies also had its own lieutenant and ensign, who were also sometimes named by the lord lieutenant himself.[57]

Regimental commands were genuine plums, and there was never a shortage of gentlemen eager to become militia colonels. So desirable, in fact, were colonelcies, that they were invariably first offered to deputy lieutenants.[58] In the local scheme of things, a place at the head of a regiment was a very high honor. It symbolized the preeminence of a gentleman over his division of the county. On muster days the regimental colonel watched as the rest of his neighbors and tenants paraded by in a demonstration of respect and obedience, duplicating, on a smaller scale, the experience of the lord lieutenant.[59] A commission as a colonel in addition to a deputy lieutenancy signaled that a gentleman had reached the loftiest heights of county society.

Other officers commanding the trained band companies hailed from less exalted society than the deputy lieutenants: usually they were members of the minor or middling gentry or younger sons of the magistracy. There were many slots for junior officers. A typical company of the Norfolk trained bands had three—a captain, lieutenant, and ensign—as well as five noncommissioned officers—a sergeant, three corporals, a lance corporal, a "harbinger," a drummer, and a clerk.[60] Despite their fairly large numbers, a captaincy lifted a gentleman head and shoulders above the crowd of status-hungry neighbors that surrounded him. The deputies of Norfolk described their officers in 1626 as all "very worthy and considerable gentlemen."[61] Junior officers were rarely in short supply; young gentlemen seemed eager to fill the available places.[62] Local men snatched at these posts, despite the often onerous work that came with them.

Bitter infighting could develop over patronage within the lieutenancy because seemingly minor offices were of prodigious importance to gentlemen in the shires. The need for an official ratification of status in a period of rapid social change gave even the lowest officers an advantage in the endless competition for place that characterized provincial gentry life. The command of a mere file of clownish, badly trained rural musketeers might be sufficient to tip the scales in a long-running battle for hegemony in the parish. For the more exalted members of the community, the ability to insert their friends and allies in these places was an important part of patronage and interest building. Gentlemen were eager for the honor and status such places conferred, and the lieutenancy entrenched itself in the shires as an indispensable social arbiter, judging the claims of competing gentlemen, rewarding the pretensions of some, and rebuffing the designs of others.[63]

The lieutenancy's patronage was not confined to grants of office. Maintenance of the trained bands and the county magazines required considerable expense for powder, match, and lead, among other miscellaneous supplies, and more than a few lieutenants were active in procuring these goods. In 1619 the council ordered the lieutenancy to buy specified amounts of powder, match, and other supplies, and the magazines that were then established were maintained through periodic purchases.[64] Although it is far from clear that the counties kept on hand the proper amounts demanded by the council, lord and deputy lieutenants did raise and spend money to keep magazines stocked.[65] The earl of Exeter arranged for powder sales in Northamptonshire, as did the earl of Northampton in his lieutenancies.[66] Moreover, some lieutenants not only laid out the county's money, they spent their own. Lord Conway promised to provide armor and weapons for forty horsemen in Hampshire, at his own charge, and the earl of Newcastle noted that he stocked the magazine in Nottinghamshire on his own credit.[67] In 1627 the deputy lieutenants of Cheshire predicted that an adequately armed trained band would cost £4,000. In 1636 the deputy lieutenants of Middlesex spent £268 on powder and match, and others spent much more.[68] Sums of this size obviously offered considerable scope for lordly patronage on the part of lieutenants, as did the lieutenancy's power to favor (or punish) when taxing the county.[69]

The lieutenancy was of crucial importance to the county community as a dispenser of honor and financial largesse, but it also had duties to perform. Although it was in essence a local institution with local priorities and attitudes, an exchange was implied by the social prominence and power conferred on it by the central government. In return, the crown expected that a passably efficient militia would be maintained. This goal was often little more than a chimera in some counties, but total neglect was very rare.[70]

By the 1620s the importance of proper military training had long been recognized, although in the first decade of James I's rule the dream was more evident than the reality. The council explained in 1603 that "reason and experience teacheth us that men well-trained and armed are the best defense," yet the government rarely pressured the provinces about the state of the militia. It was not until the mid-1620s that the crown—with important consequences—launched a campaign to reform the trained bands.[71]

Throughout most of the 1610s and 1620s, the trained bands' importance was more social and political than military. The militia bound local communities together against the omnipresent danger of faction through patronage and the highly charged symbolism of formal events like the musters. Teaching the finer points of soldiering was not what made the lieutenancy useful.

The annual muster allowed the lieutenancy to exercise its power as well as display its magnificence. A lord lieutenant like Huntingdon could sit in a silken tent amid the fluttering flags of the county and watch his neighbors parade respectfully by. Lieutenants made an effort to be present at musters. Workhorses like Newcastle, Northampton, Derby, and Maltravers attended regularly, but even that resolute courtier the earl of Pembroke could be found reviewing his men in 1629. Even Lord Conway attended musters in Hampshire on several occasions, despite his heavy work load as secretary of state.[72] Like the visits of assize judges, musters were special occasions that reaffirmed the local hierarchy. Lieutenants feasted their deputies and officers, met and socialized with many of the worthy gentlemen and yeomen of the county, and displayed their "good lordship" to the shire. At times this meant reducing the assessment of a client or turning a blind eye to the shoddy equipment that many militiamen brought with them. In 1608, in a typical example of the exchanges that went on constantly between the lieutenancy and the country, Bridget Carre wrote a Rutland deputy lieutenant asking that her tenants be relieved of their obligations.[73] Small favors were the currency of social and political life in the provinces, and the lords lieutenant went out of their way to maintain a positive balance when they could. Militia accounts also contain references to money spent on the entertainment of deputy lieutenants and officers. In some counties good lordship was expressed in the awarding of prizes for the best marksmen. Encouraging militiamen to practice at their arms as well as underscoring the benevolence of the lord lieutenant, these prizes further bound the officers of the lieutenancy to the community. Accounts of militia money spent at musters also note small amounts set aside to provide trained bandsmen with ribbons, feathers, and colors.[74] These bits of finery aided a lieutenant in his quest to satisfy the crown by creating an effective militia, while securing his own local standing by rewarding his neighbors.

Like much of premodern government, the lieutenancy sometimes seemed to lack coherence. Though its primary use was as the guardian of local stability, the social standing of lieutenants made them attractive to central government as executors of a variety of tasks. The lieutenancy's local orientation made it an obvious candidate for a whole series of nonmilitary roles.[75] These duties gradually widened to include virtually all aspects of local government, ranging from vital matters such as the collection of loans for the crown to such petty concerns as the sale of mulberry trees.[76] The gradual increase of the lieutenancy's purview was a reflection of the social and political dominance of the lords lieutenant and their deputies, as well as the ad hoc nature of early Stuart government.

The unrivaled social position held by the lieutenant made him an obvious arbiter in local disputes. In 1606 the earl of Kent, lieutenant of Bedfordshire, mediated a dispute between the bishop of Lincoln and one John Bono of Riseley; in 1613 the earl of Derby ended a dispute between Sir George Beverley and Richard Browne.[77] In 1627 the corporation of Chester asked Lord Derby to adjudicate a dispute between the town clerk and the mayor, "as lord lieutenant of our county." In 1633 Derby was ordered by the Privy Council to sort out a complicated wrangle over milling rights in the River Dee, and in 1629 the lord lieutenant of Northamptonshire, the earl of Exeter, settled a controversy involving navigation rights in local rivers. In 1637 Exeter arbitrated a Ship Money rating dispute—an unpleasant task that fell to several others during these years.[78]

Lords lieutenant took it upon themselves to preserve local harmony by settling disputes among the gentry, outside of "the ordinary course of the law" when possible.[79] Every lord lieutenant strove to preserve social harmony among the gentry. Vexatious lawsuits and even riots could result from such disagreements, and a serious quarrel could destabilize an entire county.[80] The earl of Arundel intervened in 1633 in a quarrel between Robert Garsett and a Mr. Bendish in Norfolk. He ordered one of his deputies, Sir John Hare, to call the two men together, "and hearing the whole business between them, to set a friendly end to the said differences; which if you shall not compose, then I would have you certify me the whole matter and what other circumstances you shall think fit, that thereupon I may take such order as the case and justice shall require." In a postscript, Arundel added, "Further, I require you if there be occasion to command them upon their allegiance to His Majesty not to do anything each against other in a way breaking His Majesty's peace."[81] In a society in which recourse to the duel was quick and often deadly, the exercise of the lieutenant's on-the-spot authority was essential to prevent violence when it threatened.

The search for stability and the lord lieutenant's desire to gratify his neighbors frequently led the lieutenancy into local matters that only tangentially touched its official duties. In 1611 the earl of Rutland attempted to intervene with the Board of Green Cloth in a dispute over purveyance in Leicestershire—to no avail. In 1613, west country merchants persuaded the earl of Bath to testify in their behalf against the damaging privileges granted to the company of the Merchants Trading in France. As lord lieutenant of Devon, the merchants saw Bath as a natural champion of their cause. In 1620, the council ordered the deputy lieutenants of Hertfordshire to consider how the new draperies might be advanced, and in 1637 the lord lieutenant of Essex (the earl of Warwick) conferred with the Merchant Adventurers about the preservation of the cloth trade.[82] In these cases, lords and deputy lieutenants were sought out as knowledgeable local leaders and prestigious patrons. Standing at the head of local society and possessed of an important official connection to the court, they were the obvious choice for such roles.

The crown chose the lieutenancy as its executor for a variety of reasons: its relative compactness and efficiency, its administrative experience, and, most important, its social standing. Nevertheless, any new imposition from Whitehall invariably initiated a complicated process of negotiation and compromise between court and country; in the Jacobean and Caroline state, policy decisions could not be implemented through royal diktat.[83] Policies were best enforced only after provincial concerns about traditional liberties were allayed and an elaborate search for consensus had circumvented potential opposition. The lords lieutenant, assisted by their deputies, were ideally situated to conduct these negotiations. Lieutenants' pleas on behalf of their constituents are as common as their commands to their subordinates; the earl of Exeter, a long-serving lieutenant of Northamptonshire, is a good example. Although he often chided his deputies for their lax efforts (which "I find to be very raw, and not fit for me to present to the Council Board"), he also found himself importuning the Privy Council for favors for his county. Faced with a demand for no less than two thousand pounds of butter for the court in 1613, he tried to put the government off by pleading poverty: Northamptonshire "is still rather decaying than increasing in persons of ability to defray any new charge." The earl suggested that the council find somebody—anybody—else to bear the burden.[84] The earl was providing the crown with a classic political quid pro quo: an honest effort to maintain standards in the trained bands in return for royal favor in the matter of purveyance. As inhabitants of both worlds, the courtly and the provincial, lieutenants such as Exeter could bridge the gap between the two and reconcile local with national interests. The lieutenancy, by virtue of its position at the head of county society, acted as engineer in the work of building compromises; lieutenants, because of their privileged position at court and the leadership of their shires, had in their hands all of the necessary tools for the job. Their task was difficult, and consensus was often more a goal than a reality, but even so, the king and his council looked to the lieutenancy for assistance time and again.

The lieutenancy's easy access to central power also gave it an advantage when pleading the county's case in times of crisis. In 1631, faced with a severe food shortage, the deputies of Sussex appealed to the council to relax its prohibition against the shipment of grain by sea. The regulation prevented export to the Continent, but in the case of Sussex, where a large proportion of the intracounty grain trade was carried by small coastal shippers, it severely disrupted the food supply. Acting as a kind of committee of the bench, the deputies informed the council that if the restriction remained in force, it would cause rather than prevent hardship. In January 1632, the Norfolk deputies, acting in the same capacity as their Sussex brethren, appealed to the earl of Arundel to intercede with the council to relax its orders forcing the release of all grain in store to the markets. They argued that the market would be flooded and that laborers, who generally bought their supplies direct from the farmers, would find it more difficult to get food.[85]

Although riots were comparatively rare during the early Stuart period, food shortages could give rise to civil commotion. The lieutenants' concern for social order ensured their intervention at such moments.[86] Not surprisingly, the lieutenancy was very reluctant to use the full weight of the trained bands to suppress unrest, preferring to mediate local conflict. In June 1628, the council instructed the justices and deputies to investigate reports of disturbances in Woodbridge, Suffolk, and in 1629 the lieutenancy was deeply involved in managing the grain riots that broke out at Malden in Essex.[87] At Malden the lord lieutenant, Warwick, gave a sympathetic hearing to the grievances of the rioters.[88] In some places the lieutenancy galvanized efforts to assist the poor in times of dearth. The poor harvests and trade depression of 1630–31 brought real suffering for many, and the lieutenancy played a decisive role in ensuring order and coordinating relief.[89] In December 1630 the Northamptonshire deputies were discussing means to assist the poor; in March 1631 the deputies in Suffolk spent the county's militia money on grain for the destitute.[90] Similarly, the Surrey lieutenancy collected money in July 1637 that was distributed to the sick in Southwark.[91]

The lieutenancy became involved in the enforcement of policy because of the lord lieutenant's ability to present the wishes of the king and council to a reluctant country in an informed and nuanced way. An effective lord lieutenant, relying on the contacts and prestige of his deputies, could sell an innovation or policy as no one else could. Mediation and compromise were often necessary to secure compliance, as in the regulation of grain markets and the enforcement of the Book of Orders, but a satisfactory conclusion could sometimes be reached.[92] A lieutenant could present a shire's argument at court as well as explain the rationale behind the king's actions in the provinces; in either case he was performing a vital role as a conduit of information and instruction between court and country.

A LORD LIEUTENANT in early Stuart England was a figure of special importance. He stood at the head of his county, both politically and socially. The importance of the lieutenancy lay less in its formal military duties than in its role as a vehicle for maintaining stability in the shire. For the lieutenants themselves, the position strengthened aristocratic dominance, most notably the power of their own families. In county after county, lords lieutenant followed the example of the earl of Huntingdon and used their place as a bulwark for their own local standing. In a world of rapidly rising and falling fortunes, the patronage they exercised drew many of the shire's most influential gentlemen, the parish gentry, and even prosperous yeomen into their orbit. The exercise of such authority, skillfully handled, increased a peer's influence at court, augmented his local position, and secured his house against the onslaughts of the post-Elizabethan age.

Not every lord lieutenant took advantage of the opportunities the office presented; the earl of Sussex, joint lord lieutenant of Essex, for example, rarely attended musters and relied on his deputies to do all of his work. Others were simply incapable; the earl of Banbury, lieutenant of Oxfordshire, was well into his eighties by Charles I's time, and active service was out of the question for him. Such examples do not vitiate the main point, however: a lieutenancy could be an important step forward in the search for social standing and power that dominated the early Stuart period.

That the crown was reluctant to remove such obviously inactive lieutenants as Banbury and Sussex illustrates the importance of the lieutenancy in the context of local politics. Although inactive lieutenants failed to exercise the firm control over the militia that the government wanted, displacing them could destabilize a county. This hesitancy to replace local standing with efficiency is the key to understanding the prewar lieutenancy's primary role—maintaining stability within the local community. Faction and

instability could spark disorder, and memories of the violent feuds and re-
bellions of the Tudor age lingered. Even if not every shire lived in peace and
harmony, a lord lieutenant's goal was to sustain local equilibrium.

In expanding and even improving the militia after Charles I's accession,
the lieutenancy performed a key role in accustoming local communities
to the demands of war on an unprecedented scale. The Thirty Years' War
required a higher level of readiness than ever before, and throughout the
1620s the lieutenancy oversaw a general improvement of the trained bands.
Because of the extensive system of rewards and local connections available
to them, the lords lieutenant could create a more favorable climate for
change than would have been possible through mere royal fiat. Cooperative
gentlemen could be rewarded with captaincies and enthusiastic yeomen
with places as sergeants or clerks. The increasingly rigorous demands of
the crown could be presented with greater ease or, as was frequently the
case, tempered, by local men. The council's occasional outraged rebukes
of deputies for failing to comply with some cherished scheme make this
latter tendency clear. As a persuader or, when necessary, an enforcer who
commanded local respect, a lord or deputy lieutenant had a distinct advantage over an agent of central government with no local connections. Yet
the lieutenancy's utility was not chiefly military, and intrusive centralism
hampered the institution in the pursuit of its main goal: harmony at the
local level.

Paradoxically, the advantage of the lieutenancy's local base limited the
ability of the crown to enforce all of its desires for more efficiency, for
the lieutenancy was a part of the county more than it was of the court.
Deputy lieutenants usually had little desire to coerce their neighbors.[93] The
tendency of lieutenants and their deputies to lenience toward militia defaulters was widespread and limited the crown's ability to enforce change.
The excuses, tepid responses, and outright malfeasance of deputies—and
sometimes even their lords—were not rare phenomena. The exigencies of
the harvest, the poverty of the shires, or the willfulness of underlings were
all pressed into service as excuses time and again, to the Privy Council's
exasperation.[94] The lieutenancy's official, military function often conflicted
with its informal—yet ultimately more important—local role. It dominated many shires by virtue of its ability to co-opt and compromise, but an
oppressive, centrally oriented lieutenancy had nothing to offer the country.
Its dependence on the goodwill of the gentry for the success of its affairs
was to prove the greatest vulnerability of the lieutenancy. The willingness
of the gentry to tolerate the expanding activities of the central govern-

ment was limited, and once those limits had been reached, the lieutenant was caught in a dilemma: his office was derived from a royal grant, yet its importance lay in the local standing the office provided him. Rigorous enforcement of unpopular policies undercut the lieutenancy and it stood to lose much of its effectiveness.[95] Silken tents and silver trinkets could not save the Huntingdons of the 1640s.

CHAPTER II

War and the End of the Old Regime

IF THE LIEUTENANT'S day-to-day tasks gave him a permanent place in the fabric of local society, the outbreak of war threatened both his secure position and his social utility. War tested the stability of the state as nothing else did; in no other enterprise were the tensions between the needs of central government and the hallowed traditions of local autonomy so evident. The state's need to raise larger and more lavishly equipped armies increasingly resulted in higher taxes, and local resistance impelled desperate governments to centralize.[1] The lieutenancy played an important, though very reluctant, part in this process. In the 1620s the military duties of the lieutenancy overshadowed its other responsibilities, and though the lieutenants created a more efficient military organization, they paid a high price for that success. The collection of loans and supplies for the army, the impressment of soldiers and sailors, and the maintenance of order through the use of commissions of martial law were all controversial issues and forced the lieutenancy into an uncomfortable and unfamiliar situation. For the first time, they were required to put the needs of central government ahead of local interests. Torn by divided loyalties, many lords and deputy lieutenants emerged from the political wrangles of the 1620s and 1630s with their stabilizing role in the local community in jeopardy.

The need for money to sustain the war was the most divisive factor in the relationship between country and court. From 1625 to 1628, the English government raised more money than it had for many years, and the shires faced demands for ship money, coat and conduct money, loans, benevolences, subsidies, and charges for billeted soldiers. The lieutenancy acted as both executive agent for the war effort and provincial patron, mediating compromises and attempting to shield the counties from excessive royal demands. The council reduced assessments or allowed forced loan money to be spent locally, but even so, the counties paid much higher military costs than ever before. Complete satisfaction eluded most lieutenants; the costs and inconveniences of the war lay too heavily upon many local communities. The conflict inherent in these duties ensured that the lieutenancy sometimes garnered the ill-will of both the court and the country, and as the crown became ever more importunate and the state of the exchequer ever more parlous, tension grew.

Charles I's foreign adventures dragged the lieutenancy into a series of policies about which its members felt deep ambivalence. Whatever their views on the merits or demerits of the king's war, every lord and deputy lieutenant faced a range of agonizing choices. Wholehearted support for the entire panoply of Charles's policies was rare, particularly among the deputy lieutenants, most of whom heard the complaints and grumbles of their neighbors with more immediacy than did their exalted masters. But simply rejecting the orders of the king and council was impossible. The result was an uneasy compromise that satisfied no one and left the lieutenancy confused, if still viable. The reserve of goodwill built up by the institution over the decades enabled it to survive the stresses of the 1620s remarkably well—at least on the surface. Thanks to the questions raised in the Parliament of 1628 and widespread complaints about the war's burdens, lord and deputy lieutenants welcomed the return of peace with a much greater appreciation of its benefits.

The lieutenancy's need to recover ground lost during the war doomed the king's plan for an "exact militia" from the start. Though some counties did make progress, very few in the lieutenancy were prepared to sacrifice their fragile local standing for such a goal.[2] Avoiding opprobrium was the chief occupation of many, and an officious attitude toward the trained bands was hardly the way to a neighbor's heart. As the 1630s progressed, the lieutenancy continued to be torn between its responsibilities to court and country. It served as a valuable conduit between the provinces and a Parliamentless capital but avoided, whenever it could, being saddled with new duties. The collection of ship money, for example, became a chore for the sheriff, to the vast relief of deputy lieutenants throughout the kingdom. After their poor performance as loan collectors in the 1620s, it is not at all surprising that Charles bypassed the deputies when the ship money writs went out. During the 1630s the lieutenancy walked a fine line, conciliating when it could and doing its best to ignore the rising tensions that made compromise between people of differing views more and more difficult.

The events of 1637–40 made it impossible to ignore political conflict, and the crisis engendered by the Scottish rebellion left the lieutenancy— and the political system of which it was a fundamental part—in ruins. Lieutenants were alienated from the king as well as their neighbors, and in most places the institution dwindled into insignificance or embraced the conflict it had worked so hard to avoid.

T HE OUTBREAK OF HOSTILITIES with Spain in 1625 brought home the consequences of the European military revolution with brutal sudden-ness.[3] The kingdom—and the lieutenancy—was thrown into the vortex of war ill-prepared and largely ignorant of the hardships that lay ahead. Shackled to an unresponsive and archaic military system, the government struggled from the beginning of the conflict. Most immediate was the crown's acute need for supply. Parliament voted two subsidies to prosecute the war that followed the diplomatic breakdown with Spain, an excessive sum to many members of Parliament. The crown, however, knew very well that the yield of the subsidies, at best £140,000, would never suffice.[4] A second session was called to convince the assembly of the desperate need for more money, but it soon became clear that none would be forthcoming. The king dissolved the Parliament in disgust on August 12, and two days later the council resolved upon another expedient to raise revenue: a privy seal loan.[5]

The loan would be collected by the lieutenancy; lords lieutenant would provide the names of those fit to lend and assess them individually. No doubt aware of the difficulties involved, the council framed the issue as one of loyalty to the crown. Lenders would signify their affection for the king and their concern for his honor by their generosity. The Privy Council knew that its request was a heavy responsibility for the lieutenancy and out of keeping with its traditional role. Because of the lieutenancy's local orientation, the loan was also made a test of the lieutenants' "sincerity and endeavors in furtherance of the [king's] service."[6] The defense of the king's honor took precedence over the continuation of local tradition and was not a matter for extended debate: the assessments were to be returned within twenty days. Such wishful thinking on the council's part was not to be borne out.

The council set an overall quota for each county, to be collected from gentlemen of sufficient ability. In Cheshire, the total assessed came to a substantial £2,178/13/4, in Northamptonshire, £1,500, and in Somerset £2,219/13/4. In all of these counties, the sum demanded from lenders varied widely, between £10 and £100. In Hampshire, assessments ranged from the highest, £100 (five were so charged), to the lowest of £10. In Durham, ninety-seven gentlemen and ladies were charged a total of £1,100: the highest contribution was to be £25, fifteen persons were charged £20, and twenty-four were charged at the lowest rate, £6/13/4.[7] The immensity of these assessments crippled the lieutenancy's efforts from the outset. The standard by which the gentry measured taxation was the parliamentary subsidy—a very small tax. The privy seal loans, however, were based on a much more equitable assessment of a gentleman's income than the subsidy. Rich families such as the Lancashire Traffords were expected to loan £50 or £100, and the contrast between the subsidy (which often cost no more than £5 or £10) and the loan was glaring. Success would not come easily. Even as the lieutenancy sent out privy seals, subsidy collectors were busy collecting money voted in the summer of 1625, a coincidence that highlighted the great difference in the two sums. Moreover, the loans rested far more heavily on the upper gentry than on any other group. In the subsidies, a much broader range of people, including parish gentry and prosperous yeomen, was assessed. They escaped liability in the privy seal loan, which was collected from only the most prominent gentle families.

Gentlemen were reluctant to lend, and from the very beginning bad news poured into Whitehall. As early as October 24, a very agitated earl of Exeter noted that the western half of Northamptonshire was £300 short of its quota, and he feared a sharp rebuke from the council.[8] In November, Lord Scrope wrote Buckingham that in his lieutenancy (Yorkshire), "Of the thirty men I appointed, there hath only seven returned any certificate, the rest either framing excuses, or else failing to return any answer."[9] Reluctance to lend to the crown was not wholly confined to those assessed. The lieutenants themselves were not enthusiastic about the loans, and as a result, collections lagged. As the deputy lieutenants of Devon wrote, raising loans and benevolences was distasteful to them and "against the stream of our own natures"—besides, they worried about "those storms of envy which we may chance to suffer for it."[10] In early December, the council informed the lieutenants of eight counties that money for the loan

*Blairite
view* (

was coming in far too slowly in spite of what it claimed, with characteristic
bravado, was the enthusiasm of people to lend. A week later, the council
"marvel[ed] very much" that the deputy lieutenants of Dorset had not yet
replied to the demand for assessments. On the same day, December 19, the
council wrote to the lieutenants of several other counties reminding them
that three months had passed since they were instructed to send lists of
those capable of lending and demanding replies.[11]

In Warwickshire, Lord Brooke noted that the deputy lieutenants had
resolved to allow the loan to "sleep awhile," and in other counties lieutenants or their deputies demonstrated a distinct lack of support.[12] Some
pled poverty—Nottinghamshire, its deputies asserted, was small, infer-
tile, and all its wealthiest men lived outside of the county. The deputies
of Northamptonshire gave a long list of excuses for their failure: plague,
trade depression, other taxation. They bravely asserted that "most of the
chief gentry and men of quality live at the height of their means, spending a great part thereof in His Majesty's service."[13] Lord Russell wrote a
plea on behalf of the city of Exeter, claiming that a combination of plague
and piracy made it utterly impossible to raise any money in the city.[14]
The deputy lieutenants of Herefordshire, determined to safeguard their
county's interests, seized upon a legal technicality to escape the loan. They
refused to assess the privy seals because the council's letters went to the
earl of Northampton in his capacity as lord president and lieutenant of the
Welsh counties, and "this county is none of the counties of the principality
of Wales."[15]

As these incidents illustrate, the advantages the lieutenancy had by
virtue of its compact scale and potential efficiency as a collector of loans
were offset by the deputy lieutenants' reluctance to press their neighbors
too hard. Though deputies had collected militia money for years, and therefore had a relatively well-developed administrative infrastructure at hand,
these loans were a different case. Militia money was relatively limited (a
few pence, usually, a shilling or two at most), and moreover it was spent
locally. But as subsidies, loans, benevolences, and pay for the king's soldiers mounted, so did the desire in the country to avoid shouldering such
a heavy load. Many deputies believed "that duty which we owe unto our
country" required them to favor the interests of their locality over the needs
of the central government.[16] Because of its heavy reliance on the goodwill
and cooperation of the gentry in the shires, the crown was helpless when
they would not comply with its demands. Nor were many members of the
lieutenancy prepared to abandon their paramount concern for their shires.

Their local standing depended on maintaining the trust and cooperation of their fellows, and such drastic measures as forced loans invited resistance and obstruction.

The lieutenancy's inability to collect the privy seal loan and its sequel, the benevolence, illustrates the operation of economic and social constraints on central government's authority in the kingdom. Gentlemen were simultaneously paying two subsidies, as well as coat and conduct and billet money. The plague and the slump in trade of 1625 had serious short-term consequences in some places, reducing some people's ability to contribute. Furthermore, there were the twin political problems of an ill-conducted war and an unpopular favorite. The lieutenancy could not be divorced from local sentiment.[17] Deputies pleaded on behalf of their neighbors and lieutenants on behalf of their counties; no amount of persuasion from Whitehall could force them to ignore the concerns and complaints of the country.

Unable to achieve success through the lieutenancy, in September 1626 the council decided to try a different tack. On the fourteenth, in alliance with hard-liners among his advisers, the king decided that another loan would be gathered and that this one would be prosecuted much more vigorously than the last.[18] Having learned their lesson in 1625 and 1626, the king and the loan's supporters on the council made two tactical changes in the forced loan. First, they decided to make contribution compulsory; second, they opted to spread the responsibility for its assessment and collection beyond the lieutenancy.[19] In addition to many lords lieutenant, privy councillors with local connections were made commissioners for the loan, and the deputy lieutenants were joined with the justices of the peace and other prominent local gentlemen.

Implicit in the king's decision to expand responsibility for the loan was the realization that the lieutenancy was too wedded to local interests to be a useful agent in collecting the forced loan.[20] By including a wider range of local gentlemen in the commissions, the crown hoped to increase the gentry's stake in the loan's success. Each commissioner was forced, by virtue of his appointment, to take a personal interest in the loan's progress in his own neighborhood. Failure might call into question a gentleman's honor; the refusal of his neighbors to heed his calls for contributions would be an affront to his dignity and standing. A refusal to forward the loan left the commissioner in the unpleasant position of seeming a direct contemner of the king and council, open to prosecution for his disrespect. This indirect pressure on the gentry, the government hoped, would enforce compliance.

The king released the lieutenancy from its sole responsibility when he

broadened the basis of the forced loan. The lieutenants and their deputies
had borne primary responsibility with the privy seals, but in the forced
loan the lieutenancy assisted in an ad hoc fashion, while privy councillors,
justices of the peace, and judges worked more actively. The crown's financial needs required a more forceful means of coercion than the lieutenancy,
whose true metier was compromise, could provide. At the insistence of
the king and council, imprisonment and even impressment in the army
replaced the "fair persuasion" of the lieutenants.[21] Shifting enforcement of
the loan into a broader range of hands was perhaps a shrewd notion on
the part of the government, but the need for such a move was an implicit
indictment of the policy. Whether King Charles understood it or not, his
refusal to work within the established system caused irritation and alienated
many of his subjects.[22]

The fiscal chores of the war, onerous though they were, formed only
part of the lieutenants' job. Some of their duties, though equally time-
consuming, were far less damaging to the institution's standing. For example, in addition to raising revenue and impressing troops, the lieutenancy was responsible for arming, training, and organizing the militia to
defend against an invasion. After confronting the intractable problems of
raising revenue, defending the realm came almost as a relief. The prospect
of an attack from abroad occasioned an energetic response by the lieutenancy, ever true to its accustomed tenacious defense of local interests.
This was one area in which activity—and even expenditure—was often
rewarded with success.

Although of course the government hoped to wage the war on foreign
soil, the threat of invasion was always present in the 1620s. In August 1625
the council ordered the lieutenancy to watch the coast closely and prepare
the system of warning beacons for use in case of emergency.[23] When at the
end of the month a large enemy fleet was reported off the coast of Essex,
the council ordered three thousand of the county's militia to be drawn up
to face the danger.[24] The energetic lord lieutenant, the earl of Warwick,
ably assisted by an active group of deputies, acted at once. Raising three
thousand of the trained bands, amounting to three-quarters of the county's
force, was not a simple matter; numerous special arrangements had to be
made. The sheriff was instructed to watch over "base and ill-disposed persons" in the absence of the militia, the deputies ensured that there were
sufficient markets to feed the men, who were concentrated near Harwich,
and money had to be raised for their pay. Warwick ordered £1,000 levied,
a very substantial sum.[25] Revealingly, there was no resistance to this levy,

which was clearly meant for the defense of the local community, in comparison to Essex's surly response to the loans of 1626–27. No invasion transpired, and after a month in arms, the trained bands returned home.[26] The war years in Sussex saw no less than ten landings on the coast, each one of which called out some portion of the local trained bands. Though mostly on a very small scale, these attacks nevertheless reminded the lieutenancy of the necessity of an efficient system of local defense.[27] It is clear that when directly threatened (as would also be the case after the Scottish invasion in 1639), the country could be rallied by the lieutenancy. Indeed, the enthusiastic response lords lieutenant could provoke locally stands in stark contrast to the reaction to the constant demands emanating from London.

Questions of local defense often sparked action in the provinces. Several lieutenants, acting unilaterally, engaged engineers and sent them down to the coast to assist in repair work on local fortifications. Lord Conway made repairs in Hampshire, and the earl of Warwick even sought advice from Continental experts. Warwick, who combined the lieutenancy of Essex with the governorship of the strategically vital fort at Landguard point on the Essex/Suffolk border, personally oversaw the work there. He and the deputies worked unceasingly on the project, and the council authorized them to press carts and labor to complete the job. Once again, on this matter of purely local importance, there seems to have been no resistance.[28] Essex was not, however, the only place where forts were surveyed, repaired, or erected by the lieutenancy; new fortifications were built all along the southern and East Anglian coasts. Thanks to the efforts of the lieutenancy, by 1628 the coastal defenses of England were in far better state than they had been for many years.[29]

In these areas, the lieutenancy was unquestionably acting in the local interest. Although such projects demanded further taxation of the local population, the benefits from these rates were obvious. Wages kept struggling local laborers alive for a season, and sturdy fortresses arose along the coast, providing employment for victuallers and, more important, security from the depredations of pirates. The provincial focus of these activities made them popular, and the lieutenancy lost nothing—indeed, could reap substantial benefit in the form of patronage and respect—by its efforts.

Unfortunately, many of the lieutenancy's military responsibilities were far more difficult to reconcile with the local interest. If gathering huge sums of money was the most onerous of the lieutenancy's responsibilities in wartime, impressment required the most arduous decisions. Deputy lieutenants held what in practical terms was the power of life and death over those liable to the press. The king's soldiers rarely returned from campaign unscathed; most never returned at all. Deputies decided who went and taxed the county to support the new soldiers before they left. Most worked hard to satisfy the demands of the army without alienating their neighbors, and though their power might offer the unscrupulous the opportunity to impress an enemy's clients, it also made them highly visible targets for their rivals.[30] Impressment was an unenviable task—it meant breaking up homes, sending young men to their deaths, and often leaving fatherless households to become wards of the parish.[31] The work compromised the Olympian detachment of lord and deputy lieutenants and made their enforcement of stability in the shires more difficult.

Pressing soldiers was a difficult and time-consuming business; it involved officers at every level of government from the Privy Council down to the village constable. A press began at the top, with a decision on the part of the king and council. They decided how many men to raise and apportioned the burden by county. In the years 1625–27, presses ordered by the crown ranged from a relatively painless four hundred men in June 1627 to ten thousand men in May 1625.[32] Once an overall total was decided upon, the council frequently tinkered with the numbers, usually ordering smaller additional groups of men to be raised to replace troops who had deserted or were unfit to serve.[33] The numbers were large: more than fifty thousand men were raised in the 1620s, perhaps 1 percent of the population. Such large drafts were certainly felt in the shires.

The council assigned each lord lieutenant a quota of men to raise in his county. The lieutenants, in their turn, wrote to their deputies, relaying the council's orders, which also usually contained instructions as to the rendezvous for troops and the date by which they were obliged to appear.[34] Lieutenants rarely engaged in the work themselves, although some, particularly those resident in their counties, took a close interest in the work's progress. Their role was chiefly confined to transmitting information from the council to the county, while the deputy lieutenants and local constables did the real work in the press. The lord lieutenant's instructions set off an intense round of activity in every county. Deputies organized meetings and considered how to levy their quotas; in Northamptonshire, for example, the deputy lieutenants met separately in each division, east and west, between which the burden of the press was divided equally. In Cheshire, meetings were usually held at Chester, with Lord Derby presiding. Deputies apportioned their quota among the divisions or hundreds and, further, by villages and towns. At the same time, they ordered the collection of coat and conduct money required to pay for the pressed troops' clothing and provisions until they were turned over to the king's officers. Village constables collected this money, acting on warrants issued by the deputies. A press, then, involved two separate but related tasks: raising men for the king's service and levying money to keep them until they were taken in charge by their conductor.

Of the two, raising men was ordinarily the easiest. Nearly every village had one or two young men it could safely spare for the wars; many had men they positively delighted in sending away. Impressment could occasionally be a veritable boon to the lieutenancy, always concerned as it was to tailor its activities to local needs. Deputies might seize upon the press as the perfect solution to the problem of an antisocial or troublesome neighbor. In May 1627, the deputy lieutenants of Middlesex pressed Samuel Hubbard, a wife-beater who had despoiled his stepchildren's fortunes, and who, when taken for the press, was found in bed with another man's wife, "in that open and foul manner that begat a very great offence to all the neighborhood." [35] There could have been few people unhappy to see Hubbard and others like him marched off to Plymouth. The unemployed and impotent poor were natural targets for impressment, and deputies often swept their counties clean of such men. In April 1627, for instance, the deputy lieutenants of Hampshire produced two hundred erstwhile soldiers, and their poor quality outraged the king's sergeant major general, Sir George Blundell: "You send for your 200 about 130 of the basest beggars and poorest boys and lowly rascals that I ever did see sent for soldiers," he wrote the deputies.[36] One of the king's conductors said of his charges from Suffolk in 1627 that they "are for the most part unfit for service both in respect of their age and person as also the diseases with which many of them are annoyed." The city of Leicester, too, was rather undemanding in the crown's behalf—it provided William Sparke, "lame of his right hand and left arm," Lancelot Clarke, "a great rupture in his belly," and Thomas Braunston, "his ribs broke." [37] Examples could be multiplied ad nauseam.

Those counties censured for providing the worst troops were usually those on which the heaviest demands were made, such as Hampshire and Suffolk. This tendency illustrates the point that although deputies were concerned about the impact of impressment on their counties, they did recognize a duty to the government. But there was a limit to the endurance of any county. The coastal counties provided a larger share of the king's soldiers and also bivouacked many who awaited transportation to the front. The deputy lieutenants of these counties in particular risked the displeasure of the crown in their persistent defense of the local interest. The expenses of coat and conduct money rose higher and higher as the number of pressed soldiers increased, but the government showed no inclination to meet its obligations. When in these areas the threat of an invasion sharpened the lieutenancy's desire to prepare a solid local defense, the likelihood of a confrontation between court and country increased. The deputies of Suffolk provoked the wrath of the council by daring to demand repayment of coat and conduct money from the exchequer before they raised a levy of 150 men in June 1627. The council replied curtly: "We find it strange and no way to be suffered that you should so far forget yourselves in the performance of your duties." [38] But the deputies had learned from experience not to rely on promises of recompense. In the first six months of the year, press after press had been carried out and special energy had been exerted in coastal counties like Suffolk and Essex with very little assistance from the central government.

During the war years, a harried Privy Council relied on the lieutenancy as the prime executor of its plans at the local level. To a certain degree, the priorities of the council and the local interests of the lieutenancy were harmonious—for example, the export of surplus population for the wars might suit both center and locality. The crown's need for cooperation forced the central government to compromise with provincial society just as the value lords lieutenant and their deputies placed on their power and position as honored servants of the king induced them to balance local needs with the necessities of war.

But the interests of the two institutions collided when the needs of the state intensified. The war hit some of the coastal counties especially hard. Levies of 3,800 men in June and July of 1627, following hard on the heels of a demanding series of impressments in April and May, caused the lieutenancy the greatest trouble, generating considerable resistance and obstruction. In October 1627 the deputy lieutenants of Hampshire explained to Lord Conway that raising a mere fifty men was very difficult because since 1625 "there have been impressed out of this county . . . 1500 men, and few of them returned"—creating a real shortage of eligible candidates. [39] The Dorset deputies put their own case before the council: in April they raised 250 men, in May 100 more, and in June 150. The size of this press was larger (and correspondingly more expensive) than the deputies had ever dealt with, and they found the government's demands increasingly difficult to satisfy. Meeting their June quota required four days of intense labor, and the deputies said that the county had reached its limit: "With what difficulty . . . and what lamentable cries of mothers, wives, and children we have sent away this company of men, we cannot express by writing to your lordships."[40] Continued enforcement of such harsh demands by the council increased the tension inherent in the relationship between crown and locality to an unbearable level and made the lieutenancy seem to be the instrument of an aggressive central government. This situation, said the deputies, was intolerable. It undermined the lieutenancy, depriving its members of their honor in the eyes of their countrymen. The deputies asked leave to resign.

In the end, the Dorset deputy lieutenants did not give up their commissions. Their threat was probably more a bargaining tactic designed to wring concessions from the council than an ultimatum. In this way the lieutenancy did its best to meliorate the demands of the state upon the local community. Nevertheless, the burden imposed by the campaigns of 1625–28 forced the lieutenancy to adopt the role of guardian of local interests more actively. This complicated the task of the council, whose overriding goal was the organization of a successful war.

As obstruction from within the lieutenancy increased, several counties failed to raise their prescribed quotas of troops in 1627. Wiltshire was 100 men short; Suffolk, 150.[41] Northumberland's shortfall was 27, and Surrey managed only 28 of its required 200 men. Sussex's contingent arrived at its Hampshire rendezvous 39 men short, and of 150 Norfolk troops raised in April, only 85 reached their rendezvous at Harwich. The rest managed to escape, some after turning on and beating their conductors. The men pressed in Hertfordshire were "very unwilling to go," and of a group of 685 men pressed in the midlands in September, 115 failed to arrive at Plymouth.[42]

Difficulties in raising troops were equaled by the problem of finding money to provide for them. The cost of equipping the men with their coats and conduct money could be high: coats were generally priced at twelve to fifteen shillings each and conduct money cost eight pence per day. Sometimes the authorities skimped, providing no clothing and poor rations, to save the county as much as possible. For example, the bishop of Durham spent only £19 raising fifty troops for Ireland.[43] Lonsdale hundred in Lancashire spent a mere £17 on a levy of one hundred men.[44] In other places the sums raised were more substantial; a levy of three hundred men for Cadiz in 1625 cost Norfolk £290.[45] Although some of these sums were bearable taken singly, when added to the many other charges of 1625–27, they imposed a real burden on the locality. The deputy lieutenants of Bedfordshire lamented in 1625 that the costs of outfitting two hundred men would be insupportable, but they discovered that the task was still more difficult in 1627. Two parliamentary subsidies, the privy seal loan, benevolence, and the forced loan, as well as ship money and charges for billeting in some counties, made the collection of every shilling of coat and conduct money a trial.

Billeting, the second of the lieutenancy's two main concerns when raising an army, was usually far and away the most difficult.[46] It affected everyone, not merely the unfortunates sent off to war but the entire community in which the soldiers were housed. Innkeepers provided lodging, and everyone else paid rates for food and clothing. These rates were sometimes extremely high, far higher than any subsidy or loan demanded from 1625 to 1627. Theoretically, the expenses incurred in billeting were to be repaid by the crown, and when it met its responsibilities (as it did in 1625), billeting caused no controversy. After 1625, however, repayment was at best erratic and often nonexistent. Billeting the king's forces under these circumstances was a major task for the lieutenancy and an immensely difficult one, in which the tensions inherent in early Stuart relations between the center and the periphery are most evident.

An unprecedented amount of money was required to sustain the army. In Devon, the earl of Holland, the lieutenant, told Secretary Conway that the county was spending £500 per week on billets, a huge sum, considering the realities of seventeenth-century finance.[47] In January 1627 the inhabitants of Oldham in Hampshire petitioned their lord lieutenant for relief: a company of foot was billeted upon them, at a weekly cost of £13 and 8 shillings, and the expense was so heavy that they could no longer afford to relieve the poor. The Hampshire deputy lieutenants pressed their lord lieutenant to intercede on the county's behalf and asked that the soldiers quartered on them be sent to Somerset, which had thus far escaped billeting. They were joined in their complaints by their colleagues in Dorset, likewise distressed at the strain billeting had put on their county; the latter suggested that one thousand men previously kept in Devon and Cornwall be sent to Somerset instead of their own county. As one of the deputy lieutenants of Dorset complained to a friend, Sergeant Major General Blundell was quartering his troops in the poorest villages, causing great hardship. The army, the deputies lamented, had exacerbated the situation by ignoring the lieutenancy's intimate knowledge of local conditions; Blundell had refused to listen to the deputy lieutenants' suggestions of areas better able to afford billets.[48]

Billeting was particularly onerous in the primary military staging areas along the coast. In Devon the justices of the peace and deputies joined to inform the council of their troubles: "And we are so continually molested with the cry of the poor billeters for present pay as our business is disturbed, our credits lost with our countrymen, and ourselves utterly wearied in the performance of this impossible service."[49] The Hampshire deputies worried about their local standing as well. They pleaded with Conway, their lieutenant, for permission to divert loan money destined for London to ensure that they would not "suffer very much in our reputations" in the county.[50] The deputy lieutenants of Essex avoided the risk to their reputations by paying some billeters themselves, rather than charging their neighbors, "unto whom all levies of money are at this time very unacceptable."[51] This concern for their local standing led deputy lieutenants to dig deeply into their own pockets to avoid obloquy and boded ill for the general war effort.

The king's army, raised and billeted with such effort on the part of the lieutenancy in 1626 and 1627, sailed for France on July 10, 1627. The fate of the duke of Buckingham's troops is well-known, and it fully justified the Englishman's determination to avoid the king's service. Defeat, disaster, and incompetence plagued the expedition from the outset, and no more than half of the men sent returned on the ships that sailed home again on October 10. Those who did came ashore with little more than the ragged shirts on their backs, and all were owed substantial arrears of pay. The conclusion of the campaign offered lieutenants and their deputies little relief. Their work for the king had been difficult, but no sooner was it complete than a new test arose.

The Parliament that met in the shadow of this military fiasco in 1628 was determined to vent the frustrations of an aroused kingdom. As the king's agent, the lieutenancy came in for severe criticism. "The practice of deputy lieutenants be involved with the greatest grievance" in the words of Sir Robert Phelips. Yet much of the criticism of the lieutenancy was factionally motivated, and it persuaded few members of Parliament of the need for radical reform.[52] Except for four Cornish deputies briefly confined for allegedly interfering with a parliamentary election, no deputy lieutenant or lord lieutenant suffered for committing any illegalities.[53] The inclusion of billeting in the Petition of Right and the king's acceptance of it eliminated the concerns of most MPs about the lieutenancy.[54] But the definition of the lieutenancy's powers by a new militia act, a course favored by a few members, was not necessarily welcome. Such a step might force the gentry to accept responsibilities that they might otherwise escape, and for those gentlemen who were already deputy lieutenants, a new act could be a blow to their local power and standing. After all, many members were deputies, and many more aspired to the office. The events of the Parliament of 1628 tested the lieutenancy's viability, and, on balance, the outcome was favorable. In spite of widespread bitterness in the country and among MPs about billeting and martial law, support for the institution enabled it to emerge largely unscathed. That it did so is testimony to the deep roots the lieutenancy had put down in the local community, as well as to its indispensability in the eyes of the crown.

That the lieutenancy's authority rested solidly on the prerogative and wholly outside the statute and common law concerned very few people beyond a small circle of common lawyers in Parliament. Unease with the government was focused on the small circle of advisers around the king at court and, increasingly, on the king himself.[55] The lieutenancy was widely perceived to be a provincial, rather than a central, institution. Feeble attempts to reform the militia or the lieutenancy after the passage of the Militia Act of 1558 were made seven times.[56] Only one got beyond even a first reading in the Commons, and a measure that actually passed the Lords in 1621 disappeared when sent down to the lower house. The gentry were satisfied with the lieutenancy, and even in 1628, despite violent speeches denouncing deputy lieutenants made by Robert Phelips and some of his allies, Parliament turned back yet another attempt to redefine the institution's legal standing.

The strength of the lieutenancy relied on a trade-off of benefits and responsibilities. Lieutenants and deputies were granted wide powers and had great prestige. They intervened at court in behalf of themselves, their clients, and their counties. On another level, the lieutenancy helped stabilize a community by providing an institution whose authority combined local standing and the king's benediction. It could arbitrate disputes, reconcile factions, and provide leadership for the rest of the county. Balancing these factors were the responsibilities the lieutenancy owed to the crown. It maintained the trained bands, and, most important, from 1625 to 1628 it sustained the war effort. Keeping the war going was by far the more difficult task of the two, and the heavy strain it imposed shook the consensus upon which the institution rested.

The events of 1625–28 show, however, just how broad support for the lieutenancy was. Because it embodied the resilient traditions of English local government—provincial, conservative, and attuned to the nuances of local society—it withstood a serious test. Gentlemen who might otherwise have made trouble were co-opted. Several noisy parliamentarians such as Francis Seymour, Edward Alford, and even Phelips became deputy lieutenants; Phelips resumed his place in the commission after the session. Such moves were in keeping with the lieutenancy's traditions and helped support an orderly political life in the shires. Though confronted with a new challenge from the common lawyers, the lieutenancy emerged from the Franco-Spanish war intact. The powers deputy lieutenants and lords lieutenant lost after the Petition of Right were hardly missed; deputy lieutenants took no pleasure from billeting or exercising martial law.[57] These were time-consuming, difficult, and thankless tasks, and only the most officious deputies would have been sorry to see them go. Though the king's acceptance of the petition acknowledged the extralegality of the measures used between 1625 and 1628, his lieutenants still held their commissions solely by virtue of the prerogative, a principle that Charles would never surrender. Although time and again the lieutenancy proved itself a tool of limited use, the crown remained firmly committed to its survival— possibly for lack of a better alternative. No deputy lieutenants, with the exception of the four Cornishmen, whose treatment was comparatively mild, were punished; no lord lieutenant was questioned or impeached. Despite the grumbles of some deputy lieutenants after the session had ended, most people connected with the lieutenancy had reason to be pleased with the outcome of the Parliament.[58]

A crucial factor in the debates of 1628 was the defense of local autonomy and the particularist status quo. The lieutenancy as it developed under James I was an acceptable, even welcome, addition to the political nation. An activist lieutenancy, however, was a disturbing manifestation of an increasingly vigorous and innovative king. Many felt that long-established relationships were being arbitrarily altered by his determination to sustain the war. "Reform" was decidedly not the goal of most gentlemen in 1628, at least with regard to the lieutenancy. "Reaction" better describes the gentry's mood: a desire to return to what they perceived as traditional patterns of government. Ultimately, the conflict between the king and the provinces was resolved (if only temporarily) by the acceptance of the Petition of Right and Parliament's provision of subsidies to continue the war.

T HE WAR AND THE POLITICAL STRUGGLES in its aftermath were followed by nine years of peace.[59] The lieutenancy reverted to its peacetime duties: holding musters, maintaining order in the countryside, and carrying out the administrative odd jobs ordered by the council.[60] The crown's push for a well-ordered militia in the 1620s had resulted in raised standards and greater efficiency, but the lieutenancy remained fundamentally the same localist institution it had been in the past. In the 1630s it settled into a less active, more comfortable routine.[61] The crown's need for a sufficiently trained militia and the country's desire for a quiet and inexpensive life now seemed balanced, and peace enabled the lieutenancy to maintain its distance from the increasingly authoritarian mood of the court. Burdensome royal policies such as the exact militia were deflected or lackadaisically enforced in many shires; in 1634 the council complained to the lieutenants of twenty-one counties because they had held no musters for the third consecutive year.[62] Even when musters were organized, lords lieutenant and their deputies preferred to leave the enforcement of militia obligations to the Privy Council and even intervened on behalf of alleged defaulters from time to time.[63] Moreover, the abeyance of Parliament expanded the realm of the lieutenancy's advocacy. During the Personal Rule the Privy Council was the center of authority, and the lieutenancy's easy access to Whitehall enhanced the status of the lords lieutenant and their deputies even as their ambivalence over the king's government and his ministers increased. That ambivalence extended beyond the lieutenancy; when its members did go out of their way to do the council's bidding, they sometimes encountered resistance, as in 1635, when two Norwich aldermen claimed that their lord lieutenant, the earl of Arundel, acted without legal authority. The aldermen claimed that because the lieutenancy had no statutory foundation, it was illegal. Naturally the king's response to this bold assertion, when it came before the council, was an unequivocal defense of his prerogative. Though Arundel won his point in this instance, one wonders at what political cost and how many others held similar views.[64]

The idyll, if such it was, came to an abrupt end when the king's government in Scotland collapsed in 1638. The rebellion brought to the surface all the questions, problems, and grievances that had arisen over the Franco-Spanish War. Once again the lieutenants were drafted into the uncomfortable role of agents for the crown. Shuffling responsibility off onto others—sheriffs, justices of the peace, and the like—was now out of the question. The government's plan of action against the Scots was grandiose: more troops were to be raised than in the 1620s, more money levied, and, inevitably, more pressure exerted upon the provinces from the center.

The story of the lieutenancy's role in the years 1638–42 parallels the tale of the collapse of King Charles I's government.[65] Most remarkable is the rapidity with which it fell. The lieutenancy, a prestigious, well-regarded, and useful institution, was reduced to an ineffectual ruin in less than a year, torn between the conflicting interests of center and locality. The lieutenancy's campaign in 1639 was relatively successful, perhaps indicating that the king's government had not yet tumbled over the brink of disaster at the start of the Scottish troubles. But a year of horrendous expense and uncertainty, long-standing grievances against royal policy, and, most important, the advent of a new Parliament, weakened the crown seriously. With Parliament in session, the lieutenancy was challenged in its role as principal defender of local interests, and the relatively benign conditions of the peace of the 1630s were replaced by the more threatening ones of an expensive and burdensome war—whose organizers would be, perforce, the lieutenants themselves.

From 1640 to 1642, politics, in the form of irreconcilable differences about policy and tactics, made the lieutenancy's job impossible. As an institution developed primarily to foster stability by means of social leadership while defending the interests of the country at court, it was ill-equipped to enforce obedience upon the shires. The maintenance of a delicate balance between court and country through compromise was difficult enough under any circumstances, as the experience of the latter 1620s proved. The polarization of local government required a new concept of administration, as well as new tactics. The lieutenancy, a relic of the traditional political system, was overwhelmed by the radically altered circumstances of the time and rendered largely irrelevant by events from 1640 to 1642.

The Scottish rebellion sparked the fire that ultimately consumed the Caroline lieutenancy. Disorder in the north had its roots in the king's enforcement of religious conformity in his native Scotland, another instance, like the failed plan for an exact militia, of the king's refusal to recognize the natural limits of his authority. Charles's brand of orthodoxy had a distinctly English flavor, which the Scots believed added more than a hint of popery to their church.[66] The missile that sailed across the floor of St. Giles's cathedral in Edinburgh on July 23, 1637, was meant for the king's Primate of All Scotland, Archbishop John Spottiswoode, but the blow struck at the whole religious regime erected by the Stuarts. The riot at St. Giles's launched a series of incidents that led to open rebellion in Scotland by late 1638.

As the Scottish crisis deepened in December 1638, the lieutenants in some counties strengthened their defenses. Lords lieutenant collected stores of powder and munitions, which quickly became extremely difficult to obtain. The Lancashire lieutenancy met twice in the first two weeks of December and levied £600 to buy extra supplies of gunpowder and arms.[67]

The deputy lieutenants of Sussex spent £250 on powder, buying at the very favorable rate of 10*d* per pound; most of their fellows had to pay 18*d* if they could get powder at all.[68] At the council's command, the lieutenants of several counties compiled lists of all able-bodied men aged sixteen to sixty in their shires. In Derbyshire alone the lieutenant provided the council with a list of over seventeen thousand men.[69] These unprecedented censuses, obviously intended as a prelude to raising an army, required great effort on the part of the lieutenancy, which by the opening of the new year found itself busier than it had been in a decade—busier, in fact, than it had ever been. As the war in the 1620s had shown, this sort of labor inevitably heightened the tensions between the lieutenancy's two constituencies—center and locality.

The immediate threat of attack from the north spurred a determined effort by those lieutenants who found themselves in the path of an expected invasion. The preparations being made by the Lancashire lieutenancy in early January 1639 were typical. On January 8, the deputy lieutenants assembled at Lathom House, the earl of Derby's country seat, and prepared a list of orders. The trained bands, both horse and foot, were to be increased; the money collected in December's levy kept easily accessible in Preston; magazines established or replenished in Preston, Lancaster, and Liverpool; local gunsmiths "found and set at work producing arms." Additionally, the deputies were to report on the state of the corn, butter, and cheese markets and required to see that the county's "freehold band" was trained every three weeks. For good measure, the lieutenancy took the time to order the county's horsemen to wear a red "scarf" around their waists.[70]

Preparations and fear of a Scottish invasion were understandably most intense in the north. As had been true on the southern coast in the 1620s, a straightforward defense of the local community was what the lieutenancy was best at, and northern lieutenants and their deputies worked with considerable success early in the crisis. The Stanleys, father and son, worked continuously throughout December and January. They held frequent meetings with their deputies in both Lancashire and Cheshire. Anthony Thelwall reported to Secretary Francis Windebank on January 20 that, in addition to their own personal exertions in training new soldiers, "my lord lieutenants are always present at the reviews" of the trained bands, which he found "reasonably well exercised." Thelwall, who was in the north inspecting local defenses, assured Windebank that the lieutenants and their deputies were very zealous in their duty.[71] In other counties, especially those less threatened by a Scottish descent, matters were somewhat different. Persuading locally oriented deputy lieutenants to pitch in with a will was not easy without the sight of massed ranks of Covenanters to illustrate the dangers of war. Even where experiences with the Scots were well remembered there were problems.

In Cumberland harmonious cooperation with the government was more difficult, despite the rebels' proximity. A representative from the king's army, Captain Waite, arrived there in January to inspect the trained bands and prepared to double their numbers. The deputy lieutenants rejected such a dramatic increase out of hand. Led by Sir Patricius Curwen, they explained that the county was far too poor for such a major expenditure. The muster Waite attended was shocking: "There was never a country in England so meanly provided as they were, [I] wondering at their carelessness that their men were so ignorant in the use of their arms." As Curwen (no doubt correctly) pointed out in reply, mustering was very difficult in Cumberland and Westmorland because of the local geography: "For that we live in a stormy, mountainous country." Moreover, Curwen explained, there were no old soldiers in the county to help train their men. It is clear that in Cumberland the lieutenancy's ability to create and maintain a credible militia had definite limits, and the deputy lieutenants, keenly aware of these limits, were wary about committing themselves to more than they felt their "country" could bear. Captain Waite's complaints resulted in a complicated series of negotiations in which the deputies, led by the wily Curwen, defined Cumberland's capabilities. In the end, the county restocked its magazine and increased the size of its trained bands but by much less than the council's cherished 100 percent goal.[72] The king had to be satisfied with such compromises worked out on the local level; royal orders were of little use when dealing with complex realities in the shires.

These preparations made the king's aggressive intentions obvious by November 1638, although he withheld a public declaration of his plans until February 1639. The lists of able-bodied men, imports of arms, orders to increase the size of the trained bands, and surveys of local food supplies made the crown's expectation of a coming war plain. On February 15, three months after Charles had told the duke of Hamilton, his negotiator in Scotland, that he meant to use force against the Covenanters, the king took decisive steps toward war. He ordered the lords lieutenant to raise men from the trained bands to be sent north to meet the Scottish threat. The king defended his recourse to arms with a ringing proclamation against the rebels: "The great and considerable forces lately raised in Scotland . . . by the instigation of some factious particular persons ill-affected to monarchical government who seek to cloak their too apparent designs under pretense of religion . . . hath moved us to take into our Royal care to provide for the preservation and safety of this our kingdom of England, which is . . . in apparent danger to be annoyed and invaded." [73]

This letter and subsequent orders to assemble the army at York by April 15 started the lieutenancy on its most formidable task to date. The king, following the advice of his Scottish factotum the earl of Traquair, originally foresaw an army of some forty thousand men, and though the number was gradually reduced, a force of some twenty-three thousand awaited King Charles's pleasure in the north by May. [74] This was far and away the largest single military force raised in England since the Stuart accession, dwarfing those of the 1620s. So large an army required vast sums of money for pay and equipment, as well as the execution of a myriad of administrative and logistical details. Contracts for clothing and food had to be negotiated, supplies transported and stored, and, most important, soldiers pressed. The lieutenancy was faced with a truly demanding task.

Raising an army under these circumstances was fraught with difficulty. Trained bandsmen were understandably reluctant to leave their home counties. The earl of Lindsey, lieutenant of Lincolnshire, told the council on April 6, "I find some of these trained soldiers very unwilling to go along . . . but the major part of the number which I have selected (I am confident) will be found both able and willing to do his majesty service." Lindsey's assurance was no doubt sincere, vitiated though it was by the qualifying parenthetical "I am confident," but his reference to recalcitrant trained bandsmen makes it clear that the lieutenancy had to work hard to maintain its momentum. Even before the council's order to enlist trained bandsmen, rumors in Lincolnshire worried skittish militiamen. On January 19 Francis Pelham wrote Lord Conway, "My lord of Lindsey has commanded his deputy lieutenants to [be] strict in the men, horses, and arms for war in these parts, which begins to work a fear that they must fight." [75]

Those pressed who were not trained bandsmen were just as reluctant to serve. News of the press in the countryside signaled a general panic, and eligible men fled into hiding before they could be awarded the king's shilling. The harsh life of a soldier repelled most young men, and the experiences of the 1620s, when few of those who fought for the Protestant cause returned alive, can have done nothing to fire the kingdom with enthusiasm. [76] The king's quarrel seems to have resonated with few of his subjects. A dislike of the Scots must surely have animated some, but for many others a fight against an army of godly men, Scottish though they undoubtedly were, was hardly the same as drawing the sword against papist Spaniards or Frenchmen. For many—even within the lieutenancy— a painful conundrum arose: who was at fault—rebellious Scots or devious Laudians? English Puritans had no difficulty identifying where the trouble lay—Robert Woodford, a Northampton lawyer, was not at all unusual in believing that the Scots were God's avengers.[77] These divisions made the lieutenancy's task even more difficult than it had been in the 1620s.

Ideology aside, raising an army of twenty-three thousand was expensive. Once the troops were enlisted, the county supported them until they were taken into the king's service. The lieutenancy raised this money, as well as money for coats and conduct, and the expense could be very heavy. A company of two hundred men required £208/07/04 per month in wages alone, and a troop of horse cost £365/08/0. Because of the severe shortage of money in the exchequer, the crown tried to keep the soldiers in the pay of the counties for as long as possible. A month's wages for a single regiment of foot cost the treasury £833/0/04, and parceling out these liabilities, company by company, to the shires allowed the government to avoid payment.[78] But it only added to the difficulties faced by the lieutenancy, which by the spring of 1639 had already levied large sums of money from the country.[79] Lieutenants and their deputies, who had largely avoided the job of royal tax collector throughout the Personal Rule, were now given a stiff dose of the medicine that sheriffs had been swallowing for years.

In addition to these responsibilities, the deputy lieutenants regulated local markets to prevent food shortages and high prices. Deputy and lords lieutenant shouldered a very heavy work load, certainly greater than they had borne in the 1620s. A letter from Sir Anthony Irby, a Lincolnshire deputy lieutenant, gives a good impression of the hard work done by a conscientious deputy during this spring: "Upon my coming home," he wrote, "I received a letter from their lordships for the providing of 60 horse and 20 carts which we have provided and sent to Newcastle upon Tyne; the next day I received a letter from His Majesty under his privy signet for the certifying what quantity of hemp, oats, beans, butter, and cheese we may afford His Majesty out of these parts, which certificate I am to return on the 19th of this month [he was writing on the sixteenth]. Upon Saturday I received a letter for the providing of money for payment of trained soldiers who lie for shipping at Grimsby . . . which business I am now about for the parts where I live."[80]

After a great deal of struggle, the job was done, and some twenty thousand troops were marched northward. The army the lieutenancy raised for

King Charles in May 1639 was the fruit of a heroic effort. As in the war of the 1620s, the lieutenancy responded reasonably well but was always limited by its inherent localism. The immediate threat of invasion worked most powerfully in the north, drawing local society together and encouraging northern lords lieutenant to make active preparations. Central government and local authorities worked closely together in early 1639; indeed, intense bargaining between crown and county characterized all phases of the military operation. Raising men, money, and supplies, and organizing transport, were complicated and difficult, but remarkably, counties fulfilled their quotas, fed and clothed their men, and prevented any serious disorders from breaking out among the troops.[81] And yet the victory was a precarious one, bought at considerable cost in both energy and political capital. The king failed to take advantage of this achievement, for by the first week of June, the army had been dismissed.[82] The crown could not afford to keep the men in arms while Charles waffled between war and negotiation, and so the months of hard work by the lieutenancy, the thousands of pounds spent, and the unmeasurable social disruption caused by the press went for naught.

The contrast between the relatively well-ordered, if not trouble-free, preparations for the first Bishops' War and the chaos and confusion of 1640 is striking. When the king dismissed his army in June 1639, he fully intended to assemble another the following year if need be. He planned to bide his time, raise money, and strengthen his political support before launching a new campaign. Charles and his councillors evidently believed that the lieutenancy's success in 1639 could be repeated without difficulty. That experience, however, had exhausted the goodwill of large segments of the community. The lieutenants and their deputies had struggled for nothing; their neighbors had contributed thousands of pounds to no purpose. In 1640 the king would find that there were limits beyond which his people could not be pushed—boundaries that many in the lieutenancy, as well as in the kingdom at large, could not be tempted to pass.[83]

After several months of desultory negotiation, on March 26, 1640, the council acted decisively. Hurrying lords lieutenant to their counties if they were not already there, the council gave each a quota of troops to raise. The new army was to be somewhat smaller than the previous year's, amounting to 17,600 men. This reduced number may have been an acknowledgment by the crown of the hardship involved in raising another army so soon, but Charles evidently did not realize that providing even this reduced force would be a daunting task. Quotas ranged from a tiny contingent of sixty from Rutland to no less than two thousand from Devon. The men were to rendezvous at Newcastle between May 31 and June 9. At the same time, the council ordered each shire to produce horses and carters for the army, a request that in 1639 had caused considerable dissatisfaction. The crown required fourteen hundred horses; individual counties were to contribute anywhere from twenty to seventy horses and up to twenty-three carters. Although the number of animals expected from each county was not large, the quotas were bitterly resented. A serviceable horse cost about £10, and for some counties the total expense was very high: £700 in Northampton-shire, £660 in Warwickshire, and £500 in Bedfordshire. When the pay and press money for carters was included, the counties would easily have had to provide £15,000 to furnish the king's baggage train.[84] This combined with the costs of coat and conduct money for the soldiers meant that a staggering sum of money would have to be squeezed from every county, just as it had been only a year before.

The political foundation upon which the lieutenancy rested began to crack. Lieutenants had placed tremendous pressure on their counties in 1639, and many were sympathetic to the needs of the crown. As a result, the institution's local credentials were badly dented. Northamptonshire offers a good example of the lieutenancy's political demise. The lieuten-ant there, the second earl of Exeter, successfully raised and equipped Northamptonshire's contingent in the army in 1639 but was in poor health and not in a position to repeat the performance in the spring of 1640. Ill-ness also prevented him from exerting his customary influence in the Short Parliament election in March 1640. Sinking fast, Exeter had been super-seded in all but name by the earl of Peterborough, who dominated the county's military preparations. As Exeter's heir apparent to the lieutenancy Peterborough expected to offer the lieutenant's traditional guidance in the parliamentary selection.[85] In conjunction with the deputy lieutenants and the earls of Northampton and Westmorland, Peterborough strongly urged the return of William Elmes as knight of the shire.[86] Elmes was himself a deputy lieutenant, and his fellows worked extremely hard to secure his election.[87] Ordinarily, such support would be more than sufficient to gain a place in Parliament, but the times were anything but ordinary.

On March 19 Peterborough and his noble friends wrote to the gentle-men and freeholders of Northamptonshire, canvassing for Elmes, and on about the twenty-fifth, the election unfolded in Northampton.[88] Much to the astonishment of the deputy lieutenants—and most assuredly to their extreme displeasure—the selection of members degenerated into an unruly farce. As the deputies described it, "some turbulent spirit by undue practices did cause great clamors to be raised against the authority of the lieutenancy." The "great clamors" began when a group of electors, one of whom was John Friend, a notorious Northampton Puritan, began shouting, "No deputy lieutenants!" upon Elmes's entrance into the shire hall. Adding injury to this insult, Elmes was defeated by his opponent.[89] Certain that this blow to their prestige lay at the root of their abject failure to raise the 350 troops and seventy horses demanded by the council, the deputies told their lieutenant that they were powerless, "in regard of the blemish that lies upon our reputations." Their warrants, they claimed, got "little better return than a threatening to be questioned in parliament for the same."[90] If the elections for the Short Parliament went very smoothly in most places, the opprobrium heaped upon deputy lieutenants like Elmes illustrates the corrosive effect of political conflict on the authority of the lieutenancy.

The Short Parliament dealt a crushing blow to the lieutenancy's viability. Lord Keeper John Finch's speech from the throne on April 13, 1640, dwelled on the king's needs and merely added a vague promise that the king would turn his attention to grievances "towards winter."[91] Such a weak brew was hardly likely to satisfy a Parliament that thirsted for redress as this one did, and Charles's plans were set aside in a general rush to the well of reform. On April 17, after attacks on the Laudian church and fearful pronouncements about threats to the liberty of the subject, the Commons heard petitions from the counties denouncing the burdens of war. These laments were taken up the next day by John Pym, already emerging as the most tenacious of the king's opponents in Parliament. Coat and conduct money, billets, and charges for arms and horses all became part of the debate.[92] From the first week of the Parliament, then, the lieutenancy was faced with a continuous assault on its actions of the previous year, even as it tried to repeat them to satisfy the crown's demands for a new army.

Parliamentary criticism was relentless, though it focused less on the misdeeds of lieutenants and deputies than on the burdens imposed on the provinces by the central government. On May 4 the Commons once again debated the matter of military charges, and Sir John Hotham pointed out that while ship money cost his county £12,000, Yorkshire had spent more than £40,000 supporting the king's crusade against the Scots. Charges of this magnitude would certainly have provoked tremendous difficulty even under the best of circumstances, but in the midst of a reforming parliamentary session, they spelled disaster for those charged with collecting them.

On the following day, the king, convinced after only three weeks that the Parliament was a disaster, determined to find some other way to bring the Scots to heel. Parliament was dissolved, but the damage to the lieutenancy was done.[93] Military charges had been denounced as illegal and the lieutenancy's authority called into question. Unhappily, Charles's decision to pursue the war forced the lords and gentlemen of the lieutenancy into an excruciating position: faced with resistance on every side, they were now responsible for coercing their neighbors into submission.

Never oblivious to their local standing, lieutenants and deputies failed to live up to the king's expectations in 1640. Before they even drew their warrants, the Essex deputies asked how long the county would be forced to maintain its seven-hundred-man quota before they passed into the royal army. They believed that collecting the necessary money would be impossible if the county kept the troops for any length of time, and even this assessment proved to be optimistic.[94] Resistance to the lieutenancy burgeoned after April 1640. In Dorset, the trained bandsmen resolutely refused to accept press money, alleging that they would leave the county unprotected if they went north and complaining that inland counties had borne a much lighter burden than those on the coast.[95] In Hampshire, the deputies confessed that "we find a great proportion of men wanting of the number required by reason that many are run away . . . and divers of them which were brought before us by the captains were so unfit and insufficient that we had just cause to refuse them." Furthermore, they reported, they found it impossible to raise coat and conduct money.[96] Similar problems arose all over the country, even in counties where the king had always recruited soldiers without a murmur of protest. Lord Strange worried that the five hundred men he raised in Cheshire might mutiny for lack of supply and wages. Lincolnshire, ordinarily very reliable, also had severe problems; the earl of Lindsey learned that the county's young men had fled to the woods and armed themselves with pitchforks to avoid the press.[97]

Most disturbing of all for the crown were the protests that surfaced in Hertfordshire in April: militiamen refused to serve and appealed to their lord lieutenant as leader of the local community to defend them against the demands of the government. The men claimed their traditional rights, which they expected their lieutenant to understand and defend. They broke new ground by declaring that hiring substitutes to serve in their places was a subtle form of taxation and thus a violation of the Petition of Right. They claimed that they were perfectly willing to pay taxes—but only those granted to the king by Parliament.[98] Finally, they appealed to the honor of their lord lieutenant. If they were forced to serve under strange officers, their morale would collapse, "by which the honorable title of our lord lieutenant [will be] much lessened."[99] In appealing so boldly to their lieutenant to sanction their refusal, the Hertfordshire militiamen relied on the lieutenancy's traditional stance in favor of local interests. The earl of Salisbury, the lieutenant and no great friend of the war, was expected to stand by his men.

The king's woes only increased as the spring passed into summer. County after county failed to meet its quota of soldiers. "The city of London, Kent, Surrey, Essex, Hertfordshire, Buckinghamshire, and Bedfordshire are so damnably restive that I do not think we shall get near our number in these places," wrote the earl of Northumberland, the king's general, in June.[100] According to the London artisan Nehemiah Wallington, "whereas before our soldiers would go against Scotland, now not any that I know of in this land would go."[101] On June 11 the city authorities refused to provide coat and conduct money for the troops they did raise.[102] Cheshire noblemen, knights, and gentry petitioned Lord Strange to intercede with the king and keep their trained bands within the county's borders.[103] On May 11 the Kentish militia mutinied despite the pleas of their deputy lieutenants, and the Suffolk deputies were threatened with their lives by mutinous troops.[104]

Lieutenants reported widespread resistance to the collection of coat and conduct money. On May 27 the deputy lieutenants of Middlesex told the council that they were making very little progress. Mr. Clapham, described as an esquire of Hammersmith, avoided paying his assessment of ten shillings, claiming he had no cash with him, so "the constable offering to attend him at his house for the money some other time, Mr. Clapham replied that it was labor lost, for the constable should not find him home, come when he would." A Mr. Smith of Middlesex, "assessed about 10s or thereabouts answered that he would not refuse to pay it, but he would be one of the last."[105] Robert Scott, of Coleshill, Warwickshire, was less coy. He told the constable "he cared not a fart for any warrant, nor for any man, yet, (after a little pause) he excepted his majesty." The deputies noted that Scott had prudently "since departed from his dwelling to parts unknown."[106] In Hampshire, the deputies collected only £500 of the £2,500 they assessed, and this failure "hath put the whole business [of pressing troops] at a great and unexpected stand."[107] Of the £600 levied in the west division of Surrey, the deputies raised only a pathetic £5.[108] County after county reported similar opposition.

Many lords and deputy lieutenants themselves balked at the demands of the government in 1640. In May the deputy lieutenants of Cheshire, who had raised vast sums of money over the previous year, petulantly complained to the council that their orders to levy five hundred troops provided no instructions about how to collect the necessary money for the enterprise.[109] This must have puzzled the council, for the Cheshire lieutenancy had already raised thousands without the benefit of such instructions. In August, the new lord lieutenant of Cambridgeshire, Lord Maynard, also requested an explicit warrant from the council to collect money for the army. The Surrey deputies, faced with a general refusal to contribute coat and conduct money, simply stopped pressing troops. The Hampshire deputies resisted stocking the county magazine, and the council condemned the Warwickshire deputy lieutenants for their pusillanimous support of the king's officers while they struggled to restore order among mutinous troops, "as that they [the deputies] seem rather to foment than to endeavor . . . the reformation thereof." [110]

By summer 1640, avoiding the wrath of their neighbors and protecting their standing filled the thoughts of most lieutenants and their deputies. The deputy lieutenants' desire to escape reprisals from their neighbors sometimes manifested itself boldly. The death in June of the earl of Suffolk, lord lieutenant of both Cambridgeshire and Suffolk, offered a golden opportunity for the Cambridgeshire deputies to escape their troubles. They blandly informed Lord General Northumberland that their commissions were now void and that he should not take it amiss if they ceased to answer his letters or perform any services in the king's behalf.[111] Recognizing the weakness of the lieutenancy, the government cast about for a new means to prosecute the war. In mid-August it hit upon the idea of reviving the commission of array. Based on a statute of Henry IV, the commissions seemed to offer a way around the vexed question of the lieutenancy's legal authority.[112] In a meeting held on July 1, the Privy Council considered the form of the new commissions but put off action until August 26, apparently in hopes of better success with the lieutenancy.[113] None was forthcoming, however, and the commissions were then formally issued for ten counties: Norfolk, Surrey, Sussex, Hampshire, Leicestershire, Rutland, Hertfordshire, Middlesex, Staffordshire, and Cumberland. Not surprisingly, these counties were the ones where the lieutenancy faced the most substantial resistance. The issuance of these commissions illustrates the crown's growing disillusion with the lieutenancy. Useful enough during peacetime, when it enforced a broad consensus about goals and policies, it was paralyzed by the appearance of irreconcilable political differences. By the time the Lords

and Commons assembled at Westminster in November 1640, the lieutenancy was moribund. Lord and deputy lieutenants alike anxiously avoided
association with the old institutions of the prerogative, and many fervently
hoped that the new Parliament would settle the kingdom's distractions and
allow them to return to their happy days as respected local leaders.

Once the Long Parliament began to sit, there was no question but that
the lieutenancy had collapsed. There is no evidence that even a single
county held musters at the orders of the lieutenancy between the autumn
of 1640 and the frantic run-up to war in the spring of 1642. In Parliament
itself the wide support the lieutenancy enjoyed in 1628 had disappeared.
On December 14, 1640, the House of Commons established a committee
of forty-nine members to consider "the misdemeanors of the lieutenants
and deputy lieutenants, and other inferior officers of all counties and all
others employed under them, and are to consider of the assessing, levying,
collecting, and taking of coat and conduct money, and all other levies of
monies contrary to law." [114] Once again, complaints focused on the burden of military charges, but in a reflection of the lieutenancy's drastic
decline, the misdeeds of individual members of the lieutenancy were being
scrutinized. [115]

Concern about the militia simmered while the Parliament dealt with
Strafford and the Laudian church, and the rapid increase of political tension at home sharply reminded parliamentarians of the need for a reliable
defense. For John Pym and the rest of the parliamentary leadership, this
meant a lieutenancy taken into their own hands. As Strafford's attainder
worked its way through Parliament in May 1641, the lieutenancy was once
again the object of legislative interest. The Commons instructed members
to investigate the political affections of their lieutenancy, and the House of
Lords went so far as to advise the king on the appointment of new lieutenants. [116] If in 1640 King Charles had been prepared to give up on the lieutenancy, many MPs were not. They resented a centrally directed lieutenancy,
but most were unprepared to dispense with a system of defense so long respected in the provinces, provided it was under parliamentary control. The
lieutenancy compared very favorably with the sinister commissions of array,
which smacked, many felt, of authoritarianism and innovation. [117] Murky
plans to use force against the Commons and effect Strafford's rescue—the
Army Plot—gave substance to the fears of parliamentarians and did much
to increase tensions. In this atmosphere, it is not surprising that Pym and
his confederates began to think about self-defense once Strafford was out of
the way. Pym's plans for reform, the ten propositions, were presented on

June 24, 1641. The key point at issue was the appointment of Charles's advisers, lords lieutenant included. The seventh point demanded "that there be good lord lieutenants and deputy lieutenants and such as may be faithful and trusty and careful of the peace of the kingdom." [118] There was as yet no overt demand for parliamentary control of the lieutenancy, but the implication was clear.

The Commons's attempts to settle the militia in Parliament's hands met with implacable opposition from the king, and its progress was slow. The Lords gave qualified support to the idea on July 9, and a committee was set to work on a new militia bill in August. The committee's charge was to consider "what power . . . is fit to be placed, and in what persons, for commanding the trained bands." [119] The work of the committee is obscure, and before a bill was perfected the outbreak of the Irish rebellion riveted the attention of both houses. The conflagration in Ireland revitalized the parliamentary cause and spurred the production of the Grand Remonstrance, an elaborate catalog of the king's misdeeds. The remonstrance included no less than four clauses condemning military charges and the lieutenancy's work. [120] Less than a week after the document was presented to the king, on December 7, a new militia bill was presented to the Commons by Sir Arthur Haselrig. [121] Fears for the security of Parliament impelled the movement toward a new lieutenancy. The Irish rebellion, continuing rumors of army conspiracies, and the king's manifest commitment to regaining the upper hand all contributed to the urgency of the moment. The king's attempt to arrest his five leading opponents in Parliament in January 1642 accelerated the movement toward a parliamentary lieutenancy. The leaders of the opposition were more determined than ever to take the militia in their own hands, and the king's supporters were weakened as a consequence of his rash action.

At the end of January 1642 the Commons petitioned the king to place the militia under the command of their nominees. On January 28, the king refused, saying that the trained bands were "by law . . . subject to no command but of his majesty, and of authority lawfully derived from him." This answer in no way satisfied the Commons, and along with the Lords they petitioned again on February 2. Charles was more conciliatory in his answer to this petition; he agreed to consider the Parliament's nominees, although he reserved the right to veto its choices. The debate dragged on as the nation moved toward war. On March 5 the Militia Ordinance passed the Commons, naming its own list of lords lieutenant. Without the approval of the king, Parliament ordered all previous royal commissions of lieutenancy to be surrendered and so seized control of the lieutenancy from the crown.[122]

Paralyzed by opposition and a lack of statutory authority, the old lieutenancy was useless by January 1642. Parliament's reformed lieutenancy, though it shared much in common with the old, was nevertheless a very different institution. Most striking was the change in personnel at the top. In contrast to previous commissions, the new lieutenancy involved a tremendous infusion of new blood. Twenty of the new lieutenants had never served in the office before, and of the veterans, several—Lords Strange, Hertford, and Cumberland among them—refused to serve. Many of these new lieutenants would hardly have qualified as lieutenants under the old regime: their rank or their lack of wealth would have prohibited such a lofty position. Some of those named for the lesser lieutenancies—the Isle of Purbeck, Bristol, and Lindsey—were not even nobles. Durham was placed in the hands of the elder Henry Vane, who, prominent though he undoubtedly was, could never have expected to hold a lieutenancy in earlier days. Many of the other new lieutenants were of inferior rank, such as Viscount Say, lieutenant of Oxfordshire and Cheshire, and a gaggle of mere barons: Paget, North, Robartes, and Willoughby of Parham, to name a few. The more prominent parliamentarians were forced to accept multiple lieutenancies because of the lack of suitable candidates. The earl of Warwick, for example, was lieutenant of both Essex and Norfolk, Holland became lieutenant of Berkshire and Middlesex, and Northumberland was given both Sussex and Northumberland.[123]

Although many of the lieutenants had strong local ties (Say in Oxfordshire and Brooke in Warwickshire, for example), some were little more than carpetbaggers (Say's own commission in Cheshire is an example), and others were hardly reliable parliamentarians. Like many during the months preceding the outbreak of the war, some of the new lieutenants tried to walk a fine line between poles. Chief Justice John Bankes, the parliamentary lieutenant of the Isle of Purbeck, was with the king at the time of his appointment, even though the acceptance of his new office meant that "I am here in a very bad condition where I may be ruined both ways."[124] Another parliamentary lieutenant straddling the fence was the earl of Rutland, lieutenant of Derbyshire. Though he accepted Parliament's commission, he attended Charles at York and even lent the king his personal coach.[125] Some of the new lieutenants were torn even more in their ambivalence: Lord Paget, lieutenant of Buckinghamshire, enforced the Militia Ordinance in his county, despite Charles's proclamation forbidding it, and still ended up in the Royalist camp.[126]

Charles made no serious move to rescue the lieutenancy from the clutches of a rebellious Parliament. Shortly after the Militia Ordinance was enforced (May 27), he issued his proclamation forbidding the mustering of the trained bands without a royal warrant and directed it to the sheriff and not the lord lieutenant.[127] The first commissions of array were issued on June 11, 1642. By reviving commissions of array to levy the Royalist army in 1642—as in 1640—the crown gave notice that it had abandoned the lieutenancy as an instrument of government.

The lieutenancy, however, did not disappear in the absence of the crown's favor; it lived on under parliamentary control. Enforcement of the Militia Ordinance was reluctant in many places. It seems clear that old habits of consensus and lingering hopes for a peaceful settlement continued, relics of the old lieutenancy. Before the ordinance passed, conciliatory schemes continued to surface in some areas. In Kent there was a proposal to have a dual lieutenancy, with joint royal and parliamentary lieutenants. Even after this expedient was ignored, many new lieutenants, and especially deputy lieutenants, showed a reluctance to fight a civil war.[128] Lieutenants were slow to name deputies, deputies were slow to appoint officers, and everyone was reluctant to muster. Both houses of Parliament pressed lieutenants to act, but after over a month of inactivity, little or nothing had been done in many counties. Even where action did occur, it was often tentative and explicitly defensive in nature. As Anthony Fletcher points out, the first Militia Ordinance musters were not taken as overt steps toward war but in obedience to tradition and with confused ideas about self-defense. A lord lieutenant's orders still carried considerable weight, whatever the provenance of his commission.[129]

The parliamentary lieutenancy was largely responsible for raising the army fielded against the king in 1642, and it continued to supply men and money into the later years of the war. Ironically, many of the parliamentary lieutenancy's activities during this period were precisely those that the Parliament had declared illegal in 1640—forcing the provinces to maintain troops at local expense and to provide the raw manpower for the war effort. Yet the lieutenancy's survival reflected its inveterate localism, for it placed the parliamentary war effort in the hands of local gentlemen who operated with a high degree of autonomy. Parliamentary deputies never really overcame this localism, and ultimately, even Parliament abandoned the lieutenancy when it centralized the military and created the New Model Army.[130]

The irony of the lieutenancy's collapse and rebirth from 1640 to 1642 is that an institution established to guard against rebellion, its primary duty "enemies and rebels and traitors to fight, and them to invade resist repress subdue slay kill and put to execution of death by all ways and means," became the organizer of rebellion.[131] The king was forced to fall back on medieval precedent with his commissions of array, and his war effort suffered as a result.[132] Although the institution continued to exist, the civil wars reduced the lieutenancy to irrelevance, for it never completely abandoned the defense of local interests and the maintenance of local stability. The war demanded more than compromise; it required victory, and Parliament ultimately devised methods that did not require lords lieutenant to triumph. The old lieutenancy was at one and the same time a means of cementing the loyalty of powerful nobles and a recognition of their political and social importance. The Tudor lieutenancy had allowed the crown to go a step beyond "overmighty" lords. Lords lieutenant and their deputies continued to enjoy considerable autonomy, but from 1604 it was an authority cloaked in the king's prerogative. The compromise was satisfactory all around; the crown gained an element of control hitherto unknown over its greater subjects, and aristocrats gained the additional cachet that royal favor bestowed. The bargain was equally beneficial for the relationship between province and capital. The crown created a cheap form of administration, which provided both military and civilian services. This service was paid for at the price of limited central control. The government could never push its claims too hard, for the survival of the system depended upon local cooperation.

The tradition continued after the Stuart accession—indeed, the balance tended to shift even more toward the provinces. Lieutenancies increasingly became hereditary, and deputies were appointed without reference to Whitehall. Although still useful in some areas, the lieutenancy focused on pleasing its local constituents and gradually transformed itself into a provincial advocate. Musters became rituals designed to glorify lieutenants and to reaffirm the local hierarchy, and difficult decisions (like pursuing defaulters) were passed to others or ignored altogether. When under Charles I a serious effort was made to alter this balance, it came as a profound shock. The lieutenancy had earned the respect of the provinces for its sympathy and consideration for local interests. Reconciling local differences and warding off intrusions from the outside were satisfying, if not always easy, chores. But central-versus-local tension was always inherent within the institution; lieutenants still held office by virtue of the prerogative. When Charles began pressing for reform, this congenital ambivalence came to the fore.

The lieutenancy survived the Parliament of 1628 because of the perception that it continued to be focused on the provinces. The Personal Rule did not alter this fact, although the line between satisfying the Privy Council and the community became harder to walk. But the Scottish crisis tore apart the lieutenancy. It had always been an institution delicately poised between Whitehall and the counties, and as the distance between the two widened, the lieutenancy lost its way. Attacked from one side by opponents of the crown as the agent of an iniquitous policy, it found itself simultaneously abandoned by a king who no longer trusted it. The result was oblivion— at least temporarily. The lieutenancy had been an integral part of English government for generations, and when Charles II came to restore the monarchical state, no one doubted that a revived lieutenancy would result. But restoration is not replication, and Charles II's lieutenancy proved to be very different from that of his father.

CHAPTER III

Restoration,
1660–1663

FOR TWO DAYS IN JULY 1664 some of the most prominent men in the county of Norfolk met together in a small room in Norwich Castle. The tumbledown old fortress stood atop a hill that dominated the city, and from its ramshackle collection of chambers and buildings the shire's leaders issued their orders. Grand juries, quarter sessions, county courts, and assizes had all been held there at one time or another; the castle was the heart of the local community. It was only natural that the lord lieutenant, Horatio, first Lord Townshend, would convene a meeting of his deputy lieutenants there.

The gentlemen who filed into the chamber that normally housed the county's grand jury were no strangers to the room or to Townshend. This was their seventh meeting since January, and some may have hoped that it would be a brief one. Alas for those who came from some distance over dusty summer roads, this was not to be; the meeting would last two days. There was a lot of business to attend to; the lieutenancy, once an employment full of honor but relatively free of burdensome duties, had changed dramatically since the joyous return of King Charles II.

No one in the room would have questioned the justice or necessity of the Restoration; indeed, several, not least Townshend himself, played important roles in the king's good fortune. These men were united in their

support of the restored monarchy and assumed their places in the lieutenancy with alacrity, in spite of its added responsibilities. Besides Townshend
himself there were eleven deputies present. They represented many of the
oldest and most distinguished families of the county: the roll of deputies
contained a Walpole, a Gawdy, a Holland, a Hare, and a Wodehouse, and
the others were equally distinguished. Of those in attendance, only two,
Sir John Holland and Sir Ralph Hare, had parliamentarian backgrounds,
and both had abandoned that cause long before the Restoration. Their fellow deputies were Royalists; their youth had kept many of them off the
battlefields of the civil wars, but they had suffered for their connections.
Sir Jacob Astley's father, the first baronet, had been one of Charles I's most
devoted servants; Thomas, Lord Richardson, lost his father in a Norwich
jail, where he died serving time for his role in a failed Royalist plot. And
as known Royalists, all the other deputies would have borne the intense
scrutiny of the authorities during the interregnum.

It was, then, a distinguished group that met in Norwich on July 18.
But it was a group with a cause: the survival of the restored monarchy.
The prewar lieutenancy's insouciance about its duty to the crown was gone;
after the chastening lessons of the civil war and interregnum, these men
knew how disastrous localism could be. And so they worked—they worked
harder than had their fathers, devoting great concern to details that would
have been dismissed as unimportant or burdensome in an earlier time.

On the eighteenth the deputies handled cases of assessment and default-
ing militiamen. Like deputies elsewhere, they were haunted by memories
of the inadequate enforcement of military obligations characteristic of the
prewar period, and their concern led in the 1660s to the creation of a far
more elaborate and effective system of assessment. Complex methods of
assessment helped distribute the burden equitably, but unlike their predecessors, the Restoration deputies grappled with the hard choices that
the maintenance of an effective militia required. In some counties the
lieutenancy calculated the acreage and value of every estate, an extremely
complicated business.[1] On this day, the deputies met to punish those individuals who failed to meet their obligations. Summoned by warrants issued
by the lord lieutenant, malefactors came before the deputies to answer for
their default.[2] Haling defaulters before them was a new experience for the
deputies, and it illustrated their changing role. Such routine enforcement
had been anathema to the old lieutenancy, which usually dodged this duty
and left the work of punishment to the Privy Council. In 1664, however,
the deputies berated, fined, and at times even jailed their neighbors for

ignoring their duty to the central government. A long, wearisome day passed as the lieutenant and his deputies sought to bestir the community with this mixture of persuasion and coercion. Unfinished at the close of the day, the meeting ended in an adjournment.

On the nineteenth the deputies resumed, and once again the tedious business of punishing defaulters began. Restlessness on the part of the deputies increased as the day wore on. As the commission worked, some deputies wandered in and out of the room, perhaps bored or anxious for a respite from their labors. Vexed by the flagging energies of some of the members, the commission decided to forbid anyone from leaving the table before the work was done; scheduling musters and dividing the county into administrative districts remained on the agenda. Fortified by this resolution, the deputies plowed through what remained of their agenda and at last ended their meeting before the day was out.[3]

This meeting of the Norfolk lieutenancy shows how fundamentally politics and administration had changed since the 1630s. The overwhelmingly localist bias of the old lieutenancy had been replaced by a new emphasis on the needs of the crown. Deputies were now intent on forcing the community to meet its obligations to the king as they had never been in the past. Political horizons were wider in the 1660s; lieutenants and even their deputies looked to the national stage much more often than in the past. As a result, the balance between the lieutenancy's local and central roles was gradually shifting. Other factors contributed to these changes; the existence of permanent religious and ideological differences, for example, undermined the lieutenancy's utility as a facilitator of inclusion. The kingdom now included souls who could not or would not be included in the body politic. The lieutenancy adapted to such changed circumstances in a variety of ways; although outwardly an exact replica of the prewar lieutenancy, by the 1670s, it was a very different institution in composition, function, and political orientation.

THE GROWING CIVIL UNREST in 1640 had destroyed the lieutenancy as an effective instrument of the king's government. Charles's reliance on the commissions of array to raise his armies in the fight against Parliament was an admission that the lieutenancy, as he knew it, had outlived its usefulness. Parliament, anxious to cloak all of its actions in the mantle of administrative tradition, sought to bolster its legitimacy by seizing control of the lieutenancy. The parliamentarian lord lieutenancy, however, was but a shadow of the Caroline institution. Lieutenants themselves were few;

often responsible for several counties, many lacked the local connections and high rank of most of their predecessors. In many counties the lieutenancy's very existence was tenuous after 1642; it never functioned properly in counties where a strong Royalist movement flourished. In the west and north the lieutenancy withered as soon as war began; it lingered only in areas under firm parliamentarian control. In East Anglia, deputy lieutenants continued to meet and transact business into the mid-1640s, but even there the institution died slowly. In many counties deputy lieutenants acted independently of their nominal superiors, who often had little connection with or interest in their charges. As the war continued and new forms of military organization evolved, the deputies found themselves increasingly relegated to administrative irrelevance. County associations and committees bypassed the lieutenancy, working more efficiently when they did. By 1645 the lieutenancy had become an empty shell of its former self.[4]

The abolition of the House of Lords in February 1649 provided a dramatic symbol of the eclipse of both the peerage and the lieutenancy.[5] The years of the Commonwealth and Protectorate saw many debates about the nature and control of the militia, but its traditional leaders, the nobility, had nothing to do with the experiments of the interregnum. Tainted by royalism and reluctant to serve a usurping power, they retired abroad or to their estates and waited for better times.[6]

The interregnum's closest approximation of the old lieutenancy proved to be one of its most hated innovations: the major generals. The first major general was appointed in March 1655, as Cromwell put it, to ensure "the security and peace of the nation, the suppressing of vice, and the encouraging of virtue."[7] The Protector divided England into eleven districts, each with its own major general. Although originally they were responsible for military security, within weeks of their first appointments their writ grew (as, indeed, had the lieutenancy's early in its life) to include a multitude of chores, from harassing Royalist plotters to suppressing ungodliness and disorder. Major General Edward Whalley, for example, proudly reported in April 1656, "This I may truly say: you may ride over all Nottinghamshire and not see a beggar or a wandering rogue." Major General James Berry, whose charge was the Welsh Marches, fumed over the excessive burden of civil administration he carried. He complained to Secretary John Thurloe in January 1656 that he had become little more than a "toiling magistrate."[8]

Although the regime of the major generals resembled that of the Caroline lieutenants in some respects—individuals were given wide authority over the provinces by the central government, and their duties expanded as the needs of government changed—the major generals differed radically from the old lieutenancy in both form and function. They were financed by a 10 percent tax on the estates of Royalists ("decimation"), which, unlike prewar militia rates, was raised ruthlessly and caused great hardship. Their duties involved political repression: they purged municipal corporations and county magistracies; they hunted down known or suspected Royalists. They were also political patrons, seeking out and rewarding supporters of the regime. They were chosen for their ability and, above all, for their loyalty to the government—social standing and local connections were of little importance. None were aristocrats, and some of them could advance what were at best doubtful claims to gentility. None seems to have served as even a deputy lieutenant before the wars. A Norfolk Royalist contemptuously described them as "an obscure company of mean fellows," who "lorded it over the nobility, as well as the gentry and clergy." They were also extremely unpopular. As the sectary Edmund Ludlow put it: "The major generals carried things with unheard of insolence . . . decimating to extremity whom they pleased . . . threatening such as would not yield a ready submission to their orders with transportation to Jamaica or some other plantations in the West Indies; and suffering none to escape their persecutions but those that would betray their own party."[9]

The major generals embodied the upheavals that had so altered the nature of English government since the revolution. They were agents of central authority, thrown up by events that required the creation of a wholly new structure of government. The existence of permanent opposition, whether from Royalists or the many radical sects (whose object was often the violent initiation of the millennium), required a sophisticated response from those in power. Political tests had to be placed alongside the traditional social ones. A man who craved a seat on the bench of justices now had to be politically sound, and his social standing took second place. There were, of course, gentlemen among the magistracy of the interregnum, but their social standing was not their principal qualification; their political enthusiasm was.[10] Will the candidate take the engagement? Will he accept the Westminster Confession? In the interregnum the answers to these questions were at least as important as the old ones: is he of a good family? Is he hospitable? The introduction of the major generals was the Cromwellian government's attempt to find faithful administrators of these new tests. The experiment did not outlive Cromwell and could hardly be described as an overwhelming success, but the example was not to be lost on Charles II.[11]

The decay of the Protectorate accelerated after Cromwell's death in 1658, and crisis seemed inevitable by the beginning of 1660. If many Royalists were exhausted after years of failed plots and persecution, all were not idle, and the preparations they made for action should the republic fall hinted at the course restoration of the lieutenancy would later take.[12] In January 1660 no one expected a peaceful restoration; the exiled court hoped to take advantage of the anarchic conditions that reigned in England by launching another rising.[13] In preparation, a systematic attempt was made to organize Royalists throughout the country. Reliable men—many of whom were later to become lords lieutenant—were given commissions to raise their shires for the king.[14] As the winter of 1660 came to a close, however, it became clear that such precautions might not be needed. What had appeared impossible in January or February—the peaceful return of Charles II to his throne—seemed a certainty by April. By the time the king made his entrance into London on May 29, the problems of gaining a foothold on English soil vanished and were replaced by an even more perplexing array of difficulties. Consolidation and vigilance became imperative to the success of the Restoration, and a revived lieutenancy was to play an important role from the outset of the new regime.

In some respects, the reestablishment of the lieutenancy preceded the return of the king. Still in exile in the spring of 1659, Charles received a very long letter of advice from one of his father's most devoted old servants, the marquis of Newcastle. Perhaps determined to make a mark with his young master, Newcastle took it upon himself to survey nearly every aspect of government from foreign policy to entertainment at court. But his first priority, coming before the church, the economy, and everything else, was the militia. Though the marquis was a harsh judge of London ("the bane and loss of your royal father") and advised strict control of the city's trained bands, he also called for the reconstruction of the prewar lieutenancy, which he described as "a great advantage to your majestie," provided that the new lieutenants were "well affected." This was advice that the king took to heart.[15] The decision to reappoint lords lieutenant must have come very early in 1660, as part of a general determination by the crown to revivify the ancient constitution. The first lords lieutenant received their commissions early in July 1660, and by January 1661 every English county had its lieutenant. The speed of this reconstitution testifies to the importance of the office for the crown. Although the government badly wanted a lieutenancy bolstered by parliamentary statute, and indeed made passage of a militia act one of its first priorities, the appointment of lieutenants could not wait for legislation.[16] By contrast, many offices in the central administration went unfilled for several months. While surviving officeholders simply returned to their posts, other important places waited some time for new occupants. The earl of Southampton was not appointed lord treasurer until September 1660, the chief justice of common pleas was not named until October, and the barons of the exchequer were not finally appointed until November. Likewise, there was no keeper of the privy seal and no chancellor of the exchequer until the spring of 1661.[17] These all came after the lieutenancy was revived. Locally, the reformation of the commission of the peace proceeded erratically from the summer of 1660; the government relied on the newly restored lords lieutenant to offer advice on appointments.[18] The lieutenancy, then, was one of the crown's first priorities in the reestablishment of royal government.

Of the forty-one lords lieutenant appointed in 1660, twenty-six received their commissions in July and most of the rest saw their patents pass the great seal in August.[19] The sometimes lengthy process of preparing a commission and having it sealed indicates that most of the king's choices for his lieutenants had been made within the first month of his return to England, if not before. His appointments were made with no statutory authority; for the present, the lieutenancy would continue to rely on the king's prerogative for its constitutionality. The crown had no intention, however, of allowing the lieutenancy to fall into the constitutional gray area that had undermined royal control over the prewar institution. The lords lieutenant appointed in 1660 were named by virtue of the prerogative, but King Charles would not wait long to bolster their position by statute.

The forty-one men appointed lords lieutenant in the critical opening months of the regime provide an interesting contrast to their prewar predecessors. Not surprisingly, as a group they had far more military experience than prewar lieutenants. At least half had served at some time during the upheavals of the mid-century. Of the rest, some, like Arthur Capel, earl of Essex, were too young to have fought—though it was most unusual for any lieutenant to have survived the war untouched. Essex's father, for example, had been executed for leading a Royalist rising in 1648.

The lords lieutenant of 1660 were carefully chosen for their loyalty to the crown. This alone accounted for most of the significant differences between lieutenants of the prewar period and their successors. Relatively few (only eight) were survivors of the Caroline lieutenancy. Most of these men were grandees—Newcastle, Northumberland, Hertford, and Worcester—whose continued political activity after Charles II's return made them natural candidates for lieutenancies. The overwhelming number of Charles II's lords lieutenant were Royalists. Only seven had been active against the king's father.[20] Four of these, Albemarle, Manchester, Sandwich, and Northumberland, had played vital roles in the Restoration. The others, Carlisle, Suffolk, and Fauconberg, were all important regional figures. Suffolk's former enthusiasm for the parliamentary cause had evaporated by September 1647, when the House of Commons resolved to impeach him for high treason. Carlisle and Fauconberg were former Cromwellians who faithfully served the Protector and violently opposed Richard Cromwell's radical successors. Suffolk sat the Commonwealth out quietly in the country; the other two were deeply involved in the Royalist plots that flourished in the final days of the English republic.[21] A few, such as the fourth Lord Brooke, came from parliamentarian families but had not themselves been enemies of the monarchy. Brooke, for example, though the son of the second lord, an inveterate enemy of Charles I and a casualty of the civil war, was only five when his father was killed. His lieutenancy of Staffordshire was recognition of his service as one of the delegates sent to invite Charles II's return in 1660.[22]

The rest, however, had impeccable Royalist pedigrees.[23] Some were representatives of the great noble families that had always provided the crown with its lords lieutenant: Howard, Cavendish, Seymour, and Sackville, for example. Representatives of these clans retained their preeminent places in their shires as lieutenants: the earl of Berkshire in Middlesex, the duke of Newcastle in Nottinghamshire, the duke of Somerset in Somerset, and the fifth earl of Dorset in Sussex. These men were Royalist grandees, some of whom, like Newcastle and Somerset, had worked for the Stuart cause unstintingly and suffered a great deal as a consequence. Their appointments recognized their service and standing, along with the new dukedoms and other royal favors granted upon Charles's return.[24]

Many of the new lieutenants, however, were not of great noble lineage, though nearly all boasted at least substantial gentry stock. If many were from noble houses, they ranked considerably beneath the lords lieutenant of Charles I's reign. Three of the restored king's lieutenants were commoners when commissioned: Sir John Granville, Sir Horatio Townshend, and Thomas Howard.[25] No less than eighteen of the forty-one lieutenants held ranks below that of earl—a striking contrast with the reign of Charles I. Before 1640, only three lieutenants were without at least an earl's coronet: Lord Maynard, joint lieutenant of Essex with the earl of Warwick (1635–40); Viscount Wimbledon, joint lieutenant of Surrey (1627–38) with the earls of Arundel and Nottingham; and Viscount Conway, lieutenant of Hampshire (1625–31). Conway was the only Caroline lieutenant in sole command of a county without the aid of a higher-ranking peer.[26]

New lieutenants such as Lords Belasyse, Windsor, and Newport (lieutenants of the East Riding, Worcestershire, and Shropshire) were representative of the king's choices. All were barons, all had been in arms for the king, and all were zealously committed to the defense of the Restoration. The lieutenant of the West Riding of Yorkshire, Marmaduke, first Baron Langdale, typified the new lords lieutenant. The Langdale family had resided quietly in the West Riding for generations, playing little part in county affairs—an exclusion that must have owed largely to their Catholicism. Sir Marmaduke had taken up the king's cause from the beginning of the civil wars, becoming one of the Royalists' most accomplished cavalry commanders. He fought in most of the principal engagements of the war, was exiled in 1646, and returned to raise troops in the second civil war of 1648. Langdale spent the rest of the interregnum making secret trips to England in futile efforts to organize rebellion. His estates were confiscated by the Parliament; he suffered losses estimated at £160,000. With the coming of the Restoration, his devotion to the cause required some reward. In 1658 he was ennobled, and on October 9, 1660, Langdale was commissioned lieutenant of the West Riding.[27]

Like many of his fellows, Lord Langdale received his lieutenancy as a reward for devoted service. His reliability and merit earned in the Royalist cause outweighed his relative social obscurity as well as his Catholicism. There were others; Lords Lovelace, Loughborough, Mordaunt, and Campden were given their commissions as part payment of the debts Charles II owed his supporters. Local standing and personal worth, so important in the choice of early Stuart lieutenants, were eclipsed by the crown's need to satisfy deserving Royalists, as well as by the absolute necessity of protecting the monarchy against counterrevolution from adherents of the Good Old Cause. Cavalier lieutenants, it was hoped, could be relied upon to be vigilant.

In making his appointments, the king considered absolute loyalty and former service most important. The regime wanted to promote conciliation and did so when it could: passing the Act of Indemnity and attempting to negotiate a church settlement that could satisfy moderate Presbyterians, for example.[28] But early in 1660 one of Edward Hyde's correspondents warned him, "There is so insolent a spirit among the nobility that I really fear 'twill turn into an aristocracy."[29] The king and Chancellor Hyde took the essence of this advice to heart. Neither wanted to risk placing the provinces in the hands of any but the most trusted Royalists. They were prepared to compromise on what they believed to be adiaphora—the land settlement and the precise nature of the Book of Common Prayer, for example—but they would not allow the lieutenancy to slip from the crown's grasp as it had in 1642. As the lesson of the major generals had shown, when used to police dissent, a quasi-military institution with a flexible jurisdiction could be of vital importance in ensuring the survival of the newly constituted government.

The field of candidates for the new lieutenancies was a wide one, and the king and his advisers were hard-pressed to make their choices; competition was fierce. As early as February, when choosing the king's commissioners in the counties, Hyde complained bitterly, "I have been so long broke between those two violent millstones, the Catholics and Presbyterians, that nothing they say of me doth much trouble me."[30] Aspirants for lieutenancies were legion: Royalists, Presbyterians, Catholics, and former Cromwellians all vied for places. Some were nominated by others, like Lord Herbert, the duke of Beaufort's heir. On June 15, 1660, representatives of the gentry of Glamorganshire and Monmouthshire successfully petitioned the crown for Herbert's appointment as lord lieutenant of their county; his patent passed the great seal on July 30. Others sought commissions for themselves, although few were as blunt as the earl of Bolingbroke, who wrote Secretary of State Edward Nicholas a very brief letter: "Sir, my desire is in which I beg your favor [is] to be lord lieutenant of Bedfordshire where all my land lies. My name is Bolingbroke."[31] The earl's request was denied, and the place was given to the earl of Cleveland, an elderly favorite of Charles I who had fought tenaciously for the Royalist cause. Cleveland actively supported Charles II during the interregnum, had lost his estates to Parliament, and only narrowly escaped execution in 1651 when he helped spirit the king out of England after the debacle at Worcester. Because he had also been lieutenant of Bedfordshire before the war, there was little doubt that Cleveland would receive the appointment.[32] Certainly Bolingbroke, a scion of the parliamentarian St. John family as well as a Presbyterian, had much less claim on the king.

A peer's social position no longer guaranteed his appointment to a lieutenancy. More than one man who in earlier times would unquestionably have been lieutenant of his county was passed over in 1660. The earl of Salisbury, whose family had monopolized the lieutenancy of Hertfordshire since 1588, saw the upstart Lord Capel given command there; the earl of

Warwick, whose father had been lieutenant of Essex throughout Charles I's reign and who was that county's largest landowner, was ignored in favor of the earl of Oxford; the earl of Bedford saw his old lieutenancy in Devon given to the parvenu Albemarle.[33] All of these men were the natural candidates for the lieutenancies of their shires—their families had long filled the office and they might have expected it themselves in due course. All, however, had been adherents of Parliament, all remained Puritan in their religious and political beliefs, and all, consequently, failed to receive the call to office. Another peer who would have been a lieutenant under Charles I, the earl of Pembroke, was reputed to be a Quaker; the Herbert monopoly of the Wiltshire lieutenancy was therefore broken and the impeccably Royalist duke of Somerset was appointed. In Northamptonshire the senior branch of the Cecil family had been as powerful as the junior line in Hertfordshire during the time of Charles II's predecessors: earls of Exeter had followed one another in the lieutenancy with monotonous regularity since Queen Elizabeth's day. In 1660, however, the fourth earl, John Cecil, whose father had been a moderate parliamentarian, was forced to share his authority with the former Royalist Mildmay Fane, earl of Westmorland. Exeter at least kept a partial grip on the county for the Cecils, but sharing the lieutenancy with a man who had served his grandfather as a mere deputy in the 1630s must have been galling.[34]

The tendency of the crown to avoid placing lieutenancies in the hands of former parliamentarians was not entirely the result of fear of counter-revolution or the desire to punish old enemies. As in the case of the earls of Warwick and Oxford, both of whom were socially well suited for the lieutenancy of Essex, the king's choice naturally gravitated toward former Royalists. It must be stressed that the king alone selected his lieutenants and that his personal feelings as well as political and security concerns affected his choices. Personal influence at court could provide an important boost for an aristocrat's ambitions.

Thus backstairs intrigue at court also had its part in the search for lieutenants. When, for example, in the middle of June the king was considering who to appoint lieutenant of Oxfordshire, there were rumored to be two candidates: the earl of Lindsey, whose primary interests were at court and in Lincolnshire, and Lord Say and Sele, whose local prominence in Oxfordshire balanced his parliamentarian connections and religious nonconformity. Both men had obvious disabilities as lieutenants; Lindsey was a stranger to the county, and Say was adamantly opposed by local Royalists. A friend of Chancellor Hyde's informed him of rumors he had heard at court in a letter dated June 15: "My lord of Falkland [a prominent Cavalier who also resided in Oxfordshire] met me in court this morning and told me that he had heard that my lord of Lindsey was to be their lord lieutenant of Oxfordshire, where he [Lindsey] never did anything for the king's service." Lindsey was, according to Falkland, "unworthy" of the place. Nevertheless, Falkland claimed that he was unreservedly opposed to the other candidate he had heard mentioned: "He thought my lord Say so much more unworthy . . . that in case he were the man, he would oppose whatsoever he would do by all the interest he had there, for though (said he [Falkland]) 'I cannot be so impudent and so importunate as some men are to get places, I can and shall be as sensible as any man, if I be very much disobliged.' " Such, the chancellor's correspondent reported, "is the language of very many of the king's party who think his enemies have much more favor at court than his friends." [35] Perhaps not surprisingly (despite Falkland's coy disclaimer), when the king named a lord lieutenant of Oxfordshire on July 17, it was Falkland who won the prize.

In October 1660, the Royalist gentlemen of Wiltshire were alarmed to hear that Sir Anthony Ashley Cooper was being considered as a candidate for lord lieutenant and immediately protested the possibility to their court connections.[36] Cooper was not appointed. The earl of Winchilsea, lieutenant of Kent, fearful lest his commission fall into other hands while he served as ambassador to Constantinople, complained about "underhand dealing" among his own deputies.[37] The earl of Derby was also the victim of court intrigue. In December 1662, after Derby settled an acrimonious dispute with the government over his appointment of deputies in Lancashire, secretary of state Sir Henry Bennett received a letter from Cheshire. Written by one of Derby's own deputy lieutenants, Richard Legh, it proposed toppling the earl: "There are very many persons of good quality in Cheshire who heartily wish that my lord Gerard had the command of the lord lieutenancy here, for which some good reasons might be given. . . . Divers of them have earnestly importuned me to promote their desires, the accomplishment whereof I must confess would be as great a satisfaction to me as to any." [38] The scheme failed, but that a lieutenant's own servants could be drawn into such plots illustrates the increasing complexity—not to say treachery—of Restoration politics.[39]

In light of such pressures from office-hungry Cavaliers and the security needs of the crown, it is not surprising how different the role of lords lieutenant in 1660 was from that of 1625. The transformation of the office into a reward for faithful service and its potential as a political tool in the struggle to secure the Restoration required emphasis on new qualifications. Social standing, though still a factor (those commoners appointed in 1660 were, after all, ennobled relatively quickly) became less important than Royalist pedigree and zeal for church and king. This change, so evident in the crown's choices for lords lieutenant, becomes still more obvious when the appointment of deputy lieutenants is examined.

The reestablishment of the lieutenancy in its prewar form naturally included the return of the deputy lieutenant. As before the war, the lieutenancy's need for local men to administer its responsibilities made deputies essential. The crown did make one important change: the appointment of deputies would no longer be the prerogative of the lieutenants. Charles I had abandoned his right to vet deputies in one of the first acts of his reign (and the practice had in any case become infrequent under James I); his son refused to make that concession, though it was at first assumed that the lieutenants would be allowed free choice in naming their deputies. In June 1660 Henry Townshend confided to his diary, "The parliament declines meddling with solely the militia of the nation, leaving it to the king, who intends to make deputy lieutenants in all countries according to ye old manner."[40] Nevertheless, to the discontent of a few lords lieutenant— notably the earl of Derby—it was quickly made clear that all nominations for deputy lieutenant would be carefully scrutinized. Lieutenants were to nominate candidates, and the crown would approve or reject them.

Organization of the lieutenancy got under way in the summer of 1660, and subsequent parliamentary action regularized the process. The Militia Act of 1661 gave the lieutenancy statutory authority but confirmed only its existing structure and declared unequivocally that it and the militia belonged completely in the hands of the king. According to the act, Parliament had no right whatsoever to interfere in the command of the militia or the appointment of its leaders. These statements removed once and for all the ambiguity that had resulted in the parliamentary seizure of the lieutenancy in 1642; the act was meant to prevent any repetition of that event. Deputy lieutenants were to be nominated by the lieutenants but commissioned only following the king's approval.

Hyde, already straining under the enormous work load generated by the need to appoint a wholly new government, nevertheless must have devoted a great deal of energy to sifting through the lords lieutenants' choices for deputies. Lists of nominees poured into Whitehall throughout the summer of 1660, many of which survive in the state papers. They offer an interesting insight into the government's policy for new appointments. Considerable care was taken to ensure that the men approved were ideologically sound; the lists have many insertions and deletions. Few prominent Presbyterians received commissions.[41] It is not surprising that the lieutenants, nearly all strong Royalists, nominated few Presbyterians or former parliamentarians, but it is interesting that there seems to have been no attempt on the part of the crown to intrude a few into office. The king's desire to conciliate the Presbyterians was strictly limited by a concern neither to offend the Cavalier lieutenants nor to entrust the defense of the throne to former rebels.

Some lieutenants, despite their Cavalier sympathies, nominated gentlemen whom the crown disallowed, presumably on the grounds that they had been insufficiently zealous partisans of the king.[42] The names of Sir Samuel Luke, Sir Ralph Verney, Sir George Sondes, and Robert Barnham were struck off the lists sent in by their lieutenants. All of these gentlemen had been moderates during the civil wars; Barnham was a member of the Long Parliament who ceased to attend the house after 1643; Verney, also an MP, fled abroad in 1643 rather than sign the covenant; Luke was excluded from Parliament by Pride's Purge; and Sondes sought neutrality in the wars. All had been sequestrated or imprisoned during the interregnum, but none distinguished themselves by joining the many Royalist plots of the period.[43] Though these men, and others like them, were deemed sufficiently loyal by their lieutenants to serve as deputies—in this case lords Bruce, Lovelace, and Winchilsea, Cavaliers all—the crown apparently required more reliable men.

The case of the earl of Derby's choices as deputies in Lancashire from 1660 to 1662 is instructive.[44] Charles Stanley, eighth earl of Derby, took the place of his executed father as the lord lieutenant of Cheshire and Lancashire at the Restoration. Successive earls of Derby had held the office since 1585, and there was no question but that the eighth earl would also receive the honor when commissions were granted in 1660. The Stanley monopoly of the lieutenancy might well have encouraged the earl to assume that he was on safe ground in his nominations for deputies, but he provoked the king's fury by his obstinate refusal to abandon the old-fashioned ways of a great northern magnate.[45] Derby had been unhappy with the government's insistence upon reviewing his appointments in 1660, and subsequent events did nothing to endear him to the king.[46] The earl's high-handed persecution of the former parliamentary governor of the Isle of Man (ignoring the Act of Oblivion, which Derby held did not apply to acts committed on the island [47]) irritated Charles; meanwhile, the failure of Derby's private bill for compensation in Parliament further alienated the earl.[48] Additional complications in the relationship between subject and sovereign ensued.

The passage of the more comprehensive Militia Act of 1662 voided the commissions of the deputy lieutenants named before it came into effect; thus lords lieutenant were required to name a new set of deputies. Derby had his nominees in very quickly. He chose to continue those who were already in office and wanted to add several others. Two of his choices met with the violent opposition of a local faction led by Sir Roger Bradshaigh and Colonel Richard Kirkby. Both lifelong Royalists and longtime sufferers in behalf of the Stuart cause, they felt that they themselves deserved recognition in the form of a deputy lieutenancy and were outraged that Derby had chosen two former rebels instead.[49] Derby supported Sir Gilbert Ireland and Sir Richard Houghton. Houghton, a former member of the Long Parliament and servant of the Protector, sustained many Lancashire Presbyterian ministers in their hour of need. Ireland's nomination was even more galling for the former Royalists. He had been a captain in the parliamentarian army, an unshakable Presbyterian, and a vigorous supporter of the Protectorate, and his association with Sir George Booth's abortive Royalist rising in 1659 did nothing to satisfy the old Cavaliers.

Kirkby and Bradshaigh set to work at court to undermine Derby's position, and in October 1662, Ireland and Houghton were rejected. Derby had testified to the loyalty of his nominees, "whereunto I was advised by my lord chief justice of the common pleas, as considering the one [Houghton] a real convert, and the other a man of estate and interest (and so they both are) and fit (and probably by this means) to be reclaimed."[50] Nevertheless, the court was ill-disposed to support former Cromwellians over Royalists, and the lord lieutenant's candidates were rebuffed. Although this was mortification enough for Derby, the king ordered him to appoint the Cavaliers as deputies. In an attempt to display his authority still further, shortly afterward the king ordered Derby to appoint Alexander Rigby, who, Secretary Bennett said, "is . . . very able and right well-affected to his majesty's person and government" to a deputy lieutenancy.[51] Rigby had strenuously opposed Derby's recent political interference in the corporation of Preston and boasted that "whatsoever business he the said earl did appear in he would oppose him to the utmost of his power."[52] Rigby, however, like Ireland and Houghton, was a Presbyterian, and when the court made this discovery his nomination was dropped.[53]

Derby responded by absolutely refusing to cooperate. Kirkby and Bradshaigh, he claimed, succeeded by persuading the court that "they are the leaders and managers of the affections and interests of all the gentry of this county." Through their insinuations, the king had been convinced that Derby was "last in the affections of the gentry" in Lancashire. This was completely false, he said, and indeed the earl took credit for Bradshaigh's election as knight of the shire. According to the lieutenant, Kirkby and Bradshaigh were engaged in a factional attempt to displace him: "Now because they could find nothing immediately to object against me, they have gone mediate ways, to find fault . . . with the persons of some of my deputies."[54]

Derby fought vigorously but failed. The king was determined to control the lieutenancy, and submission to his will was simply a lesson that future lords lieutenant would have to learn. In fact, one memorandum produced during the dispute faulted the crown for even explaining its reasons for rejecting Derby's nominees: "But this showing reasons against private particular persons may increase the king's enemies. His commands of this nature will not admit of debates." The anonymous writer went on to admit that Derby's violent reaction was perhaps understandable because "anciently the lord lieutenant gave his commissions to his deputies without expecting the king's approbation."[55]

Provincial faction was not the only factor involved in the naming of deputies, as the Lancashire case illustrates. The central government's determination to keep the lieutenancy in its hands meant that lieutenants were under much closer scrutiny from Whitehall than ever before. The earls of Derby were no longer "kings of Lancashire"; Charles II was the only king in England. The struggle highlights some of the issues involved in the reestablishment of the lieutenancy. Faction within counties developed rapidly, particularly between "old" Royalists, who had supported and suffered for Charles II's father, and "new" Royalists, whose support for the crown began after the war—or even later. Kirkby and Bradshaigh are representative of the old Royalist style of politics, easily recognizable in every county. They meant to be obliged and were contemptuous of the Presbyterians, who welcomed the king back to his throne. As Sir John Bramston of Chelmsford wrote, "And they [the Presbyterians] were too crafty for the king . . . for they persuaded the king and Sir Edward Hyde that the king could not come home but by the Presbyterians, who all truckled for employments and honors, whereas it was the Cavalier party, the loyal gentry that brought him in in truth."[56] The sentiment of one Lincolnshire Cavalier who had been left out of the restored commission of the peace in June 1660 was typical:

"I am ashamed to appear anywhere with such a disgrace on me." Naturally, he blamed his exclusion on a "Presbyterian meddler."[57] Gentlemen continued to associate local officeholding with status and honor, and their desire to hold places under the crown was sharpened by the bitterness of civil war divisions. In their eagerness to share in the spoils of office, they were prepared to go to great lengths; court intrigue became a standard part of the repertoire of a gentleman in search of a deputy lieutenancy. The government, already accused of neglecting its most deserving supporters, was anxious to conciliate as many of them as possible.

The exclusion of most prominent Presbyterians and former parliamentarians had been completed by 1663, when the governor of Chester Castle, Sir Evan Lloyd, wrote: "The dangers threatening Chester do all proceed at this time from one party or faction called Presbyterians." Further, he said, "The Presbyterian gentry in these parts are discontented seeing themselves out of the commissions of peace and lieutenancy, and other employments in the state, and like to continue so their religion and nature agreeing well with ruling and not obeying."[58] And even though the Cavalier gentry had triumphed by 1663, the volume of their complaints had not been appreciably reduced. The government never satisfactorily recognized their service, and, moreover, the ghosts of the past, in the form of dissenters and republicans, lingered everywhere.

One of the lieutenants' most difficult tasks when naming deputies was the sheer number of deserving candidates. Lord Falkland sent in his nominations for Oxfordshire in the summer of 1660, but by September he was asking for more deputies: "Though the last list that I gave you," he wrote Secretary of State Nicholas, "was larger than usual, yet I must humbly beg the addition of Sir Francis Wenman, Sir Thomas Chamberlain, Sir Thomas Pope, and Rowland Lacy esq. The reason is it is now the case in our county to have a great number of young gentlemen of equal fortune, quality, age, and interest, and persons that have been near equally concerned in the restoration of his majesty, so that I am forced to desire this to prevent faction in this county, which we are now totally free from."[59]

As a result of this pressure, the size of the commission of lieutenancy increased all over the country. The number of deputies had increased notably during Charles I's reign, but the trend accelerated after 1660. Government efforts to check the growth of the commission were made from time to time; in 1668 Secretary Arlington transmitted the king's annoyance at a list of twenty-odd deputies submitted for Kent. Charles believed that such large commissions "in other counties . . . rather lessens their [the deputies'] activity than increasing it."[60] Despite these strictures, however, the number of deputy lieutenants continued to multiply. Lincolnshire had twelve deputies in 1629 and twenty-two in 1662, and in Staffordshire, which had six deputy lieutenants in 1627, the list grew to fifteen by 1677 and twenty-three by 1689.[61] The number of deputy lieutenants, which had averaged between five and ten before the civil wars, by 1663 reached a median of ten to twenty; some, like Lincolnshire and Devon (with twenty-two deputies), had even more. By 1662 their numbers were such that the government could hardly keep track of them and began identifying the "principal" deputies in each county.[62]

The increase in the numbers of deputies reflects the desire of the gentry for office after long years of political exclusion or exile; the Restoration released their pent-up demand for power and status. The addition of some new deputies also throws light on the changing nature of the lieutenancy itself. Before the civil wars, deputy lieutenancies offered great power and responsibility; their holders represented the inner circle of a county's leadership. The deputy's function was to administer the business of the lieutenancy and, more important, to maintain harmony in the shire. After the Restoration, at first subtly and later much more noticeably, the deputies played a different role.[63] They still performed their military duties and in many cases with far greater success than their predecessors, but they were no longer the conciliators and consensus builders that they had been.[64] Before the wars the lieutenancy had often acted as a referee or arbiter in local disputes; after 1660 that role increasingly seemed to fall to others. Divisions within the kingdom made such tasks virtually impossible to sustain. Lords lieutenant were now concerned with building an interest, with rewarding political allies, and with advancing political protégés. The patronage power of their office was a crucial means of maintaining political hegemony; the increase in the number of deputy lieutenants was a consequence of their desire to extend this self-serving hand to a rising contingent of local claimants.

Some gentlemen accepted their appointment as a natural right; Sir Edward Bagot of Staffordshire accepted his lieutenant's offer of a deputy lieutenancy "though I am not upon any vainglorious score ambitious of it . . . finding it so long performed by my ancestors as if it [were] inherent in the family."[65] More common, however, were men like Thomas Colepepper of Kent, who in 1662 wrote letter after letter to Secretary Bennett detailing his work as an enemy of sectaries and asking for a commission. Colepepper did not refer to family tradition or honor in his bid to become a deputy; it was the service of the king and church for which he aimed: "I hope you will pardon my ambition in aspiring to be one of the deputy lieutenants because I believe by being it my service may be more acceptable to his majesty."[66] The ideals of men like Bagot, better suited to an earlier time, were rapidly being replaced by those of the Colepeppers. Their political vision was much more commonly directed toward the court and metropolis than that of their predecessors. Although natural leadership and social standing were still important marks of a deputy lieutenant, these increasingly antiquated factors often conflicted with vigorous service for the crown and tolerance for the intrusion of royal power in local affairs. Before 1660 appeals to the secretary of state for a deputy lieutenancy would have been fruitless, and as lieutenants such as the earl of Derby now well understood, the new efficacy of such appeals could have troubling consequences for the old-fashioned.

The government was not unconcerned with the traditional requirements for a deputy lieutenancy. Deputies were not of obscure family, though many had never been represented on the commission before the civil wars. Wealth remained important; one of the earl of Westmorland's candidates in Northamptonshire was rejected by the crown in 1662, "believing him not of fortune answerable to that employment." Derby was chagrined to discover that the £500 estate of one of his Lancashire nominees was not enough to qualify him.[67] Deputies were rich men, and from the scattered evidence available, they seem to have been at least as prosperous as their predecessors before the civil wars had been. The earl of Cleveland noted that two of his Bedfordshire nominees, Sir John Duncombe and Steven Anderson, were endowed with £2,000 and £3,000 per annum respectively, and the incomes of the Staffordshire deputies ranged from £700 to well over £2,000. Three Wiltshire deputy lieutenants were allegedly worth between £4,000 and £6,000 per year.[68]

Deputy lieutenants were still men of high social standing, although the expansion of the commission diluted the status of the deputies as a whole. In Norfolk, for example, in the commission named by the earl of Arundel in 1626, Norfolk had eight deputies, all of whom were knights and three of them baronets. By contrast, of sixteen deputies appointed in 1660, eleven were knights and one a Scottish peer. By 1678, furthermore, the commission had grown to include twenty-nine men, of whom only twelve were knights.[69] The deputy lieutenants of Norfolk in the 1670s and 1680s were still men of great wealth and status—they included representatives of the Walpole, Knyvett, Coke, and de Grey families, all of whom had been prominent in the county for generations—but the expanded commission included a wider range of gentry fortunes.

Northamptonshire offers a similar illustration. In 1607, when a new commission of lieutenancy was issued to the first earl of Exeter, all seven of his deputies were knights. Under his son William, lieutenant from 1623 to 1640, the commission grew to include thirteen deputies, one of whom was an earl (the earl of Westmorland), five baronets, five knights, and only two esquires. In the first commission issued after the Restoration, fifteen deputies were named: one Scots peer (Lord Cullen), one English peer by courtesy (Lord Despenser, the earl of Westmorland's heir), seven knights, and six untitled gentlemen. By 1680 Northamptonshire had seventeen deputies: one Scots peer (Cullen's successor), two courtesy lords (Burleigh and Fitzwilliam), seven knights and baronets, and seven mere gentlemen.[70]

The prime factor in the choice of deputy lieutenants upon the reestablishment of the lieutenancy was political: did the subject merit the office by virtue of his service to the Royalist cause? Many of the nominations of the lieutenants detail the records of their candidates. Sir John Duncombe had been a servant of Charles I during his confinement on the Isle of Wight in 1648: "His father and grandfather of perfect loyalty to his majesty of blessed memory, as is this person to your majesty." Steven Anderson was "of perfect integrity" and had been "several times sequestered for his loyalty to your majesty's father of blessed memory."[71] John Lane of Staffordshire was noted as "very loyal and orthodox and stout. Intelligent and active"; his colleague Sir Walter Wrottesley was "very sober, loyal, and orthodox. Very intelligent."[72] Orthodoxy and loyalty was sometimes enough to secure a man a place on the commission; Sir John Prettyman of Leicestershire inherited a £700 estate in 1638 and by 1663 had amassed debts of over £20,000. A strong Royalist and active plotter during the interregnum, he won a baronetcy and deputy lieutenancy at the Restoration despite his shaky financial position. Prettyman's final ruin followed in the 1670s, when, jailed for debt, he disappeared from the commission.[73] The new circumstances created during the interregnum, in which loyal service was rewarded with office and opposition was punished by exclusion, made such appointments, impossible before 1640, a feature of political life.

Filling the lieutenancy with reliable and deserving officers was the first priority of the restored monarchy. The tone of the revived institution was set during the summer and autumn of 1660, establishing it as a powerful representative of the Cavalier gentry. In spite of the crown's rhetoric about reconciliation with its former enemies, the lieutenancy was placed in the hands of the Stuarts' oldest supporters: Royalist Anglicans. To be sure, some adherents of former regimes and parliamentarian sympathizers were included as deputy lieutenants. Furthermore, there were a handful of former rebels acting as lords lieutenant—Albemarle and Sandwich being the most prominent. But these were exceptions that proved the rule. The government vetted the deputies with great care, rejecting many prominent Presbyterians whom even the most stolid of Royalist lieutenants had recommended. In this way royal government adapted the pattern of politics forged during the revolution to its own ends.

The king's appointment of deputy lieutenants accomplished two important objectives: the militia was kept securely in loyal hands should there be a republican rising, and Cavaliers were rewarded for their services. Both objectives were essentially aimed at the establishment of security: safety against a sectarian rising and safety from disillusionment among the Cavaliers. Either could be fatal, and Charles II went far toward his ultimate goal—a secure throne and the preservation of the ancient constitution—by his appointments to the new lieutenancy.

THE RESTORATION of the lieutenancy was a first step toward the reestablishment of the regime, but it was of little value without an effective militia.[74] The king's guards, though an important hedge against rebellion, could not contain serious trouble in the provinces—a not unlikely prospect in the early years of the Restoration. The officers and men in the royal army totaled fewer than eighty-five hundred in 1663; thus the militia formed the government's primary defense against civil disorder, and, as always, the lieutenancy was responsible for its organization.[75]

The chief duty of the lieutenants appointed in 1660 was to organize their county's forces. Officers had to be named, regiments formed, and militiamen mustered and armed. The Privy Council followed up the appointment of new lieutenants with instructions to reembody the local militia. Lieutenants and deputies were obliged to meet frequently until the business was done, and most set to work immediately.[76]

The appointment of militia officers took first priority. The government attempted to increase their number by insisting that each county maintain forces of at least pre-1642 strength while reducing the size of individual militia units. A troop of horse was to consist of no more than fifty men, and a company of foot should not exceed eighty.[77] Though these orders must have greatly expanded the officer corps, competition for places was fierce. As with the deputy lieutenancies, the number of eligible gentlemen exceeded the number of places available. The appointment of Staffordshire's muster master, for example, was highly controversial. The deputy lieutenants were not happy with their lieutenant's choice, but as Lord Brooke explained, "There were so many competitors that it was impossible to satisfy any considerable part in any one of them."[78] Competition for commissions was accompanied by the jostling for precedence that had been such a common feature of the prewar period. The lord and deputy lieutenants of Lincolnshire spent weeks attempting to untangle a dispute among their officers over who was to be senior captain and which company commander ranked over which in the militia regiments.[79]

As before the war, militia officers enjoyed a high standing in their communities: commissions continued to be marks of favor. A major difference between the two periods, however, was that before 1642 lords lieutenant (and their deputies) were substantially free to appoint whomever they pleased to local military commands. After the Restoration the increasing politicization of local government limited the lieutenants' choice to the "loyal and orthodox." The crown's scrutiny of officers was of course not total; the militia contained too many captains, lieutenants, and cornets to vet each one. Nevertheless, the government's concern with the political character of its servants made a difference. The earl of Derby, ever out of touch with new realities, was threatened with dismissal when he chose a gentleman unacceptable to the king as a militia colonel. And Lord Newport made sure to inform Secretary Nicholas in November 1660 that his officers were all perfectly fit for service: "I can assure you they are such as have been ever faithful and loyal to his late majesty and his majesty as now is."[80] Although the men who served as lieutenants were unlikely to recommend the disloyal, the political test their nominees had to pass meant that they no longer had the freedom of choice of their predecessors.

With the aid of their officers, the lieutenants began the formidable task of constructing a serviceable militia. The militia bill introduced into the Convention Parliament in November 1660 was probably the result of resistance the lieutenants encountered in several counties when they began enforcing militia obligations.[81] Complaints of overassessment came from Wiltshire; the deputies of Monmouthshire reported that some dozen people refused to contribute to the militia, claiming that the lieutenancy had no right to act without parliamentary authority. Instantly jailed on the deputies' orders, most then conformed, but the deputies worried about the consequences of their actions. The October musters in Cheshire were undercut by a number of people who refused to appear.[82] These problems were temporarily resolved in the Militia Act of 1661, Parliament's interim solution to the problem of the lieutenancy's legal standing.

The 1661 act settled the constitutional questions surrounding the lieutenancy, giving unequivocal control of the institution to the crown. But it failed to establish any clear set of duties and responsibilities for either the lieutenancy or militiamen. The power of deputy lieutenants to punish defaulters remained undefined, as did the amount of service expected from the militia. Rates were still to be fixed by deputy lieutenants as in the past and arms assessed according to the lieutenancy's judgment. Because these areas were left vague, although the new act solved a long-standing constitutional problem, it did little to guide the lieutenancy in the performance of its duties. The government meant to provide this guidance, but the race against the parliamentary clock forced it to compromise in 1661. The most important principle—for the crown, at any rate—had been secured. The rest would have to wait for a propitious moment, and a permanent act was finally passed in the spring of 1662 which provided for all that the earlier one did not.[83]

The terms of the Militia Act of 1662 delineated the lieutenancy's powers for the first time since Philip and Mary's act expired in 1604.[84] Lieutenants were authorized to arm and lead their troops anywhere they were needed during a rebellion and to muster and train them at any time. Two deputy lieutenants could carry out most of the main functions of the lieutenant in his absence. These provisions merely confirmed the lieutenancy's authority as exercised under the early Stuarts—in the past they had been included in the text of the king's commission. It was in the specific areas of assessment and default that the act broke new ground.

The lieutenancy was empowered to punish defaulters by fine—one pound for horsemen and ten shillings for foot soldiers and, in extraordinary cases, up to twenty pounds—and it could also jail offenders for up to five days. These provisions ended the confusion over the lieutenancy's right to punish, an ambiguity that had been a continuing problem during Charles I's reign. The Privy Council, formerly the principal enforcer for deputies reluctant to punish their neighbors, was relieved of the time-consuming business of citing gentlemen for nonpayment of trifling sums for militia horse; the lieutenancy assumed that role from 1662. The deputies who toiled away in the grand jury chamber at Norwich were fulfilling the terms of an act that required far more commitment to the wishes of central government than anything their fathers had accepted. Although the institution's ability to discipline defaulters was limited, the new measure had the advantage of being unquestionable. This firm grounding in law enhanced the authority of the lieutenancy in the provinces, where deputies exercised their power to punish those who failed to fulfill their obligations to the crown. But it also subtly altered the relationship between local and central government by imposing responsibilities upon the lieutenancy (and the provinces) that could not be evaded.

The Parliament that passed the act of 1662 was nothing if not sensible of the interests of the shires, and its provisions for assessments ensured that the militia would rest lightly upon the country, whatever power the lieutenancy had to punish defaulters. The lieutenancy was authorized to levy an annual "week's tax" for the maintenance of the militia—officers' salaries, trophies, clerks' wages, and other miscellaneous items. Spread over the entire kingdom, the week's tax amounted to £17,500 and so was a relatively light charge, especially in comparison with other parliamentary taxation such as the hearth tax and excise.[85] The 1663 and 1666 assessments in Norfolk, for example, brought in just over £430 each.[86] In addition to the week's tax, the Parliament granted the king a total of £70,000 per annum for three years in the form of a month's assessment, which was to be raised by the lieutenancy "in case of apparent danger."[87]

The lieutenancy also assessed the county for militiamen and horsemen, an activity for which the act established detailed guidelines for the deputies to follow. A gentleman had to have a minimum of £100 in land or £1,200 in goods to be assessed for the horse and £50 and £600 respectively to be obliged to provide a foot soldier.[88] Each of the troops raised by those assessed at the lieutenancy's order was required to provide his own equipment (which was specified in the act) and was to be paid a wage set by the deputies for his services. Although Richard Gough, writing in the early eighteenth century, remembered a time when gentlemen and prosperous farmers served in the militia, throughout most of the Restoration period militiamen were of lower social status and were hired by those assessed.[89]

Once in place and working, these acts formed the basis of the lieutenancy's administration until Parliament passed a series of reforms in 1757. The impetus for the passage of the acts of 1661 and 1662 had been gathering momentum for decades, but the revolution and the interregnum were crucial in changing the attitude of the gentry. The repeated failure to pass a statute formally establishing the lieutenancy during the reigns of James I and Charles I reflected the gentry's general satisfaction with the traditional arrangement. Bills failed in 1604, 1624, 1626, and 1628—all backed to one degree or another by the crown—but even in 1628, when complaints against the lieutenancy were at their most strident, none was passed. Gentlemen preferred the locally oriented lieutenancy and wanted as few statutory responsibilities laid on them as possible. The events of

1642–60 inspired a change of opinion among the gentry. The crown's posture remained the same: it wanted an act. The seizure of the lieutenancy by the Parliament made the king even more anxious for an unambiguous statement of his control of the militia (this was provided by the Militia Act of 1661). For the gentry, the arbitrary assessments and decimations of the Protectorate and republic made the need for specific limitations on the authority of the lieutenancy clear. The concerns of both crown and provinces combined to ensure the passage of the militia legislation, a series of acts that defined—to the mutual satisfaction of both—military obligations that had been unclear for generations.

By late 1663, the lieutenancy had begun to enforce the terms of the new acts, and the administrative routine it established continued unchanged for the rest of the century. In July 1662 the council sent the lieutenants a series of instructions which initiated a general overhaul of the militia as it had been reestablished in 1660—if in fact it had been reestablished at all. Complaints were made about the state of the militia in several counties in 1662 and 1663. In Westmorland, where enthusiasm for the militia had always been muted at best, Sir Christopher Musgrave worried that rebellion might break out unchecked because "the trained bands are so much out of order, many companies are armed but have no officers." A Wiltshire gentleman condemned the state of the horse there: "Now indeed both horses and furniture are so extreme bad that an officer [who] ever saw anything of war or discipline may be ashamed to muster them." One of Secretary Joseph Williamson's correspondents reported to him that there was no militia at all in the eastern rape of Sussex.[90]

The council's orders enjoined the lieutenants and deputies to meet frequently until the new militia was organized, to keep in touch with neighboring lieutenancies, and to keep a careful watch on the disaffected.[91] In an illustration of the changing nature of central-local relations and increased regard for orders from Whitehall, most lieutenants set to work immediately and with a will. Lord Fauconberg in the North Riding, the deputy lieutenants of Bristol, the earl of Derby in Lancashire and Cheshire, and the joint lieutenants of Northamptonshire all met with their new militia officers and deputy lieutenants to put the new force in order.[92] Such tender regard for the wishes of the council would have been very rare before the civil wars. A few lieutenants had to be prodded into action by the council, like the duke of Ormond, whose failure to organize the Somerset militia promptly "occasioned much complaint."[93] Most, however, were more like Lords Brooke in Staffordshire and Derby in Cheshire and Lancashire, who devised a list of standing instructions for their deputies shortly after the passage of the new legislation.

Brooke's instructions were typical. The deputies were to hold two general musters of the militia annually, one on Whitsun Tuesday at Lichfield, the other at harvest time in Stafford. The deputies were to meet within one week of each general muster to make arrangements and to prepare warrants—and as many were to appear as possible, "to add reputation and solemnity to the affair." Further, they were to give Brooke a detailed report of their meetings and the progress of their musters.[94] Once these initial arrangements had been made, the lieutenancy settled into a routine that rarely varied through the remainder of Charles II's reign.

In Norfolk, the deputy lieutenants met regularly to conduct militia business, usually in conjunction with quarter sessions; when in Norwich they met in the castle (in the "little grand jury chamber") or at an inn called the King's Head, where they had worked since at least the 1620s. When sessions were held in other Norfolk towns, as they were on occasion, the deputies met there.[95] From 1670 on, the deputies decreed that they would meet at two in the afternoon on the first day of every quarter session. The lord lieutenant joined his deputies when he was in the county, and meetings were usually well attended.

Some lords lieutenant were active in the militia's administration even when they were not in the county. In Hertfordshire, Lord Capel, who spent much of his time in London, was closely involved in militia business, as the accounts of the county treasurer from the mid-1660s show. He habitually authorized the expenditure of militia money involving sums as trivial as six pounds "paid by the lord lieutenant's order" to Corporal John Wingfield "for his service in the militia."[96] A lieutenant's role in the day-to-day administration of the militia varied considerably; some, like the duke of Ormond (lieutenant of Somerset) took little interest in their charges. Ormond, lord lieutenant of Ireland and a major political figure, had other important business to follow. Others, for whom a lieutenancy was their most important political employment or who were determined to build a local interest, were far more active. Such lieutenants—Townshend in Norfolk, Capel in Hertfordshire, Bruce in Bedfordshire, Falkland in Oxfordshire, and Fauconberg in the North Riding of Yorkshire, to name a few—were deeply involved in all of the activities of the militia in their shires.

The main business of the lieutenancy's meetings, except in times of crisis, consisted of matters of routine militia administration.[97] The Restoration lieutenancy spent far more time dealing with administrative matters than its prewar predecessor. Assessing for arms was a time-consuming business, requiring many letters to and from militia officers and head constables, who were obliged to provide the deputies with lists of those liable to service. Deaths, removals, and rating disputes had to be settled, often many at each meeting. In March 1666 eight deputies attended an archetypal meeting at Thetford, where they reviewed the assessments of at least two dozen people, reducing some and increasing others. One, Dr. Wotton, a clergyman, had his contribution changed from finding foot arms to half a horse; Thomas Wright's assessment was delayed "till his estate be further discovered"; and the contribution from the city of Norwich, which owned land in the Thetford area, was fixed at two horsemen. Frequently the deputies were called upon to make complicated decisions regarding the obligations of their subordinates. At this meeting, for instance, a single set of foot arms charged on Stoake Holy parsonage was divided five ways, between the dean and prebends of Norwich and several other gentlemen.[98]

In addition to charging the county for the militia, the deputies dealt with those who failed to appear at musters or pay their rates. In Norfolk the deputies either failed to record or did not prosecute defaulters until 1665, but thereafter an increasing amount of space in their lieutenancy book was devoted to detailing the deputies' prosecutions. The deputies levied fines on defaulters and occasionally distrained the property of those who refused to pay.[99] As was the case with assessments, handling defaulters could be complex. In July 1674, Stephen Cullen appeared at his company's muster without his arms—an offense for which he or his "providers" (those obliged to equip him) could be fined. Cullen's providers were Quakers who refused to pay or equip their soldier. The deputies excused Cullen but fined his masters 16 shillings and 6 pence each for their offense. At the same time three other Quakers were summoned before the deputies for failure to show their weapons. Their case was postponed because they claimed that bearing arms had been forbidden them, "which was the occasion of their default." The deputies resolved to investigate the truth of their story with the men's captain.[100] The summoning and dispatching of such cases constituted a large part of the lieutenancy's normal business.

Possibly the most difficult of the lieutenancy's everyday business was the collection of the week's tax and its companion, the month's tax. Dozens of constables, collectors, and subcollectors worked in every parish and hundred throughout the county raising the money. In Norfolk the fixed sum rated for the month's tax was £3,662/3/4. These collections were sometimes in arrears, and the deputies often had to untangle shoddy accounts and pursue negligent constables. One constable, Mr. Bilby, died insolvent and six pounds in arrears on his collections, and another, Thomas Sutton, "is broke and is run away." [101] Some collectors were up to five years in arrears, and a few never did pay over their collections.

The model provided by Norfolk's lieutenancy was repeated elsewhere—by the terms of the militia acts, the procedures in widely scattered counties were much the same. The legislation allowed the crown to enforce its will much more vigorously than it had been before the wars, whereas the lieutenancy enjoyed less latitude in its conduct but more power in its administrative and policing tasks. In neighboring Suffolk the lieutenants met regularly, following the example of their neighbors in Norfolk, and in Lancashire, deputies held meetings four to six times per year, usually coinciding with assizes or quarter sessions. [102] Unlike their brethren in Norfolk, the Lancashire deputy lieutenants spent less time harrying defaulters in the 1660s, preferring to keep a sharp eye on local dissenters. In 1669, when assessing arms and hearing cases of default, they noted that they had "found that by the long intermission of a meeting to that purpose, there hath appeared many defects which we have to our best power taken course to prevent for the future." They kept their word, and the Lancashire lieutenancy records show considerable interest in defaulters from 1669 forward. [103]

All over the country the lieutenancy worked conscientiously throughout the 1660s to keep the militia in order, and in this it enjoyed considerable, although by no means universal, success. [104] John Milward reported that in the spring 1665 musters in Derbyshire, both the horse and foot that assembled at Bakewell were well turned out, and even more surprisingly, there was no default severe enough to be punished with a fine. [105] By 1664 the foot in Lincolnshire was in better condition than ever: "By exercising together [they] are become good firemen and fit for services." [106] By the time of the invasion scares of 1666 and 1667, the new militia was well organized and prepared to perform its duty. Gloucestershire was perhaps better organized than some counties, but John Herbert's report of June 1666 illustrates the general success of the lieutenancy in organizing the militia after 1662: "The lord lieutenant of Gloucestershire hath been here several times this two months last past mustering his militia, which are all in very good equipage, having in his lieutenancy 5,000 foot and a regiment of horse . . . and I believe as good officers and as well disciplined as most in England." [107] Similar compliments were made about the lieutenancy's handiwork in Dorset, Kent, Yorkshire, and Warwickshire.[108] By the late 1660s the lieutenancy had forged a militia that, despite its problems, was an institution of significant value to the crown; well-organized and well-equipped, it was prepared to face the many dangers that threatened the Stuarts. Those dangers loomed on every side, and the lieutenancy proved to be remarkably adept at securing the survival of the Restoration monarchy.

CHAPTER IV

Internal Security, 1660–1674

CHARLES II'S PROMISES of reconciliation and the quick passage of the Act of Oblivion by the Convention Parliament were designed to include as many of the republic's former adherents as possible in the Restoration settlement. Despite the national rejoicing at the return of the king in 1660, however, many greeted the restored monarch with hostility. Fears for the survival of the new regime were widespread. The quick reestablishment of the lieutenancy was one of the first measures taken by the government to confront the danger posed by the plots of unregenerate republicans; the crown's deliberate policy of restricting control of the militia and lieutenancy to men of proven loyalty made these institutions an ideal base from which to defend the throne against subversion and rebellion.

The reestablished lieutenancy was well-equipped for its role as guarantor of the Restoration. The lords and deputy lieutenants maintained the dominant position in the social fabric of the shires that they held before the wars; places in the commission continued to hold the same status and allure of earlier decades. What some lieutenants lacked in ancient lineage was compensated by the statutory authority of the militia acts and the force of an unregenerate Cavalier ideology. Like the majority of the gentry in the 1660s, lieutenants held firmly to what has been described as the "myth of the Royal Martyr"—essentially a nostalgic vision of a perfect

Royalist Anglican state torn to pieces by irrational fanatics.[1] The restored lieutenancy was carefully crafted to provide the force, ideological as well as physical, to ensure the survival of the Stuart dynasty against its many enemies.

The prewar lieutenancy had sometimes played a part in internal security matters, harassing Roman Catholic recusants from time to time.[2] Yet such duties never demanded much consistent effort, and indeed it is doubtful, given the localist nature of the institution, that the prewar lieutenancy would have been capable of frequent and efficient persecution. Firm action against local recusants would have entailed an uncharacteristically heavy-handed approach toward people who were often, after all, gentlemen, and the deputy lieutenant's neighbors as well. The Restoration lieutenancy was untroubled by such social considerations. The interregnum had taught that political and religious dissent led to subversion and threatened another eclipse of constitutional government. Under the changed circumstances, the lieutenancy became a much more vigilant servant of the center; in fact, the diligence of the deputies and their masters at times even exceeded the wishes of the king himself. The political views of the gentry had changed radically: defense of the central government and its priorities had become the only sensible way to protect a gentleman's local standing and power.[3] The consequences of the wars and interregnum were revolutionary indeed, for they turned the gentry's inward-looking, conservative traditionalism upside down, transforming these gentlemen—many of whom did not understand the nature of the change—into advocates of centrally directed, activist order. At the root of this change was the survival of republicanism and religious dissent.

There were some two thousand former republican officers in England in 1660, many of whom would never be reconciled to the new regime and all of whom were well acquainted with the use of arms.[4] The radical sects, too, numbered their adherents in the thousands, and many a Cavalier firmly believed that each one of them presented a serious threat to the government. There were twenty to thirty thousand Baptists, some ten thousand Fifth Monarchists, and an unknown—but undoubtedly substantial—number of Quakers.[5] In 1663 the deputy lieutenants of Staffordshire could report that no less than 1,128 men in their county had "served against the king."[6] A community of radicals of this size was more than enough to give the newly established government pause and to give its loyal supporters in the provinces nightmares.

The euphoria that accompanied the king's landing in May 1660 lasted until the autumn. Some of the most prominent republicans fled the country; some were captured and jailed; the rest lay low, awaiting further developments. Their spirit smothered by the events of the winter of 1659–60 and their confidence shattered by popular rejoicing for the new king, the radicals remained quiescent. As the Yorkshireman Sir John Reresby wrote, "The kingdom was at this time very rich, and all people well-satisfied with the king's return; or such as were not durst not oppose the current by seeming otherwise. . . . All things went on calmly and easily." But Reresby and many like him were not sanguine: "Not but that it was likely that a considerable number could have wished it otherwise, such as had lost commands in the army which was now disbanded, or estates which they had quietly enjoyed in the late time out of the crown lands, the bishops', the deans' and chapters', or the delinquents'; dissenters in religion, and those of commonwealth principles."[7] This was a formidable set of characters.

Once the new commissions of lieutenancy had been issued, deputy lieutenants named, and militia officers appointed, attention shifted from celebration of the Restoration and the pursuit of reward to the losers of the struggle between monarchy and republic. Even though those considered most dangerous had done little to warrant suspicion over the course of the summer, the lieutenants were not slow to exercise the power of their new commissions. The fragility of the Restoration, as it was unanimously perceived by the lords and deputies of the lieutenancy, made vigilance against subversion appear vital, and they acted accordingly. The broad agreement among the gentry as to the threat represented by sectaries and republicans added force to the lieutenancy's determination to destroy the regime's most dangerous enemies.[8]

By October 1660 former servants of the republic found themselves under the close scrutiny of the authorities. Many of those with the strongest connections to the old regime or who remained uncompromising in their disdain for the king's government were arrested or harassed. A Major Creed, for example, was jailed at the order of the earl of Bath, the lieutenant of Cornwall. Creed had served under the infamous republican general John Lambert, and Bath felt Creed was a serious threat.[9] Captain Robert Hope, a former officer in the republican army, claimed that he was persecuted beyond civilized limits. His entire arsenal, he said, amounted to a single birding gun and one light rapier, and yet "my house was searched . . . nine times in one week, to the great terror of my wife and then sickly family."[10] For one Wiltshire man, Edward Herbert, the vainglorious boasts of yesterday came back to haunt him. Once a tenant of the Protector, he had bragged that he was Oliver's "right hand man"; in 1661 that information resulted in his arrest by Sir Robert Mason, a local deputy lieutenant.[11]

The lieutenancy's action against these potentially dangerous men was encouraged by the Privy Council's original circular letters to the new lords lieutenant. The council instructed the lieutenants to prevent the meetings of illegal conventicles and to watch the disaffected closely. Most did so with enthusiasm, for they shared the council's concerns about the potential for counterrevolution. As early as September, in Derbyshire the high constables of each hundred were given copies of the council's letters and strict orders from the deputies to watch for any suspicious activity.[12] The deputies there conducted searches in December and just after the New Year assured their lord lieutenant (the marquis of Newcastle), "We will not fail to . . . suppress and prevent all numerous and unwarrantable meetings and assemblies of ill-affected persons, and to secure both their persons, arms, and ammunition."[13] The deputy lieutenants of Cheshire did the same in late December, warning colonel of militia Thomas Leigh to command his soldiers "to be very civil in the search, without offering abuse to any person."[14] Fear of sectarian revolt was widespread, but in most places, as in Cheshire, the lieutenancy avoided unnecessary provocation. Even the Derbyshire deputies were reluctant to act unwarrantably and asked their lieutenant for more precise instructions "to impower us to discharge that duty." The lieutenancy's diffidence indicates the survival of prewar ideas about its role in internal security and the deputies' desire to avoid alienating their community. But it became obvious early in the new year that such notions were out of date.

Official equivocation about how to respond to dissent vanished in January 1661, when all of the government's worst fears seemed about to be realized. In London a small group of Fifth Monarchists led by Thomas Venner resolved in December 1660 to deal "a blow for king Jesus" against Charles II, "a professed enemy, a rebel, and traitor to Christ."[15] Venner had already been jailed under the Commonwealth for plotting the Protector's demise, and as far as Thomas was concerned, the Stuarts deserved no better. On January 6, some thirty-five to fifty Fifth Monarchists, who truly deserved the Cavalier sobriquet "fanatic," met in Swan Alley, where they armed themselves and set out for St. Paul's Cathedral, determined to conquer the world and usher in the millennium. Arriving at the cathedral after dark, they broke in and awaited the dawn. A passerby, when asked "who he was for" replied—most unluckily—"King Charles." He was murdered on the spot by an assailant who demanded allegiance to King Jesus.[16] News of the citizen's death spread quickly, and the city authorities responded by calling out the trained bands. Pursued by the militiamen, Venner and his compatriots withdrew to the woods north of London. Marching beneath a banner proclaiming "the Lord God and Gideon," the rebels slew several hapless constables who crossed their path and vanished into the darkness.[17]

The pathetic rising came to its inevitable conclusion three days later, when the remnants of Venner's group, driven by hunger and desperation, burst back into the city. They fought a sharp—though brief—engagement against a force of militiamen and Life Guards, led by the lord mayor, Sir Richard Browne. All the rebels were killed or captured, and Venner was taken alive. Twenty-two Fifth Monarchists died in the fighting, and twenty were taken prisoner; the captives were quickly tried, and many suffered traitor's deaths.[18]

The rising electrified the country. As Pepys noted, the city was thrown into a panic: "In the street I find everybody in arms at the doors. . . . In our way, the streets full of trained bands . . . the shops shut and all things in trouble."[19] Throughout the country the lieutenants called out trained bands in anticipation of a widespread revolt. The lieutenancy in Surrey and Middlesex joined with the city and the royal guards to provide troops, but lieutenants in more remote counties also reacted quickly.[20] In Derbyshire, the deputy lieutenants ordered out the militia, which appeared in force and with high morale; expresses were sent to the deputy lieutenants of Northamptonshire, Leicestershire, and Staffordshire to coordinate local defense.[21] Rumors of sectarian risings cropped up in Northumberland, Lincolnshire, Cheshire, and Flintshire.[22] The lieutenancy raised the militia in each of these counties and added to their strength by calling upon the many troops of volunteer horse that had been formed in 1660.

Venner and his followers did not threaten the overthrow of the state, but the response to the revolt illustrates the widespread uncertainty about the stability of the government and worries about the intentions of those who opposed it. The months of peace that followed the king's return had not diminished the Royalists' fear that the battle had been won too easily. Cavaliers feared that republicans were merely gathering strength for a decisive blow; indeed, many republicans actually were busily plotting to overthrow the king. Venner's attack strengthened the conviction of the Cavalier gentry that stern measures had to be taken before a general rebellion of all the regime's enemies ensued. It was in this highly charged atmosphere that the lieutenancy began its transformation into an institution whose primary goal was to enforce political conformity and suppress dissent.

On January 10 the king issued a proclamation forbidding the meetings of "Anabaptists, Quakers, and Fifth Monarchy Men." The lieutenancy was busy for weeks suppressing unlawful meetings.[23] As Lord Brooke told his deputy lieutenants in Staffordshire, nonconformist meetings offered a clear danger: "For should the pulpit be allowed a sanctuary for sedition or treason, we must expect quickly to see the kingdom again in a flame."[24] Most lieutenants and their deputies performed their duty enthusiastically. As one Wiltshire deputy told a friend, "The king's affairs will scarcely permit me to present my service to you. What with the taking up of Quakers in the country . . . I have not time to untruss my breeches between meals."[25]

Suspected persons were arrested everywhere. In Oxfordshire Lord Falkland, at the head of 250 volunteers, led a raid on nonconformists' homes; in Leicestershire, Gloucestershire, Essex, and Yorkshire thorough searches and many arrests were made.[26] By March well over four thousand Quakers had been jailed, and the government decided that the reaction in the country had gone far enough. Within a week of the revolt, the king, alarmed at the number of illegal searches which were being carried out, issued a proclamation against arbitrary procedure, and on January 25 he ordered the release of most of the Quakers held in London jails.[27] Many of those jailed in the panic that had followed the rising remained in prison for weeks. On January 2, Adam Martindale, a prominent Cheshire Presbyterian, had been imprisoned by the deputy lieutenants for refusing to read a notice forbidding "all manner of persons (of whatsoever opinion they be)" from assembling upon "pretense of preaching." He languished in Chester Castle until the end of February, when he was at last released by order of the earl of Derby, upon condition of his appearance at the Easter Assizes. Although he had no connection with Fifth Monarchists or republican plotters, Martindale was a victim of the heightened fear caused by Venner's revolt.[28]

The Quaker leader George Fox dated the end of sectarian peace from the moment of Venner's quixotic rebellion; from that time until the rise of political strife in the 1670s, nonconformists were subject to persecution by a vigorous lieutenancy.[29] The worries of the Cavalier lieutenancy were not unfounded; there were many dissenters and former republicans in the country, some of whom never ceased plotting against the crown. One sectary allegedly warned that he and his fellows were ready "to sheath our swords in the bowels of [the king] and his council."[30] Another typical example was a Wiltshire man who proclaimed, "If this wicked king do reign as he begins, I hope I shall see his head cut off as his father's head was, then there will be no king, no bishop, no book of common prayer." In August 1661 the council warned the lieutenancy of "the frequent meetings and complottings of some persons of dangerous principles, of the seditious pamphlets which are daily published and dispersed to prepare and mold people's minds to new troubles, and of the more than usual confidence and presumption that at present appears in many of those who were active instruments in the late times of usurpation and tyranny." It was plain, the council went on, that "there is still an unclaimable mutinous spirit in some persons in the kingdom who endeavor to dislike our peace and quiet."[31] In August 1661, the marquis of Newcastle's Gloucestershire steward reported to his master that tenants were very hard to find, "especially since every day here is preaching and rumors of rebellion."[32]

Parliamentary measures taken against nonconformist meetings—the Act of Uniformity, the Conventicle Act, and the Five Mile Act—passed largely as a result of the link Venner's rising had forged between radical religion and treason. Dissenters' meetings, the lieutenants firmly believed, were the nurseries of sedition. The lieutenancy saw in conventicles a threat to the very existence of the government; for the deputy lieutenant in the shires, the line that divided peaceful meetings of nonconformists from nests of revolutionary agitators was very thin. Indeed, for some, there was no division whatever. Reminders of the dangers of sectarian meetings from the council were hardly necessary. The number of illegal meetings and the undeniable connections between some radical sectarians and treasonous plotting bred fear and uncertainty among loyal men throughout the kingdom. Complaints about conventicles flooded into Whitehall, and lords lieutenant were besieged by news of arrogant dissenters meeting in defiance of the law. It was reported that Suffolk "swarms with thieves, with factions, and schismatical persons, insomuch that if great care be not taken to prevent, and suppress it, that county will be overrun with fanatics, separatists, and Quakers."[33] A gentleman in Sussex believed that the dissenters there were out of control, many in Cheshire were allegedly "vehemently infested with the principles of disobedience to king and church," and the Kentish fanatics "are very high and insolent, and threaten all persons that have been in any way loyal." In Hampshire the deputy lieutenants worried about the activities of "many unquiet heads" that were "continually active."[34]

Sir Justinian Isham, a deputy lieutenant in Northamptonshire, summed up the feelings of the gentry about conventicles in 1662. A nonconformist, Benjamin Morley, had been arrested during a raid conducted by Isham and afterward sent the deputy a letter arguing the dissenters' case. Morley wrote that he hoped that "the Lord [may] direct your heart into the knowledge of His truth . . . so you may be directed by divine guidance that you may understandingly know how to wield the sword of justice." Isham was a thoughtful man, an amateur philosopher and scientist—but he was also a lifelong Royalist. After Morley's arrest, Isham took his prisoner home and attempted to reason with him, to no avail. Isham's answer to Morley's plea illustrates the potential danger many deputy lieutenants saw in dissenting meetings. Was it, Sir Justinian asked, "against the law of God or natural reason to restrain the assembling of any such people in multitudes in a doubtful time when many of the same principles have lately been abettors and fomenters of a civil war, and of those principal leaders who have disturbed the peace of an ancient and careful government?" On the matter of those innocent believers who might be unduly harassed for their essentially harmless principles, he wondered "whether the simple and innocent carriage of some few who only pretend liberty of conscience ought to make all their people stand to their mercy by suffering of their public assemblies, who have already suffered, in all that is done to them by the cruelties of those who went upon the like principles?" [35]

For Isham and his contemporaries the answers to these questions were clearly negative. Serious Anglicans viewed schism as both a dreadful sin and a political crime; indeed, the two were merely opposite sides of the same debased coin. [36] The horrors of civil war and sectarian rule were still so vivid in the memories of the gentry that extreme measures in defense of the Restoration were almost inevitable. As Sir Philip Musgrave, a prominent Cumberland deputy, wrote in 1663, "I will rather be in His Majesty's mercy for some irregular proceedings than hazard the peace of the kingdom by too strict an attendance on the rules of law." [37] It was the task of the lieutenancy to "inquire into men's principles" and to suppress those whose opinions were considered dangerous. [38] Such inquiries would have been inconceivable before the civil wars, but in the 1660s they seemed essential to the survival of the social and political order.

The lieutenancy's policing role was carried out with the assistance of other local authorities—magistrates and constables—and frequently involved use of the militia. In October 1663 the Norfolk deputy lieutenants ordered Captain Day's company of foot to quarter at Wymondham for nine days, "for the preventing and suppressing of all conventicles and unlawful meetings." [39] In November 1662 Colonel Thomas Colepepper, one of Kent's most active Cavaliers, broke up a meeting of some two hundred dissenters with his troop of horse, and in 1664 two hundred Somerset militiamen broke up a very large meeting that was being held less than a mile from the soldiers' camp. Another meeting was disrupted in Norwich in November 1663. Captain William Cowell's company surrounded the meetinghouse and after fruitless knocking broke down the doors of the building. Inside they found two to three hundred people, of whom the captain claimed one hundred were "stout men, capable of bearing arms." Questioning about the purpose of the meeting revealed nothing, and eventually those in attendance were released after promising to attend no more.[40] As late as 1670 the trained bands were harassing dissenters. Lord Roos's accounts for the summer of that year list payments "for the hire of a soldier to go out two days when they went about the conventicles, five shillings, the hire of a sword, powder, and the muster master, 2/6."[41]

In September 1661, the Wiltshire deputies, who were already on the trail of what they thought was a dangerous plot against the government, raided a Baptist meeting.[42] They found eight hundred to a thousand people in attendance and arrested four: a physician named Allen, two "teachers," who may in fact have been ministers, and a gentleman named William King, who allowed the conventicle to be held on his property, "in a place which he built on purpose with galleries round about it (he calls this meeting place a barn)." The four were held without bond, and the deputies reported that King had letters "of dangerous consequence" in his pocket. The arrested men maintained that they had come together with no political purpose in mind and had heard that the king was about to offer an indulgence to dissenters. The deputy lieutenants, however, were not prepared to accept their excuses. They asked the Privy Council "whether those tumultuous meetings, their letters, their words, and et cetera do not amount unto treason?" In arresting such suspicious characters, the Wiltshire deputies acted with the full support of their neighbors. "And if you give a good account of your trust," one gentleman wrote a deputy, "you will be both an honor to your own and a good example to other counties to copy after you. God bless your intentions."[43]

Other counties followed the Wiltshire example, and throughout the rest of 1661, the lieutenancy harried dissenters unmercifully. The behavior of some dissenters provoked persecution and heightened the zeal of the deputies. In Middlesex, Sir Richard Browne, lord mayor of London and a deputy lieutenant, was in May 1662 confronted by a Quaker who had been arrested at a conventicle. The Quaker, "a sturdy knave," refused to doff his hat, whereupon Sir Richard, enraged, yanked the offender's hat down around his ears. In reply, the Quaker "caught the alderman's chain (which was about his neck) in both his hands, with such violence that he almost laid his worship on the ground." The Quaker was carted off to New-gate, "with a kick in the breech" from the deputy.[44] In Yarmouth, a town notorious for dissent, "the Independent faction is grown so high that our minister is forced to lay aside the performing of his duty in the burying of the dead. . . . They not only jeer and laugh at him but make a noise that he may not be heard. Some have been so impudent as to lay their hands upon his book."[45] In Northamptonshire the deputy lieutenants informed their master that "the sectaries are so obstinate and numerous that . . . we find them unwilling to forbear, the consequence whereof we leave to your lordship's consideration."[46] In London the militia locked up a Quaker meetinghouse, but to the vexation of the lieutenancy, they continued to meet in the street.[47] In Derbyshire the high constables received detailed instructions on how to handle dissenting congregations—those who wor-shiped "in any . . . fanatic form"—first commanding them to disperse and, should they refuse, arresting the minister. If, however, "the company be so great that you dare not proceed in execution of your warrant," the constable was to notify the nearest magistrate or deputy lieutenant. The trained band would then arrive to enforce the law.[48]

The lieutenancy's constant pressure had its effect. Dissenters curtailed their activities and became much more sophisticated in their attempts to avoid disturbance. Some Presbyterians were reported to have disguised their meetings as feasts so that if a militia company or deputy lieutenant should appear, they could hide away their Bibles and take up their pots of ale. Some met in the early morning hours, some in secret rooms; some min-isters were known to travel disguised as tinkers or laborers. The dissenters of Olney met at a point where the three counties of Buckinghamshire, Bedfordshire, and Northamptonshire converged—a strategy that enabled them to flee into another jurisdiction at the first sign of trouble.[49] In 1664 the deputy lieutenants of Lincolnshire reported that their efforts had made a difference. The fanatics there had been "by reason of the checks that have been given them, and the constant power that is upon them, more modest and less frequent in their meetings than formerly."[50]

The lieutenancy's efficiency as a scourge of dissenters in the 1660s owed to a variety of factors. Most important was the strongly held belief among the lords and deputy lieutenants that dissent was subversive. A reflection of the convictions of many gentlemen (and common people as well), this belief made it imperative to curtail nonconformist meetings and break up dissent-ing organizations whenever possible.[51] The Cavalier position was expressed politically by the passage of the Act of Uniformity and the Conventicle Act, and it was given practical life by the activity of the magistracy and the lieutenancy. The lieutenancy's efforts to eradicate dissent were buttressed by the organizational structures of the lieutenancy and militia themselves; lieutenants could levy funds to pay spies for information and troops for raiding congregations. The Cavalier sentiments of its officers made it all the more willing to do so. As long as the link between dissent and treason remained strong, the lieutenancy enjoyed considerable success in its war against nonconformity.

The persecution meted out by the lieutenancy was constantly spurred by the regular discovery of plots against the government. The detection and prevention of treasonable conspiracy, however, was a daunting task, for a bewildering variety of schemes surfaced and required scrutiny, though most amounted to little more than alehouse talk. Large amounts of gossip and rumor were sifted for a few nuggets of hard fact. "Night riders" might be phantoms or genuine troublemakers, but each report was investigated by dedicated lords and deputy lieutenants.[52] Venner's rising was only the first of a long series of plots the government uncovered at regular intervals. The general roundup of suspects and close surveillance of anyone with radical leanings or connections after the 1661 rising formed a pattern for following years. Some deputy lieutenants were virtual spymasters; Sir Edward Bagot of Staffordshire was one who received regular reports from informers about suspicious activities.[53] Sir Thomas Gower, a deputy lieutenant in the North Riding, headed an extensive network of spies throughout the north, which functioned with admirable efficiency.[54] Similarly, the bishop of Durham acted as his lieutenancy's chief spymaster.[55] Yet if spies, intercepted letters, and informers became important tools in the battle against rebellion, the lieutenancy most often employed more prosaic tactics: searches, tours of guard duty, and patrols intended to foil seditious plots long before they came to fruition.

One of the more spectacular episodes in the lieutenancy's antisedition campaign took place in the summer of 1662, when rumors of a possible Presbyterian rising were rampant. The council ordered the lieutenancy in several counties to take preventive measures: the walls of three towns, Northampton, Gloucester, and Coventry, all known for their unregenerate attitudes, were to be demolished. The government would not take the chance that the towns might be fortified and held against the king. In all three counties, the lieutenancy worked throughout the summer to level the city walls. The destruction of the ancient defenses of these towns symbolized the readiness of the crown to disregard the rights and traditions of corporate bodies when issues of state security were concerned. As with the Corporation Act—usually administered by the lords lieutenant—and the later campaign against borough charters, the government was prepared to act vigorously to protect itself, and the lieutenancy assisted without regard to local interests.[56]

Demolition proceeded without incident in Gloucester; in Coventry, however, problems arose. The lord lieutenant of Warwickshire, the earl of Northampton, supervised the work personally and informed the king that many in the town were very unhappy about the fate of their walls. He blamed resistance on the Presbyterians, one of whom left an anonymous letter at his lodgings "that hath in it the whole spirit of pagan presbytery, without the least tincture or mixture of Anabaptists' or Quakers' schism. By it your Majesty may see that those [the Presbyterians] are your only implacable enemies."[57] At Northampton the fears of resistance were such that the council's order, treated in Gloucester with near indifference, resulted in a hurried display of the lieutenancy's power. The lieutenants ordered out the county's militia, which was to march immediately upon Northampton and search every suspected house for arms. In a letter dated midnight on July 10, 1662, the deputy lieutenants reported that they had assembled 130 soldiers. They had expected more, though the harvest prevented some men from appearing. A search was conducted, and the number of arms discovered in private homes was found to be "inconsiderable." The town hall's magazine yielded two hundred muskets, and a few more were found in a church vestry. The deputies assembled the sleepy town magistrates and informed them of the king's orders. Despite some initial protest, the work on the walls began the next day and continued all summer.

Once the lieutenancy concluded that no local conspiracy threatened, the greatest problem became the council's allotment of only £50 for the demolition of the walls. Labor had to be hired from the countryside in the midst of the harvest. In the end the lieutenancy had to promise to give the stones to anyone who would remove them. Even so, the lieutenant estimated that the job would cost £500.[58] Like the earl of Northampton in Coventry, the earl of Westmorland (one of the county's two lieutenants) remained in the town until the job was completed.

Searches, examinations, and preventive arrests continued almost unabated into the mid-1660s. Night riders worried deputy lieutenants, former republicans sent letters full of cryptic messages "darkly expressed," and sectaries met in violation of the Conventicle Act. Radicals who had always been suspected by the Royalist gentry were joined after the passage of the Act of Uniformity (in 1662) by Presbyterians, who many feared would ally themselves with "fanatics."[59] Of course, many of the schemes uncovered proved to be mere fantasies; the lieutenancy expended considerable energy chasing ghosts. In 1662, many counties were thrown into a ferment by reports of the presence of Edmund Ludlow, the former republican radical and regicide. His presence was confidently—and simultaneously—reported in Cheshire, Sussex, Kent, and London; in appearance he was, variously, forty years old and black-haired, or squat and sixty, or silver-haired and tall. The two-month search resulted in the arrest of a justice of common pleas in Sussex who was accused of being the regicide. The incident was rendered still more farcical by the fact that Ludlow had been living in quiet exile in Switzerland for two years.[60]

Notwithstanding overzealous bungling of this sort, the lieutenancy's vigor paid benefits to the government. In September 1663, Sir Thomas Gower's informants gave him news of a revolt planned for the next month. This conspiracy was very real. Most of the action was confined to the north, although there is evidence that some of those involved—all of whom were former soldiers in the republican army—had contacts elsewhere.[61] The duke of Buckingham, lord lieutenant of the West Riding, hurried north to take command of the county's defense. The rising was due to take place on October 12, and the duke raised two regiments of foot—one regular militia and the other volunteers—to meet the expected attack. Lord Belasyse, lieutenant of the East Riding, offered another thousand foot and three hundred horse, and all the neighboring counties called out their militia in anticipation of a general rebellion.[62] The earl of Derby, marquis of Newcastle, Lord Belasyse, and the bishop of Durham all personally commanded the units raised to put down the revolt, and even in the south deputy lieutenants secured suspicious characters and prepared to strike against known radicals.

The actual outcome of the Derwentdale Plot was, like Venner's revolt, something of an anticlimax. About fifty horsemen, some of whom were unarmed, gathered in a wood near Leeds on the night of October 12 and were so dispirited by the pathetic show of force they made that the group broke up, afraid of capture by the vastly superior forces of the duke, which were searching for them not far away.[63] Not a shot was fired or a man lost, but the conspiracy was riddled with spies and in the aftermath twenty-one men were hanged. Like the Fifth Monarchists, the Derwentdale plotters were crushed by the efficiency of the lieutenancy's intelligence operation and the zeal of its leaders.

The lieutenancy's success in dealing with sedition and treasonous plots in the 1660s was a function of the almost unanimous conviction of the gentry—especially those who served as deputy lieutenants—that dissenters offered a clear danger to the throne.[64] During the 1660s the traditional English fear of popery was overlaid by fear of Protestant dissent and republicanism.[65] Although their predecessors in Charles I's reign had seen Roman Catholics in the same light, the old lieutenancy had never pursued recusants with much vigor. The gentry's views had changed, and, moreover, the problem in the 1660s was far more acute; now there actually were sectarian plots against the government. Aside from the famous episode of 1605, the English Catholic laity had resolutely avoided political activity and had lived peaceably among their neighbors. Republicans and dissenters were far more visible than Catholics had been, and the lieutenancy was better equipped, both ideologically and physically, to pursue them. Before the wars, many gentlemen had been reluctant to prosecute their Catholic neighbors because of their social standing as well as their quietude.[66] The sectaries of the postwar period were different. Most were of lower rank socially, and gentle consciences rarely suffered when a meeting of Quakers or Baptists was broken up.

Anglicans and Royalists chafed at their monarch's lenient stance toward dissenters. By the time of the Derwentdale Plot, Clarendon reported that the king was heartily sick of the constant accusations that flooded in from informers: "The continual discourse of plots and insurrections had so wearied the king, that he even resolved to give no more countenance to any such informations, nor to trouble himself with inquiry into them."[67] The crown, much to the horror of some deputies, continually ordered the release of arrested sectaries, as in the aftermath of Venner's rising and after the Derwentdale affair.[68] In 1662, rumors of a royal indulgence for dissenters caused the Hampshire deputy lieutenants and militia officers to declare that should such a thing be granted, they would resign their commissions in protest; two years later the Oxfordshire deputies likewise complained that Charles was far too lenient toward fanatics.[69]

The gentry's unanimous determination to suppress nonconformity was the engine that drove the lieutenancy in its war against sedition. By the later 1660s, however, that consensus had begun to fragment. For some, old enemies, in the shape of Catholic recusants, had begun to resume their role as the political nation's principal bugbear.[70] Anti-Catholicism had always been present in England; its potential strength had been illustrated in the hysteria that gripped the kingdom in the tense months of 1642. Antipopery, overshadowed in the first years of the Restoration by fear of

Protestant dissenters, rebounded as the sects began to withdraw from politics and republican plots dwindled. Old habits reasserted themselves; the attention of the political nation, fixed for so long on the doings of the supporters of the Commonwealth, began to wander.[71]

The last great antisectarian convulsion of the decade came in 1666, the result of the burning of London. The Great Fire that consumed most of the City in the first week of September was quickly recognized by the king and council as the result of an accident, but the lieutenancy immediately suspected a conspiracy.[72] As the earl of Carlisle, lieutenant of Cumberland and Westmorland, said when he called out his lieutenancy's militia, London was clearly the victim of "anabaptists and other ill-affected persons."[73] The militia was summoned in every county as word of the calamity spread, and lieutenants acted quickly, rounding up the usual suspects: in Norfolk, Cheshire, and Yorkshire sectaries and former republicans were jailed.[74] A Northumberland gentleman believed that "the plot was not only for London but the destruction of the principal cities and towns in England," a theory that was widely held.[75] The lieutenancy's vigorous response illustrates some of the changes in the kingdom's attitudes toward dissenters. For the first time since the Restoration, the blame for a supposed plot was not laid exclusively at the doorstep of the "fanatics." Some people chose to blame sectaries, some posited a weird alliance of Quakers, Jesuits, and Dutchmen, but, significantly, many firmly believed the responsibility lay exclusively with malevolent Catholics.[76]

Fortunately for the Restoration lieutenancy, its views on the suppression of dissent could easily be transferred from sectaries to recusants; now the gentry was prepared to act against all those it believed posed a threat to the state, Catholic or Protestant. As a consequence of the great surge in popular antipapist sentiment occasioned by the Great Fire, the king issued proclamations banishing priests and ordering that papists be disarmed, the first active steps against Catholics the crown had taken since 1660.[77] Some lieutenants were clearly ready to transfer their suspicions. Comparatively few dissenters were jailed after the news of the fire spread, and in other counties, where arrests were made, most of the prisoners were released quickly. Lord Townshend, for example, released all but three of those he ordered held in the Norwich jail within a week of the fire.[78]

Foreshadowing the bitter divisions that would rend many counties in the 1670s and 1680s, a deputy lieutenant in Warwickshire found himself accused of conspiring to destroy Warwick. Fear of a possible plot panicked Warwickshire; on September 9, 1660, Secretary Joseph Williamson was informed of "a strange kind of robbing" that had appeared in the county. Sheep were found dead in their pastures, missing nothing but their tallow—the essential ingredient of an incendiary device ("fireballs," as they were called). A deputy lieutenant, Thomas Norton, investigated the robberies and apprehended a man who claimed that he had nothing to do with a plot but stole to relieve his poverty.[79] The lieutenancy was satisfied with this explanation, but its efforts to calm the populace were ruined by an incident that took place in Warwick less than a week later.

The city was alarmed when a little boy out gathering blackberries spied a stranger lurking in a ditch, "very busy doing something." Spotting the boy, the man fled, carrying a bag from which dropped "a ball of blackish brown color, bigger than an egg." Upon his return to town, the boy presented his find to the city magistrates and deputy lieutenants, who were then meeting to secure the county against plots. The suspected item "was presently concluded to be a fireball . . . but that it was not yet fully finished" because it stubbornly refused to burn when the deputies put it to the ultimate test. The news of an incendiary skulking around the town threw Warwick into turmoil. As one of Williamson's correspondents described it, "the town continued all that day in a strange kind of tumult, every man in arms, besides the militia horse that were there, keeping strong and strict guard all night." On the following morning, Sir Henry Packering, one of Warwickshire's senior deputy lieutenants, arrived with a troop of horse. Seeing the panic and disorganization that prevailed, and no doubt skeptical of the danger from arsonists, he ordered the citizens back to their homes. A confrontation resulted. The local men refused to obey Sir Henry, declaring "that for ought they knew he had a design himself to betray their town." Packering threatened to order his troops to fire upon the men, who responded by cocking and aiming their muskets at the horsemen.[80]

Bloodshed was eventually avoided after lengthy negotiations, but Warwick's desperate fear of Catholic incendiaries is indicative of a decisive change in public attitudes toward dissent. "It is unimaginable," said Ralph Hope of this incident, "what panic fears and animosities the generality hereabouts are possessed with, it being I believe as possible to persuade them out of their Christianity, as into any belief but that the papists have a desire to rise and cut their throats."[81] The town remained in an uproar until the arrival of the earl of Northampton a week later. Northampton held a meeting of the principal gentlemen of the shire, reviewed the county militia, and ordered the severe punishment of anyone who spread false rumors.

Furthermore, the earl proclaimed that anyone who dared disparage Sir Henry Packering would deeply regret such action.[82]

The kingdom's response to the Great Fire of London marks a turning point in Restoration politics. Divisions that had been submerged in the face of the threat posed by the survival of the Good Old Cause had begun to reappear by 1666. These divisions were stimulated by the disillusionment of many with Charles II's government, the first stirrings of parliamentary opposition, and the resurgence of the nation's traditional fear of popery.[83] The repeated failure of republicans and sectarians to generate any serious opposition to the monarchy, largely a result of the vigilance of the lieutenancy, was also a factor. The last act of the misnamed Clarendon Code, the Five Mile Act, was passed by Parliament in 1665, but the impetus for persecution was already fading. Only one prosecution was made under the act in its first year of operation, and the number of prosecutions under the Conventicle Act declined precipitously after 1665. By this time, sectaries were meeting openly in many parts of the country.[84] Weak and divided as the sectaries were, many in the country were able to dismiss the threat they represented as a minor one when compared with the dangers of resurgent Roman Catholicism.

The upshot of these increasing divisions was that the lieutenancy no longer represented a united political nation. Although many more people in Parliament and the nation at large began to question the Cavalier orthodoxy that had reigned in the early years of the Restoration, lords lieutenant and their deputies, who were directly accountable to the crown, began to take on a more explicitly partisan role. The lieutenancy was by now well-versed in new methods of political action and was prepared to turn the tactics it had learned against anyone who presented a potential threat— including supporters of Exclusion or other opponents of the king's will. The persecution of Protestant dissent continued after 1666, and vigorous campaigns against dissenters were launched in 1670 and during the Exclusion Crisis. The most sweeping of all came in 1681–83, in the aftermath of the last Exclusion Parliament and the Rye House Plot.[85] All of these activities were intimately connected to the political battles of the day; the lieutenancy in the 1670s and 1680s no longer acted as the instrument of gentry consensus as it had in the early 1660s; it had become the representative of Royalist Anglicanism in its struggle against the Exclusionists. Although not yet presiding over a one-party monopoly of power, the lieutenancy's campaign against sedition in the early 1660s was clearly a crucial step marking the institution's abandonment of its traditional localism in favor of allegiance to the central state, a shift that became even more evident in the lieutenancy's conduct of the Second Dutch War.

T HE S ECOND D UTCH W AR officially began in March 1665, after English naval attacks against Dutch interests pushed tensions between the republic and England to the breaking point.[86] As in the 1620s, the lieutenancy was responsible for a considerable part of the kingdom's war effort, although differences are noteworthy. The Second Dutch War was a naval one; no English soldiers were sent abroad to fight on the Continent. Consequently, the Restoration lieutenancy was spared the problem of billeting soldiers which had so vexed its predecessors in the previous reign. The large numbers of men needed to man the army in the 1620s and the huge sums of money that had to be extracted from the local community to feed and house them did not plague Charles II's lieutenancy. Even more novel, the war against the Hollanders began as a popular one, with the wholehearted support of most of the country. In November 1664, Parliament expressed the determination of the nation to meet the Dutch challenge by granting the king—without a dissenting voice—the unheard-of sum of £2.5 million, the largest supply ever given to an English monarch to that time.[87]

The conduct of the war offers an interesting contrast with Charles I's European wars. In both cases the lieutenancy bore the prime responsibility for local defense, but because the conflict against the Dutch was almost exclusively naval, the burden was shared more fully with the naval administration.[88] The lieutenancy helped with provisions for the fleet and, more important, pressed seamen, but its role was somewhat more restricted than it had been in the 1620s. There was another important difference between the two wars: the danger of invasion. Although some coastal counties were panicked by rumors of French attacks in the 1620s, in the 1660s the threat from the Dutch was much more immediate. The Dutch raided port towns on several occasions and, most spectacularly, attacked the royal fleet in the Medway and Landguard Fort in Suffolk in 1667. Defending native soil against an enemy invader proved to be an easier task than billeting thousands of troops had ever been. Finally, the spirit of Cavalier solidarity that animated the pursuit of sectaries and former republicans in the provinces helped ensure the lieutenancy's success in the conflict.

The first months of the Second Dutch War weighed lightly upon the lieutenancy, and it brought successes for English arms that rivaled those of Cromwell. Dutch possessions and shipping were seized, and the navy won a significant victory off the Suffolk coast in April 1665 at the battle of Lowestoft. The victory resulted in France's entry into the war on the Dutch side, but the lieutenancy's work load did not increase until the later months of 1665. In October the council warned the East Anglian lieutenants that the Dutch fleet was prowling near their coasts. One of the duke of Ormond's correspondents noted on the sixteenth that "the Dutch have lately been upon the coast of England, and have put . . . several of the small sea-towns in great apprehensions of their landing." Coastal counties prepared their militia to march on short notice, but apart from several insignificant landings by longboats full of sailors in search of provisions, the crisis passed without incident.[89] By November, the weather ended the annual campaigning season, and the lieutenancy turned from defending against invasion to assisting in the outfitting of the next season's fleet.

The task of preparing the fleets for this war rested largely with the officials of the navy: victuals and supplies were contracted for in London, and many of the sailors needed were pressed in the city by naval officers.[90] But the lieutenancy still had much to do. Pressing sailors was an occasional duty; Lord Lovelace oversaw the impressment of three hundred Berkshire men in the summer of 1666, and Lord Townshend was on hand for a press of two hundred in Lynn at the same time.[91] The task was simplified by the relatively small numbers of men involved and also by their unwonted enthusiasm for the king's service. An Oxfordshire gentleman noted that the deputy lieutenants there had had great success in their efforts: they sent off a company of "lusty young bargemen; it pleased us much to see their willingness and resolution, singing and shouting along the streets as they passed for London." A few days later, 150 soldiers were sent away, "who marched with the same jollity." Even some of the local women were enthusiastic: "There is a sturdy brave girl of about twenty years of age that has habited herself in men's apparel and is gone aboard the fleet. . . . If other counties had the same zeal," he said, "within seven years we might drown Holland and fire down France."[92] The contrast with the lieutenancy's experience in 1627–28 is remarkable and must in part be credited to new respect for its active enforcement of the priorities of central government.[93]

The need for men was matched by the crown's need for money, and the lieutenancy was called upon to help as it had been so many times in the past. The huge parliamentary supply granted in 1664 took time to collect, and the war, as ever, was very expensive. Early in 1665 the government solicited a "Royal Aid"—loans that were to be made on the security of the money voted the previous November.[94] Responsibility for collecting the aid was given to local commissioners, many of whom were deputy lieutenants. Despite the popularity of the war and the victories of the summer, money was slow in arriving. By the early spring of 1666, only one-third of the aid had been paid into the exchequer. The council resolved to encourage payment by appealing to the lords lieutenant. Lieutenants wrote their subordinates and traveled around their shires in an effort to raise money, with some success.

In Nottinghamshire the duke of Newcastle was especially active, as was Lord Brooke in Staffordshire.[95] Brooke found that many gentlemen were reluctant to loan money, but after speaking with the king he arranged a compromise: rather than raising a loan, Brooke gained the king's permission to encourage Staffordshire gentlemen to pay their regular taxes six months to a year early.[96] John Bentham wrote to Secretary Williamson in July 1666 to say that people were ready and willing to oppose an enemy invasion but were reluctant to loan money before an actual landing occurred.[97] Reluctance to lend to the crown was of course a long-standing tradition and was exacerbated by the economic dislocation that had followed in the wake of the plague epidemic that decimated London in 1665. The funds came in slowly, but in the end nearly 98 percent of the loan was gathered.[98] The lieutenancy was again ordered to promote a loan in the summer of 1667, when another fleet had to be supplied. Lord Brooke held a public meeting of the gentry in Lichfield in July, to "persuade all . . . to a compliance to these his majesty's reasonable desires," and the earl of Rutland, among other lieutenants, was importuned by the king to encourage a good response in Leicestershire.[99]

In addition to loan money, in 1666 the lieutenants forwarded funds collected under the Militia Act to London for "safe keeping." Through this method—one of dubious legality—the government gained the use of several tens of thousands of pounds.[100] The state of the exchequer in 1666 made the money a welcome relief for the hard-pressed officials of the Royal Navy. The expedient was not tried again, however, because in the next year the bulk of the money raised under the Militia Act was spent locally for wages and supplies for the militia.

Raising men and money for the crown was not, however, the lieutenancy's prime responsibility during the Second Dutch War. Lieutenants and deputies all over the country, but especially in the south, worked hard to fortify their coasts and repel hostile invaders. The first alarms came in 1665, but the lieutenancy busied itself inspecting and improving local defenses for weeks before the first enemy sail was spotted. By early 1666 the effort

was in full swing. In late January the earl of Oxford toured Essex, his lieutenancy, and issued orders to begin a strict watch of the beacons as well as
increased training for the militia.[101] The Suffolk militia was called to arms
and marched down to the coast in February after reports of a Dutch fleet
reached the lord lieutenant.[102] As the weather improved, and with it the
likelihood of enemy raids, the lieutenancy's activities increased.

By June the danger was such that the king instructed all lords lieutenant
to return to their shires: "We do hereby require and expressly command
you forthwith to repair to some convenient place within your lieutenancy
thereby to unite the gentry and quicken those under your command to
the discharge of their various duties."[103] Secretary Henry Bennett told the
duke of Ormond that the king was devoting as much time to preparing the
nation's defenses as were the lieutenants: "His majesty hath sat in council
much of the morning and afternoon disposing of the militia as usefully
as he can order it towards repelling an invasion."[104] All rose to meet the
danger. Those lieutenants who were in London when the king issued his
order hurried to the country, and those who were already on the scene redoubled their efforts.[105] Activity was naturally most intense along the coast.
In Gloucestershire the militia was drilled on several occasions as a body
in the presence of the lieutenant, as it was in Dorset, Cornwall, Norfolk,
and Devon.[106] As happened elsewhere, the Hampshire militia mustered
together in early July, and the more remote and inland counties did their
part as well; the Staffordshire horse was ordered by Lord Brooke to proceed
to Northampton, from whence they would be dispatched in case of an invasion.[107] In the earl of Derby's lieutenancies, the militia was called out in
July, and at a meeting of the Lancashire gentry in Preston, the assembly
resolved to raise six companies of volunteers for the king's service. Even
in Cumberland the earl of Carlisle had no difficulty raising a company of
volunteers.[108]

Most striking about the preparations the lieutenancy made in the summer of 1666 was the enthusiastic cooperation of the populace. In virtually
every county attendance at musters was high, as was the morale of those
who appeared. A Dorset gentleman claimed that he had not seen such a
complete turnout of the militia in years; the Gloucestershire militia was described as "in very good equipage"; the Cornish troops were "very zealous";
the Yorkshire trained bands declared that they were ready "in a trice" to sacrifice their lives in the king's service.[109] According to the *Oxford Gazette*, the
Kentish horse, under the direction of Lord Winchilsea, was "unanimously
well-appointed, and are at a day's warning, which gives an assurance how

ready all this county will be to manifest their faithfulness to their king and country; as also their care and diligence that is used in siting the beacons, and whatsoever may conduce to the well-managing of his sacred majesty's concernments in these parts." [110]

In Lancashire, where Lord Derby ordered one-quarter of the militia horse to Northampton to join those waiting there for an enemy attack, the biggest problem the deputies faced was not reluctance to serve but how to prevent every horseman in the county from appearing. [111] John Herbert told Secretary Williamson that the same occurred in Gloucestershire, where the lord lieutenant, his deputies, and the most important local gentry presided over a muster of the horse. [112] In another example of the country's enthusiasm, in June a report reached the local population of a French assault on Pendennis in Cornwall. The report was mistaken, but every man for miles sprang to arms, and the militia marched hurriedly to the coast. Hugh Acland reported that within three hours of the alarm, ten thousand Cornishmen were prepared to throw back the invaders. [113]

The war at sea in 1666 was not a happy one for the English; a major defeat in the Four Days' Battle in June was followed by a draw—which was perceived as a defeat—on St. James's Day in the following month. [114] These setbacks triggered the invasion scare of the summer, although they did not result in any major enemy landings. The danger from abroad induced solidarity, as had the fear of sectaries, and this perceived threat helped the lieutenancy carry out its duties with greater success. The performance of the summer of 1666 was impressive; the lieutenancy organized, within a very short time, a credible home defense. The fact that in the Second Dutch War the enemies were both republican Holland and Catholic France helped unite the kingdom, despite the growing tension between those concerned more with Catholicism than with dissent. The lieutenancy led the way in 1666, yet the true test of its effectiveness as guardian of the national defense was to come the next year.

High morale played an important role in the lieutenancy's efficiency, but the foundations of its success were laid in the first years of the Restoration. Lords and deputy lieutenants carefully chosen for their loyalty and zeal for the Stuart monarchy inspired extra effort from the provinces. In the 1630s Charles I's service suffered from his failure to mold a lieutenancy willing to override local interests in pursuit of a successful war effort. His son's government took the lesson of 1640 to heart, and the king's choices of lieutenants, as well as his careful supervision of the appointment of deputies, was intended to prevent a repetition of previous experience. The increased number of deputies also eased the burden on the lieutenancy. Directing preparations for a war was an exhausting enterprise, and the deputies of the 1620s and 1630s had often found themselves overwhelmed by the multiplicity of their tasks. What had once been done by six or eight men was in the mid-1660s the job of fifteen or twenty. The result was a better-organized war effort. Finally, the militia acts gave the lieutenancy the leverage it had lacked in previous conflicts. Money to pay militiamen and officers was available, and the undisputed authority to punish the slack offered further incentive. The Restoration lieutenancy's organizational strength created a formidable military institution.

As usual, in 1666–67 the autumn and winter seasons saw a diminution of military activity. In Norfolk, Lord Townshend took a tour of inspection near Yarmouth, and the Suffolk deputies occupied themselves by searching for deserters from the fleet. Throughout most of the country, however, attention turned to other matters.[115] Lord Brooke, considering the trouble and expense the county had borne during the summer, decided to cancel the regular autumn musters of the militia and set his deputies to providing uniforms for the troops—buff coats and gray caps.[116] During the Great Fire the trained bands of Hertfordshire and Surrey were called out to perform firefighting duties, and the subsequent hunt for Catholic arsonists kept many lieutenants and deputies busy until winter set in.[117]

The spring of 1667 passed quietly, but on May 29, the king's birthday, the council sent an express to the lieutenants of all the coastal counties. The Dutch fleet was preparing to leave its ports, and the lieutenancy was once again to ready the counties for an invasion. The council expected enemy landings in force—the lieutenants were especially reminded that "in places where you shall be obliged to make head or appearance to the enemy, you make the greatest show you can in numbers, and more especially of horse, even though it be of such as are otherwise wholly unfit and improper for nearer service, horse being the force that will most discourage the enemy from landing."[118] As a result of these instructions, the militia from Cornwall to Northumberland stood to arms and waited anxiously for the Dutch.[119]

The blow fell early in June. Admiral Michael De Ruyter's fleet was spotted in the Thames estuary on the ninth, and the militia forces of Kent, Essex, Hertfordshire, Surrey, and Middlesex were ordered to march to the defense of the capital.[120] Pepys lay awake on the night of the eleventh and listened to the frantic preparations of the city militia for the attack. He noted "the beating up of drums this night for the train bands upon penalty of death, to appear in arms tomorrow morning, with bullet and powder and money to supply themselves with victuals for a fortnight." [121] A small party of enemy troops landed on Canvey Island in Essex, where they burned several buildings and killed livestock before a contingent of the Essex militia drove them off. [122] The earls of Oxford and Winchilsea, lieutenants of Essex and Kent, both played active roles in defending the shoreline from further depredations; Winchilsea was given the command of all the forces in Kent, both regular and militia, and Oxford performed a similar function on the opposite bank of the Medway.

Unfortunately, none of the care and vigor displayed by the lieutenancy could prevent the disaster that befell the king's fleet riding at anchor in the river. The Dutch broke through the chain strung across their path and brushed aside the boom of sunken ships that barred their way, falling upon the ships laid up in the harbor. The navy's most important ships were anchored there, virtually defenseless. Expecting the conclusion of peace—the terms of which, unknown to both sides at this moment, had already been concluded at Breda—the government had economized and left the ships in the Medway unmanned and unprepared for action. The result was disastrous: the Dutch destroyed all of the important vessels there and, most humiliating of all, captured the pride of the navy, the *Royal Charles,* towing her away in triumph to Holland. [123] London, afraid that the enemy fleet would continue up the river and raid the city, panicked. "The distraction and consternation in court and city was so great," wrote Clarendon, "as if the Dutch had not only been masters of the river, but had really landed an army of 100,000 men." [124]

Luckily for the city, the Dutch withdrew, peppered all the way back down the river by shots fired from companies of militia lining the banks. Meanwhile, the rest of the country braced itself for further landings. The earl of Bath sped away to Cornwall within six hours of the first Dutch attack, Lord Burlington marched his forces to the Yorkshire coast, and the militia in virtually every other county stood ready to assist wherever they were required. [125] The lieutenancy was responsible for the defense of most of the crucial points on the coastline; the tiny forces that made up the regular army were spread far too thinly to manage the job. Dover Castle, Landguard Fort, Exeter, and the Isle of Wight—as well as the Channel Islands—were all garrisoned during this emergency by the militia, who answered to their deputies and lords lieutenant. [126]

The danger of attack continued after De Ruyter left the Medway. He carried some three to four thousand soldiers in his fleet, under the command of a renegade Englishman, Colonel Thomas Dolman, and was anxious to put them to good use.[127] After prowling along the East Anglian coast for almost two weeks, he chose a target: Landguard Fort. The fort protected Harwich, where a large fleet of merchant vessels had taken shelter after the appearance of the enemy. If De Ruyter could seize it, Harwich would be defenseless—dozens of ships would be at the mercy of his fleet, and a prosperous port town lay open to total destruction.

The Dutch believed that the fortress, which stood on a spit of land near the harbor, on the Essex-Suffolk border, was poorly defended. The fort had been erected in 1626, under the supervision of the then lord lieutenant of Essex, the earl of Warwick, and was well built and sited. Furthermore, unknown to the Dutch, it was garrisoned by several hundred Suffolk militiamen and well prepared for the arrival of the enemy. The lord lieutenant of Suffolk, James Howard, earl of Suffolk, had been in the county for several weeks, feverishly working to guarantee a warm welcome for the Dutch should they attempt a landing. By the time De Ruyter appeared on July 1, Suffolk had assembled two of the county's militia regiments, the Yellow and his own White regiment, all of the county's horse, and additional reinforcements from Cambridgeshire.

Not knowing the strength of the opposing forces, Colonel Dolman landed about 1,700 to 2,000 soldiers and marines the next day. They quickly discovered that the fort was much better fortified than they had anticipated, but nevertheless they pressed forward and made an unsuccessful attempt to scale the walls. The first assault was driven back with light casualties, but Dolman had already decided that Landguard Fort was too well defended for his small force. The Dutch withdrew to the beach, where they were engaged by the militia regiments under Suffolk's command: "A smart skirmish began between them which continued until ten in the evening."[128] There were few casualties on either side, although the exact number of soldiers who fell is unknown. The action was over by the evening of the second. A rumor of another landing circulated on the third, and Suffolk's troops were hastily reinforced by huge numbers of men from the surrounding countryside who armed themselves with whatever was available—scythes, halberds, and birding guns—and rushed to the area. But there was no attack. Satisfied with their triumph in the Medway and convinced that the coast was too well defended to make any more raids worthwhile, the Dutch returned to port in Holland.

The news of the attack and defense of Landguard Fort set off another vigorous campaign by lieutenants to prepare their counties. In Yorkshire

Lord Fauconberg was reported to have taken great pains to ensure the safety of Scarborough and Whitby, where he spent several weeks personally inspecting fortifications and training militiamen.[129] The duke of Richmond traveled down to Dorset—a comparatively rare event, for Richmond was not an active lord lieutenant—where he reviewed the militia and toured the defenses on the coast.[130] The Cornish lieutenancy garrisoned Falmouth with three thousand infantrymen, four troops of horse, and 150 guns in anticipation of an attack.[131] Although the war had all but ended, the summer's lessons made the lieutenants of every coastal county extremely cautious.

Reports of enemy fleets continued to alarm the country; on July 11, a hostile force was reported off Milford Haven. The deputy lieutenants quickly called out the militia, which, according to Francis Malory, appeared promptly and in very great numbers. The alarm proved to be false, however: the ships the deputies feared were Dutch turned out to be a convoy of cattle carriers bound for Ireland.[132] At the same time, a similar incident occurred in Hampshire. A sighting of forty or fifty sail off Portsmouth resulted in a general mobilization of the militia. Again, the enemy proved to be a phantom. One of Pepys's friends, Sir William Batten, expressed pungently what many deputy lieutenants must have felt at this time: "By God! I do believe the Devil shits Dutchmen!"[133]

The Restoration lieutenancy retained the primary responsibility for the defense of the realm it had been charged with under Charles I. If the institution had sometimes worked effectively in the 1620s, the problems of 1628 and 1640 had shown that the Caroline lieutenancy was unable to sustain a modern war. Its improved efficiency in the 1660s was aided by the immediate threat of invasion and the fact that the kingdom's leaders—the gentry and peerage—were solidly united behind the crown. Indeed, the response of ordinary militiamen to the call of the lieutenancy indicates that that support extended far beyond the manor house. In Cornwall and Lancashire, gentlemen noted that even nonconformists vied to offer their services— offers that were pondered with considerable wariness by the lieutenancy.[134]

In spite of all the false alarms, however, the lieutenancy acquitted itself remarkably well in the Second Dutch War. The vigor of the lords lieutenant in their preparations and the performance of the militia when threatened with invasion illustrate the effectiveness of the new lieutenancy as a military institution. The battle at Landguard Fort marked the first significant seaborne invasion of English soil since the arrival of William the Conqueror, and although it was hardly an action of epic proportions, the militia stood up well under enemy fire. The county, under the direction of its lord lieutenant, responded enthusiastically to the challenge from seasoned Dutch soldiers, and the sheer weight of numbers forced the enemy to withdraw. The Restoration settlement had succeeded in strengthening the lieutenancy by ensuring its ideological reliability as well as by revamping its practical organization and reasserting its authority, a success pointedly illustrated by its performance in the Second Dutch War.

But the Second Dutch War was not a lasting triumph for the lieutenancy. If the success of the lieutenancy was in the short term encouraged by the disaster in the Medway, that defeat held within it the seeds of future trouble. The inability of the government to protect the most important part of the Royal Navy, the general perception of scandal and incompetence that surrounded the conduct of the war, and the huge expense involved in keeping the war effort going encouraged dissatisfaction in the provinces. As in the case of the pursuit of nonconformity, Cavalier zeal began to dissipate, and with it vanished the ability of the lieutenancy to marshal unanimity among the gentry.

The Third Dutch War, which began in 1672 and ended with the signing of the Treaty of Westminster on February 9, 1674, was fought halfheartedly by the government, weakly supported by the people, and symptomatic of the decline of the Cavalier supremacy.[135] The following years saw the rise of party and ideological conflict in England; the lieutenancy was again to play a vital role in this transformation of the political scene. Though the institutional strengths of the Restoration lieutenancy would remain, the political developments of the 1670s and 1680s would drastically alter both the public perception of the institution and its role in society.

CHAPTER V

Politics and Rebellion, 1660–1685

POLITICAL TENSION IN ENGLAND peaked in 1681. Revelations of popish conspiracy and conservative fears of a revival of the "Spirit of '40" created a climate of distrust and suspicion. One man who was swept up in and ultimately destroyed by the furious struggle over the succession was a London craftsman, Stephen Colledge, the "Protestant Joiner." The campaign to send Colledge to the gallows would involve many of the king's supporters: his judges, his legal officers, and, not least, his loyal lord lieutenant in the county of Oxfordshire, James Bertie, Lord Norreys.

Bertie succeeded as lord lieutenant of Oxfordshire in 1674 at the tender age of twenty-one. The second son of the first earl of Lindsey, a Royalist general and one of the more illustrious casualties of the civil wars, Norreys boasted a distinguished pedigree in the service of the Stuart dynasty. A firm opponent of Exclusion, he turned his considerable vigor to the pursuit of the king's enemies in the late 1670s. The third Exclusion Parliament, held in his own bailiwick at Oxford, gave Norreys a personal stake in the political issues of the day. Stephen Colledge began his last act on the public stage at the same time, unluckily at the very moment that the government decided to crush its opponents. Norreys, consequently, played an instrumental role in the sacrifice of the hapless tradesman.

Stephen Colledge was a passionate London Protestant; the revelations of the Popish Plot left him bewildered, frightened, and determined to defend his religion against the machinations of the Catholic conspiracy.[1] But Colledge was also venturing into very deep waters. A full-fledged member of the remarkably open London political scene in the late 1670s, Colledge made the usual round of the Exclusionist coffee houses and taverns, where he mixed with many of the leading spirits of the movement to unseat the duke of York as the king's heir.[2] He eagerly participated in the intrigue surrounding the Exclusion Parliaments, and he clearly enjoyed making his own mark among such company. At a meeting at the Sun Tavern, near the Exchange, attended by "several lords and, I believe, above a hundred parliament-men of the Commons," Colledge experienced his own political epiphany: "The duke of Monmouth called me to him, and told me he had a good report of me, and that I was an honest man, and one to be trusted . . . and from thence I had, I think, the popular name of the 'Protestant Joiner.' "[3] With such high praise from the idol of godly Exclusionists, it is not surprising that Colledge devoted himself to the cause with such ardor.

Convinced of the righteousness of his goals, Colledge bustled about town bidding defiance to those he saw as Protestantism's enemies. Indiscreet words—he allegedly announced that the king's council required a purge, or "we will make England too hot for him"—and his indefatigable support for Exclusion kept Colledge in the public eye. He distributed ribbons embroidered with the legend "No popery!" and "No slavery!" to all and sundry and shocked strangers by announcing that the Long Parliament was not responsible for the death of "his late sacred majesty," Charles I.[4] Such behavior made Colledge an obvious target for the government's wrath.

Unfortunately, unlike his patrons, Colledge was hardly a man whose social position or political prominence offered protection. When the dissolution of the Oxford Parliament afforded the king the leisure to pursue those who threatened to destroy the monarchy, the Protestant Joiner was one of the first to suffer. Colledge was arrested in London and held in the Tower to await indictment. To the irritation of the crown, the Middlesex grand jury, under the control of London Exclusionists, refused to indict him. The bill was rejected, and the government, undeterred, searched for a new way to proceed. The prosecution's solution was to seek a new indictment, but this time in a more congenial locale: Oxfordshire, where some (though not all) of Colledge's alleged offenses took place.

The government refused to contemplate the possibility of failure, and, as lord lieutenant, Norreys eagerly joined the pursuit. On July 11, 1681,

Sir Leoline Jenkins, the king's secretary, sent Norreys a reminder of what was expected from him. The king expected Norreys to ensure that "a good honest substantial grand jury" was impaneled.[5] The lord lieutenant did as he was told, and the jury, dominated by anti-Exclusionists, duly returned a true bill. In fact, the grand jury went farther still and published a public address directed at the Middlesex grand jurors, scolding them for their failure to act. "Let not the ill and nauseous scent of Protestant coffee houses poison your affections to the established government," the jurors sententiously pronounced, "but . . . put your hands and hearts to the support of thy monarchy and church."[6] The indictment returned, the king's judges made short work of the Protestant Joiner. Prisoners charged with treason were always at a distinct disadvantage under the law, and Colledge was no exception. His trial began on August 17 and finished the next day, almost certainly with Lord Norreys in attendance.[7] Although the king's evidence was flimsy, the jury obliged the government by rendering a guilty verdict.

The final act of the tragedy took place on August 31, when Colledge mounted the scaffold erected near the castle in Oxford. Accompanied by a minister and his son, the Protestant Joiner lamented the unfairness of his trial: "I could not tell the witnesses that were to swear against me; I could not tell what it was they swore against me . . . I could get no copy of the indictment, nor . . . make any preparation to make my defense . . . I had no liberty to do anything." Colledge denied to the last his treason, forgave the hangman, and threw himself upon the mercy of the Lord before the grisly business of execution began. In an act somewhat inappropriately described as "mercy," the king allowed Colledge's family to take possession of their father's mangled remains for private burial.[8]

The destruction of Stephen Colledge was a political act, commanded by the king and aided and abetted by the lieutenancy. But it was by no means a unique case of cooperative effort on the part of the lieutenancy and the monarch. The lieutenancy played an important part in the king's offensive against political dissent and seemed, at times, to lead the way for a monarch ambivalent about persecution. Although Norreys's role in the Colledge case remains shadowy, his efforts earned him effusive compliments from Secretary Jenkins: "It was a serious truth and no compliment that Mr. Justice Raymond spoke when he said, 'That such a lord lieutenant, such a sheriff, and such a grand jury would keep the king's crown fast upon his head.' Posterity will judge that we owe these subordinate men to a good lord lieutenant."[9] The king shared Jenkins's good opinion and shortly thereafter made Norreys earl of Abingdon.

The Exclusion Crisis saw the frequent intervention of the lieutenancy as an active player in the political struggles of the time. Lords lieutenant, through their choices of "subordinate men" and the persecution of those who stood in the way, became the political overlords of their shires. Through them the king vanquished the men who hoped to alter the succession and ensured the complete dominance of Royalist Anglicans in the kingdom.

THE TIES OF COMMUNITY and interest that bound the gentry, already weakened by the civil wars and interregnum, came under extreme pressure in the age of party inaugurated by the Exclusion Crisis. Although it has recently been argued that Exclusion was merely a symptom of a wider crisis upon which far too much emphasis has been laid, the fact is that it did have a transformative effect on politics in England. Though rooted in traditional English fears of popery, and so part of a series of anti-Catholic convulsions stretching back into the sixteenth century, the Exclusion Crisis nevertheless gave rise to a new politics.[10] Gentlemen who under Charles I's regime would have had a prescriptive right to a role in county society were from the 1670s denied that role because of their political—not religious— views. Before 1660 some (though by no means all) gentlemen were denied a role in local government because they were Catholics; yet Protestants, even those with distinctly Puritan views, were not excluded for their beliefs. By the time of the Exclusion Crisis, however, Protestant monarchists were excluded for their whiggery and, after the Glorious Revolution, for their Tory principles.

The advent of party struggle under the later Stuarts completely altered British politics. Old forms and traditions were abandoned or reshaped to fit new circumstances, new lessons were assimilated, and old verities discarded. The pre–civil war concept of the "county community" could not survive the elevation of Parliament and central government that followed the Restoration.[11] The crucial role Parliament came to play in government and politics required the mobilization of all of the crown's resources— including the influence of the lieutenancy—to manage parliamentary elections.[12] The traditional system, in which a lord lieutenant's local concerns were paramount, was replaced by one in which local interest was employed to affect the outcome of events at Westminster and Whitehall. The localist attitude of the lieutenancy changed dramatically following the Restoration; the Royalist lieutenancy consistently acted much more forcefully in the crown's behalf, even when—as was sometimes the case—the king himself was reluctant to use partisan tactics. This commitment to a vision of the crown's interest without reference to the man who wore it is one of the more striking developments of the Restoration; it created passionately "loyal" monarchists whose royalism seemed too stern even for the king. It was only by climbing onto the back of this bumptious tiger that Charles II managed to subdue his opponents. Charles knew what he was doing; he did not act blindly or haphazardly. He appointed Royalist Anglican lieutenants and deliberately excluded others from the lieutenancy from the start. Whatever their disagreements over religion or policy, it was clear that this alliance was a mutually beneficial one. Indeed, Royalist Anglican dominance raised the king to heights of authority which no Stuart before him had reached. An unintended consequence of this reluctant, but unavoidable, move was a new political structure in England.

The lieutenancy was one of the most effective architects of this structure. Lords lieutenant became political bosses—some, such as the earl of Bath in Cornwall and Devon and the earl of Yarmouth in Norfolk—of enormous local influence.[13] They ensured the selection of members of Parliament sympathetic to the court and kept a watchful eye on the crown's opponents. Military duties took second place to politics, and local interests were sidetracked by the more pressing needs of the crown.

This changed focus had been apparent since 1660; the reconstruction of the lieutenancy after the Restoration initiated the first halting steps toward politicized local government. The king's deliberate choice of Royalist Anglican lieutenants and deputies laid the foundation for the institution's use as a weapon in party warfare. The lieutenancy's activity in the persecution of republicans and nonconformists reflected a struggle between rival political views in England after the Restoration. The stubborn resistance of what Royalist Anglicans called "fanaticism" and its eventual alliance with Exclusion created a movement of frightening proportions for them. The continued survival of the Stuart monarchy, and with it the Church of England, required action. The successful campaign against dissent and, later, the destruction of Exclusion was the result of several factors, among them the new militia acts and the better organization of the lieutenancy, but it owed not a little to the determination of lord and deputy lieutenants alike to stamp out what they believed to be the dangerous set of political opinions at work in dissenting churches.

Although the political and ideological struggle of the 1670s greatly differed from that waged in the 1660s, the lieutenancy was no less a part of it. As the Cavalier consensus crumbled, the scene of conflict shifted from the provinces to the Houses of Parliament, where opposing views received public utterance and the crises of the decade were played out most dramatically. As a result, the focus of the lieutenancy shifted from preventing sedition in the pulpit to squelching it at the hustings and on the bench. The lieutenancy's targets, once mostly peripatetic ministers and defiant Quakers, now included gentlemen who no longer supported the goals of the once-solid Royalist ascendancy. That ascendancy was characterized by two overriding objectives: the protection of the Church of England from sectarian attack and the preservation of the monarchy from republicanism. In the 1660s the dangers of those near relatives, dissent and treason, had seemed self-evident, but by the mid-1670s that was no longer the case, and many began to see danger from other quarters—Rome and York House, for example. The politicization of the lieutenancy in the immediate post-Restoration period was born of necessity; after all, many would have welcomed the overthrow of the Stuarts. But once begun, the process was virtually unstoppable. When ideological opposition to the crown broadened from a small number of unrepentant republicans to include gentlemen who feared the accession of the duke of York, the lieutenancy found itself once again acting as the guardian of a party orthodoxy.

The first important political duty given the lieutenancy after the king's return was the enforcement of the Corporation Act in 1662. The act excluded dissenters and former republicans from borough government by requiring all town officers to take communion in the established church, thereby proving to the commissioners their loyalty to church and king. The crown nominated groups of prominent local gentlemen—most of whom were not residents of the corporations they scrutinized—as commissioners. Many were deputy lieutenants, and the lord lieutenant was almost invariably the president of the commission.[14]

The lieutenancy's interest in the loyalty of the corporations began even before Parliament considered the issue. In Berkshire, the deputy lieutenants were so eager to purge Wallingford of its unacceptable members that they unilaterally displaced the mayor and had installed another in his place a year before the Corporation Act passed. Sir George Fane, who led the deputies, was severely censured by the council for his illegal action and ordered to reverse it forthwith.[15] A similar incident took place in Bath, where Henry Chapman used his trained band captaincy and the warrant of two deputy lieutenants to arrest four of his factional opponents in the corporation.[16] Elsewhere the lieutenancy waited for the law to sanction its actions. In the autumn of 1662, the commissioners for each county began to visit local corporations. One of the first lieutenants to begin work was the earl of Derby. On August 26, 1662, he and his fellow commissioners visited Chester. Their execution of the act devastated the corporation: the recorder, John Reynolds, lost his place, as did ten aldermen, twenty common councilmen, the two treasurers and coroners, and the town clerk. Not even the corporation's menial servants were spared; both the sword bearer and the mace bearer lost their places.[17] Some were removed because they refused to denounce the covenant, but Derby did not stop there. Writing Secretary Nicholas, he said that "all who had ever been against the king, or given no testimony of loyalty before the restoration should be turned out, even though willing to take the oath."[18] After they had done their work in Chester, the commissioners proceeded to the other Cheshire boroughs, where they acted with no less vigor. On September 9, Lord Brereton, the joint lieutenant of Cheshire, informed Lord Norwich, "Having been at Chester and regulated that corporation, we are now at Congleton where we find the town according to their proportion as rotten as Chester, and I fear we shall not find the other towns much better. We are resolved to visit as many of them as we can this week."[19] By October, Derby was at work in neighboring Lancashire, although with considerably different results. The purges carried out in the Lancashire boroughs were not nearly as severe as the ones in Cheshire; when, on October 10, for example, Lancaster came under the earl's scrutiny, only one alderman and the town clerk fell victim to the Corporation Act.[20] Preston received a similarly lenient visit two weeks later.

Differences in the treatment of boroughs in Lancashire and Cheshire indicate the continuing importance of local alliances and personal politics for such tradition-minded lieutenants as Derby. The Lancashire boroughs were no less tainted than those in Cheshire, yet while in Lancashire many men with questionable pasts survived, in Cheshire they were uniformly ejected. The explanation for these differences lies in the social and political position of the earl of Derby in the northwest. Lancashire remained the earl's center of power; his clients were numerous and the web of local allegiance was delicate and complex. Every displacement had to be carefully weighed for its potential effects on local politics and social relations. In Cheshire, by contrast, the Stanley influence had declined disastrously in the course of the seventeenth century; virtually all that remained was the Stanley town house in Chester.[21] The Corporation Act offered the eighth earl of Derby an opportunity to rebuild the Stanley influence by inserting clients into local boroughs. Furthermore, because he was essentially reconstructing the family interest from the bottom up, the complications of disrupting established patronage networks were less significant. For Derby, then, the Corporation Act could be used in a very traditional way—as a means of building family influence. His enforcement of the Corporation Act illustrates the tenacious survival of many prewar traditions; for Derby, as for some others, the political world created in the aftermath of the Restoration had not eradicated all traditional practices.

Other lieutenants, too, were busy purging the unreliable in their counties. The earl of Northumberland turned thirteen aldermen out of their places in Arundel; Lord Lovelace cast out nine members of the corporation of Reading, including the mayor. Like Derby, Lovelace excluded members without giving them the opportunity to take the oaths. Other corporations were struck as hard as Chester had been. Kidderminster was deprived of all of its magistrates, with the single exception of a former Royalist officer, and even the earl of Clare found himself removed from his position as recorder of Nottingham by his lord lieutenant, the marquis of Newcastle.[22] Similarly, the boroughs in Wiltshire, Somerset, and Dorset endured a purge unlike any they had experienced during all the upheavals of the civil wars.[23]

The regulation of the corporations in 1662–63 was undoubtedly, as one historian has written, "a preliminary step in the politicization of local government," but in comparison to the purges of the 1680s this vetting of local officials was a rather halfhearted and unhurried affair. Clare, deprived of his recordership, was reinstated at the king's command—a consideration that the Holles family would certainly not receive after the Exclusion Crisis. Lieutenants of the 1660s, like Derby or Lord Brooke, who wrote his deputy lieutenants that he found the task of regulating Tamworth in Staffordshire "too great a burden for me to undertake," were as intent upon serving their own interests as serving the crown's.[24] The rigor of these changes, therefore, was sometimes mitigated. An attitude as relaxed as Brooke's would certainly cost a lieutenant his place in the 1680s.

Traditional patterns continued in other areas as well. Many elections to the Convention and Cavalier Parliaments went uncontested, and in the elections lords lieutenant acted much as they had before the Long Parliament: they ratified the choice of the community or worked to construct a general consensus among possible candidates. The earl of Devonshire, lieutenant of Derbyshire, might have been writing in James I's time when in February 1661 he told John Milward, "I pray you let me know whether my son may be acceptable to the county" as its knight in the Commons. A few days later the hint was taken and the deed done. The gentry met at

Derby on February 26, "and we have without any contradiction fixed upon my lord Cavendish and Mr. Freschville to be the knights for our county to serve in the next parliament."[25] Unlike the vast majority of selections for Parliament, the Derbyshire election of 1661 was contested. Devonshire's son Cavendish was indeed returned at the head of the poll, but the gentry's "unanimous determination" failed to keep Sir John Curzon from standing.[26] Polite hints from lords lieutenant, effective as they were in 1661, would in the future not be enough to ensure harmonious selections.

In Staffordshire, Lord Brooke secured two uncontested elections to the Convention and the Cavalier Parliaments by relying on his powers of persuasion. The death of Sir Thomas Leigh, one of the knights of the shire, in April 1662 resulted in months of hard work on the lieutenant's part. Finding a successor was not easy. "Upon the death of Sir Thomas Leigh," Brooke wrote Clarendon, "I heard of great contests like to be between the gentry there about the choice of another which (because I know they were apt to beget animosities which in length of time prove very prejudicial to his majesty's affairs) I did endeavor to settle and appease, which happened to have so good success that all the parties agreed in Sir Edward Littleton to be the man." Brooke's work was nearly destroyed when Littleton was placed among the nominees for sheriff of the county. The lieutenant testified that if Littleton were chosen, "the contests must needs return again, which I dare not promise myself so much happiness as to be able to compose a second time."[27] Littleton was not chosen sheriff and there was no contest. In fact, Brooke's efforts were unusually successful—Staffordshire proved to be one of the only shires whose county seats went uncontested until the Glorious Revolution.

The periodic by-elections held throughout the life of the Cavalier Parliament saw lieutenants employing both old but, increasingly, new tactics.[28] The rising incidence of contests and the increase of political divisions worked to transform the lieutenancy's role in local and national politics; as a place in the House of Commons rapidly became an end in itself, rather than an extraneous certification of honor, lieutenants found themselves in a pivotal place between center and locality. The elections and by-elections of the 1660s and 1670s illustrate the uncertain state of English politics, a curious combination of innovation and tradition. The Corporation Act, too, was a hybrid of pre- and post-Restoration developments. It was a political purge, but it was also a reaffirmation of the dominance of the gentry and nobility over the towns. Some lieutenants, like Derby, used their power as commissioners as much in their own interests as in that of the crown. Most of those who lost their places had deliberately put themselves beyond the pale when they refused to conform to the reestablished Church of England. Like Roman Catholics in times gone by, their exclusion from the political nation was self-inflicted. By the end of the Cavalier Parliament's life, following the arrival of more clearly defined political parties, things would be very different.

THE FALL OF THE EARL OF CLARENDON in 1667 was later seen by the exiled James II as the beginning of the end for the crown's prerogative.[29] Whether this was the case or not, it was unquestionably true that the pace of political change increased after the former chancellor fled the country. The struggle among court factions for dominance sharpened political debate, though conflict remained essentially factional. Courtiers jockeyed for the king's attention and favor, and every faction worked to build a base of support in both Parliament and the country. Ideological division remained inchoate through this period; the by-elections to fill vacant seats in the Cavalier Parliament in the 1670s demonstrate the confusion that dominated national politics. Lords lieutenant became increasingly involved in attempts to influence the outcome of elections held within their shires, but they did so with little reference to the wishes of the crown. The disposition of the lieutenant to various court factions was most often the decisive factor in his choice of candidate. The Liverpool by-election of 1670, for example, indicated the confusion wrought when party organization did not accompany increased interest in parliamentary seats.

The earl of Derby's brother, William Stanley, had represented Liverpool since 1661. He died in 1670, thereby initiating a by-election in which no less than fifteen possible candidates were named. As lord lieutenant of the county and the former member's close relation, Derby was involved in the choice of a new member from the start. He held a meeting among various interested gentlemen in an effort to sort out the many nominations that quickly issued from court. The duke of Monmouth, the duke of Ormond, and a host of their friends and allies, ranging from the locally influential Lord Molyneux to the duke of York, recommended competing candidates. It was left to Derby to arrive at an amicable solution. In this parliamentary selection the lieutenant stood in a far different position than had his father and grandfather in the early years of the century. Now, with parliamentary seats the object of intense competition, the lieutenant faced a much more delicate task. Not only were competing interests within the county clamoring for support, but there was the added complication of outside power brokers intervening. Managing a parliamentary election had become infinitely more complex.[30]

The role of the lord lieutenant in by-elections grew steadily during the life of the Cavalier Parliament. When Sir Thomas Osborne became lord treasurer and was promoted to the House of Lords in 1673, he hoped to have his eldest son elected to the seat he vacated in York.[31] The new Viscount Latimer had been a longtime ally of the duke of Buckingham, the lord lieutenant, and his son desired the duke's speedy assistance: "Send my lord duke of Buckingham's letter to the city with all speed, being the only thing that . . . will do the work, the people being possessed his grace is for Sir Henry Thompson."[32] In an example of the increasing difficulty of maintaining unchallenged supremacy in many boroughs, Buckingham's letter, dispatched soon afterward, failed to sway the corporation.[33]

The lord treasurer was not always so unlucky; two years later (by then Latimer was earl of Danby and assured of the king's full support at court), the Norfolk borough of King's Lynn had a seat to fill. Lord Townshend, lieutenant of Norfolk and also the borough's recorder, supported alderman Simon Taylor for the place, but Danby was determined that his son-in-law, Robert Coke of Holkham, would have the seat. Townshend nearly succeeded. He visited the town personally and canvassed for Taylor, which one man said "gives some probability whereas few days past it was concluded at most indifferent hands Mr. Coke would carry it." Nevertheless, once again a lieutenant was bested; Coke, backed by Danby and the expenditure of no less than £7,000, won out.[34]

The by-elections of the 1670s show the political process in a state of transition. Lieutenants became increasingly active in the race to fill vacant parliamentary seats, but they did not act systematically or support any "party line"; nor were they always successful. Sons and personal dependents remained the most frequent recipients of a lieutenant's patronage. Some supported Clarendon, some Buckingham; later, some allied with Danby and others with Ormond. The result was a confused series of choices in which any group might gain the upper hand. As long as the king himself stayed out of the process—which he did until at least 1679—the lieutenancy continued to perform an ad hoc function in parliamentary selection.

It was the earl of Danby who first began to organize a "court interest" that could be relied on to support his policies in Parliament, and from the beginning the lieutenancy occupied an important place in his plans. From 1674 until his fall and imprisonment in 1679, Danby tried to create a solid block of support through by-elections and the manipulation of the bench.

Lords lieutenant served as the treasurer's eyes and ears in the provinces.[35] They provided the court with the names of those who were thought to be Danby's enemies or otherwise unreliable. As the earl of Lindsey, Danby's brother-in-law and lord lieutenant of Lincolnshire, said, the use of the lieutenant as the minister's deputy in the shires would be "a very powerful and engaging argument for persons to adhere to our party, for the world will be governed by interest."[36] The treasurer himself, in a failed attempt to urge the king to purge his opponents in 1677, said, "Let the world see the king 'would reward and punish.'"[37]

An essential goal of Danby's faction was the dismissal of political opponents from the bench. Nevertheless, the regulation of the magistracy under Danby was quite limited; no more than eighty-two justices were sacked between 1673 and 1678, thirty of whom lost their places for malfeasance, two of whom were Catholics, and two others who were sacked at the request of the House of Commons.[38] Most of the recommendations for dismissals came from a few especially zealous lieutenants. In Norfolk, where Lord Townshend had been replaced by Viscount (soon to be earl of) Yarmouth in 1676, the purge was more extensive than in most counties.[39] Yarmouth sent a list of gentlemen he wanted made justices of the peace, "for the king's immediate service and the strengthening of my own interest in a greater capacity to serve the crown." Additionally, the new lieutenant left out "the four great dissenters, namely Sir John Hobart, Sir John Holland, Sir Robert Kemp, and Sir Peter Gleane."[40] The four "dissenters" were allies of Danby's enemy Townshend and would all later strongly support Exclusion. A few of Danby's opponents elsewhere also fell victim to this rather tentative purge: the earl of Bath had four justices of the peace dismissed in Devonshire in 1675; the earl of Lindsey dismissed one in Lincolnshire in 1676; and the marquis of Worcester had twelve removed from the Welsh bench between 1674 and 1677.[41] All of these nobles were lords lieutenant of these shires, and all strongly supported Danby. Nevertheless, it is the general stability of the bench during Danby's ascendancy that is most noticeable. Although some lieutenants such as Bath and Yarmouth believed that a purge was needed, even they did not go far toward that end.

As long as Danby remained at the head of the king's administration, and despite his desire for a more thorough sweep of the commissions, progress remained slow. Traditional factional disputes continued to be as significant a problem as fledgling party warfare. In Cumberland, for instance, Sir Philip Musgrave, a deputy lieutenant and prominent magistrate, became involved in a fierce battle with his lord lieutenant over the composition of the local bench. The lieutenant, Lord Carlisle, nominated two of Musgrave's most bitter enemies to the bench and worsened matters by appointing another enemy a deputy lieutenant. The dispute threatened to split the county: "It is most industriously endeavored by my Lord Carlisle and Sir George Fletcher," wrote Musgrave, "to make me insignificant in these parts, as well as themselves a terror to those that will not truckle under them . . . I know the greater part of the justices of both counties [Cumberland and Westmorland] dislike their arbitrary proceedings."[42] Both Carlisle and Musgrave supported the court; Musgrave was marked as "thrice vile" by Shaftesbury, and Carlisle worked actively in the Royalist Anglican behalf in later years.[43] Although the two men were eventually reconciled, the dispute that separated them was more common in the period before the Exclusion Crisis than after it; here local power brokers were more concerned about their own positions and reputations than those of Lord Danby.

These considerations applied in the management of by-elections to the Cavalier Parliament as well. The careful policy Danby followed with regard to the bench was applied to parliamentary elections, and, again, lieutenants were increasingly expected to act as the minister's agents. As in the case of Lord Townshend in Lynn, expectations might not be met, but the appointment of Yarmouth in Townshend's place indicated Danby's desire to influence the composition of the House of Commons. Andrew Browning calculated Danby's potential strength in the Commons: through lords lieutenant who were in some way connected or allied to him, he was in a position to influence 350 seats; the eight lieutenants allied to opposing factions, 82.[44] These numbers come from a Namierite compilation of connections and relationships, and thus their meaning is hard to interpret, yet it is clear that Danby relied on his allies and connections to help return supporters to a new Parliament.

The vigorous new role of the lords lieutenant was apparent in one of the last by-elections to the Cavalier Parliament, in Leicester. Sir John Prettyman, one of the town's members, died in a debtor's jail late in 1676, and John Grey wanted to succeed him. One of his first actions was to write the earl of Rutland, lord lieutenant of the county, asking for his support. In a letter written in January 1677, Lord Roos, Rutland's heir, gave notice to the county of the lieutenant's desires: "My uncle Mr. John Grey is standing for burgess for Leicester, who is a very loyal subject to his majesty. I desire you all and every of you who have any commission from my father in the militia or have any dependence upon him in the said militia or otherways, to give your votes to Mr. Grey at the election, and in the meantime use your best endeavors to procure others to do the like." [45] Grey was handily chosen over Heneage Finch, and a few weeks after the election Lord Roos was joined with his father in the Leicestershire lieutenancy—possibly a comment on Danby's need to win active supporters in both the country and Westminster. Roos thanked Danby effusively: "I had not been thus long without giving your lordship my humble thanks . . . absolutely unmerited favour brings so much confusion with it that I could not say what I ought." Roos remained a loyal, if erratic, friend of Danby until the minister's fall. [46]

Roos also played a supporting role in the election to fill a vacant seat in Grantham, Lincolnshire, in March 1678, although the most important player in Danby's interest was the earl of Lindsey. Lindsey, Danby's brother-in-law as well as lord lieutenant of Lincolnshire, strained every nerve to see the treasurer's candidate elected. As in many elections held before party polarized the kingdom, the issue was not merely one of court versus country. Lindsey's principal opponent at Grantham was Sir Robert Carr, with whom he had struggled for hegemony in Lincolnshire since the early years of the Restoration. Both had unimpeachable Cavalier backgrounds, and Carr had been on the Privy Council since 1672. The two men were bitter enemies, and so Carr's stance with relation to Danby's ministry was dictated by Lindsey's relationship with the treasurer. These circumstances made the Grantham election essentially a factional one which neither side was content to lose. [47] Sir Robert Southwell described the battle over the seat as "at bottom . . . a contest of that county between the lord lieutenant [and Carr], each drawing in all their strength and relations." [48]

In such a factional battle, Lindsey had the advantage. His power as lord lieutenant offered considerable leverage in the county, and his relationship with the king's most important minister made him a force to be reckoned with at court. Lindsey applied direct pressure on the corporation at Grantham by mustering the militia in the town—a tactic he had employed two years earlier in Stamford. [49] Writing Lord Roos in neighboring Leicestershire to request his support, Lindsey reminded him that the Manners's standing was at stake. A victory for Carr's candidate, Sir William Ellis, would be "the greatest wound in the world . . . for the king will then observe that notwithstanding he hath lately conferred the recordership of Grantham and the lieutenancy of Leicestershire, yet that Sir Robert Carr hath a greater interest, and this I look upon as not for your lordship's service." Furthermore, Lindsey told Roos that several gentlemen with influence in the election were from Leicestershire and a little persuasion from their lord lieutenant would bring them around. [50] In the election that followed, Lindsey's man, Sir Robert Markham, was sent to the house on a disputed return. Carr's defeat came at great expense; his attempt to unseat Markham by petition failed, and he was removed from the Privy Council.[51] Thereafter, Lindsey, with the power of his lieutenancy and the backing of the court, occupied a virtually unassailable position in Lincolnshire.

These halting efforts toward the creation of a reliable political interest were important, but their impact was restricted. The success of Danby's limited attempts to influence local government and the House of Commons was not enough to save him from the chaos that followed in the wake of the Popish Plot and Ralph Montagu's exposure of the treasurer's secret negotiations with Louis XIV. The efforts of allies such as Yarmouth and Lindsey were of no use when the king abandoned their mentor in 1679. In the end, it would be the support of the king himself for Danby's policy of purge and patronage that would allow the crystallization of party, but in 1679 the time for such tactics had not yet come.

The horrifying tales of Israel Tonge and Titus Oates catalyzed the reaction that sent Danby to the Tower and transformed the lords lieutenant into political bosses. In October 1678, the revelation of a plot to murder the king and place the duke of York on the throne initiated a series of events that culminated in the triumph of the anti-Exclusionist party in 1685.[52] The plot turned the once-acquiescent Cavalier Parliament, which was already uneasy about the duke's open Catholicism, into a ready instrument in the hands of the earl of Shaftesbury and his allies in their campaign to oust York from the king's councils. A month after Oates first laid his charges before an astonished Privy Council, Sir Henry Coventry wrote the duke of Ormond, "I never wrote in a worse humor to you in my life. All things, both in court, parliament, town, and country, full of confusion."[53] By the end of 1678 the delicate position of the Danby ministry and the court was in danger of collapse.[54]

Danby's proposed solution to the crisis entailed a new Parliament, coupled with a compromise with the duke of York's opponents. The Cavalier Parliament was finally dissolved on January 24, 1679, almost eighteen years after it first assembled. The lord treasurer's confidence in his ability to construct a new majority based on a strong anti-Catholic policy and the imposition of restrictions on a popish successor was such that he made no concerted effort to influence the new elections. Typical of his lackluster style was a letter he wrote to the duke of Newcastle, lieutenant of both Nottinghamshire and Northumberland and influential in a number of boroughs. The king, he wrote, "commanded me to let your grace know from him that he desires you will promote as much as you can the choice of good members in those places which are influenced by your grace."[55] Danby offered no suggestions as to who might be fit to serve, nor did he offer any other advice or instructions before the elections took place.

Once again, some of the most partisan lieutenants attempted to broker elections in their lieutenancies, but these were relatively few and their success limited. Yarmouth was enraged by opposition to his anointed candidates in Norfolk, Sir Neville Catelyn and Sir Christopher Calthorpe. In an open letter to the gentry, he wrote, "I understand that there is great interest making for the setting up of some persons for knights of the shire without acquainting me therewith, which I think ought not to be done without my knowledge, bearing that office I do under his majesty in this county . . . I shall vigorously oppose their designs to their disrepute . . . you may acquaint any of your or my friends how ill I resent such proceedings and that I will have it known what office I bear."[56] A master of political maneuver, Yarmouth secured the support of the sheriff and under-sheriff and deployed the militia in his candidates' behalf. Sir John Hobart, leader of the opposition and himself standing against Yarmouth's nominees, recognized his disadvantage: "To oppose an interest set up by the civil and military government of the country is called faction by some, inconsiderate by others, and very improbable of success by most." Calthorpe and Catelyn were duly returned, and in a practice that was to become more and more frequent, the result was contested in the Commons.[57] In Oxfordshire, Lord Norreys— who was Lord Lindsey's brother and thus also one of Danby's brothers-in-law—combined with the bishop to work in the treasurer's interest.[58] As in the later by-elections of the Cavalier Parliament, Norreys's activity was largely dictated by his personal relationship with the earl of Danby.

But the success of some of the minister's most active partisans was not enough to shape the new Parliament. Danby's unstable position is illustrated by the failure of Lord Roos to survive a challenge for his place as knight of the shire in Leicestershire from Sir John Hartopp. Hartopp, a stepson (and son-in-law) of Major General Charles Fleetwood, supported Exclusion; Roos's position as joint lieutenant and scion of the largest landowning family in the shire was of no avail.[59] The new House of Commons was no more tractable than the last had been. For lack of a systematic effort to send his friends to the lower house, Danby neglected an important element in his scheme to carry on his administration.

Danby's failure to provide guidance to the lieutenancy hampered the choice of suitable members, in part because the lord treasurer, a court politician with tenuous local connections, continued to think of the lieutenants in traditional terms as powerful local figures who needed no direction from court. Lords lieutenant played a transitional role in the selection of the members of the first Exclusion Parliament. Although many labored to return men who would be friendly to the ministry, local interests continued to be very important. Even though he had been the lord lieutenant of the West Riding since 1674, Danby had not taken any discernible interest in the post and had confined himself to rubber-stamping the decisions of his deputies and occasionally advancing his claims to local parliamentary patronage. Had Danby recognized the importance of cultivating a local interest, he would have offered guidance to other lieutenants as well as strengthened his own position in Yorkshire.

The new Parliament ignored the ministry's efforts at compromise and proceeded to insist upon the exclusion of the duke of York from the succession. The result was a swift prorogation and dissolution. By the end of the spring a new set of writs was in preparation, and Danby was determined to try again. The time seemed right for a rigorous effort to punish the duke's enemies; in the words of the earl of Yarmouth, writing with regard to the corporation of Norwich in 1678: "Norwich could be the loyallest city in England if a few were out of it who in fact [are] a party with antimonarchical principles."[60] But the king preferred another approach. To Danby's dismay, Charles attempted conciliation. Danby was sacrificed and soon took up residence in the Tower. The court won over several prominent members of the opposition in April, and Shaftesbury himself was given the presidency of the council.[61]

Ironically, it was Shaftesbury who first initiated the policy that Danby had long advocated: a purge of the bench. On May 21, the council ordered that a committee consisting of the chancellor, local bishop, lord lieutenant, custos rotulorum (who was frequently also the lieutenant), and circuit judges examine the list of justices with an eye toward removing unsuitable members.[62] The inclusion of lieutenants paid tribute to their importance in the provinces. Their customary role in the nomination of magistrates was well established and could not be ignored, though Shaftesbury well knew the Royalist predilections of the lieutenants and did his best to circumvent them.

Shaftesbury intended to control the purge by adding political allies as ex-officio members. The official members of the committee were to be joined with several other local noblemen, solid supporters of Shaftesbury such as Lords Russell, Cavendish, Monmouth, Essex, and Holles. Thus

Shaftesbury hoped to alter the magistracy in his own favor.[63] It was clear that the real powers on these committees were Shaftesbury's allies; Royalist lieutenants and friends of the lord treasurer would not be consulted in the real deliberations over a revised bench. The earl of Lindsey, for example, was completely excluded from the process. Lindsey flew into a rage: "The king hath been pleased to lay a new indignity upon me by not sending me a letter as to other lords lieutenant as to their approbation or dislike of justices in their respective lieutenancies, and hath put out some of my friends and added those who have very little respect for me." [64] In fact, the Exclusionist attempt to remake the magistracy failed because the king refused to accept most of the recommendations of the committees.[65] This abortive regulation was abandoned after Charles decided that further compromise with Shaftesbury was impossible and the Exclusionists on the council were dismissed in October 1679. Nevertheless, it illustrates the increasingly complex relationship between the court and the country. The traditional balance of politics, in which lords lieutenant were largely free to select whom they pleased as justices of the peace in their shires, was changing, and the vagaries of court and party politics began to intrude as they had not done before. Conversely, however, as Shaftesbury recognized in his attempt to prevent some lieutenants from influencing the selection process, movement toward a more politicized magistracy gave lords lieutenant more leverage than ever. They were in a better position than anyone else to judge who was ideologically sound enough to serve on the bench, a factor that enhanced their importance in the emerging system of party politics.

The gradual intrusion of party politics in the selection of justices of the peace had its counterpart in the choice of members of Parliament. The elections to the second Exclusion Parliament in August and September 1679 indicated a quickening of the lieutenants' activity in the court's behalf. At last an attempt was made by the duke's allies to swing some elections, although once again, the effort was not a systematic one. More lieutenants acted to ensure the return of members favorable to the court, but pressure from Whitehall was relatively slight. The king urged some of his supporters to stand for election but made no sustained effort to see that lieutenants labored in his behalf.[66]

Some lieutenants did act vigorously, however. They relied on many of the tactics developed during the life of the Cavalier Parliament: their natural influence as the leaders of their shires, lavish entertainment, cunning tricks, and, at last, the naked power of the militia. In Essex, the duke of

Albemarle led a parade of anti-Exclusionist gentlemen and some two hundred clergymen in behalf of his candidates, Sir Thomas Middleton and Sir Eliah Harvey. Harvey had formerly been "very adverse to the court," but the lord lieutenant's persuasion (and possibly the offer of the lieutenancy of Waltham Forest) convinced him to stand with the duke. Although the lieutenant's appearance at the head of the "loyal party," along with his patronage power both in the county and at court, made a formidable combination, the opposition was not overborne. His opponents were led into the fray personally by Lords Grey of Warke and Chandos, accompanied by the bulk of the Exclusionist gentry in the county.[67] And, needless to say, the earl of Yarmouth was hard at work in Norfolk, aided by the sheriff and his own possession of the writ of election. Success came in Norwich, but Yarmouth failed in a fiercely contested county election.[68]

As in the elections to the first Parliament of 1679, the lack of a centrally organized effort on the part of the court led to the return of a hostile House of Commons. When the new Parliament met on October 7, there was but one item on its agenda: exclusion of the duke of York from the succession. The king responded with an immediate prorogation, repeated several times over the course of nearly a year. Dissolution was avoided so as to give the court the opportunity to prepare for a new general election. For the first time, the government abandoned all attempts at compromise and, by employing its natural advantages of patronage and organization, crushed Exclusion once and for all.

Shaftesbury's dismissal from the Privy Council proved to be the opening salvo of the court's attack; with him went the duke of Monmouth, who held the lieutenancies of Staffordshire and the East Riding. Monmouth was the only lieutenant to lose his place before the elections to the third Exclusion Parliament. Several lieutenants who leaned toward exclusion remained in commission: the earls of Northampton, Suffolk, and Manchester, for example, all wavered on the issue. At the end of 1679 it may have seemed possible to sway them to support the crown. In fact, most lieutenants opposed the move to disinherit the duke. From the most violent anti-Exclusionists, such as Yarmouth and the earl of Peterborough, to moderates who would have preferred an accommodation, such as the earls of Sunderland and Bath, the lieutenancy could be relied on in the upcoming struggle.

A review of the magistracy was the first task the government undertook. As far as the government was concerned, Exclusionists—like republicans and dissenters—were disloyal and subversive, and they could have no place in the government of the realm. Depriving them of their seats in Parliament was only a start. Beginning in November and December 1679, lords lieutenant were solicited for their opinions of their local bench; this process continued until the early summer of 1680.[69] The duke of Albemarle, in a letter praising the zeal of his Devonshire deputies in August, reminded them to keep him fully informed about local politics; he wanted "some of you to give me a constant account of public affairs."[70] By March every English county had received a new commission, followed by a series of minor adjustments. The crown asked for suggestions from local Royalist magnates, but the lords lieutenant played the most important role in selecting new justices and marking Exclusionists for dismissal. In January 1680 the clerk of the Privy Council requested up-to-date lists of justices from several lieutenants, and in April the earl of Rutland received a list of proposed justices for Leicestershire for his "perusal and consideration . . . as lord lieutenant of that county."[71] The duke of Newcastle received the same letter for his lieutenancies and provided the council with a list of magistrates who should be put out of the commission.[72] The duke of Ormond was informed on April 18 that "this day the council spent in purging the commission of all counties, leaving none but who were loyal and conformable to the church."[73] The court and the lieutenancy posited an irreducible link between Exclusion, religious dissent, and treason, and so close scrutiny of all of the king's servants was necessary. In all, between December 1679 and July 1680, 272 justices of the peace (of 2,559) were cast off the bench at the instigation of the lieutenancy.[74] The purge was the most dramatic since the king's return in 1660.[75]

An attempt was also made to revise the lieutenancy itself before the return of the second Exclusion Parliament. No lords lieutenant were displaced, but a few deputies fell victim to the purge that had swept the bench. In Wiltshire, the earl of Pembroke received an order from the king in March to dismiss Thomas Thynne, a deputy and MP whom Shaftesbury noted as "doubly worthy." Two other Exclusionist MPs, Thomas Mompesson and Edward Hungerford, were also removed from the commission. They were to be replaced by Sir John Talbot, John Wyndham, and Richard Lewis, all three of whom were anti-Exclusionist MPs resident in Wiltshire. Pembroke, a notoriously difficult man, evidently ignored the king's instructions, because a month later Secretary Jenkins sent the earl a stern rebuke: "My lord, I hope that this delay, which is more taken notice of to your disadvantage than I could wish, will be repaired by your giving these commissions with all dispatch possible and sending them to these gentlemen. I should be extremely sorry this should have any mention given before the king otherwise than by way of account that you have fully obeyed his commands."[76] Although the deputy lieutenants were in any case overwhelmingly pro-York even before the purge, by the middle of 1680, no lieutenant could safely ignore the central government's commands to remove prominent Whigs.

In conjunction with the purge of the bench, the council turned its attention to local corporations. A circular letter sent out to the lieutenants in May ordered them to ensure that local boroughs were complying with the terms of the Corporation Act. This order and the reports of the lieutenants that followed may have been intended as a first step in the general alteration of corporate charters that followed in the next several years.[77] In Norfolk the council's instructions were vigorously implemented. The lord and deputy lieutenants met on May 21 to organize their response and formed a committee of deputies to inspect each of the county's corporate boroughs.[78] Not all lieutenants responded as forcefully as the earl of Yarmouth, but the council's instructions did produce action. The response of the earl of Derby was perhaps more typical; he sent a letter to the mayor of Chester ordering him to prepare a report on the state of the corporation there, to be passed on to the king.[79] The deputy lieutenants of Devon urged that strong measures be taken with the corporation of Tiverton, where the "increase of conventicles, faction, and disorder" alarmed them. Although they lamented the situation in the town, they wrote their lieutenant, Albemarle, that "we have no powers to reform matters of this nature; the redress is solely in his majesty's power and prerogative." They wanted a new charter for the town and a wholly remodeled magistracy.[80]

The purge of the bench and the scrutiny of corporate charters were clearly designed to put the government in a better position should the necessity of another Parliament arise. The body elected in the autumn of 1679 did not return to Westminster until October 21, 1680; by that time nearly all of the most violent Exclusionists had been removed from their local offices. On November 11, a second Exclusion bill passed the Commons and was sent up to the Lords, where it lost by a vote of sixty-three to thirty. The result was a stalemate, during which the Commons voted one inflammatory resolution after another. The second Exclusion Parliament was peremptorily dissolved on January 18, 1681, and the campaign to lock Exclusionists out of local government intensified.[81]

Some of the first to feel the effects of their defiance of the king were the three lords lieutenant who voted in favor of Exclusion. The earl of Man-

chester was replaced by the ultra-Royalist earl of Ailesbury in Huntingdonshire, and the earl of Suffolk lost two lieutenancies, Suffolk and Cambridgeshire. His replacements were Lords Arlington and Alington, respectively.
The earl of Essex was also deprived of his authority in Hertfordshire. The
reliable earl of Bridgewater, who had already given the crown good service in Buckinghamshire, took Essex's position.[82] Although relatively few
changes were made in the commissions of the peace, the lieutenancy was
extensively remodeled for the first time, and several deputies were deprived
of their commissions. The council ordered the lieutenants to dismiss every
deputy lieutenant or militia officer who had already been removed from the
bench; apparently a few displaced justices had managed to cling to some of
their local authority through the militia.[83]

The purge was widespread. Most of Essex's deputies in Hertfordshire fell
victim along with their master. Sir Harbottle Grimston, whose family had
provided deputies in Hertfordshire and Essex for generations, was uncere-
moniously excluded, as was Silius Titus, who had been a faithful client of
the Capel family since the civil wars.[84] They were replaced by staunch anti-
Exclusionists: Ralph Freeman, Sir Thomas Feilde, and Thomas Halsey.
Such changes were repeated over and over again throughout the country.
In Somerset, Sir Haswell Trent was succeeded by Francis Luttrell, MP for
Minehead, at the king's command. Luttrell's appointment might well have
been his reward for failing to appear on the floor of the Commons when
the second Exclusion bill came to a vote.[85] Sir Robert Filmer was added
to the commission in Kent, and in June 1681 the marquis of Worcester
visited the king at Windsor with a list of likely candidates and victims in
his lieutenancies.[86] Many of the changes in the commissions of lieutenancy
were mandated by the crown. In such cases the lieutenants were merely
the recipients of orders from above and had little room for maneuver. In
November 1681 the lord lieutenant of Wiltshire was instructed to dismiss
Colonel Thomas Thynne from the command of his cavalry regiment, and
the earl of Bridgewater was required to appoint Sir Nicholas Miller as a
deputy lieutenant of Hertfordshire a month later.[87] There was nothing a
lord lieutenant could do in such circumstances but obey.

Widespread though this purge of provincial government was, considerable room remained for local interests to make themselves felt. In consequence, lords lieutenant found their influence increased. Whitehall was in
no position to scrutinize the appointment of every officer; it usually had to
rely on the lieutenants' judgment.[88] A lieutenant's scrutiny could go quite
far down the social scale; in March 1681, for example, the earl of Win-

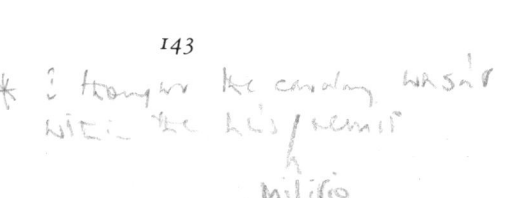

chilsea proudly announced that the militia captains in Canterbury were all "truly loyal and of the Church of England."[89] The marquis Worcester, when he attended the king with his lists of deputies and justices of the peace, noted that he had been lenient: "All that are tolerable, and possible to be reclaimed are left in [the lists]."[90] Whether the marquis succeeded in his attempt to limit the scope of the "reformation" is not known, but not all lieutenants saw themselves transformed from independent actors into conduits for royal instructions. Many lieutenants were trusted to make their own decisions, such as the earl of Ailesbury in Huntingdonshire, where "his majesty was pleased to leave all to your lordship's discretion to do as you should find things to be best for his majesty's service," and the earl of Rutland, the lord lieutenant of Leicestershire, who was consulted by the secretary of state before any candidates for a new commission of the peace were chosen.[91] Furthermore, increased turnover in local office gave lieutenants more opportunities to appoint clients and allies to vacant places, thus strengthening their own interest.

The new commissions of lieutenancy issued between 1680 and 1681 were still overwhelmingly appointees of the lieutenants. The state papers offer many examples of the king approving new lists of deputies nominated by lords lieutenant without demur.[92] In some places, changes in local government were initiated by the lieutenancy itself; in June 1680, the Devon deputy lieutenants launched an attack on Tiverton, petitioning their lord to secure a quo warranto against its charter. They claimed that the town was in the grips of factious dissenters and needed to be remodeled.[93] The duke of Albemarle passed on the request; the result was an investigation by the attorney general, who recommended a new charter.[94] Here, as elsewhere, the court recognized the value of the lieutenancy's service in the provinces and acted on its suggestions.

The nature of the relationship between court and lieutenancy at the time of the Exclusion Crisis is made evident in a letter from Secretary Jenkins to the earl of Peterborough, written in 1682. Peterborough had been busy overseeing the destruction of the Exclusionist interest in Northampton, for which he received the king's thanks: "It was a matter of particular satisfaction to him to find by your lordship's letter that the city of Northampton is by your lordship's care rendered to so good a temper." The earl's recompense for his efforts, in addition to the king's good opinion, was the speedy appointment of two new deputy lieutenants in Northamptonshire.[95] Each side benefited; the crown gained a foothold in the notoriously anti-Royalist city of Northampton, and Peterborough added to his local network of clients.

In spite of the heightened importance of the lieutenancy, however, the campaign against the Exclusionists from 1679 to 1681 tied it much more firmly to the crown. The enhanced influence of the institution was strictly bounded by the realities of the national political situation; it had to be exercised within an Anglican anti-Exclusionist framework. The personal desires of a lord lieutenant were sometimes forced to take second place when they clashed with the interests of the crown. When Sir George Fletcher was deprived of his deputy lieutenancy in Cumberland as a result of a personal feud with the earl of Carlisle in 1683, Carlisle was pressed to reinstate Fletcher against his wishes. The king was anxious to maintain Fletcher's considerable influence in the north, even if it meant offending such a loyal servant as Carlisle.[96]

By 1682 the Royalist interest—always dominant—reigned supreme within the lieutenancy, preparing to carry out its new function as policeman of a one-party state. In July 1682 Sir Edward Harley remarked that "there was not as he believed one lord lieutenant or militia officer in England, but what was a damned papist."[97] For Harley, papists and Yorkists were synonymous, and though he was hardly correct when he described the lieutenancy as dominated by Catholics, it certainly was an overwhelmingly anti-Exclusionist institution.

Many of the changes in the commission of the lieutenancy and the bench were undoubtedly made with an eye to the creation of a new House of Commons. The crown had already been at least partly successful in its attempt to influence Parliament; the second Exclusion bill failed in the House of Lords by a wide margin and on its first reading. The punishment of those lords lieutenant who defied the king followed rapidly, and the dismissal of many deputy lieutenants and justices of the peace formed part of the crown's effort to advertise its determination. Once purged, the lieutenancy was ready to be employed in the new elections.

The elections for the third Exclusion Parliament took place in the winter of 1681, and once again the lieutenants were as active in the duke's interest as they had been in 1679. Despite the extensive remodeling of local government and the efforts of the lieutenancy, the newly erected Yorkist interest had not had time enough to take advantage of its position, and the opposition rode a tide of Exclusionist sentiment into Oxford. In Worcestershire, Lord Windsor convened a meeting of the local gentry in an attempt to head off the selection of Thomas Foley and Bridges Nanfan, both committed Exclusionists. He failed to persuade Foley to stand down, following "some warm talk," and failed again when he tried to convince the gentlemen present to promise money to support a Royalist candidate.

When "some gentlemen began to reflect smartly upon the project," the lieutenant's effort collapsed, and Foley and Nanfan were returned without opposition.[98] In Cheshire the attendance of the earl of Derby at the county election was to no avail, and the county selected a pair of Exclusionists; in Kent Lord Winchilsea was unable even to find a pair of Yorkists to stand for the county. The frantic efforts of Lord Abingdon in Oxfordshire likewise failed to secure an anti-Exclusionist victory, and the duke of Albemarle had no more success even after he led another parade of churchmen and magnates to the poll in Essex.[99]

Some lieutenants had better luck. In Gloucestershire the marquis of Worcester managed to get his son returned for Gloucester, and there was a Royalist victory in Bristol. The Exclusionist defeat in Bristol was attributed to the intervention of the Bristol Artillery Company, which was under the command of Worcester as lord lieutenant. In Norfolk, Lord Yarmouth directed a successful campaign for Norwich's two seats, although Exclusionists were returned for the county.[100] These favorable results for the court, however, did little to alter the final outcome of the elections. The Parliament that assembled at Oxford in March was as committed to Exclusion as were its two predecessors.

The Parliament met in the febrile atmosphere of the Oxford schools on March 21.[101] One week later the Commons read its third attempt to deprive the duke of York of his birthright. The assembly was dissolved the same day, and the king ended the session with what proved to be his final word on the subject of Exclusion: "Let there be no delusion. I will not yield, nor will I be bullied. . . . I have law and reason and all right-thinking men on my side."[102] With these words, the battle against the Exclusionists shifted from the hustings and the floor of the House of Commons to the world beyond. Barred from office and politics, Exclusionists became not merely opposing candidates at the polls but, like the republicans excluded from government at the Restoration, security threats. The lieutenancy, which had long experience in the art of suppressing sedition, was to return to its earlier role. The fate of political dissenters like Stephen Colledge would now rest in the hands of a partisan lieutenancy. The guardian of the restored monarchy became the aggressive defender of the Royalist Anglican ascendancy.[103]

THE LIEUTENANCY PLAYED an important part in the triumph of the king's party which followed the Exclusion Crisis. It began working toward that goal before the dissolution of Charles II's last Parliament, dividing its activities between the persuasive and the repressive. Before the end of the Oxford Parliament, the former was most in evidence. Lords lieutenant tirelessly promoted the Royalist Anglican cause and were very important in organizing its interest in the provinces. Besides their work at the polls, the lieutenants were the prime mover of loyal addresses to the crown, as well as other public demonstrations of loyalty such as bonfires celebrating the anniversary of the Restoration. After the dissolution, however, the political theater came to occupy less time than the pursuit of sedition. The result was a period of persecution not unlike that which followed the Restoration. The lieutenancy's methods were similar—searches and preventive arrests—but the targets were much different. It was no longer the middling to lower-order dissenters who bore the brunt of the government's ill-will but peers and gentlemen. The gentry community was rent by the political strife that accompanied Exclusion, and the years from about 1680 to 1687 were dominated by Royalist attempts to recreate Cavalier solidarity through both rhetoric and repression. The lieutenancy was central to this campaign.

Lords lieutenant began acting as propagandists during the early days of the Exclusion Crisis. In November and December 1679, the Exclusionists mounted a series of petition drives, the object of which was to garner support for their cause.[104] The initial response on the part of some lieutenants was simply to halt the Exclusionist petitions. In Essex, for example, the duke of Albemarle rushed out from London to quash the anti-York movement as soon as he got word of it.[105] It was not long, however, before lieutenants were organizing their own counterpetitions. These documents "abhorred" the popular and subversive nature of the Exclusionists' efforts and became known as "abhorrences." Lieutenants in most counties worked diligently to promote them. By the time of the dissolution of the Oxford Parliament, loyal addresses had become common tools in the hands of Yorkist lieutenants. In 1681 the earl of Winchilsea produced an effusive one in Kent, and Lord Yarmouth passed on the king's compliments to his deputies for similar service: "By his majesty's express commands I am to present you with his kindest respects, and with his thanks for your affectionate loyalty to him."[106] Typical of the sentiments in these addresses were those from the Norfolk deputies praised by the king: "We beg the favor of your lordship [Yarmouth] to assure his majesty that we will never be wanting upon all occasions to preserve his undoubted rights and prerogative with that zeal and obedience which becomes those loyal subjects who are willing to sacrifice their lives and fortunes to such a gracious prince."[107] Additional campaigns were conducted after the discovery of the Rye House Plot in 1683 and the accession of James II in 1685.[108]

Loyal addresses were important for several reasons. They were of considerable importance in organizing local Royalists and giving expression to their views. They served as an invaluable source of propaganda for a government that could not rely on the giant pope-burnings and demonstrations so popular with the Exclusionists. Lieutenants enlisted many of their most prominent neighbors, leaders of the church, and respectable gentlemen in behalf of the king's cause. The loyal address symbolized the weight and solidity of the king's interest; the duke of Newcastle boasted that his address of 1681 had received the signatures of eight hundred of Northumberland's most important men.[109] Royalists contrasted the significance of their supporters to those of the Exclusionists; while Exclusionists courted the mob, the lords lieutenant appealed to men of substance.[110] Recognizing the importance of these addresses, the king himself frequently received them personally from the lord lieutenant, very often with a considerable show of approbation, while Exclusionist petitions were ignored or shunted aside with a royal sneer. Moreover, the government frequently ordered the publication of the lieutenancy's productions in the official gazette, where their impact could be expanded far beyond the borders of the county from which they originated.[111]

The loyal address proved to be useful as an organizational tool in the provinces and as a propaganda weapon against Exclusion. It had other implications as well. Its widespread use made it something of a test of a lord lieutenant's abilities; the failure to promote one successfully might be interpreted as an indication of incompetence or disloyalty. Newcastle, whose promotion of addresses by his lieutenancies on appropriate occasions was most diligent, was perturbed when in August 1683 one of them, sent from Nottinghamshire following the king's safe deliverance from the Rye House Plot, went five weeks unpublished. He wrote Secretary Jenkins: "I have watched in my reading the gazettes to see our address to his majesty from our lieutenancy of Nottinghamshire, which was delivered five weeks since and is not printed. We have little encouragement for our loyalty—those that come after us shall be printed before us, and we shall be disgraced because others are not as vigorous in their loyalty."[112] The ability to promote successful addresses reflected well on the lieutenant who organized them, and at least one was so determined to impress the court that he was gently discouraged. Secretary Jenkins informed Lord Yarmouth that though his address from Norfolk in July 1683 (his second since the news of the Rye House affair broke) was welcome, he should not deliver it personally because he was needed more at home. The king, said Jenkins, might not have time to arrange an audience.[113]

Addresses had another use—with them a lieutenant might identify potential opposition. Those who refused to sign or who attempted to obstruct the progress of an address could be marked as men of questionable loyalty. When Newcastle instructed the deputies and justices of Northumberland to produce an address in 1681, the text he had prepared (which was modeled after the address sent from Nottinghamshire) engendered resistance. Newcastle's letter arrived in time for the assizes, and the justices resolved to consider it privately. Sir John Fenwick, Northumberland's chief gentleman, refused to allow the magistrates to retire and produced a text of his own. With the assistance of a like-minded grand jury and seven justices, Fenwick's petition prevailed. In the end, the Royalists ignored Fenwick's version and went ahead with their own, gathering a large number of signatures. The lord lieutenant, however, carefully noted the names of the justices who supported Fenwick. They would not long remain in the commission.[114]

In the use of the loyal address as a gauge of affections for the crown, the lieutenancy's persuasive and repressive sides shaded into each other. There could be little question about the nature of its performance when faced with the danger of treasonous conspiracy by Exclusionists. Royalists' suspicions ran high from the very beginning of the Exclusion Crisis and increased as Charles's reign drew to a close. Lord Norreys was one of the first to act when he engineered the indictment of the Protestant Joiner, but he had many subsequent imitators. If Colledge's death was one of the more egregious uses of a lord lieutenant's authority in the pursuit of political opponents, there were many other victims of the lieutenancy's zeal.

Traditional suspects—religious dissenters—continued to undergo harassment. In 1681, for example, Newcastle launched a major campaign against nonconformists in Northumberland; the Kentish deputies closed conventicles, threatened to burn down meetinghouses, and roughed up insolent Quakers in Canterbury. The Somerset militia demolished the dissenting chapel in Bridgewater and made a bonfire of the contents.[115] But for the first time since the interregnum, gentlemen were subjected to the sort of scrutiny previously meted out to religious fanatics and former republicans; the homes and gathering places of the Exclusionist gentry were not spared. In 1682 a Royalist cleric in Cheshire remembered how during Cromwell's time Royalist gentlemen often met under cover of horse races and cockfights. He noted that many Exclusionists attended similar events and that the duke of Monmouth, their great hope for a Protestant succession, had also attended many as he made his pseudo-regal way through the midlands. Charles Bertie urged the lord lieutenant of Leicestershire, the earl of Rutland, to suppress horse races altogether—"they lead into such distances and beget such jarring among neighbors." [116]

The fears of plotting that arose from the Exclusion Crisis seemed confirmed in June 1683. A murky conspiracy to murder the king and the duke of York was uncovered; it involved a collection of radical Exclusionists and former republicans, including Lord Russell, Lord Grey of Wark, and John Wildman. Monmouth, who was also implicated, was to have assumed the throne. In a letter to the lieutenants on June 23, the plan to murder Charles, combined with a "general insurrection of the disaffected," was revealed, and the news electrified the nation, triggering the lieutenancy's vigorous response.[117] Some lords lieutenant immediately called up their militias in expectation of the "general insurrection"; all of them embarked upon extensive searches of suspected persons. Lieutenants along the coast ordered their deputies to close the ports and search them for fugitive conspirators—Monmouth and Grey had fled and were at large.[118] In Warwickshire the lord lieutenant, the earl of Conway, ordered a general search of Coventry, a city with a long-standing reputation for disaffection; in Oxfordshire Lord Abingdon conducted a series of searches in the homes of local nonconformists.[119] The primary targets of the searches and seizures of arms, however, were prominent Exclusionists. The earl of Dorset, lord lieutenant of Sussex, announced that in his county the "disaffected" would be searched "without shewing favor to any (tho they be my near neighbors) who may be justly suspected." [120]

Former leaders of the Exclusion party in the House of Commons were among the first to win the attention of their lieutenants. In Norfolk Sir John Hobart's house was searched, as were the homes in Northamptonshire of former MPs Miles Fleetwood and John Holeman and of Thomas Mainwaring in Cheshire.[121] Little was found. The lieutenancy discovered no stockpiles of illegal weapons or secret stores of powder laid aside for use in a rebellion. After two weeks of unceasing effort in Norfolk, the deputies had found a total of thirteen people suspicious enough to warrant a confiscation of arms; in the port of Yarmouth, they seized six bird guns and ten blunderbusses. Some lieutenants were not surprised by the paucity of arms found. As a deputy lieutenant in Warwickshire remarked following his fruitless search of Coventry, anyone who had sufficient knowledge of the plot would certainly have been clever enough to find some safe place to hide his arms.[122] For the solidly Yorkist lieutenancy it seemed impossible that prominent Exclusionists knew nothing about the Rye House Plot.

Those searched had a different opinion. Complaints and charges of misconduct on the part of the lieutenants and their deputies were widespread. William Harbord, an Exclusionist who had represented Thetford in all three Exclusion Parliaments, had his arms seized from his Northamptonshire home by Sir Roger Norwich. He complained bitterly about the incident to the secretary of state. Norwich, who himself had stood in the king's interest for Northamptonshire in 1679 and managed the subsequent campaigns there in 1680 and 1681, wrote: "Give me leave to say that no man can act briskly for the king's service in this county where there are many ill-affected gentry (tho at present all are loyal or seems so) but must be hated or evil spoken of." [123] Other complaints came from Lincolnshire, where not only did Lord Lindsey order the confiscation of arms, but he also imprisoned one suspect, Sir Drayner Massingberd. Massingberd had in his possession five pairs of pistols, three rapiers, and three muskets. Such an arsenal was more than enough to make him dangerous in the eyes of his lord lieutenant. Massingberd was held in Hull until at least August, when he petitioned the Lincolnshire deputy lieutenants for his release. [124] In Cheshire Thomas Mainwaring was also searched by the deputies and lamented in his diary: "But God Almighty knows my innocence and that I had not given them just occasion." Although they found no weapons in their search, the Somerset militia demolished the dissenting chapel in Bridgewater and made a bonfire out of its contents. [125]

Even some in the lieutenancy were reluctant to enforce the new Royalist hard line. This might be particularly true when the pursuit of Exclusionists clashed with long-standing social attitudes. In Leicestershire, Lord Beaumont, a deputy to the earl of Rutland, refused to search Lord Stamford's house for arms without a written order for, "though you are pleased to say . . . that a verbal order is enough to any in the militia, I am not of that judgment." [126] Although in this case Beaumont must have been considering his legal position should Stamford question the deputy's authority, he was also concerned about the propriety of the militia searching the home of a peer on very thin evidence. The earl of Derby was also evidently slow to accept his new role as Royalist enforcer. He was alleged to have acted too slowly and too leniently in the aftermath of the Rye House Plot. [127]

The targets of the lieutenancy's crackdown, as well as a few of the players on the government side such as Derby, were drawn into a game whose rules were unfamiliar. Association with Exclusion was enough to convict anyone of disloyalty, even though virtually everyone involved was a conforming Protestant monarchist. Such a turnabout baffled many such as Mainwaring, who had welcomed the Restoration and execrated the Cromwellian regime. In some ways it was a continuation of the almost irresistible inclination of early modern English society to enforce unanimity. That impulse had characterized previous governments, and the Royalists were no less eager to stamp out dissidence than Henry VIII or the Rump had been. The lieutenancy's response to the Rye House Plot was something of an object lesson in the seventeenth century's perception of opposition to the policies of the state: opposition, here, was evidence of disaffection, and disaffection was to be rooted out. If that could not be managed through persuasion—by the distribution of favor and office or the production of propaganda—then force would be employed. The men who served in Charles II's lord lieutenancy were not yet ready to accommodate the notion of legitimate political dissent.

Even after Exclusion was defeated and the Rye House Plot failed, Royalist Anglican dominance had to be maintained. The crown needed to exercise a degree of control over local affairs to forestall an Exclusionist revival; once assured of a loyal lieutenancy and magistracy, it set to work to achieve that goal. The lieutenancy became intimately involved in the enforcement of political conformity in the shires. Some lieutenants were more than willing to act ruthlessly in defending the duke's interest, and no misstep was too small in the eyes of the most zealous defenders of the crown. We have already seen Lord Norreys's work in the Colledge case. In Coventry two years later, three aldermen of the city were summarily removed from their places at the instance of Sir Robert Townshend, a local deputy lieutenant. Their only offense proved to be that they had presented their respects (and a gift of wine) to the duke of Monmouth when he passed through the city.[128]

The politicization of local government encouraged the lieutenancy to assert itself in other ways. In Cheshire the deputy lieutenants attempted to enforce an early form of gun control in 1683. They planned to order all of the county's gunsmiths to attend their monthly meetings and report on who had purchased or had had guns repaired over the course of the month. In Somerset the deputies suggested that the sale of gunpowder be strictly controlled and licensed by the lieutenancy.[129] Neither of these schemes was implemented, but both illustrate the tendency of the lieutenancy to intervene more aggressively in local government. In Lincolnshire, Lord Lindsey even believed that his place entitled him to a sort of supervision of the church: "Ever since his majesty has been pleased to make me lord lieutenant of Lincolnshire," Lindsey wrote in May 1683, "I have made it my business not only to observe amongst the clergy and laity who is most active to promote the king's interest and the public good of the Church, but also have endeavoured to have them encouraged and gratified." The duke of Beaufort made a similar plea later the same year: "I hold myself obliged, in those places which the king has put under my care for his temporal service [he was lord lieutenant of Wales and the Marches], to give testimony of men as I have found them ready and able to serve him."[130] An obvious corollary of this increased interest was increased power and patronage in the locality: Lindsey's object in writing his letter was to recommend a client to a deanery, and Beaufort's candidate aspired to the see of St. David's. Had control of the arms market been given to the lieutenancy as the deputies in Cheshire and Somerset suggested, the institution would have assumed still more importance.

The crown's new reliance on the lieutenancy to enforce its ascendancy and the corresponding expansion of the lieutenancy's role were also evident in the remodeling of the borough charters between 1682 and 1687. The new charters that the crown issued in the 1660s were chiefly concerned with removing the radical elements that had infiltrated borough government over the course of the interregnum.[131] In this earlier period the lieutenants had played only a minor part; they had been chiefly occupied with the enforcement of the Corporation Act and the harassment of local radicals. In the 1680s, however, lords lieutenant were central to the political remodeling of the boroughs—just as they were in the reconstitution of the county bench.

Lieutenants reported to the secretary of state those corporations which they felt were insufficiently loyal; in 1683, the earl of Yarmouth told Secretary Jenkins that the borough of Yarmouth required a quo warranto, and the duke of Beaufort saw to it that Malmesbury's charter was revoked.[132] Yarmouth also played a large part in the surrender of Thetford's charter in 1681 and of Norwich's a year later. The duke of Newcastle acted similarly in the corporations under his supervision in Nottinghamshire and Northumberland.[133] Other lieutenants acted in the same fashion: Ailesbury in Bedfordshire, Bath in the west, and Jeffreys in Shropshire and Buckinghamshire. Bath was probably the most successful; between 1682 and 1685, he secured the surrender of thirty of the thirty-two charters held by parliamentary boroughs in Devon and Cornwall, his two lieutenancies.[134] Action against some charters was initiated by other individuals: assize judges and other interested local magnates played a role, but it was the lieutenants who were most active. In those counties where the lieutenants showed little interest in their duties, corporations often went unscathed—Sussex and

Wiltshire, for example, in the care of the earls of Dorset and Pembroke, had eight and ten towns respectively whose charters survived the campaign. Neither Dorset nor Pembroke took any significant part in the management of their lieutenancies. Both much preferred an indolent life at court or in the country to the cares of local politics—an exceptional life-style for the remodeled lieutenancy.[135]

The key position of many lieutenants in the surrenders gave them considerable influence in the preparation of new charters.[136] They stood between the court and the borough, and when confronted with the inevitability of a quo warranto, many local magistrates preferred to rely on their lieutenants as patrons. In November 1684 the corporation of Berwick, which had resisted surrender for months, finally recognized the futility of its struggle and surrendered its charter to its lieutenant, asking for his "especial consideration." Newcastle, irritated by the town government's obstructionism, was unimpressed. In his letter to Lord Sunderland announcing the surrender, Newcastle wrote, "I confess I can say nothing for the town of Berwick for the people there is [sic] very disaffected."[137] The duke of Beaufort was caught in a complicated dispute about the surrender of Bristol's charter in April 1683. The corporation voted down a Royalist proposal to surrender the charter, even though it had the support of the mayor, bishop, and "most of the considerable people in town." Even though the duke led the attempt to force the surrender, those who opposed it voted to appeal to Beaufort to present an address in behalf of their old constitution to the king. Unlike Newcastle in the case of Berwick, Beaufort argued that with more persuasion, a voluntary surrender might be effected. He recommended against a quo warranto.[138] In Bedford, the magistrates worked assiduously to cultivate their lieutenant, the earl of Ailesbury. The town had anti-Royalist antecedents; Lord Russell, executed for his part in the Rye House Plot, had been a freeman of the corporation, and it had elected, without opposition, Exclusionists to all three of Charles II's final parliaments. A realization of the perilous state of their 1664 charter induced a swift change of heart in the autumn of 1683, when Ailesbury began to receive the regular compliments of the borough thanking him for his attendance at sessions and earnestly requesting his patronage.[139]

The lieutenants' relations with the court made it possible—if they were so inclined—to obtain favors for boroughs in their new charters. Many towns were concerned about fees payable to chancery for the preparation of a new charter, and some lieutenants promised reduced charges for those who

¶ I'm not clear what the relationship
is between magistrates & boroughs.
* See next page margin *

surrendered quickly. Ailesbury told the town clerk of Bedford, "I can give you some perfect assurance that very small fees will be expected as things are ordered, so that you may surrender the charter at a cheaper rate." [140] The duke of Newcastle, who also oversaw the issuance of a new charter for Nottingham, interceded in behalf of the town and requested that expenses be held down. [141] When Lord Yarmouth reported the surrender of Norwich's charter, Secretary Jenkins asked him to assure the corporation that any reasonable changes the town wanted (such as additional fair days) would be made. [142] The crown's chief interest was to continue its political dominance in the boroughs, and it was prepared to make some sacrifices to ensure its success. Buckingham, to take one example, was granted two extra fairs as well as a new weekly cattle market. [143] Thus the lieutenants once again became brokers between court and country, offering favors in return for cooperation.

In some cases, the consequence of intervention on a corporation's behalf was a boost in the standing of the lieutenant himself. Some took advantage of the new charters to have themselves appointed to important local offices as recorders or stewards—as did Newcastle in Berwick and Peterborough in Northampton. Others preferred to impose clients or relatives on the towns. Yarmouth, for instance, had his son made recorder of Norwich. [144] In some towns the increased power of the lieutenant was also expressed in symbolic terms. Elaborate ceremonies were sometimes staged in which a lieutenant would accept, in the king's behalf, the surrender of a charter, or bestow a new one. At these moments the importance of the lieutenant's role in the 1680s was given symbolic expression. Bedford, for example, received its new charter on July 19, 1684, from the hands of Lord Ailesbury. Two years earlier, Ailesbury had seen all of his attempts to advance the king's interest in Bedford rebuffed; his personal influence in the borough had been virtually nonexistent before the fall of the Russells from political grace. Now, named recorder in the charter, Ailesbury arrived accompanied by his deputy lieutenants, justices of the peace, "and a very great number of gentlemen." They were met two miles out of town by the whole body of the magistracy in full regalia and formed a procession of some five hundred horsemen into the city. There the charter was read publicly, and Ailesbury made a speech: "His lordship was pleased to let us know how great his majesty's grace and favor had been to us (although undeservedly) and how highly we were obliged from thence to approve ourselves eminently loyal, and to continue so for ever." [145] Ailesbury's dominance in Bedford was ensured by the charter of 1684 and, combined with his power over the rest of the shire, made him—like many of his fellow lieutenants—a potent political force.[146]

The campaign against the borough charters was part of the general reorganization of government on partisan lines. It complemented the purges of the lieutenancy and magistracy which preceded it and was meant to ensure the dominance of the king's supporters, both locally and in Parliament. Charles II, and for a time, James II, relied on the largest and most important class of gentlemen to enforce their wishes: the "church and king" interest, as the earl of Danby had urged years before. They were numerous and influential, and when combined with the institutional strength of the lieutenancy and the bench, they held an almost impregnable position. The political situation at the start of Charles II's twenty-fifth year as effective king of England was one of complete Royalist dominance. Within this seemingly unshakable edifice, however, lay flaws that portended disaster for the crown. The culmination of the extensive political changes of the early 1680s came immediately after the succession to the throne of James II. The unexpected death of Charles II in February 1685 resulted in a general election during which Royalist political dominance in the boroughs and countryside was dramatically illustrated, and the role of the lord lieutenant as a political boss working in the king's behalf reached its apogee.

The elections of 1685 illustrated the radical change that the lieutenants' political role had undergone since the Exclusion Crisis. They were no longer the consensus builders they had once been. They were now partisans, and it was their duty not to promote harmony but to ensure the defeat of their political opponents and the victory of their allies. Fairness and consensus were casualties of the new political process; they had no place when the most important goal of a parliamentary election was to maintain the dominance of a political party. In the minds of the Royalist Anglican majority, the stakes were very high: success or another revolution. The transition from Charles II to James went more smoothly than many feared. That there was no immediate anti-Yorkist uprising is testimony to the efficiency with which the lieutenancy and its allies had cowed the opposition. After the initial concern about the possibility of rebellion in the days following Charles's death, the lieutenants began the work of organizing the return of "loyal" members to the new Parliament.[147]

In 1685 lieutenants worked much as they had during the elections of 1679–81—although they enjoyed more success. As a result of the many

new borough charters issued during the last years of Charles's reign, lieutenants occupied a better position to influence elections for burgesses. They
were now serving as recorders and stewards, and they exerted considerable
influence on the choice of members. In Leicestershire the earl of Rutland
was asked "to give order to your officers to bespeak what assistance they
can" for the election of a member acceptable to the court.[148] In Staffordshire
and Essex, the settlement of the elections for both the shire and the county
town awaited the arrival of the lieutenant.[149] The earl of Bath worked
diligently to secure the election of a solid phalanx of reliable men from
Cornwall. "In some boroughs," wrote Gilbert Burnet, "they [the court]
could not find a number of men to be depended upon, so all neighboring
gentlemen were made the corporation men. . . . This was practiced in the
most avowed manner by the earl of Bath."[150] The crown urged the return
of "honest members," in many cases leaving the choice of such candidates
up to the country.

In other places the king ordered lieutenants to see that specific men
were elected. In Grantham, Lord Lindsey received "his majesty's positive
commands to be assisting with all of my interest I have to the electing of
Mr. Graham burgess for Grantham. . . . I never saw the gentleman in my
life, but since the king judges him fit for that service, I acquiesce in his
majesty's commands."[151] In Hampshire the lord lieutenant was instructed
to give his support to Roger L'Estrange in the Winchester election.[152] In
Essex, the duke of Albemarle was told by Sunderland to support Samuel
Pepys for a place at Harwich, where the duke had been made recorder by
the terms of the borough's 1684 charter. Although Albemarle had initially
intended to place a client of his own in the seat, Pepys was duly elected.[153]
Most of the crown's nominees were returned, and, in those counties where
the government merely left the management of the elections in the hands
of the lieutenancy, none but the reliable were chosen. The result was by far
the most "loyal" Stuart Parliament ever assembled. The revolution in local
government and the management of the Royalist Anglican interest in the
provinces by the lieutenancy proved to be a triumphant success, and the
new regime, now bolstered by an acquiescent Parliament, appeared almost
invulnerable.

The first real test of the reign, however, was not long in coming. The
new Parliament had only just begun its work when news reached the government of an impending invasion. The attack was anticipated on two
fronts: in the north, where the duke of Argyll had assembled a small force

of covenanting Scots, and in the south, where the duke of Monmouth was expected to land from Holland. On May 19, 1685, Sunderland warned the lieutenants of the far northern and western counties of the imminence of a landing, and within a month Monmouth too had appeared.[154] For the first time since the Second Dutch War, the lieutenancy was called upon to repel an invasion.

The rebellion in the west was the most serious of the two risings. Argyll, who had little support and less luck, was quickly crushed. Monmouth's attempt, however, was more threatening. Although he landed with a small force, there was considerable apprehension that he might gather many recruits to his cause in the west country. He did win the support of many dissenters and poor peasants, but the local power structure remained solidly loyal, or at least refused to assist the rebels openly. The government moved swiftly to neutralize those whom it feared might favor the duke and mobilized the militia under the lieutenants to meet the military threat posed by the rebel force.

The counties nearest the landing bore the brunt of the military action. The militias of all the western counties mustered immediately and marched toward Devon. Additionally, the forces of Berkshire, Surrey, and Middlesex were ordered to Reading to block the path of the rebel army toward London.[155] These orders were carried out hurriedly but with a minimum of trouble. The rebellion showed that even after years of political upheaval in the shires, the lieutenancy was still able to deploy the militia quickly in the defense of the realm. Though Monmouth undoubtedly did have the support of some, even within the militia, it seems clear that most of those involved in the rebellion saw the campaign as action against foreigners and traitors.

The militia under the lieutenants performed with mixed results during the revolt. The Dorset militia met the rebels in several small skirmishes on June 13 and 14, when a local deputy lieutenant reported that the duke's men had been put to flight. By June 15, four days after Monmouth landed at Lyme Regis, the first substantial meeting of the militia and the rebels occurred. It was inconclusive. The duke of Albemarle, lieutenant of Devon, commanded some four thousand men but chose to await further reinforcement rather than engage the enemy. Some Somerset militiamen deserted to Monmouth, and others fled. Lord Lumley, a Sussex deputy lieutenant commanding a unit against the rebels in Hampshire, reported that some of the men raised by the mayor of Leamington had deserted but was pleased by his own men: "We have 400 foot and 150 horse—they are but indifferent to look to, but all are very willing, and more orderly than I expected from such a sort of people." [156] Nevertheless, despite desertions and their less-than-regimental appearance, many militiamen acquitted themselves well. The Gloucestershire militia under the command of the duke of Beaufort prevented a rebel march on Bristol; a group of Oxfordshire, Wiltshire, and Somerset militiamen held Bath in defiance of the duke, and the earl of Pembroke personally led some of the Wiltshire militiamen against a force of a thousand rebels, routing them. [157] Although the militia's success on the battlefield was limited by the ambivalence and poor training of some soldiers, its contribution was not as negative as the king and some later historians have claimed. Incidents of desertion were often balanced by the dutiful performance of others, and it is certainly true that the officers, chosen with such care by the Royalist Anglican lieutenancy, remained loyal.

Away from the battlefield, the lieutenancy had the task of forestalling sedition or assistance for the duke from the discontented. On June 20, the lieutenants were ordered to arrest everyone likely to be dangerous. [158] In Norfolk, those arrested included all nonconformist ministers and everyone who could be found who had served against Charles I in the civil wars. [159] Many of the same people harassed following the Rye House Plot were arrested. Once again, for example, Sir Drayner Massingberd found himself jailed in Hull Castle at the orders of the earl of Lindsey, where he and several other Lincolnshire suspects remained long after prisoners from other counties were released. [160] "Many men are clapt up," wrote Katherine Gough in July, "and many more withdraw from their families." [161] Throughout the summer of 1685, the jails were filled with the lieutenancy's suspects, and many were not released until long after Monmouth's capture and execution.

After the failure of Monmouth's rebellion, James II's throne seemed more secure than ever. The lieutenancy had mobilized the support of the country in the king's behalf and, despite occasional lapses on the field of battle, vindicated itself as a valuable prop of the regime. Indeed, the relative ease with which Monmouth was crushed may have inspired a dangerous overconfidence on the king's part. The institutions of the monarchy had performed splendidly: Parliament responded to the rebellion by voting gratifyingly large sums of money; the magistracy remained firmly supportive of the government; and the lieutenancy mustered a considerable part of the force necessary to defeat the rebels militarily. James's position was so strong that it may have appeared to him that nothing was out of reach—including the relaxation of restraints against Catholicism. His mistake was to assume that the support of the gentry—the support that ensured the efficacy of the lieutenancy—was unconditional. In the months following the victory over the rebels at Sedgemoor, the magnitude of that mistake would become apparent.

CHAPTER VI

Revolution:
The Deposition of James II

MONMOUTH'S RISING THREATENED James II's regime, but its failure assured the king of his subjects' basic loyalty. The gentry sprang to the defense of the legitimate succession, and Parliament seemed determined to support vigorous royal action against traitors. In the provinces, local government remained in the hands of loyalist Anglicans, whose commitment to the preservation of the legitimate Stuart line remained inviolate. As in the previous reign, the lieutenancy, in its zeal to vindicate the new king's rights, represented the consummation of the relationship between crown and Royalist gentry.

After an adjournment during the summer of 1685, James's first Parliament returned to Westminster in November. Contrary to the king's expectations, it offered determined resistance to royal policy from the start. It was James's ambition to end the isolation of his Catholic subjects from the political nation; he wanted to include them once more in the governance of the kingdom. Ultimately he hoped that the example of truly loyal, godly Catholics, serving the crown and living in harmony with their neighbors, would bring about a gradual, spontaneous counterreformation. England would return to the true faith peacefully and without rancor.[1]

What the king did not understand was the horror with which the Royalist Anglican establishment viewed civil equality for Catholics. Charles II had emerged the victor in the tumultuous struggle with the Exclusionists because he had recognized that building an alliance with the Royalist gentry required more than simply fighting in behalf of the hereditary succession.[2] The duke of York's undoubted claim was inextricably connected to the position of the Church of England as the sole legitimate faith. Charles used the gentry's devotion to an Anglican supremacy for his own ends by co-opting the most vigorous and influential leaders of the cause. Although he seemed oblivious to his limitations in this regard, James II could hardly rely on the Royalist Anglicans mustered by his brother to assist in his campaign to dismantle the edifice of Anglican hegemony. He soon discovered that his brother had left him a ready-made opposition firmly entrenched in the provinces.

The king had his first encounter with the champions of Royalist Anglican orthodoxy in the fall of 1685. James wanted to increase his standing forces. He argued that the militia had performed poorly during Monmouth's rebellion and that a reinforced standing army—in which Catholics would hold commissions—was vital to the security of the crown.[3] The issue was debated in November 1685, following a speech the king made from the throne. James thanked God that Monmouth had been defeated but raised serious concerns about the utility of the militia: "When I reflect what an inconsiderable number of men began it, and how long they carried it on without opposition, I hope everybody will be convinced that the militia . . . is not sufficient for such occasions."[4]

Neither house of Parliament showed much sympathy for this course of action. The idea of arming Catholics was reason enough to oppose the plan, and moreover the personal interests of many Parliament men were involved: a weakened militia meant a weakened lieutenancy. Both houses contained many lord and deputy lieutenants who had an interest in avoiding such an outcome; consequently, opposition to a standing army was fierce. Edward Seymour encapsulated the feelings of many gentlemen more conservative than himself when he declared that he would prefer to vote twice as much money for the use of the militia than to support the establishment of an army.[5] The debate, on November 12, revealed such strong sentiment for Seymour's view that even the king's supporters found it necessary to treat the issue gently. The earl of Ranelagh, who supported an increased standing force, prefaced his argument with the statement, "I do not intend to arraign the militia."[6] Sir Thomas Clarges noted that the militia "did considerable service in the late rebellion"; Sir Hugh Cholmondeley, a North Riding deputy lieutenant, claimed it "as good as any army we can raise";[7] Serjeant Maynard also spoke against the army, saying that it was unnecessary: "There is already a law that no man shall rise . . . against the king; lord lieutenants and deputy lieutenants have power to disarm the disaffected."[8] Led by an ominous alliance of the whiggishly inclined and deputy lieutenants, the House of Commons was determined to defend the militia and its members' own interests.

The house, however, was not anxious to force a breach with the king over the issue of supply for the army. A compromise, offered by Sir Richard Temple, was adopted, despite the uneasiness of many MPs: temporary supply for the army until a thorough reform of the militia could be made.[9] When coupled with the king's expressed desire to repeal the Test Act, the plan to replace the militia with a standing army as the chief guarantor of internal security alarmed the most cooperative Parliament of the century. Members were willing to compromise with the king, but the possibility of a Catholic-dominated army was a threat to the constitution as they saw it; it posed a clear breach of the settlement made by Charles II in the early 1680s. James, however, was adamant that he would not part with his Catholic officers: "I think them fit to be employed under me, and will deal plainly with you . . . I will neither expose them to disgrace nor myself to the want of them."[10] The result was an unsatisfactory compromise, magnifying parliamentary concern for the integrity of the Royalist Anglican constitution. Before the session had lasted three weeks, the king, enraged by the obstinacy of the members, prorogued it.

What followed in 1686 was an attempt on James's part to get his way by persuasion and the gradual inclusion of Catholics in local government. "The king," said Reresby, "gave all the encouragement he could to the increase of his own {i.e., Catholics}, by putting more papists into office . . . and many other things."[11] The year 1686 saw a series of provocative gestures by the crown, all of which evoked concern on the part of the Royalist Anglican lieutenancy. Charles II's deathbed conversion was publicized; judges who refused to sanction the king's right to dispense with the Test Act were dismissed; and, acting on the advice of William Penn, the king ordered the release of twelve hundred Quakers from prison.[12] All of these actions struck at the cornerstones of the Royalist Anglican ideology: the sanctity of the Church of England and the safety of the monarchy. Papists and Quakers were avowed enemies of both, and the king appeared dangerously oblivious to the threat they posed to the constitution.

These fears were worsened by the regulation of the bench which commenced in late 1686. For the first time since Shaftesbury's presidency of the council, most lords lieutenant were left out of the process of nomination. The similarity between Shaftesbury's schemes and James's new policy must certainly have redoubled Royalist Anglican alarm. Shaftesbury, a confirmed enemy of the church and crown, had aimed at both in his attempted regulation of the magistracy. Now the king himself appeared to be following the same evil precedent. A committee of the Privy Council was established in October to review the commissions, led by Jeffreys and Sunderland and including several members of the Catholic junto in the council: Tyrconnell, Powis, and Arundell of Wardour. With the exception of the crypto-Catholic Peterborough in Northamptonshire, lieutenants were not asked for their nominations; the committee evidently relied on the knowledge of local Catholics. The primary goal of the remodeling was the inclusion of Catholics, who made up over 60 percent of the new justices.[13]

Although the 1686 regulation of the bench was made for what the king felt were good and necessary reasons—the restoration of worthy Catholics to their rightful places in the community—by ignoring the Royalist Anglican interest he provoked widespread unrest from those who were, until then, temperamentally the least likely to resist. Aside from the ideological objections advanced by Anglican lieutenants, James's new course threatened the local order. Many lieutenants had carefully built an effective political machine in their shires, based firmly on the dominance of church-and-king men. Keeping that organization in good order depended in large part on the lieutenants' ability to control local patronage, as well as to maintain a good relationship between the crown and gentry. Lords lieutenant knew very well that the wholesale appointment of Catholics to local office would cause great disquiet among the gentry, and when the king bypassed the lieutenants and forced the inclusion of Catholics, he undercut the lieutenancy's patronage power. Lords lieutenant found themselves reduced to spectators and began to lose influence to other men upon whom the king relied for advice—Catholics on the Privy Council and in the provinces—many of whom, they felt, were far less well placed to understand the local consequences of the king's actions.[14]

James was alienating the most powerful group in the political nation: the Anglican nobility and gentry and their creature, the lieutenancy. His brother had recognized the importance of conciliating them and relied on them to defend the legitimate succession. Charles's primary goal, the maintenance of the traditional constitution, not only included upholding the hereditary right of the duke of York but also entailed defending the supremacy of the Church of England, a combination central to the lieutenancy's success in the early 1680s. James, however, was determined to weaken the Protestant establishment. The new Commission of the Peace was a definite sign that he was prepared to scrap the pact his brother had made with the Royalist Anglican gentry, although in December 1686 the consequences of his policies remained unclear. Lords lieutenant clung to the hope that James would see the error of his ways and reverse himself, and James expected that the long-proclaimed loyalty of Royalist Anglicans to the sovereign would overcome their fear for the church.

But by early 1687 it was obvious to the king that neither persuasion nor gradual Catholicization would be enough to sweep aside Anglican objections to royal policies. James's new resolution was to replace the loyalist-Anglican dominance that brought him to the throne with a new one based on Catholic and dissenting support. By giving Catholics and dissenters the same solid grip on the institutions that had enforced the loyalist hegemony—Parliament, the bench, borough corporations, and the lieutenancy—James believed that he could force his will on the kingdom. The Royalist Anglican ascendancy would be recreated, but as a mirror image of its Caroline incarnation.

The half-measures of 1686 were abandoned in early 1687. The Declaration of Indulgence in April and the final dissolution of the much-prorogued Parliament on July 2 decisively signaled a new policy.[15] The connivance of the clergy and magistracy in the widespread opposition to the Indulgence was probably a major factor in James's decision to send his Parliament home; the massive purge of local government that followed was no doubt intended to punish the recalcitrant as well as to ensure a more pliable new legislature. If the king could not advance his religion by means of the prerogative, then he would do it by statute, as his Tudor predecessors had done. The result was a concerted effort to ensure the selection of favorable Parliament men. Such an effort would require the assistance of the lieutenancy.

King James had seen the positive effect of the lieutenancy's activities on the crown's behalf in 1685, and he believed that it could once again be turned to good account. Not the institution, but rather the individuals in it, posed a problem for the king. In 1685 the lords lieutenant had successfully organized parliamentary selections throughout the country; unfortunately, as James discovered in 1686–87, many had chosen the wrong candidates in that election. The lieutenants themselves had to be proven trustworthy before the great institutional strengths of the lieutenancy could be used effectively. The need for loyal lords lieutenant was self-evident; if they could not be relied on, they must go. Several Exclusionists had fallen victim to the same principle in Charles II's reign. As the king wrote to the duke of Beaufort, lieutenant of Herefordshire, no one could oppose "my so reasonable desires" and expect to remain in service.[16]

The first dismissals came in August 1687. The earl of Thanet, typical of many of the victims of this purge, lost his lieutenancies in Cumberland and Westmorland. Thanet had been a firm anti-Exclusionist member of the Commons before he succeeded to his title. He had also held a place in the duke of York's household before Charles II's death. His services to James had been rewarded by his appointment to the lieutenancy in March 1685. He raised a regiment in the king's behalf against Monmouth, but by the end of 1686, James's Catholicizing policies had alienated the earl, and he resigned his colonel's commission in the royal army while continuing to hold his lieutenancies. He was an obvious target for removal when the purge came and did not have long to wait.[17] The earl of Pembroke, lieutenant of Wiltshire, had also served with distinction in the suppression of Monmouth's rebellion, but his differences with the king over religion ended in his removal. Other casualties of the first wave of dismissals were Lords Roos and Newport in Leicestershire and Shropshire and the duke of Somerset in Somerset. All three were firm Royalist Anglicans; Roos and Newport had long experience as lieutenants: Roos boasted ten and Newport no less than twenty-seven years of service. The first month's changes were followed by a series of other removals spaced between September 1687 and March 1688. A total of twenty-one counties changed hands during these months as James searched for more amenable lieutenants.

This was by far the most radical purge the lieutenancy had ever experienced, and it had a disastrous impact on both the institution and the king's support among Royalist Anglicans. The dramatic alterations of late 1687 and early 1688 seriously weakened the lieutenancy, as many of the most experienced lieutenants, representing the kingdom's most influential families, were turned out of their places. In addition to Lord Newport, ten more of these lieutenants had over a decade's experience, and some, like Lord Windsor, Viscount Fauconberg, and the earl of Oxford, had been lieutenants for over twenty years. Among those with fewer years in office, several belonged to families that had regularly held lieutenancies in the past, such as the duke of Somerset, the earl of Bridgewater, Viscount Campden, and the earl of Shrewsbury. Of the nineteen new men appointed to the lieutenancy, perhaps only three, Viscount Preston, Lord Jeffreys, and the earl of Sunderland, were talented enough to be effective. Of these three, only

Preston had significant connections with the counties he was given charge of, Cumberland and Westmorland.[18] In short, James deprived himself of an important pool of talented and effective men when he excluded these lieutenants from office. In the process he created ill-will and bitterness. Somerset, for example, was sacked after a rancorous exchange over the reception of the papal nuncio. James insisted upon the duke's presence, Somerset absolutely refused, and as a result lost his place—and his respect for the king.[19]

Sixteen of the nineteen newly appointed lieutenants had little to recommend themselves. Some owed their positions to their close relationship to the king: the earl of Lichfield and the duke of Berwick, James's illegitimate sons, acquired the important lieutenancies of Hampshire and Oxfordshire; his son-in-law Lord Waldegrave, that of Somerset; and his bosom friend the earl of Peterborough, Rutland. All three replaced lieutenants whose commitment to the Royalist Anglican cause had never flagged and who had been very effective in their places: the earls of Gainsborough and Abingdon and Viscount Campden. Many new lieutenants gained preferment because of their religion; Peterborough, Berwick, and Waldegrave were all Catholics. James was willing to entrust a lieutenancy to almost any of his coreligionists, however obscure. Though it was hardly a surprise given the rigid exclusion of Catholics from most places of power in England for a century or more, many of the new lieutenants came to their office with virtually no experience in government. Some bore titles that conjured visions of influence in the remote past—the marquis of Powis and Viscount Montagu, for example—but the families of most, such as Lord Petre, Lord Carrington, Lord Aston, and Lord Ferrers, had lived in quiet obscurity for generations. A very few, such as Lord Molyneux, had some local pretensions (Molyneux had dabbled in politics in Lancashire), but most were far inferior to the men they replaced in both stature and experience. In all, thirteen Catholics were appointed lieutenant over fifteen counties.[20] Along with his effort to press into service every available Catholic, the king also gave some of his patronage to Protestant dissenters, the earls of Huntingdon and Mulgrave and viscount Fairfax being the most prominent.

The resulting group of lords lieutenant was a weak one; few could enforce the king's will in the provinces. Their Catholicism, their lack of experience, and their obscurity combined to ensure the futility of their struggle to overcome the gentry's opposition to the king's policies. Some of the new lieutenants recognized their own poor qualifications; Lord Petre candidly informed Sir John Bramston, an Anglican deputy lieutenant in

Essex, that "the king had put an employment upon him he was in no way fit for, but his majesty had commanded, and he must obey."[21] The twenty lieutenancies these new men held covered every region of the country from Essex to Somerset and Hampshire to Cumberland, but in all of them the local response to the king's policies was the same: rejection.

Fourteen lords lieutenant survived the purges. Most of them were men of tested loyalty, but few were wholly pleased with the direction the king had taken. They included the earls of Ailesbury and Lindsey (lieutenants of Bedfordshire, Huntingdonshire, and Lincolnshire), the dukes of Norfolk and Newcastle, and the earls of Bath, Rochester, and Dover. Although most of the lieutenants in this group had their doubts about the king's policies—and some expressed them openly—they were willing to serve the crown as best they could. The grumblers seem to have survived for no other reason than that the king simply could not do without them. The earl of Bath, as well as the dukes of Newcastle and Norfolk, were the most obvious examples of this type. Without the active assistance of these three, it would have appeared impossible to secure the king's goals in the North, West, and East Anglia. Try as they might, however, they could do very little in the face of the almost unanimous opposition of the country, a reality that was clearly illustrated in their disastrous attempt to secure the election of a Jacobite Parliament.

King James's purge of the lords lieutenant took place in conjunction with his attempt to influence the upcoming parliamentary elections. The lieutenancy was to continue its role as electoral organizer in the shires, as it had done in 1685. Initially, in the early months of 1687, the king pressured lieutenants individually, bombarding them with letters and closeting them at Whitehall. The letter Beaufort received in February 1687 was a typical example of the king's style early in the process. Beaufort's influence in his western lieutenancies was wide, and James made the royal wishes clear: "I intend . . . to have the two tests and penal laws repealed that my Catholic subjects may be in the same condition as the rest of my subjects are. Therefore pray take pains . . . [to] get as many of them as you can to promise you positively that they will do it."[22] Later, however, a much more systematic attempt was launched.

The king's determination to remove anti-Catholic laws from the books called for new tactics. On October 25, 1687, all lords lieutenant were instructed to ask their deputies and justices of the peace three questions: Would they agree to the repeal of the Penal and Test acts should they be elected to Parliament? Would they support the candidacy of gentlemen who did promise repeal? Would they "live peaceably" with their non-

Anglican neighbors in the event of a declaration of indulgence?[23] Moreover, the lieutenants were instructed to report on the state of the corporations in their charge—who had "credit enough of their own to be chosen parliament men, or may be chosen if assisted by their own friends." Last they were to list "what Catholics and what dissenters are fit to be added either to the list of deputy lieutenants, or to the commission of the peace throughout the said lieutenancy."[24]

The project astounded the already nervous lieutenancy. "In most of the counties," wrote Bishop Burnet, "the lords lieutenants put those questions in so careless a manner, that it was plain they did not desire they should be answered in the affirmative." Lord Preston, lieutenant of Cumberland and Westmorland, was described as "not very well pleased" with his instructions, a feeling shared by many.[25] The lukewarm response of many lieutenants was the direct cause of their dismissals between October and February. The earl of Northampton, for example, felt that it was his duty to obey the king's commands and put the questions, but he frankly informed his deputies that he himself could not agree to repeal. He was soon replaced by the earl of Sunderland.[26] Curt letters to the lords lieutenant informing them that the king "has commanded me to let you know that he had thought fit to dispose otherwise of your lieutenancies so that you are to act no more in that capacity" was the result of their lack of enthusiasm.[27] A survivor, the earl of Ailesbury, was hardly more pleased with the plan; in his memoirs, he described the three questions as "a most damnable project."[28] The duke of Norfolk, faced by widespread resistance in Norfolk, seriously considered going abroad to escape his dilemma.[29] Nevertheless, the crown continued to press ahead.

The new lieutenants and those who had not been displaced were expected to question their subordinates in both the lieutenancy and the magistracy and remove from office any who continued to resist the king's policies. The result of the canvass greatly disappointed the crown and illustrates the precarious position of the new lieutenants at the time. Deputy lieutenants and justices of the peace refused to satisfy their new masters. Most had no difficulty answering the third question in the affirmative; living in peace with their neighbors did violence to few men's consciences. The other two queries presented different problems. Deputies commonly replied that they could not promise their vote in Parliament without hearing the debates on repeal, and many simply said that they had no intention to stand. As for their support in selecting MPs, most replied that they could give no assurances until they knew who was standing.[30]

The deputies were as evasive as they could be; a Bedfordshire deputy was typical when he said to his lieutenant, "My lord I pray you to assure the king that if I am chosen a member, my resolution shall be to come into the house absolutely with a most loyal temper, and no wise prepossessed, and that my intentions are to act in every sense according to honor and conscience, hoping that the king can never be able to ask anything but what I can cheerfully comply with."[31] Sir John Knatchbull, a longtime deputy lieutenant in Kent, responded in a similar manner when his new lord lieutenant, the Catholic Lord Teynham, questioned him. He could not, he said, make any commitments about what he might do in the House of Commons before he had heard all of the arguments both for and against repeal.[32]

In many places the respondents were not at all circumspect in their answers and responded with a flat "no" to the first two questions. Sir John Stonehouse of Berkshire thought "the test was made for the support of the Church of England, of which he has always professed himself a member, and cannot give his consent to repeal without doing a great deal of injury to his religion." John Bigg of Huntingdonshire was recorded as saying, "To the first [question], he cannot consent. To the second he is of the same mind," and Sir William Gostwick of Bedfordshire held to a typical position when he said that he did not plan to stand for Parliament, "but if he be chose, he cannot part with the penal laws and tests. Second, that he cannot contribute to the election of any such as will."[33] Ailesbury noted that in his lieutenancy (Bedfordshire) "the negative was given almost unanimously, save as to the last question . . . those very few who complied were persons very low in fortune and of little credit in their county."[34] The duke of Norfolk reported a similar experience in Norfolk, where the three questions were presented at a general meeting of the deputies and justices.

Negative replies far outnumbered positive ones, and in many counties it was clear that the deputies and justices concerted their answers. In Somerset twelve deputies answered identically; when Sir John Holland in Norfolk added a parenthetical "as my judgment at present is" to his written refusal to support repeal, Sir William Coke and Sir Neville Catelyn, both Royalist Anglicans of long standing, suggested that he delete it "because the best way to preserve a unity throughout the county is to avoid all ambiguity and doubt."[35] The united stand of so many gentlemen in the lieutenancy and on the bench ensured that the changes in their composition made by James in 1687–88 would have to be a radical ones.

Those few who answered positively were either Catholics or, as Ailesbury said, men of little account. In Somerset one of the only deputies who consented to all three questions was Francis Paulet, a Catholic relation of the marquis of Winchester. In Staffordshire there was an unusually large number of positive replies; six deputies agreed to accept the king's terms. Four of these six are noted as Catholics.[36] But there were simply not enough Catholics in the commission for the lieutenancy to remain effective as a political force in the kingdom.

Those who refused to cooperate had to be dismissed and replaced with more pliable deputies, nominated by their lieutenants.[37] Judging from the number of new nominations sent in to Whitehall, the number of dismissals was very high. In Ailesbury's words, "Generally speaking all the deputy lieutenants and justices were removed."[38] In Lincolnshire, only four of the old deputies survived the purge; they were to be supplemented by eleven new men. In Northamptonshire two old deputies were joined by six new ones; in Berkshire only one deputy remained. Some counties were left virtually without experienced deputy lieutenants. The entire commission was replaced in Bedfordshire, Cheshire, Lancashire, and Sussex, and other counties fared almost as badly; Buckinghamshire, for example, was left with only a single deputy lieutenant from the previous commission.[39]

The new deputy lieutenants began their careers under inauspicious circumstances; the administrative difficulties that such a sudden and massive purge involved were in themselves enough to destroy the institution's effectiveness for a long time to come. The old lieutenants and their deputies were not disposed to cooperate with their successors, whom they viewed as usurpers, if not traitors. Lieutenancy records were usually kept by clerks employed as personal servants of the former deputies or lieutenants, and after the lieutenancy had fallen into other hands, the new appointees often faced great difficulty in wresting these documents, vital to the continued functioning of the lieutenancy, from the grasp of the disfranchised. The new lieutenants, aided by even the most vigorous and able deputies, found their business very difficult with nothing but the text of the militia acts to guide them.

Unfortunately, the new deputy lieutenants were hardly better qualified than the newly appointed lords lieutenant. Again, the government relied as much as it could upon Catholics to fill vacant positions. In Sussex, where the Catholic community was very old and prominent, the new list of deputies contained several: Sir Richard Shirley, Sir John Gage, Sir John Shelley, and Richard Caryll. These men came from families whose breeding and estates might have qualified them for a commission but who had been excluded from local government as recusants. Their lack of experience could

hardly have helped their new lord lieutenant, Viscount Montagu, himself a Catholic of ancient lineage. In Buckinghamshire Lord Jeffreys chose
nine Catholics for his deputies, and other lieutenants nominated as many
Catholics as they could muster. The Catholic deputies did not serve alone,
however. To their number was added a contingent of dissenters. Buckinghamshire's nine papists, for instance, were joined by seven dissenters.[40] The
names of other dissenting or Exclusionist families occur in the nominations:
Strode, Syderfin, and Bampfield in Somerset, Parker in Sussex, Standish
and Gerard in Lancashire, and Hobart and Potts in Norfolk. Some of these
deputies had sat in one or another of the Exclusion Parliaments and been
dismissed from the lieutenancy in the purges of the 1680s. One such was
Silius Titus, a deputy lieutenant for Huntingdonshire. Sacked in 1680 at
the command of Charles II for his advocacy of Exclusion, Titus was not only
restored to his old place but found himself sitting in King James's Privy
Council as well.[41]

During the months from August 1687 to March 1688 the lieutenancy
was completely restructured. Lords lieutenant who survived the purge were
unenthusiastic about the crown's policies, and those who were appointed
for the first time lacked the stature and experience necessary to carry out
their responsibilities. The posing of the three questions was a disastrous tactic which inflicted tremendous damage upon the king and his government.
The removal of all opponents to royal policies was the natural consequence
of James's determination to have his own way, but he failed to recognize
that without Royalist Anglican support he could not hope to succeed. A
lieutenancy in the hands of Catholics and dissenters would never be as
effective as it had been under Charles II. In the short space of six or seven
months, James had inadvertently kicked away one of the strongest props
that supported his throne.[42]

The reconstruction of the lieutenancy was accomplished concurrently
with a vigorous attempt to pack the upcoming Parliament. The lords lieutenant played little part in this new campaign; they were circumvented by
the appointment of a group of organizers the court sent into the provinces.
The decision of the crown to use these agents implicitly acknowledged the
unreliability of the new lieutenancy; preparations continued in the spring
of 1688 with very little input from the institution.[43] The earl of Ailesbury
ruefully noted that "I was become very insignificant in the counties where I
was lord lieutenant." The agents sent into the country to manage elections
were for the most part dissenters, and William Penn was charged with
coordinating their activities.[44]

The organizers of the king's campaign were not far wrong in distrusting the lieutenancy as an electoral agent. In Somerset, where the senior deputy lieutenant, Lord Fitzharding, had remained in the commission despite his distinctly lukewarm assent to the three questions, opposition to the king's plans came from within the lieutenancy itself. The new sheriff of the county, Edward Strode, a dissenter who had also been named to a deputy lieutenancy in the new commission, accused Fitzharding of leading the opposition to the king's candidates. Fitzharding presided over a dinner of the county's most prominent gentlemen in January 1688, where, Strode reported, "I was sufficiently abused and teased by them, having nobody there of the king's side with me." Fitzharding dismissed his guests' behavior as a minor offense and made no attempt to hide his contempt for Strode: "If any heat of word passed between him and other gentlemen, who have ever been as eminently loyal as he and his family were otherways, I never knew my country famed for good breeding."[45] In Bedfordshire, John Eston, who was working among the dissenters to return suitable members, implied to the earl of Peterborough that Lord Ailesbury was dragging his feet. In Bedford the dissenters stood solidly behind the king's candidates, "but the churchmen are implacable against us." Ailesbury was the only man who could secure their support; the Anglicans were "the lieutenant's votaries," and apparently Ailesbury had done nothing to sway their opinion in the king's favor.[46]

Understandably, Ailesbury and the other lieutenants were dismayed by the course of events. The lieutenant of Bedfordshire loathed the king's agents. "It was my lot," he wrote bitterly, "to have a broken fanatic shoemaker, one Roberts, whom I never saw, that purged the corporation of Bedford." Describing another of the chief executors of the king's policies, Sir Nicholas Butler, Ailesbury wrote "that he had been a stocking merchant, and a bankrupt—a man that had wit and sense, but else little or no morals."[47] It was no surprise that Anglican grandees like Ailesbury were contemptuous of the king's new allies and that they did little or nothing to assist them in their work.

The attempt to return a Jacobite Parliament was never put to the ultimate test, but it seems clear that the gentry would not have supported the outcome of any such election. The alienation of the gentry from the crown was completed by the king's attempt to ally himself with Catholics and, even more damaging, with dissenters. Considering the horror with which the Restoration lieutenancy viewed dissent, it is possible that in his tactical embrace of dissenters James had committed a sin that could never be expiated. Royalist Anglicans supported and, by their actions in Monmouth's rebellion, proved that they would not hesitate to defend a Roman Catholic monarch. The radical course the king's policies took in 1687, however, transformed the political landscape. King James was threatening to pull down the twin pillars upon which Royalist Anglicans had constructed their political world. The Church of England was under assault from Rome; Catholics were even intruded into the nursery of the clergy, the universities. Declarations of indulgence and papal nuncios raised the specter of a counterreformation. Furthermore, by allying himself with dissenters, confirmed rebels all—former parliamentarians, republicans, supporters of the late duke of Monmouth—James threatened the very institution of the monarchy. Some in the lieutenancy, like the duke of Newcastle and the earls of Bath and Ailesbury, remained at their posts despite their fundamental disagreements with the king, but virtually everyone ceased to regard him as the champion of the established order that he had once seemed.

The crown's purge of the lieutenancy was a failure: the result was not a more motivated, firmly committed institution but a powerless one. All over the kingdom musters of the militia ceased to be held, as did meetings of the lieutenancy. The militia of the West Riding was not mustered once after the summer of 1686; in 1688 the lord lieutenant of Lincolnshire noted "the long absence of musters" in his shire, which met only once after the spring of 1686.[48] The situation in other counties was little better; Norfolk went musterless for two years, for example.[49] Even the most vigorous lieutenants and deputies were unfamiliar with their duties and feared the consequences of neglecting the militia. Lord Aston, the Catholic lieutenant of Staffordshire, noted in September 1688 that his command was completely disorganized, "by which really there is no militia at all."[50]

Moreover, there were many who chose to avoid acting altogether. They were well aware of the hostility of their neighbors and had no desire to encourage it further with a display of Jacobite bluster. Many, after all, had accepted their commissions reluctantly; their appointments had been dictated more by their Catholicism than their enthusiasm for the king's policies. It was clear by the spring of 1688 that local government—particularly the lieutenancy—was paralyzed.[51] The king had lost the support of his subjects.

As early as April 1688 the Prince of Orange had probably made the decision to intervene in England, and by summer plans for an invasion were well in hand.[52] It was not until September that James finally realized the precariousness of his position. In the face of impending disaster he reversed his policies and attempted to undo the damage he had wrought in the preceding two years.[53] Late in September the king ordered the lieutenants to restore to the commission "such as will in their judgment serve the king without any more ado."[54] The crown at last recognized its inability to maintain a viable administration in the provinces by relying solely on Catholics and dissenters.

Expecting a landing on the East Anglian coast, the king replaced the ineffectual Lord Petre in Essex with the popular earl of Oxford and removed Lord Teynham in Kent in favor of the earl of Feversham, a professional soldier. The earl of Derby was reinstated to his lieutenancy in Lancashire, succeeding Lord Molyneux, and all three of the Yorkshire Ridings were united and given to the duke of Newcastle. Feversham's appointment was obviously a move to guarantee the military security of a strategic county; the other appointments were motivated by political calculation and were intended to rout unpopular and ineffective lieutenants. These new appointments did virtually nothing to remedy the king's situation. Feversham found that none of the old deputy lieutenants, whom he proposed to restore, would serve under him, despite the lieutenant's solemn promise that "he would admit no papist, and that if the gentlemen would accept of him they should govern him in everything."[55] The earl of Oxford also attempted to reemploy the old deputies and was informed by Sir John Bramston that "he would find gentlemen not forward to take commands; some would think one kick in the breech enough for a gentleman."[56] The duke of Norfolk met with fourteen former deputy lieutenants on October 7 and attempted to persuade them to return to the commission, but they unanimously refused to do so until all Catholics were removed from office.[57] The approaches of lieutenants throughout the country were similarly rebuffed.[58] Some, like the bishop of Durham, merely ignored the prevailing sentiment of the gentry. On October 5 he blandly informed his old deputies that he wanted to prepare the militia "in case of some sudden use" and that they had been forthwith reappointed. It seems unlikely that the bishop's efforts had any good effect.[59] There was little that loyal lords lieutenant could do in the king's behalf so late in the game.

After an abortive attempt to sail on October 29, William's armada left Holland early the next day and landed—contrary to expectations—at Torbay in Devon on November 5.[60] The final outcome of the conflict was by no means preordained nor did the days following the prince's landing determine the victor. The king commanded a large army, and it was still unclear how far discontent would lead gentlemen into active support for the invasion.[61] The response of the lieutenancy to William's arrival would tell much about the prospects for King James's survival. The duty to repel invasion and suppress rebellion lay at the heart of the lieutenancy's function; thus there could be no question about the action the crown expected. The lieutenants were to raise their forces and come to the defense of the throne. Yet this time the institution did not fulfill the crown's expectations as it had in 1685. Already weakened by the upheavals of the previous year, by November 1688 the lieutenancy was incapable of effective action—or unwilling to undertake it. The earl of Bristol, lord lieutenant of Dorset, told the king just a week before the landing that although he had convinced some of the old deputies to serve, the militia, having been neglected for some time, was not fit to oppose the enemy; it would take at least three months to prepare. It seems clear that the former deputies, who returned to their posts only under the condition that the king "might not expect more from them than they could perform," did their best to avoid taking any action. In Cheshire the newly restored Derby claimed on October 28 that because he had not received a commission under the great seal he could not legally act; in Cornwall, the earl of Bath announced that he could not hope to prevent a landing.[62]

Some lieutenants attempted to put a brave face on the situation. On October 28 the earl of Lindsey in Lincolnshire assembled the militia horse and found them to be in better condition than he had hoped, "there having been such a long omission of musters." The duke of Norfolk attempted to rally his forces in Norfolk, but he was skeptical of the loyalty of the people there. The previous deputies had already proved unreliable when they refused to return to the commission, and the duke was no less concerned about the common people. He advised against firing the beacons in case of invasion because the "rabble, who are so unsteady, and in some parts so ill-affected that it [the beacons] might as well guide them where we would not have them as show them where we would." [63] Former deputies continued in their refusal to accept office, and many new deputies deliberately lay low for fear of provoking their neighbors. John Herndon noted on October 25 that deputies "generally refuse to act," and many lords lieutenant temporized or simply did nothing.[64]

A few lieutenants made preparations. The duke of Norfolk, having failed to persuade his former deputies to return to their duty, arrived at his palace in Norwich and took personal control of the situation. In the last week of October he mustered four troops of horse and two infantry regiments and called his deputies and ten prominent justices of the peace together for a meeting. The duke's moves must have been very encouraging to the king, but it seems that there was more behind Norfolk's activities than steadfast loyalty. As the Prince of Orange's army steadily increased in size, Norfolk, commanding his regiments of militia, remained on the side-lines. On November 28 the duke called for a general meeting of the gentry, and it seemed that he was at last ready to choose sides. When the assembly met in Norwich on the first of December, the lord lieutenant announced his support of William: "And since the coming of the Prince of Orange has given us an opportunity to declare for the defense of [the laws, liberties, and the Protestant religion], I can only assure you that no man will venture his life more freely for the defense of [them] than I will do."[65] Norfolk unilaterally brought his county over to the prince's side and demonstrated the potency of the Royalist Anglican lieutenancy in defense of the ancient constitution.

Undoubtedly Norfolk was deeply unhappy with King James and his policies, but it also seems certain that the duke was acting with an eye to his own interests. The refusal of the Royalist Anglican establishment to take up James's cause for the third time threatened his position as the preeminent aristocrat in East Anglia. Developments might have left him behind, but his quick action in raising the militia and holding it out of the fray gave him the upper hand. Norfolk made shrewd use of his office in his declaration for the prince. As lord lieutenant he assembled the gentry of the shire and directed their deliberations. The Norfolk gentry would almost certainly have declared for a free Parliament in any case, but in siding with his county against the king, the duke placed himself in a position to control the process.

Even more spectacular defections occurred in the west. The earl of Bath, lord lieutenant of Cornwall and Devon, as well as governor of Plymouth, realized where his interests lay and also took up the prince's cause. This was a devastating blow to James, who relied on Bath more than any other lieutenant in the field. Bath was nearest the scene of the Dutch landing and had hitherto been a loyal servant, surviving the purges of 1687–88. He had consistently striven, against the odds, to implement all of the changing decrees that descended from Whitehall, and his desertion of the king was as sudden as it was unexpected. Throughout the latter half of October he was in his lieutenancy, ostensibly attempting to prepare for the coming attack. Charles Hatton, with the earl at Plymouth, was very impressed by the lieutenant's work: "I think myself more happy to be under his [Bath's] command, than under that of any other person on earth. . . . Should the Dutch think fit to attack us here we think ourselves very secure under his conduct and are well assured that by his care and interest in these parts we shall be . . . so powerful as to enable us to make a vigorous defense." [66] Despite Hatton's confidence, however, others were reaching different conclusions. A letter from Exeter strongly hinted at Bath's unreliability. "The king," wrote John White, "is very insecure in these two counties whatever he may be told. . . . I may say scarce any care is taken for his majesty's service in this part of the kingdom. I would not have you think I mean the mayor for he is a little inconsiderable fellow. . . . I mean a person in a much higher station." [67]

White meant Bath, and he was correct, for the earl had been playing a double game all along. He had been in contact with one of William's agents, Henry Sidney, and though he had not yet committed himself to support the invasion, it is certain that he made no serious attempt to prevent it. [68] Bath informed Whitehall of the prince's landing on the night of November 6, and his assessment was not very positive. Exeter, he said, was not able to "resist the force of an army," and "the common people are so prejudiced with the late regulations, and so much corrupted that there can be no dependence at present on the militia." [69] It took Bath less than two weeks to make his final decision. On the nineteenth, just after William had occupied Exeter without resistance, the prince received a letter from the earl assuring him of his support and offering to assist in the capture of Plymouth. On the twenty-eighth Bath surrendered the city; on the same day the duke of Norfolk set in motion his plan to deliver East Anglia to the prince. [70]

The final blow to the king's authority in the west came on the same day, November 28, when the duke of Beaufort surrendered Bristol. Beaufort had shown little inclination to fight on the king's behalf, and, following his surrender, he retired to Gloucester, where he hoped to "continue to keep that county and the rest of my lieutenancy . . . from any rising." The sentiment was commendable, yet Beaufort's letter reads more like an excuse to avoid any serious action in the king's behalf than a pledge of loyal service. [71]

The actions of these three lieutenants, Norfolk, Bath, and Beaufort, illustrate the vital importance such magnates attached to maintaining control over their local power base, as well as the ability of a lord lieutenant to mobilize his shire against the crown and deliver it to the Prince of Orange. All three had objected to King James's policies, and thus their actions were at least partly motivated by their principles. Nevertheless, the landing of the prince was an event fraught with both danger and possibility. A lord lieutenant could choose the wrong side and lose everything, including his life. He could, as many did, do nothing at all—simply sit tight and wait for a victor to emerge. This tactic had its own danger, however—the lord lieutenant who failed to seize his opportunities might easily find himself swept aside by the course of events; his carefully constructed position of local preeminence could be swiftly demolished by an astute rival. Norfolk, Beaufort, and Bath acted to prevent such an outcome. In other counties the timid or uncertain who refused to make a bold stand were circumvented; in Oxfordshire and Buckinghamshire militia forces were raised by the prince's supporters without legal authorization from their lieutenants. In Cumberland several of the old deputy lieutenants did the same and arrested a number of Catholics in the county besides.[72] By the end of November, the militia was being raised in William's behalf, often without authority, in many counties.

The fate in store for a lord lieutenant who failed to negotiate the perilous weeks following the Dutch landing is exemplified by the duke of Newcastle. Appointed to the combined lieutenancies of the three Yorkshire ridings on October 6, as well as his old places in Northumberland and Nottinghamshire, Newcastle was poised to exert enormous influence. The choice between king and prince was more complicated for the duke than for others such as Norfolk and Beaufort. Newcastle could not present himself as the leader of the Orangist cause in his counties as they could—positions that made the switch much easier for them—for Newcastle had a rival in the north: the earl of Danby. Danby was one of the prime movers in the conspiracy against the king, and as a Yorkshireman he expected that the reward for his service would include a dominant position in his home county. Newcastle had no desire to see his place usurped by Danby, and his decision to support the king was certainly influenced by his determination to safeguard his political position.

Danby and his fellow conspirators made every attempt to win the duke over. When Newcastle took up residence in Yorkshire after his appointment, he received a steady stream of visits from the prince's partisans. Still he refused to cooperate and continued in his efforts to rally the gentry against an invasion.[73] Newcastle's chief supporter in Yorkshire was Sir John Reresby, a deputy lieutenant and governor of the castle at York, but aside from Sir John, the duke made very little progress in his work.

Danby's northern conspiracy unfolded swiftly following William's landing in the west. On November 13, eight days after the prince's arrival, the lieutenancy met to consider how to respond. Newcastle ordered a regiment of militia and two troops of horse to be stationed in York, and, at the urging of one of the deputies, Sir Henry Goodricke, a general meeting of the gentry was scheduled for the twenty-second in York. The purpose of the meeting, so Newcastle and Reresby thought, was to declare "our adherence to the king according to the laws of the land and the obligation of our religion."[74] In fact, Goodricke was a key member of Danby's organization and intended to use the meeting as an opportunity to appeal to the gentry over Newcastle's head.[75] Reresby's suspicions of a plot were aroused when at a dinner on the fifteenth, some present supported a declaration for a free Parliament. Goodricke, who was there with Reresby, "absolutely denied it" and temporarily allayed the governor's fears.

Newcastle, however, had evidently learned that the coming meeting would offer anything but loyal support to the king, and he arrived in York intent upon discovering the truth. On November 20, he called all of his deputies together and confronted them with his information. The result was a declaration by the deputies that they would support a petition for a free Parliament—essentially a declaration for the Prince of Orange. The lord lieutenant found himself in a very difficult situation; his deputies refused to acknowledge his authority, but he could not bring himself to throw in his lot with Danby. The very fact that the conspiracy went so deep made it still more difficult to switch sides gracefully as Bath and Norfolk had done. Newcastle had been publicly affronted by his subordinates, and sheepish acquiescence in the plot would have completed the destruction of his influence. Over the strenuous objections of Reresby, the duke took what must have seemed to him the only way out. He withdrew from the contest in an attempt to avoid further humiliation. He told his rebellious deputies that they could rethink their decision and meet him the next day, but it seems clear by his actions that he was abandoning the field. He refused Reresby's entreaties to dismiss the militiamen already under arms, and on November 21 he left York for his estate at Welbeck, leaving the troops under the command of his deputies.[76]

His rival vanquished, the earl of Danby then made a triumphant entry into York on the twenty-second, where at a meeting of the deputy lieutenants and gentlemen the north was delivered into William's hands. Reresby made a last, ineffectual effort to prevent the coup, but Danby "told me that to resist was to no purpose; that he and these gentlemen were in arms for a free parliament, and for the preservation of the Protestant religion and the government, as by law established, which the king had very near destroyed, and which the prince of Orange was come to assist them defend." [77] The governor still refused to cooperate and was arrested by the conspirators.

The duke of Newcastle had lost control of the situation, and the result was the complete eclipse of his political fortunes. His lieutenancies of Nottinghamshire, Northumberland, and all three Ridings of Yorkshire made him, in theory at least, the most powerful man in the north. If he had been shrewd enough, or if he had been able to work out a suitable compromise with the earl of Danby, he might well have turned the revolution to his advantage. It is certain, however, that he could never have used his lieutenancy in a successful defense of James II, and his attempt to do so resulted in personal disaster. In a feeble last attempt to regain a semblance of control in his own lieutenancy, on November 27, the duke ordered the militia horse in York to return home, "but they refused to obey him, and laughed at him for his message." [78] The demise of Newcastle as a political player was finalized when, on December 3, following orders from Danby, a party of militiamen arrived at Welbeck and confiscated the duke's horses and arms. The lord lieutenant of Yorkshire was a helpless prisoner.

The lieutenancy's utility as a political instrument in the hands of the Prince of Orange's supporters was unquestionable; through the complicity of lieutenants in the West and East Anglia, William was given valuable aid. The Norfolk declaration dealt a crushing blow to James's rear, while the surrender of Exeter and Gloucester immeasurably complicated the military tasks facing the king. The end came when elements of the royal army defected, but the assistance of politically astute lieutenants and deputy lieutenants made William's task far simpler. The lieutenants who supported the king discovered that the purged and powerless institution of James's creation could not withstand the opposition of the well-connected Anglican magnates. The duke of Newcastle found that the lieutenancy could be a threat to the king; James, as his father had done in 1641–42, had forfeited the loyalty of a large part of the gentry in the pursuit of his ill-considered policies, and the price he paid was an unreliable lieutenancy in a moment of crisis.

Those few lieutenants who weathered the crisis emerged with their influence strengthened, and their example reinvigorated the lieutenancy. Four lieutenants survived all of the tergiversations of the period from 1686 to 1689: Bath, Norfolk, Bristol, and Lindsey. The first three played key roles in the Orangist victory, and Lindsey saved himself by a last-minute switch and the intercession of his brother-in-law, the earl of Danby. The part the first three played in ensuring William's success served as a lesson to the new monarch, who saw how effective the lieutenancy could be, and to the lieutenants themselves, who saw the dividends firm control of a shire might pay in the right circumstances.

The reconstruction of the lieutenancy after the revolution followed the pattern set under Charles II and his brother; there was no effort, as there had been in 1660, to return to the prewar model. Changes in the commission were extensive, and new lieutenants were chosen on largely political grounds. All but a handful of counties received new lieutenants in the year after William and Mary's accession. Nine of them, about a third of the total, had been victims of James's earlier purges and were restored to their positions. Lieutenants such as the earls of Bridgewater, Abingdon, Winchilsea, and Pembroke, were all Royalist Anglicans but were not tainted by James's excesses. Most of the new commissions, however, went to the victors in the struggle against Yorkism and fell into the hands of peers who had been shut out of government for some time. Names that in the next century would become synonymous with "Whig Oligarchy" made their initial appearances as lords lieutenant in 1689–90: Delamere, Lowther, Lumley, Macclesfield, Brandon, Bedford. Conservative peers such as the earl of Shrewsbury, the newly appointed lieutenant of Hertfordshire and Worcestershire, would learn soon enough that limited though the revolution was, it certainly did create a new ruling order.[79] The lieutenancy's politicization made Whig dominance of the institution, and all that that implied, inevitable under the new regime.

See p. 142

When James fled England in December 1688 he left behind a lieutenancy prepared to act independently of the crown in defense of the constitution, and thereafter the institution remained of central importance in the governance of the provinces. The political struggle over Exclusion had proved the lieutenancy's worth in the political arena, and the sensitive management of the events surrounding William's invasion by such lieutenants as Bath and Norfolk further illustrated its political importance. The successful management of the transition from James to William and Mary was the culmination of a process by which grandees like Norfolk took on party political rather than old-style sociopolitical roles in their shires, a process that had its beginnings in the immediate post-Restoration period but clearly foreshadows the world of the eighteenth century.

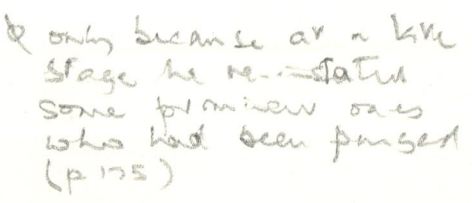

& only because at a late stage he re-instated some former ones who had been purged (p. 175)

Conclusion

LOOKING BACK OVER the previous seventy-five years from a vantage point in the early eighteenth century, an elderly English peer in a reflective mood could point to many alterations in his country. The duke of Leeds, to take an example, was born in 1632 and entered public life at the age of twenty-eight; he rose to become Charles II's lord treasurer and then served briefly as one of Queen Anne's chief ministers before his retirement in 1699. Leeds began life as plain Thomas Osborne, son of Yorkshire gentry. Had he written his memoirs, he could have said much about the changes the seventeenth century had wrought.

Osborne was born into a highly conservative and hierarchical world rooted in medieval assumptions about place and social standing. He was fortunate; his family stood high in local society. Like his father and grandfather before him, he was able to start his public career as an officer in the local trained band, and after several years of service, he could expect a place on the bench and a commission as a deputy lieutenant. To these full-time posts would very probably be added occasional trips to Westminster as a member of Parliament and appearances at Whitehall, where the monarch graciously received the scions of the gentry. After decades of devoted service to crown and community, organizing musters, resolving disputes, and preserving order in the countryside, Osborne could expect to end his days, full of years and respected by all, as had his father and grandfather before him. As it happened, Osborne's life took a radically different course, as did England itself.

Osborne's personal experience was bound up with the history of the lieutenancy, as was the experience of the bulk of the peerage and thousands of country gentlemen. He was the son of a deputy lieutenant, deputy himself by 1661, and later lord lieutenant of three counties, and the lieutenancy loomed large in his life. Although politics and society were transformed during his lifetime, the lieutenancy remained an institution central to political administration, military organization, and local governance throughout his career.

The lieutenancy of the 1620s and 1630s reflected the values of the early Stuart era; the social characteristics of standing and connection were paramount. Lords lieutenant were high-ranking nobles, mostly from old houses: names like Howard, Stanley, Cecil, and Sackville abound. The few exceptions, such as Yorkshire's earl of Strafford, were the focus of unease and malice; their appointment violated the standards custom had imposed on the office. Deputy lieutenants, like their superiors, belonged to the inner circle of county society; they were placed high on the bench, their families controlled the widest estates, their fathers and grandfathers boasted the most distinguished family trees. All, lieutenants and deputies alike, were born to their offices, which were routinely handed down from father to son.

The social prominence of the lieutenancy before the Restoration was crucial to its effectiveness; the office entailed a wide variety of duties, but all required the ability to reconcile individual communities to the demands of central government. The crown's policies ranged from the relatively innocuous sale of Virginia Company lottery tickets under James I to the organization of Charles I's wars. The provision of money, men, and supplies for the royal army was the most burdensome task the lieutenants were required to accomplish; the wars of the 1620s proved how difficult a task this could be. Only the prestige, connections, and power of the lieutenants could persuade the reluctant. Whitehall could rely on the lieutenancy to accomplish things mere bureaucrats from the capital could not.

Moreover, their close relationship with the court offered the localities the promise of royal favor and special consideration. Lieutenants were very often privy councillors or court officers; Viscount Conway, secretary of state and lieutenant of Hampshire, was in a position to favor his own countrymen when in 1626 the charges for billets began to roll in. The earl of Northampton secured favorable conditions for his own lieutenancies during the campaign of 1627. Optimally, the lieutenancy's function as a link between court and country operated for the benefit of both.

The lieutenancy's focus remained provincial throughout the early Stuart period. Although lieutenants were at times prepared to antagonize their neighbors in the king's behalf, for the most part their local ties took precedence. A lieutenant's (and even more, a deputy's) worth was a function of the esteem with which he was held by his countrymen. A centralizing lieutenancy that overrode the interests of the shire would have had very little standing. In this way the lieutenancy reflected a deeply held view about the proper balance between the county and Whitehall; the scale always tilted toward the provinces.

Despite the localist orientation of the lieutenancy, lord and deputy lieutenants provided services to the king as well as to their neighbors, and their efforts did not go unnoticed from either side. Their intercessions on behalf of local interests were rewarded with respect and obedience; members of the lieutenancy became acknowledged mediators in local disputes, nominators of Parliament men, and sought-after patrons. The king compensated them with the power of their office and his personal countenance. Easy access to Whitehall was the privilege of every lieutenant, and some, like the second earl of Exeter or the first earl of Newcastle, used it to advantage in the scramble for honor.

The attractions of the lieutenancy for the gentry survived the difficult period from 1627 to 1628, when members of Parliament, some motivated by factional disputes at home, and others, chiefly lawyers, attacked the institution. It was denounced as unconstitutional and arbitrary, but the charges failed to convince the political nation, though they had some resonance because of legitimate grievances over the costs of billeting. In the end, members saw no reason to weaken an institution that represented their interests with such efficiency.

The lieutenancy began the years of Personal Rule in a strong position; the nation was at peace, the parliamentary test had been passed, and without the prospect of a new assembly in the near future, the lieutenancy became one of the few points of contact between court and country, and thus the lord lieutenant's preeminent local standing was further enhanced. The onerous duties of the 1620s had been cast off—the lieutenancy of the next decade managed to avoid all responsibility for financing the king's government. In the 1620s raising money for loans and billets damaged the institution's standing; in the 1630s such tasks fell to others. It was the shrievalty, following the advent of ship money, that was forced to shoulder the heaviest load. Lieutenants and deputies undertook to improve the militia and enjoyed some success, but even here the problem of enforcing

compliance was passed on to the Privy Council. In some counties the lieutenancy circumvented royal instructions to press for improvements in the
trained bands, putting local interests above national policy.

The Personal Rule was not a golden age, however, and the tensions
it engendered came into the open following the first Bishops' War. War
against the Scots forced the lieutenancy once again into the distasteful business of raising troops and money and made neglecting the interests of the
crown impossible. Although the lieutenancy was successful in its first effort
to supply the king with an army, its second, in early 1640, exposed the
precariousness of Charles's regime. The divisions that appeared among the
gentry shattered the political harmony upon which the viability of the lieutenancy depended. Compromise and conciliation, which had always been
at the heart of the lieutenancy's success, by 1641–42 seemed impossible.
The lieutenancy effectively collapsed; Charles himself recognized the fragile state of the institution and illustrated his lack of confidence with the
issue of commissions of array in 1640.

The king's expedient was ineffective; the demise of the Caroline lieutenancy was a symptom of the fatal weakness that had overcome his government. Both Royalists and parliamentarians fought to maintain what each
side believed was the traditional constitution; indeed, the civil wars were
the result of a desperate attempt to restore unanimity to a divided society.
As the champion of consensus, the lieutenancy could play no significant
part in this process. Both sides had to invent new forms and new means
to accomplish the work of self-destruction. County committees, commissioners of array, and the New Model Army were the new instruments, and
the old were eclipsed.

The lieutenancy, at first simply overtaken by events and then officially
abolished, disappeared from the scene—but it was not forgotten. After
twelve years of experiment and crisis, an exhausted England attempted to
recapture the spirit of the old constitution, not through another instrument
of government or military dictatorship but through restoration. The settlement of 1660 was a valiant attempt to return the kingdom to its former
harmony, to an era when virtuous monarchs ruled over a pious people,
united by a single faith. Central to the rebirth of the constitution was the
return of many of those institutions that had fallen victim to the mid-
century revolution. And so, in one of Charles II's first acts, the lieutenancy
was revived. That this was done, and that the lieutenancy was not relegated
to the historical rubbish heap like the Court of Wards, Star Chamber, and
other relics of the prerogative, is testimony to its prewar importance. It

was a powerful symbol of the way things ought to be—locally controlled, consensus-oriented, and tradition-minded. These attributes assured the lieutenancy's revival.

Restoration does not mean recreation, however, and circumstances had changed greatly since the 1620s and 1630s. The office remained nominally the same; the lords lieutenant were assisted by deputies as before, their commissions were worded no differently, and the militia remained their primary duty. But the crown's priorities had changed; Charles I's lieutenancy had been concerned with Continental war, and as the Bishops' War and civil wars showed, its ability to crush enemies within was limited. The Restoration lieutenancy, however, was dedicated from the outset to the suppression of dissent. Fanatics and former republicans, enemies of the monarchy, were watched closely and harassed mercilessly. Rather than practicing a politics of inclusion and compromise, as had been the goal before the civil wars, the lieutenancy became the enforcer of a system that rigidly excluded a large part of society from participation.

This new mission is reflected in the composition of the new lieutenancy. Historians of the Restoration have stressed the crown's attempt to include many former enemies of Charles I in the settlement, but in the case of the lieutenancy, the principle of exclusion operated from the very beginning. With only a very few exceptions, commissions went to men of proven loyalty. Presbyterians, Cromwellians, and neutrals were kept out of the lieutenancy, despite their rank or status. Peers who before the civil wars would have unquestionably been awarded a lieutenancy—such as the earls of Bolingbroke and Pembroke—found their claims disregarded. Others were commissioned who before the wars could never have aspired to a lieutenancy. Mere barons like Lords Lovelace, Capel, and Newport were elevated to a position far higher than their social standing could account for. Deputy lieutenants too were subjected to an ideological test, and many country gentlemen, eminently qualified in other ways, were denied the places their forebears had filled.

The need for a trustworthy lieutenancy was self-evident; King Charles had many enemies and only a tiny standing army (many of whose members had served the usurpers) to protect the throne. The Cavalier interest was solidly behind the Restoration and, moreover, deserved some recognition for its suffering. Entrusting the lieutenancy to the Cavaliers was good policy and inevitable, for no other part of the political nation was as loyal. Charles may have been reluctant to entrust his government to his Cavalier supporters, but his abortive attempts to ameliorate the plight of dissenters by proclaiming an indulgence forced him to recognize that he could not hope to maintain himself in the face of their opposition.

Charles's understanding of the power of the Cavaliers to serve his interest and his own skill as a politician enabled him to harness that force in the crisis of his reign: the attempt to exclude the duke of York from the succession. Though few historians have remarked on it, the history of the lieutenancy in the 1670s and 1680s throws the importance of loyalism into sharp relief. Growing from the Cavalier reaction to the civil war and interregnum, a body of beliefs centering around the monarchy and Anglican church gradually coalesced in the reign of Charles II. Loyalists, or perhaps more accurately, Royalist Anglicans, outnumbered those of opposing views, and with the aid of the king, and using the lieutenancy as an instrument, fastened the dominance of their party on the kingdom with what seemed to be an iron grip. Although the elements of this dominance were present for some time, the Exclusion Crisis acted as the catalyst for a dramatic political change.

The rise of Exclusion as an issue was in part owing to the efficacy of the lieutenancy in destroying the immediate threat offered by Protestant dissenters to the monarchy. As the fear of dissent faded, the old terror of popery reasserted itself, and many began to see the prospect of a Roman Catholic sovereign as a threat to the constitution. Initially, few in the lieutenancy shared these fears; their attention remained focused on dissenters. The loyalist gentry and the king both saw the constitutional threat in the desire to meddle with the legal succession, and Charles enlisted the Royalist Anglican lieutenancy in his brother's cause.

The Exclusion Crisis was a great watershed in the reshaping of English politics and society. The expulsion of political dissenters from the body politic had begun in the 1660s with sectaries and Presbyterians, but the defeat of Exclusion demanded a thoroughly refined and politicized system. In Charles I's time mounting such a response would have been unimaginable; political dissent could not be marginalized, it had to be destroyed. Divisions in the kingdom as wide as those that separated Exclusionists and Yorkists resulted in civil war in the 1640s; in the 1670s they did not. The kingdom had come a long way from the day when dissent could be managed only through recourse to the sword. The peaceful resolution of the Exclusion Crisis was not achieved through the eradication of dissent, which would have been the goal of the 1620s, but rather was ensured through the erection of a new political system that recognized that although dissent was inescapable, it could be overborne through marginalization. Dissenters were to be identified and removed from influence everywhere; when they were denied favor, standing, and place, the threat they posed would wither and die.

The lieutenancy performed a key function in this new system. From the beginning of the crisis it was solidly behind the crown. Those few who supported Exclusion were quickly removed, and the lieutenancy became the crucial agent in enforcing the Royalist hegemony. Lords lieutenant propagandized in their shires, producing lists of loyal supporters as well as dissenters; they organized parliamentary selections; they nominated trustworthy magistrates. Exclusionists were hounded out of office by the lieutenancy, and the most tenacious among them fell victim to harassment and persecution.

Charles II, with the invaluable assistance of the lieutenancy, saved the constitution, but in doing so he paid a price. Most important, he was forced to tie himself evermore tightly to the values and priorities of Royalist Anglicans. Though inclined toward religious toleration himself, the king had to subordinate his desires to the Anglican monopoly that formed a central tenet of his allies' loyalist philosophy. He was faced with a straightforward choice: to protect the legitimate succession or to champion the interests of Catholics and dissenters. He chose the former course. Such compromises gave the Royalist Anglicans strength and influence independent of the crown. Charles was forced to concede authority to lords lieutenant that, if exercised in opposition to the crown, could be very dangerous; becoming political bosses in their regions, lieutenants were now offered many opportunities to use their power to build a personal interest. Some, such as the duke of Beaufort and earl of Bath in the west and the earl of Yarmouth in East Anglia, were extremely effective. As long as the interests of crown and lieutenants coincided, the king's position was secure. Without it, the dynasty was in peril.

Charles's death in February 1685 was followed by the smooth accession to the throne of the duke of York, and the allegiance of the Royalist Anglican interest was transferred from elder to younger brother without incident. The lieutenancy organized the return of a hyperloyal Parliament and rallied to the throne against the duke of Monmouth; it remained wholly committed to the Stuarts. The events of 1685 illustrate the strength of the interest Charles II had allied himself with; under a more serious threat than any since the Restoration, Royalists delivered the scepter to

James II. The king's enemies, denied influence and authority for so long, could not overcome him, and by the autumn of 1685 James II was at the height of his power.

The relationship between the crown and its erstwhile allies soured, however, over James's determination to restore his coreligionists to their rightful place in society. The circumvention of lieutenants in the appointment of new magistrates, the gradual insinuation of Catholics into office, and the apparent subversion of the Church of England's sacred hegemony alienated more and more of the king's former supporters. Facing the implacable opposition of Royalist Anglicans, James hoped to imitate his brother through the construction of a new political constellation that would turn the tables on the old establishment. Anglican lieutenants and deputies would be replaced by Catholics, and the Caroline ascendancy would be marginalized and replaced by a new Jacobean one.

The plan was in some respects a logical one; it was, after all, what Charles II had done to the Exclusionists. But unlike Charles, James refused to recognize that the Anglican interest was too powerful to overturn so easily. The experience of the late 1670s and early 1680s had made supporters of church and king even more important, as lords lieutenant built independent power bases of their own. Their replacement by Catholics of little stature and less interest was by no means a satisfactory solution, and the new men found themselves to be strangers in their own lieutenancies. The purges of 1686 and 1687 merely drove home the point that a victory for the king would be a very difficult proposition.

Whatever chances for success the king might have had were destroyed by the intervention of the Prince of Orange. Despite a desperate effort in October 1688 to reverse his course and restore the Royalist Anglican supremacy that had won him his throne in the first place, James discovered that it was too late. The years had created a powerful, as well as an independent, Anglican interest, and its most important guardian, the lieutenancy, threw its weight behind the prince. Those who did not, like the duke of Newcastle, were helpless to prevent the shift from Stuart to Orange. The defection of the lieutenancy was a decisive blow from which the king could not recover. The crown's servant had developed an agenda of its own.

The history of the lieutenancy from the reign of Charles I to the Glorious Revolution reflects the gradual emergence of the modern political system in England. The process was slow, marked by crises that accelerated or altered it—the mid-century revolution, Exclusion, the Orangist intervention. Lords lieutenant played an essential role throughout the period, and their part in the transformation of politics stretched beyond 1688. Many questions about the progress of this evolution, of course, remain unanswered. Future work might profitably focus on the continuing role of Royalist Anglicanism as an ideology, the place of the peerage in government, and the impact of the wars of the 1690s on politics and society. All these developments, however, have their roots in the fundamental transformations that took place in the decades following the Restoration—the problems they raise are the problems of the postrevolutionary state.

Surveying the changes of his lifetime, the duke of Leeds would have had cause for some satisfaction. A participant in all of the changes since the 1630s, Leeds was a great beneficiary of them, rising far higher than he could have expected, given his birth and circumstances. The premodern state into which he was born collapsed as a result of irreconcilable divisions that made political choices necessary. As an adult, Thomas Osborne was one of the men who built a new edifice on the ashes of the old, a system that neutralized dissent not through violence or civil war but politically, through expulsion. He lived through the elaboration of the new politics and witnessed its triumphs over Exclusion and James II's attack on the church. The duke led those who deprived James II of his throne by seizing the Yorkshire lieutenancy from Newcastle, and he welcomed the proclamation of a new monarch. Neither crisis provoked civil war; the chaos and bloodshed that had plagued the kingdom in the past were avoided. England had indeed, Leeds might have reflected, come a long way since 1642.

NOTES

Abbreviations

APC	*Acts of the Privy Council*
BIHR	*Bulletin of the Institute for Historical Research*
BL	British Library
Bodl.	Bodleian Library
BRO	Bedfordshire Record Office
ChRo	Cheshire Record Office
CRO	City of Chester Record Office
CSPD	*Calendar of State Papers, Domestic*
DNB	*Dictionary of National Biography*
DRO	Derbyshire Record Office
EHR	*English Historical Review*
GEC	George Edward Cokayne, *The Complete Peerage*
HLQ	*Huntington Library Quarterly*
HMC	Historical Manuscripts Commission
JBS	*Journal of British Studies*
JMH	*Journal of Modern History*
LAO	Lincolnshire Archive Office
LRO	Lancashire Record Office
NH	*Northern History*
NNRO	Norfolk and Norwich Record Office
NRO	Northamptonshire Record Office
PRO	Public Record Office
SJ	St. John Manuscripts
SRO	Staffordshire Record Office
THSLC	*Transactions of the Historical Society of Lancashire and Cheshire*
TRHS	*Transactions of the Royal Historical Society*
VCH	*Cheshire. Victoria County History of Cheshire*
VCH	*Leicestershire Victoria County History of Leicestershire*

Introduction

1. J. C. D. Clark has noted the paucity of historians working on the period 1660–1832 in his historiographical survey, *Revolution and Rebellion: State and Society in England in the Seventeenth and Eighteenth Centuries* (Cambridge, 1986), p. 7, although recently there has been a vigorous revival of Restoration studies, with a group of younger scholars adding to the valuable work of a previous generation. See my review essay, "Reconstructing the Restoration," *JBS* 29 (1990): 393–401.

2. The standard modern version of Pepys's *Diary* is Robert Latham and William Matthews's monumental edition, 10 vols. (Berkeley, 1970–83). The definitive edition of Evelyn's *Diary* is by E. S. deBeer, 6 vols. (Oxford, 1955). Celia Fiennes's *Journies* has been edited by Christopher Morris (London, 1947).

3. Evelyn, *Diary*. For the czar's riotous stay at Sayes Court, and the house in general, see John Bowle, *John Evelyn and His World* (London, 1981), p. 220. Pepy's description of the Great Fire can be found in his *Diary*, 7:267–79. The best biography of Pepys remains Sir Arthur Bryant, *Samuel Pepys*, 3 vols. (Cambridge, 1933–38).

4. Mark Kishlansky, *Parliamentary Selection: Social and Political Choice in Early Modern England* (Cambridge, 1986). Professor Kishlansky is currently engaged in a study of the origins of majoritarianism in English politics.

5. See John Miller, *Charles II* (London, 1991); Ronald Hutton, *Charles II* (Oxford, 1990); J. R. Jones, *Charles II: Royal Politician* (London, 1987); Hutton, *The Restoration* (Oxford, 1985); Paul Seaward, *The Cavalier Parliament and the Reconstruction of the Old Regime, 1661–67* (Cambridge, 1988), and also his *The Restoration, 1660–88* (New York, 1991), which contains an up-to-date bibliography; R. W. Harris, *Clarendon and the English Revolution* (Stanford, 1983).

6. The stress here will be on the lieutenancy—lords lieutenant and their deputies—rather than the militia itself, for the lieutenancy transcended the militia, which was only a part (though usually the main part) of its responsibilities. The militia has been treated at much greater length in Lindsay Boynton, *The Elizabethan Militia, 1558–1683* (London, 1967); J. R. Western, *The English Militia in the Eighteenth Century* (London, 1965); and in my Ph.D. dissertation, "The Lord Lieutenancy in Stuart England" (University of Chicago, 1988). Anthony Fletcher has also written a chapter on the Stuart militia in his *Reform in the Provinces: The Governance of Stuart England* (New Haven, 1985).

7. For the origins of the Tudor lieutenancy, see Gladys Scott Thomson, *The Lords Lieutenants in the Sixteenth Century* (London, 1923), and "The Origins and Growth of the Office of Deputy Lieutenant," *TRHS* 4th ser., 5 (1922): 150–66.

8. For the view emphasizing consensus, see Kishlansky, *Parliamentary Selection*. A recent synthesis of the opposing view may be found in Ann Hughes, *The Causes of the English Civil War* (London, 1991), esp. chap. 2.

9. See David Rannie, "Cromwell's Major Generals," *EHR* 10 (1895): 471–506. For a look at major generals in a local context, see S. K. Roberts, *Recovery and Restoration in an English County: Devon Local Administration, 1642–1670* (Exeter, 1985), esp. chaps. 2 and 3.

10. Anthony Fletcher has noted this important change in his study of Stuart local government, *Reform in the Provinces*.

11. Kishlansky describes the same process in electoral politics in *Parliamentary Selection*, pt. 2. In his discussion of Horatio, Lord Townshend, James Rosenheim shows how difficult the transition could be for an aristocrat used to older ways (*The Townshends of Raynham* [Middletown, Conn., 1989]). Andrew Coleby provides insights into the process on the county level in *Central Government and the Localities: Hampshire, 1649–1689* (Cambridge, 1987).

12. See Jonathan Scott, *Algernon Sidney and the Restoration Crisis, 1677–1683* (Cambridge, 1991), and his articles, "England's Troubles: Exhuming the Popish Plot," in Tim Harris, Paul Seaward, and Mark Goldie, eds., *The Politics of Religion in Restoration England* (Oxford, 1990), pp. 107–31, and "Radicalism and Restoration: The Shape of the Stuart Experience," *HJ* 31 (1988): 453–68.

13. P. J. Norrey reached the same conclusion in "The Relationship Between Central Government and Local Government in Dorset, Somerset, and Wiltshire, 1660–1688" (Ph.D. dissertation, Bristol University, 1988).

14. County studies are abundant. Some of the best are Anthony Fletcher, *A County Community in Peace and War: Sussex, 1600–1660* (London, 1975); T. G. Barnes, *Somerset, 1625–1640: A County's Government During the Personal Rule* (Cambridge, Mass., 1961); Ann Hughes, *Politics, Society, and Civil War in Warwickshire, 1620–1660* (Cambridge, 1987); Roberts, *Recovery and Restoration;* and Coleby, *Central Government and the Localities*. Of these, Coleby does most to place his county in a wider national context. Broader studies are Fletcher, *Reform in the Provinces;* G. C. F. Forster, "Government in Provincial England Under the Later Stuarts," *TRHS* 5th ser., 33 (1983): 29–48; Sir Geoffrey Elton, "Tudor Government: Points of Contact," in his *Studies in Tudor and Stuart Politics and Government,* 3 vols. (Cambridge, 1974–83).

15. For the bench during this period, see Norma Landau, *The Justices of the Peace, 1679–1760* (Berkeley, 1984), and Lionel K. Glassey, *Politics and the Appointment of Justices of the Peace, 1675–1720* (Oxford, 1979).

16. Although the idea of the Restoration as a critical point has grown stronger thanks to some of the recent works cited above, the view can be traced back to the works of scholars such as John Miller, John Kenyon, J. R. Jones, David Ogg, and, more remote still, George Trevelyan.

17. Christopher Hill, *The World Turned Upside Down* (Harmondsworth, 1972); Hill, *The Experience of Defeat: Milton and Some Contemporaries* (London, 1984).

18. See Bernard S. Capp, *The Fifth Monarchy Men: A Study in Seventeenth Century English Millenarianism* (London, 1972); Barry Reay, *The Quakers and the English Revolution* (New York, 1985); J. R. Jones, *The First Whigs: The Politics of the Exclusion Crisis, 1678–1683* (Oxford, 1961); Gary deKrey, *A Fractured Society: The Politics of London in the First Age of Party* (Oxford, 1987); and Jonathan Scott, *Algernon Sidney and the English Republic, 1623–77* (Cambridge, 1989). Richard Greaves has published two impressive books on Restoration radicalism: *Deliver Us from Evil* (Oxford, 1987), and *Enemies Under His Feet* (Stanford, 1990). A broad survey of religious dissent in England is Michael Watts, *The Dissenters: From the Restoration to the French Revolution* (Oxford, 1978).

19. Michael Heyd makes a similar point in his article "The Reaction to Enthusiasm in the Seventeenth Century: Towards an Integrative Approach," *JMH* 53 (1981): 258–80. He argues that studying the reaction of society to religious enthusiasts like the Quakers might reveal more about the seventeenth century than studies of the Quakers themselves (p. 259).

20. For divine right before the wars, see J. P. Sommerville, *Politics and Ideology in England, 1603–1640* (London, 1986). See also S. C. A. Pincus, "Popery, Trade, and Universal Monarchy: The Ideological Context of the Outbreak of the Second Anglo-Dutch War," *EHR* 105 (1992): 1–29, which stresses the importance of loyalist ideology in the 1660s, and Mark Goldie, "John Locke and Anglican Royalism," *Political Studies* 31 (1983): 86–102. John Kenyon has noted the continued strength of loyalist principles in the years after the revolution in his *Revolution Principles: The Politics of Party, 1689–1720* (Cambridge, 1977), esp. chaps. 5 and 6.

21. See J. C. D. Clark, *English Society, 1688–1832* (Cambridge, 1985). The best analysis of Filmer is James Daly, *Sir Robert Filmer and English Political Thought* (Toronto, 1979); see also Gordon Schochet, *Patriarchalism in English Political Thought* (Oxford, 1975), esp. chaps. 10 and 11.

22. For a good statement of this view, see Colin Lee, " 'Fanatic Magistrates': Religious and Political Conflict in Three Kent Boroughs, 1680–1684," *HJ* 35 (1992): 45–61.

23. See Mark Goldie's essay "The Political Thought of the Anglican Revolution," in Robert Beddard, ed., *The Revolutions of 1688* (Oxford, 1991), pp. 102–36, in which he skillfully analyzes the paradoxes of the Anglican reaction to James II's policies.

24. See below, Chapter 6, where this theme is developed more fully. For a thoughtful summary of recent historiographical trends on the Revolution of 1688, see John Morrill, "The Sensible Revolution," in Jonathan Israel, ed., *The Anglo-Dutch Moment* (Cambridge, 1991), pp. 73–104.

25. For the decline in the aristocracy's fortunes, see Lawrence Stone, *The Crisis of the Aristocracy* (Oxford, 1965), and David Cannadine's account of its final eclipse in *The Decline and Fall of the British Aristocracy* (New Haven, 1990).

26. For the aristocracy from the Restoration to the eighteenth century and beyond, see J. V. Beckett, *The Aristocracy in England, 1660–1914* (Oxford, 1986), and Cannadine, *Decline and Fall*.

1. The Early Stuart Lieutenancy

1. *VCH Leicestershire*, 2:106. Huntingdon's abrasive personality led to a series of feuds with local gentlemen, most spectacularly with Sir Henry Shirley. Thomas Cogswell is currently working on a study of Huntingdon's political life. Until the 1410s the family's principal sphere of influence was in the North Riding. For the family's move to Leicestershire and early importance there, see Eric Acheson, *A Gentry Community: Leicestershire in the Fifteenth Century* (Cambridge, 1992).

2. The castle's fortifications were razed in 1648. See P. Johnson, *The National Trust Book of British Castles* (New York, 1979), pp. 138–40.

3. *VCH Leicestershire*, 2:106–10.

4. Claire Cross, *The Puritan Earl: Henry Hastings, Third Earl of Huntingdon* (New York, 1966), pp. 64–66, 69–71. For the financial problems faced by other nobles at the same time, see Stone, *Crisis of the Aristocracy*, esp. pt. 2, and his case studies in *Family and Fortune: Studies in Aristocratic Finance in the Sixteenth and Seventeenth Centuries* (Oxford, 1973).

5. For a discussion of the concept of "worship" in early modern politics, see Mervyn James, *Society, Politics, and Culture: Studies in Early Modern England* (Cambridge, 1986).

6. Even his keepership of the long-vanished "forest" of Leicester was lost when the crown disaforested it in 1627. See *VCH Leicester*, 2:267; PRO, SP16/67/2, for the earl's account of his services to the crown.

7. HMC, *Hastings Manuscripts*, 4 vols. (London, 1928–47), 4:194. Years later Huntingdon greatly displeased the council by his unenthusiastic response to the forced loan, and for a time his dismissal seemed imminent (PRO, SP16/67/2). See Richard Cust, *The Forced Loan and English Politics* (Oxford, 1988).

8. Leicestershire muster return, PRO, SP16/32/64.

9. Leicestershire Accounts, PRO, SP16/70/70. For early Stuart musters in general, see Boynton, *Elizabethan Militia*. Barry Coward gives a more focused view in "The Lieutenancy of Lancashire and Cheshire in the Sixteenth and Early Seventeenth Centuries," *THSLC* 119 (1967): 39–64. See also Stater, "Lord Lieutenancy."

10. PRO, SP16/70/70. Huntingdon's lavish use of the county's funds provoked some dissent: see SP16/67/2, 65/3, 55/23.

11. *VCH Leicestershire*, 2:106–7. For early Stuart elections in general, see Kishlansky, *Parliamentary Selection;* J. K. Gruenfelder, *Influence in Early Stuart Elections* (Columbus, Ohio, 1981); and Derek Hirst, *The Representative of the People?* (Cambridge, 1975). For the influence of peers in particular, see Vivienne Hodges, "The Electoral Influence of the English Aristocracy" (Ph.D. dissertation, Columbia University, 1977), V. A. Rowe, "The Influence of the Earls of Pembroke on Parliamentary Elections, 1625–1641," *EHR* 50 (1935): 242–56; and Lawrence Stone, "The Electoral Influence of the Second Earl of Salisbury, 1614–68," *EHR* 71 (1956): 384–400.

12. PRO, SP16/83/29; HMC, *Hastings Manuscripts*, 4:206–7.

13. For the Tudor lieutenancy, see Thomson, *Lords Lieutenants*.

14. Ibid., pp. 31–32, 48. This fact might also reveal a resurgence of aristocratic power in the country, although, in theory at least, this power was under the immediate control of the crown. Although I do not agree with the position of J. S. A. Adamson, whose vision of the peerage ascribes more influence to it than I would, a study of the lieutenancy might modify the picture of an enervated nobility as presented in Stone, *Crisis of the Aristocracy*, chap. 5. For some of the controversy surrounding Adamson's views, see Mark Kishlansky, "Saye What?" *HJ* 33 (1990): 817–37; Adamson's reply, "Politics and Nobility in Civil War England," *HJ* 34 (1991), and Kishlansky, "Saye No More," *JBS* 30 (1991): 397–448. See also the exchanges in the *Times Literary Supplement* for February 7, 14, and 21, 1992.

15. C. W. McIlwain, ed., *The Political Works of James I* (Cambridge, Mass., 1918), pp. 24–25.

16. Ten thousand men raised for the Continent in 1624 were not actually in

the king's service, but rather were under the command of Count Mansfield, a military entrepreneur who fought on behalf of the elector Palatine. See Thomas Cogswell, *The Blessed Revolution: English Politics and the Coming of War, 1621–24* (Cambridge, 1989).

17. Nottinghamshire, the last exception, would have its own lieutenant by 1626, while the City was in the hands of a commission. Middlesex, another county that had traditionally been left in commission, had been awarded to Buckingham in 1622. See J. C. Sainty, ed., *Lieutenants of Counties, 1585–1682*, Bulletin of the Institute of Historical Research, Special Supplement 8 (London, 1970). John Chamberlain noted that "the lord of Buckingham is made lieutenant of Middlesex, a place I have not known given before unless it were to ye lord chancellor Hatton" (PRO, SP14/131/24).

18. Sainty, ed., *Lieutenants of Counties,* pp. 12, 21. Wallingford, who lived to an incredibly old age, remained as lieutenant until 1632, although he was joined with the earl of Holland in 1628.

19. For example, the earl of Newcastle received the lieutenancy of Derbyshire during the minority of the earl of Devonshire, a post he vacated upon Devonshire's majority in 1638.

20. See below, Chapter 3.

21. Sainty, ed., *Lieutenants of Counties,* pp. 37, 33. See also *DNB*, s.v. "Thomas Jermyn." Jermyn was joined with the distinctly un-common third earl of Suffolk. In 1603 there were 55 peers; by 1628 there were 126. See Stone, *Crisis of the Aristocracy,* pp. 99, 104.

22. Stone, *Crisis of the Aristocracy,* pp. 99, 104. Of those below the rank of earl, only Viscounts Conway and Wimbledon were appointed before 1640. Some of those counted as earls include heirs appointed jointly with their fathers and a few who were raised in the peerage after they assumed the office.

23. The single exception to the general equation of high rank and multiple lieutenancies was the marquis of Winchester, an ostentatious Roman Catholic. The third marquis, who died in 1598, was lieutenant of two counties. For more on officeholding in general under the early Stuarts, see Gerald Aylmer, *The King's Servants* (London, 1961).

24. Stone, *Crisis of the Aristocracy,* Appendix 8, p. 106.

25. Some of these, such as the earl of Sussex and Viscount Wallingford, had held significant posts in previous reigns but had been eclipsed by 1625. Interestingly, most of these peers were of the ten families with the smallest landed incomes of the lords lieutenant—Grey (earls of Kent), Hastings, Wentworth (earls of Cleveland), Radcliffe, Howard (earls of Nottingham), and Maynard. See ibid.

26. See the essays on the Privy Council and court politics in Kevin Sharpe, ed., *Faction and Parliament* (Oxford, 1978), especially Sharpe's "Parliamentary History: In or Out of Perspective," "The Earl of Arundel, His Circle, and the Opposition to the Duke of Buckingham," and Derek Hirst's "Court, Country, and Politics Before 1629."

27. For Suffolk, see *DNB,* s.v. "Theophilus Howard," and for Holland, ibid., "Henry Rich." Some aspects of Holland's subsequent career are detailed in Barbara

Donagan, "A Courtier's Progress: Greed and Consistency in the Life of the Earl of Holland," *HJ* 19 (1976): 317–53.

28. Lindsey was named general of all the king's horse at the outbreak of the civil war and died of his wounds at the battle of Edgehill.

29. The best account of the forced loan is Cust, *Forced Loan.*

30. PRO, SP16/334/51, 335/21. Hertford's lack of standing probably contributed to his ill luck in raising troops for the king in his former lieutenancies at the start of the civil wars. For this, see Joyce Malcolm, "A King in Search of Soldiers: Charles I in 1642," *HJ* 21 (1978): 251–74; and Ronald Hutton, *The Royalist War Effort* (London, 1982). Anthony Fletcher, *The Outbreak of the English Civil War* (New York, 1981), also examines the creation of a Royalist army.

31. See Clive Holmes, *Seventeenth Century Lincolnshire* (Lincoln, Eng., 1980), and *DNB,* s.v. "Robert Bertie, first earl of Lindsey."

32. Sir Anthony Hungerford, deputy lieutenant of Wiltshire, for example, resigned his commission in favor of his elder son, Edward, in 1624 (PRO, SP14/159/43).

33. Linda Peck, " 'For a King Not to Be Bountiful Were a Fault': Perspectives on Court Patronage in Early Stuart England," *JBS* 25 (1986):31–61. 33–35. See also her *Court Patronage and Corruption in Early Stuart England* (Boston, 1990). Sociological studies of exchange and patron-client relationships include Erich R. Wolf, "Kinship, Friendship, and Patron-Client Relationships in Complex Societies," in Michael Banton, ed., *The Social Anthropology of Complex Societies* (New York, 1966), pp. 1–22; S. N. Eisenstadt and Louis Roniger, "Patron-Client Relationships as a Model of Structuring Social Exchange," *Comparative Studies in Society and History* 22 (1980): 42–77.

34. Thomson, "The Origins and Growth of the Office of Deputy Lieutenant."

35. *APC,* 1625–26, p. 24. The order was made on April 12, barely a week after James's death.

36. HMC, *Lothian Manuscripts* (London, 1905), p. 83. Other seventeenth-century Norfolk papers, mostly of the Hobart family, have been noticed in the First and Seventeenth Reports of the HMC. Most of these papers are now in the Norwich and Norfolk Record Office (NNRO) in Norwich.

37. R. H. Silcock, "County Government in Worcestershire, 1603–1660" (Ph.D. dissertation, University of London, 1974), p. 61.

38. William Rye, ed., *State Papers Relating to Musters, Beacons, and Subsidies in Norfolk* (Norwich, 1907), p. 5. For the Book of the Peace, 1 Car I, see BL, Harl. MSS 1622. There were a total of forty-nine men on the Norfolk bench.

39. G. P. Higgins, "The Government of Early Stuart Cheshire," *NH* 12 (1976): 33; Hughes, *Politics, Society, and Civil War,* pp. 112–14.

40. W. E. A. Axon, *Echoes of Old Lancashire* (London, 1899), pp. 80–81. The Trafford family continued to reside at Trafford Hall well into the nineteenth century.

41. The number of hearths at Trafford Hall comes from the 1666 Hearth Tax assessment, in James Tait, ed., *Taxation in Salford Hundred, 1524–1802,* Chetham Society, n.s. 83 (1924), p. 86. Interestingly, the house with Lancashire's largest

hearth tax assessment was Lathom House, home of the earls of Derby, the lords lieutenant. It was charged with seventy-three hearths. The list of Trafford's property was made in 1639; see *The Royalist Composition Papers*, vol. 6, Record Society for the Publication of Original Documents Relating to Lancashire and Cheshire, vol. 95 (1941), pp. 219–20.

42. *Miscellanies Relating to Lancashire and Cheshire*, vol. 1, Record Society of Lancashire and Cheshire, vol. 12 (1885), p. 151.

43. Edward Baines, *History of the County Palatine and Duchy of Lancashire*, ed. James Croston, new ed. (London, 1888), 1:84–85.

44. Ernest Axon, ed., *Manchester Quarter Sessions*, vol. 1, 1616–22/23, Record Society of Lancashire and Cheshire, vol. 42 (1901), pp. v, 152; John Harland, ed., *The Lancashire Lieutenancy Under the Tudors and Stuarts*, Chetham Society, vols. 49–50 (1859), pp. 53 and passim.

45. Axon, *Echoes of Old Lancashire*, pp. 96–97, 101–2. Trafford was unusual in one respect: in the 1620s he converted to Catholicism. Nevertheless, he remained a deputy lieutenant and justice of the peace until at least 1639, when he ceased to be active in the county. He was prosecuted for his recusancy in 1639 and imprisoned as a Catholic by Parliament in 1642. He died in 1672. See D. J. Wilkinson, "The Commission of the Peace in Lancashire, 1603–1642," *THSLC* 132 (1983): 66. Trafford's ability to escape the penalties of his recusancy until 1639 may have been the result of his solid political and familial connections.

46. PRO, SP14/28/48 (Herefordshire), and SP14/33/2 (Shropshire).

47. Book of the Peace dating from May 1608, PRO, SP14/33/2.

48. BL, King's MSS, 265 f. 268v (for 1588), 308v (for 1605), 322v–323 (for 1615); and Rye, ed., *State Papers*, p. 5. For more on late Tudor Norfolk, see A. Hassell Smith, *County and Court: Government and Politics in Norfolk, 1558–1603* (Oxford, 1974).

49. Barnes, *Somerset*, p. 103; Higgins, "Government of Early Stuart Cheshire," p. 44.

50. For example, Berkshire had five in 1626, Northamptonshire eleven in 1627, Lincolnshire twelve in 1629, and Suffolk thirteen in 1625. See PRO, SP16/44/40; NRO, Brudenell MSS o/i/14; LAO, Yarborough MSS 8/2/3 (Pelham Family Papers); BL, Harl. MSS 305 f. 208v.

51. See *DNB*, s.v. "Henry Grey, first earl of Stamford."

52. Huntington Library, San Marino, Calif., Temple MSS, HA 12541. I would like to thank Professor Kishlansky for providing me with a photocopy of this document. Spencer's prediction came true after 1642, when the Hastings led the Royalist cause in Leicestershire and the Greys championed Parliament. See *VCH Leicestershire*, 2:108–15.

53. For an example of one lieutenant's intervention in a parliamentary election, see the exchange between Huntingdon and the corporation of Leicester in January 1621 (HMC, *Hastings Manuscripts*, 4:204). The earl of Rutland, lieutenant in neighboring Rutland, was also approached for other nonmilitary posts such as the clerkship of the peace (HMC, *Twelfth Report, Appendixes 4 and 5—Rutland Manuscripts*, 4 vols. [London, 1888–1903], 1:431).

54. For more about the lieutenants and parliamentary selections during Charles

I's reign, see Hodges, "Electoral Influence," pp. 96–105, and Kishlansky, *Parliamentary Selection*, pp. 15, 126. For developments during the Restoration period, when the lieutenancy would occupy a much more formal place in the distribution of office, see Chapters 3 and 6 below.

55. For the most complete account of the militia and trained bands, see Boynton, *Elizabethan Militia*, esp. chaps. 7 and 8.

56. PRO, SP16/381/66.

57. PRO, SP16/158/12, for the Huntingdonshire establishment; Barnes, *Somerset*, p. 115; Rye, ed., *State Papers*, p. 31; and PRO, SP16/241/55. More often these minor posts were filled by the captain himself. A typical Norfolk company of foot was composed of one hundred men and several officers (NNRO, Walsingham MSS xvii/2 (William de Grey's Official Letterbook).

58. This was the case in virtually every county with a militia force large enough to be divided into regiments. See Barnes, *Somerset*, p. 115; Rye, ed., *State Papers*, p. 31; BL Add. MSS 21922 (Hampshire); BL Harl. MSS 703 (Sussex). This lieutenancy book was probably the property of Sir Walter Covert, deputy lieutenant. Covert also collected official correspondence to other local officers such as magistrates and sheriffs in this volume.

59. Except on those few occasions when they had to compete with resident peers, who in this period rarely served as colonels.

60. NNRO, Walsingham MSS xvii/2, ff. 1–3.

61. Deputy lieutenants of Norfolk to trained band captains, March 26, 1626, Bodl. Tanner MSS 72/118.

62. Fletcher, *County Community*, p. 177. Barnes noted the same phenomenon in Somerset. See *Somerset*, pp. 116–17.

63. Two other offices in the lord lieutenant's gift, the provost marshal and muster master, are discussed in Lindsay Boynton, "The Tudor Provost Marshal," *EHR* 77 (1962): 437–55, and Esther Cope, "The Debate over Muster Masters," *Huntington Library Quarterly* 45 (1982): 271–84.

64. *APC*, 1618–19, p. 363. The amounts of powder ranged from 3 lasts 15 hundredweight for Norfolk to ¼ last 125 pounds for Leicestershire and Rutland. A last was a measure amounting to about 2,000 pounds.

65. Boynton, *Elizabethan Militia*, chap. 8.

66. HMC, *Buccleuch and Queensbury Manuscripts*, 3 vols. (London, 1899–1926), 3:190–93, 199; PRO, SP16/104/1.

67. PRO, SP16/33/75, 31/101, 33/126. See also Margaret Cavendish, Duchess of Newcastle, *Life of William Cavendish, Duke of Newcastle* (London, 1667), p. 6.

68. PRO, SP16/312/66. See, for instance, the accounts for Leicestershire, SP 16/70/70.

69. PRO, SP16/72/24. A considerable amount of money must have been raised in Cheshire because the quality of its trained bands improved dramatically in the later 1620s and 1630s. See John S. Morrill, *Cheshire, 1630–60: County Government and Society* (Oxford, 1974), pp. 26–27, and Higgins, "Government of Early Stuart Cheshire." For some of the difficulties involved in maintaining standards, see Richard Stewart, "Arms Accountability in the Early Stuart Militia," *BIHR* 57 (1984): 113–17, and J. N. N. McGurk, "The Clergy and the Militia, 1580–

1610," *History* n.s., 60 (1975): 198–210. For more on the complexities involved in rating the local communities for militia money, see Stater, "Lord Lieutenancy"; A. Hassell Smith, "Militia Rates and Militia Statutes, 1558–1563,"and in Peter Clark, A. G. R. Smith, and Nicholas Tyacke, eds., *The English Commonwealth, 1547–1640: Essays in Politics and Society* (New York, 1979), pp. 93–110; Boynton, *Elizabethan Militia.*

70. Westmorland and Cumberland were two salient examples of complete neglect; in these counties, the militia seems to have been virtually nonexistent by the 1630s. See below, Chapter 2.

71. PRO, SP14/4/55. For a more detailed account of the militia in King James's reign, see Boynton, *Elizabethan Militia,* chap. 7.

72. For Northampton as lord lieutenant, see Hughes, *Politics, Society, and Civil War,* pp. 59–60, 114, 135. The extent of Derby's activity can be seen in CRO, Earwaker MSS 63/2/6. For Newcastle, see Cavendish, *Life of William Cavendish,* and the many letters from him about trained band matters that have survived in the state papers. For Maltravers, see Rye, ed., *State Papers,* passim; BL, Add. MSS 27447 (Paston Correspondence).

73. HMC, *Twelfth Report, Appendixes 4 and 5,* 1:417.

74. PRO, SP16/70/70; Joan Wake and H. I. Longden, eds., *The Montagu Musters Book,* Northamptonshire Record Society Publications, vol. 7 (1932–33), p. 84. Among prizes for marksmanship established were those in Derbyshire in 1624 (PRO, SP14/158/18, 175/11) and Cornwall in 1626 (SP16/33/111). For examples of trivial expenses see the Leicestershire trained band accounts in SP16/70/70, and Wake and Longden, eds., *Montagu Musters Book,* pp. 87, 109.

75. For the lieutenancy's role in civil affairs before the turn of the seventeenth century, see Thomson, *Lords Lieutenants,* esp. chap. 5.

76. See Cust, *Forced Loan,* for the lieutenancy's involvement in this controversial duty. In 1607 the government required the deputy lieutenants to organize the sale of ten thousand mulberry trees to their neighbors at six shillings per hundred (PRO, SP14/26/6).

77. BL Lansdowne MSS 89/69; *APC, 1613–14,* p. 109. For an early instance of the lieutenancy's role in mediation, see David Dean, "Parliament, Privy Council, and Local Politics in Elizabethan England: The Yarmouth-Lowestoft Fishing Dispute," *Albion* 22 (1990): 46.

78. PRO, SP16/71/32; PC2/42/406, 47/348.

79. This was the phrase the council used when ordering the earl of Bath to settle a dispute in Devon in 1615 (*APC, 1615–16,* p. 58).

80. For the consequences of local faction, see Barnes's description of the Poulett-Phelips feud in *Somerset,* and my essay "War and the Structure of Politics: Lieutenancy and the Campaign of 1628," in Mark Fissel, ed., *War and Government in Britain, 1598–1650* (Manchester, 1991), pp. 87–109.

81. Rye, ed., *State Papers,* p. 190.

82. HMC, *Twelfth Report, Appendixes 4 and 5,* 1:430; *APC, 1613–14,* p. 247; *APC, 1619–21,* p. 132; PRO, SP16/354/92.

83. For the growth of central-local tensions, see Perez Zagorin, *The Court and the Country* (New York, 1970). For a thoughtful assessment of recent works deal-

ing with provincial government, see Derek Hirst's review essay, "Local Affairs in Seventeenth Century England," *HJ* 32 (1989): 437–48.

84. HMC, *Buccleuch and Queensbury Manuscripts*, 3:148.

85. Rye, ed., *State Papers*, p. 178.

86. For a view of the London lieutenancy's response to disorder, see K. J. Lindley, "Riot Prevention and Control in Early Stuart London," *TRHS* 5th ser., 33 (1983): 109–26.

87. For Woodbridge, see PRO, PC2/38/239, 251. For Malden, see John Walter, "Grain Riots and Popular Attitudes to the Law: Maldon and the Crisis of 1629," in John Brewer and John Styles, eds., *An Ungovernable People: The English and Their Law in the Seventeenth and Eighteenth Centuries* (New Brunswick, N.J., 1980), 47–84; *APC*, 1631–32, p. 382; PRO, PC2/41/27, 44; *APC*, 1631–32, pp. 284, 294; PRO, SP16/193/11; Silcock, "County Government in Worcestershire," pp. 119, 162; PRO, PC2/41/509. See also Andrew Charlesworth, ed., *An Atlas of Rural Protest in England, 1548–1900* (London, 1983).

88. *APC*, May 1629–May 1630, p. 24; PRO, PC2/39/265.

89. For a general survey of agricultural conditions, see Joan Thirsk, ed., *Chapters from the Agrarian History of England and Wales, 1500–1750*, 5 vols. (Cambridge, 1990), esp. vol. 1, *Economic Change: Wages, Profits and Rents*, ed. P. J. Bowden, and vol. 4, *Agricultural Markets and Trade*, ed. John Chartres.

90. BRO, SJ MSS 1328 (letters of Sir Rowland Watson, deputy lieutenant of Northamptonshire); *APC*, June 1630–June 1631, pp. 268–69.

91. PRO, SP16/363/27.

92. For the Book of Orders, see Paul Slack, "Books of Orders: The Making of English Social Policy, 1577–1631," *TRHS* 5th ser., 30 (1980): 1–22; and B. W. Quintrell, "The Making of Charles I's Book of Orders," *EHR* 95 (1980): 553–72.

93. See, for example, Exeter's exemption of eight Northamptonshire gentlemen for assessments, dated September 25, 1626 (HMC, *Tenth Report, Appendix 6* [London, 1887], p. 114).

94. For some samples, see HMC, *Buccleuch and Queensbury Manuscripts*, 3:148 (poverty), p. 161 (the harvest), p. 202 (refractory militiamen). Among many other rebukes delivered by the council, see *APC*, March 1623–March 1626, pp. 69–70, 163–64, 484; *APC*, September 1627–June 1628, pp. 140, 260–61.

95. For the impact of some of these policies, see Cust, *Forced Loan;* Cope, "Debate over Muster Masters," and Boynton, *Elizabethan Militia*, chap. 8.

2. War and the End of the Old Regime

1. See C. S. R. Russell, "Monarchies, Wars, and Estates in England, France, and Spain, c. 1580–1640," *Legislative Studies Quarterly* 7 (1982): 205–19, and Ann Hughes on the concept of functional breakdown in *Causes of the English Civil War*, esp. chap. 1.

2. For a detailed look at the exact militia and its fate, see Boynton, *Elizabethan Militia*, and Stater, "Lord Lieutenancy."

3. See Michael Roberts, "The Military Revolution," in Roberts, *Essays in Swedish*

History (Oxford, 1967), and Geoffrey Parker, *The Military Revolution: Military Innovation and the Rise of the West, 1500–1800* (Cambridge, 1988).

4. I am following C. R. S. Russell here; see his *Parliaments and English Politics, 1621–29* (Oxford, 1979), pp. 204–52. For a different perspective on the background to this war, see Cogswell, *Blessed Revolution,* and the essays in Richard Cust and Ann Hughes, eds., *Conflict in Early Stuart England* (London, 1989).

5. S. R. Gardiner, *A History of England from the Accession of James I to the Outbreak of the English Civil War,* 10 vols. (London, 1884–1909), 6:3.

6. *APC,* 1625–26, p. 168.

7. CRO, Earwaker MSS 63/2/6 ff. 6v, 7–10; HMC, *Tenth Report, Appendix 6,* p. 112; Silcock, "County Government in Worcestershire," p. 223; BL, Add. MSS 21922 ff. 16–17; *APC,* 1625–26, pp. 454–55. Assessments in Dorset totaled £1,788/6/8 (ibid., p. 288). The various county assessments ranged from the highest (Middlesex), £10,335, to the lowest (Huntingdonshire), £555 (PRO, E401/2586).

8. HMC, *Tenth Report, Appendix* 6 (Lord Braye's MSS), p. 113. Exeter offered to make up the shortfall himself if necessary.

9. PRO, SP16/9/42.

10. PRO, SP16/34/76. Some assessments and a few related papers for the loan may be found in PRO, E401/2590.

11. *APC,* 1625–26, pp. 276, 288.

12. Hughes, *Politics, Society, and Civil War,* p. 163.

13. HMC, *Tenth Report, Appendix* 6 (Lord Braye's MSS), p. 112.

14. PRO, SP16/10/61, 9/68.

15. PRO, SP16/18/72I; BL, Loan MSS 29, vol. 202, f. 197 (Portland Papers). Needless to say, the Privy Council was not convinced by this argument.

16. So wrote the deputies of Glamorganshire when explaining the poverty of their shire (PRO, SP16/18/5).

17. See Paul Slack, *The Impact of the Plague in Early Modern England* (London, 1985), for a general discussion of the disruption caused by this epidemic. For discussions of the nature—often hard to recover—of popular sentiment in the localities, see F. J. Levy, "How Information Spread Among the Gentry, 1550–1640," *JBS* 21 (1982): 11–34; and Richard Cust, "News and Politics in Early Seventeenth Century England," *Past and Present* 112 (1986): 60–90.

18. Richard Cust, "Charles I, the Privy Council, and the Forced Loan," *JBS* 24 (1985): 209–12.

19. Compulsion in loans and benevolences was not unknown; for earlier examples, see G. L. Harriss, "Aids and Benevolences," *HJ* 6 (1963): 1–19. See also Harriss, "Medieval Doctrines in the Debates on Supply, 1610–1629," in Kevin Sharpe, ed., *Faction and Parliament* (Oxford, 1978), pp. 73–103.

20. See Derek Hirst, "The Privy Council and the Problem of Enforcement in the 1620s," *JBS* 18 (1978): 46–66, for the council's difficulties in enforcing its will upon recalcitrant provincials. Compare Hirst with Kevin Sharpe, "Crown, Parliament, and Locality: Government and Communication in Early Stuart England," *EHR* 101 (1986): 321–50.

21. Some lieutenants and deputies were sacked for opposing the loan, including

the earl of Warwick in Essex and four Northamptonshire deputies (*APC*, September 1627–June 1628, p. 98; Northamptonshire lieutenancy commission, BL, Additional Charters, Charter 2146; Althorp MSS, Box A3, Sir William Spencer to Exeter, February 14, 1626, and March 1626).

22. For the king's persistent refusal to recognize the political costs of his actions in this period, see L. J. Reeve, *Charles I and the Road to Personal Rule* (Cambridge, 1989); the same disastrous habits are apparent in Peter Donald, *An Uncounselled King: Charles I and the Scottish Troubles* (Cambridge, 1990). C. S. R. Russell addresses the same issue in his *Causes of the English Civil War* (Oxford, 1990). For an interesting picture of Charles's lack of sensitivity to the desires of his people, see Judith Richards, " 'His Nowe Majestie' and the English Monarchy: The Kingship of Charles I Before 1640," *Past and Present* 113 (1986): 70–96.

23. *APC*, 1625–26, p. 146; BL, Harl. MSS 6988 f. 7.

24. BL, Add. MSS 21922 f. 9 (Sir Thomas Norton's Letterbook).

25. Bodl., Firth MSS c4, pp. 147, 155, 156 (Essex Lieutenancy Book).

26. *APC*, 1625–26, p. 182.

27. Fletcher, *County Community*, p. 189.

28. *APC*, June–December 1626, p. 21.

29. Boynton, *Elizabethan Militia*, p. 245. For more on the state of coastal defense in this period, see David Hebb, "The English Government and the Problem of Piracy, 1616–1642" (Ph.D. dissertation, University of London, 1985), and Howard Colvin, ed., *History of the King's Works*, vol. 4 (London, 1982).

30. There was always the potential for financial corruption as well, though no deputy lieutenant was ever found to have taken bribes. Most deputies were far too well off to be tempted by such petty crimes, but no doubt some of the constables and clerks in their employ were.

31. For the problem of poverty in early modern England, see A. L. Beier, *Masterless Men: The Vagrancy Problem in England, 1560–1640* (New York, 1985).

32. *APC*, January–August 1627, p. 480.

33. In 1627, for example, orders to press men were issued in February (2,000), April (1,500), May (2,000), June (1,400), July (2,000), August (400), and September (2,000) (ibid., pp. 100, 216, 271, 374, 455, 480; *APC*, September 1627–June 1628, p. 60). For lists of county quotas for men to be sent, see PRO, SP16/63/92I. See S. J. Stearns, "Conscription and English Society in the 1620s," *JBS* 11 (1972): 1–23, and my "The Lord Lieutenancy on the Eve of the Civil Wars: The Impressment of George Plowright," *HJ* 29 (1986): 279–96. For the work of the constables see Joan Kent, *The English Village Constable, 1580–1642* (Cambridge, 1986), and Kent, "The English Village Constable, 1580–1642: The Nature and Dilemmas of the Office," *JBS* 20 (1981): 26–49.

34. An example, of Exeter to the Northamptonshire deputies, orders one hundred men to be sent to Plymouth by September 12, 1625 (BRO, SJ1289).

35. PRO, SP116/64/38.

36. BL, Add. MSS 21922 f. 96 (Norton Letterbook).

37. PRO, SP16/58/35; Helen Stocks and W. H. Stevenson, eds., *Records of the Borough of Leicester* (Cambridge, 1923), pp. 222–23.

38. PRO, SP16/66/53; *APC*, January–August 1627, p. 335.

39. PRO, SP16/82/86. The deputies in Sussex raised seventeen hundred men between 1624 and 1628 (Fletcher, *County Community*, p. 193).

40. PRO, SP16/66/41.

41. *APC,* January–August 1627, p. 304.

42. PRO, SP16/73/44; *APC,* January–August 1627, pp. 239, 250, 257; PRO, SP16/76/17, 61/56, 63/76, 78/2. Some counties managed to get most of their men (though Pembrokeshire was the only one to provide all of its quota of fifty). Ninety-five of one hundred came from Herefordshire, forty-seven of fifty from Huntingdonshire and Nottinghamshire. More, however, performed poorly— Bedfordshire could only manage twelve of thirty-eight, Buckinghamshire thirty-seven of fifty, and Staffordshire seventy-two of one hundred.

43. HMC, *Fourth Report—House of Lords Manuscripts* (London, 1874), p. 6. From May to October 1627, the city of Reading spent £42/0/9 on raising troops (J. M. Guilding, ed., *Reading Records: Diary of the Corporation,* 4 vols. [London, 1895], 2:472).

44. LRO, MF13/3, p. 25 (Sir Alexander Rigby's Lieutenancy Book, 1627–40).

45. Rye, ed., *State Papers,* p. 60.

46. See Lindsay Boynton, "Billeting: The Example of the Isle of Wight," *EHR* 74 (1959): 24–40.

47. PRO, SP16/84/12. See C. S. R. Russell's essay on Caroline finance in Russell, ed., *The Origins of the English Civil War* (London, 1973), pp. 91–118, and also his Ford lecture, "The Poverty of the Crown and the Weakness of the King," in his *Causes of the English Civil War,* pp. 161–84.

48. PRO, SP16/52/49, 41/133, 35/7, 62/57.

49. PRO, SP16/82/82.

50. BL, Add. MSS 21922 f. 31 (Norton Letterbook).

51. PRO, SP16/59/31. The Essex deputies faced a particularly volatile situation; riots involving billeted soldiers and exasperated townspeople broke out in Witham and threatened elsewhere. See Gerald Aylmer, "St. Patrick's Day, 1628, in Witham, Essex," *Past and Present* 61 (1973): 139–48.

52. Robert C. Johnson et al., eds., *Commons Debates, 1628,* 6 vols. (New Haven, 1977–83), 2:79.

53. See Stater, "War and the Structure of Politics," pp. 87–110. For the Cornish election, see Kishlansky, *Parliamentary Selection,* pp. 74–75. See also Harold Hulme, *The Life of Sir John Eliot* (London, 1957).

54. For the Petition of Right, see John Guy, "The Petition of Right Reconsidered," *HJ* 25 (1982): 289–312.

55. See Reeve, *Charles I and the Road to Personal Rule,* esp. chap. 1.

56. See Smith, "Militia Rates," pp. 93–110.

57. See Lindsay Boynton, "Martial Law and the Petition of Right," *EHR* 79 (1964): 255–84. Boynton found no evidence to indicate that a single soldier or civilian was executed under martial law. He argues convincingly that deputy lieutenants were extremely reluctant to enforce it.

58. See PRO, SP16/150/74, for Sir Bernard Grenville's bitter complaints about the state of affairs in Cornwall.

59. For a detailed treatment of the period immediately following the dissolution of the Parliament of 1629, see Reeve, *Charles I and the Road to Personal Rule,* and Kevin Sharpe, *The Personal Rule of Charles I* (New Haven, 1992).

60. For the lieutenancy's peacetime duties, see above, Chapter 1.

61. See Boynton, *Elizabethan Militia,* chap. 8. For a local perspective, see D. P. Carter, "The Exact Militia in Lancashire, 1623–1640," *NH* 11 (1975): 87–106.

62. Boynton, *Elizabethan Militia,* p. 271, and chap. 8, passim. For a more positive view of the exact militia, see Sharpe, *Personal Rule.*

63. For samples of the council's actions against defaulters, see *APC,* June 1630– June 1631, items 85, 741, 775, 781, 910, 997, and 998. For examples of deputies intervening for a defaulter, see *CSPD,* 1634–35, p. 486; *CSPD,* 1633–34, pp. 261, 475, 561. For a more detailed view of the problem of militia defaulters, see Stater, "Lord Lieutenancy," and Boynton, *Elizabethan Militia,* pp. 272–80.

64. Boynton describes this incident in *Elizabethan Militia,* pp. 271–72; for the Privy Council's decision, see PRO, PC2/45, ff. 69, 101.

65. See C. S. R. Russell, *The Fall of the British Monarchies, 1637–42* (Oxford, 1991), for a detailed narrative of the political history of this period.

66. For Charles I's rule in Scotland, see Maurice Lee, *The Road to Revolution: Scotland Under Charles I, 1625–37* (Urbana, 1985). Donald, *Uncounselled King,* offers an excellent account of the high politics of the crisis. See also Russell, *Fall of the British Monarchies,* and Mark Fissel's forthcoming book about the Bishops' Wars, to be published by Cambridge University Press.

67. LRO, MF13/3 pp. 138, 140b (Rigby Lieutenancy Book).

68. PRO, SP16/355/61. The Cheshire lieutenancy bought more than three lasts of powder in September (SP16/354/123).

69. PRO, SP16/405/pt. II. Although the lists for two hundreds were missing, Suffolk provided a roll of 19,712 names (SP16/411).

70. The freehold band was composed of men who were not in the trained bands but were still liable for military service—a kind of untrained reserve. For the scarf order, see LRO, MF13/3 p. 142 (Rigby Lieutenancy Book).

71. PRO, SP16/410/102.

72. SP16/410/32, 412/144, 410/172.

73. The king to the Northamptonshire lieutenancy, NRO, Finch-Hatton Papers, 2843.

74. John Rushworth, *Historical Collections,* 7 vols. (London, 1659–1701), 3:926– 27. The number of foot is given as 19,614 and horse as 3,260.

75. PRO, SP16/417/41, 409/105.

76. For the early modern military experience, see Charles Carlton, *Going to the Wars: The Experience of the British Civil Wars, 1638–51* (London, 1992).

77. Woodford wrote this in April 1639. See John Fielding, "Opposition to the Personal Rule of Charles I: The Diary of Robert Woodford, 1637–41," *HJ* 31 (1988): 769–88. Ann Hughes discusses another group of godly gentlemen who favored the Scots in "Thomas Dugard and His Circle in the 1630s: A Parliamentary-Puritan Connection?," *HJ* 29 (1986): 771–93.

78. Rushworth, *Historical Collections,* 3:1046–50.

79. Lancashire, for example, raised £2,700 for the army from December 1638 to May 1639 (LRO, MF13/3 pp. 138, 140b, 148b, 151b, 152b [Rigby Lieutenancy Book]).

80. PRO, SP16/417/109.

81. See also Carlton, *Going to the Wars,* chap. 2. Carlton argues that although the army was adequately equipped and clothed, it was badly trained.

82. BL, Add. MSS 15084 f. 2.

83. For an overall view of the decline and ultimate collapse of the king's government, see Fletcher, *Outbreak of the English Civil War,* and Russell, *Causes of the English Civil War* and *Fall of the British Monarchies.*

84. PRO, PC2/51/393–400. For the price of horses in general, see LRO, MF13/3 (Rigby Lieutenancy Book), and P. W. Edwards, *The Horse Trade in Tudor and Stuart England* (Cambridge, 1988).

85. Peterborough was named lieutenant immediately after Exeter's death in July (Sainty, ed., *Lieutenants of Counties,* pp. 28–29).

86. HMC, *Ninth Report, Appendix 2—Woodforde MSS* (London, 1883–84), p. 498; HMC, *Twelfth Report, Appendix 9—Ketton Manuscripts; Beaufort Manuscripts* (London, 1891), p. 491. For some of the circumstances surrounding this extraordinary election, see Fielding, "Opposition to the Personal Rule of Charles I," and his "Conformists, Puritans, and the Church Courts: The Diocese of Peterborough, 1603–42" (Ph.D. dissertation, Birmingham University, 1989).

87. See, for example, Sir Rowland St. John's draft letter in Elmes's behalf, BRO, SJ1363.

88. HMC, *Ninth Report, Appendix 2,* p. 498.

89. PRO, SP16/449/4, 473/24. Interestingly, the council—in the king's presence—examined thirteen men accused of the disruption and allowed itself to be convinced that the shouts of "No deputy lieutenants" were not meant against the lieutenancy per se but rather were to distinguish one candidate—who just happened to be a deputy lieutenant—from another. The men were released unpunished (SP16/473/24).

90. PRO, SP16/450/24. The deputies in Kent suffered as well; as Sir Edward Dering said, "In times so desperate I would contribute no help to any privy councillor or deputy lieutenant." It is interesting that by September, Dering himself was a deputy lieutenant for Kent, and this seemingly had no effect on his decision to stand for the county in the election for the Long Parliament. See also Alan Everitt, *The Community of Kent and the Great Rebellion, 1640–1660* (Leicester, 1966), esp. chaps. 3 and 4; ibid., p. 130, n. 111.

91. Quoted in Russell, *Fall of the British Monarchies,* p. 102.

92. Gardiner, *History of England,* 9:101, 104–5, and see also C. S. R. Russell, "The Scottish Party in English Parliaments, 1640–42," *Historical Research* 66 (1993): 48.

93. Gardiner, *History of England,* 9:114–15, 117–18; Russell, *Fall of the British Monarchies,* pp. 122–23.

94. PRO, SP16/451/74, 457/23. The county was marginally better disposed toward traditional demands such as coat and conduct money than the innovative such as draft horses.

95. PRO, SP16/451/5.

96. BL, Add. MSS 26781 f. 73 (Sir Edward Dering's Lieutenancy Book, 1630–40).

97. PRO, SP16/454/85. One of the few counties to report any success was Leicestershire, where the earl of Huntingdon managed to raise four hundred men and even equipped them with knapsacks (SP16/458/4).

98. PRO, SP16/466/42; see also BL Add. MSS 34729, f. 104.

99. PRO, SP16/466/42.

100. PRO, SP16/457/5.

101. Quoted in Paul Seaver, *Wallington's World: A Puritan Artisan in Seventeenth Century London* (Stanford, 1985), pp. 163–64.

102. Gardiner, *History of England*, 9:153.

103. CRO, Earwaker MSS 63/2/6 f. 18v.

104. PRO, SP16/453/11; for Suffolk, see Gardiner, *History of England*, 9:160.

105. PRO, SP16/455/30.

106. PRO, SP16/455/71.

107. BL, Add. MSS 26781 f. 104 (Hampshire Lieutenancy Book), and ibid., f. 98.

108. PRO, SP16/454/71.

109. PRO, PC2/52/663; SP16/454/85.

110. PRO, SP16/465/57, 454/71, 468/113; PC2/52/586–87.

111. PRO, SP16/458/77.

112. Gardiner, *History of England*, 9:162.

113. PRO, PC2/52/610, 700–701.

114. Rushworth, *Historical Collections*, 4:98–99.

115. Russell, *Fall of the British Monarchies*, pp. 234–35.

116. Ibid., pp. 298–99.

117. For an account of the formation of the Royalist army and the use of the commissions of array, see Hutton, *Royalist War Effort*.

118. Gardiner, *History of England*, 9:312–17, 400–401; Russell, *Fall of the British Monarchies*, pp. 392–96, 351. For the complete text of the ten propositions, see S. R. Gardiner, ed., *The Constitutional Documents of the Puritan Revolution, 1625–1660*, 3d ed. (Oxford, 1906), pp. 163–66, and Rushworth, *Historical Collections*, 4:66.

119. Russell, *Fall of the British Monarchies*, p. 357. Quote from Lois Schwoerer, "The Fittest Subject for a King's Quarrel: The Militia Controversy, 1641–42," *JBS* 11 (1971): 49.

120. For the text of the Remonstrance, see Gardiner, ed., *Constitutional Documents*, pp. 202–32.

121. Schwoerer, "Fittest Subject," pp. 47–48. The bill did not proceed beyond a second reading.

122. *Journal of the House of Lords*, 4:518–19, 534.

123. For a list of the parliamentary lieutenants see *Journal of the House of Lords*, 4:577–79. For Vane's nomination, see ibid., p. 578. Say was named lieutenant of Cheshire after Lord Strange committed himself to the king's cause (ibid., p. 670).

124. Quoted in Fletcher, *Outbreak of the English Civil War*, p. 278. For Bankes's

efforts to mediate between king and Parliament, see Russell, *Fall of the British Monarchies*, p. 513.

125. Fletcher, *Outbreak of the English Civil War*, p. 279.

126. Russell, *Fall of the British Monarchies*, p. 512. For the text of the king's proclamation, see Gardiner, ed., *Constitutional Documents*, pp. 248–49.

127. Russell, *Fall of the British Monarchies*, p. 512.

128. For the Kentish scheme see ibid., p. 472n.

129. For examples of parliamentary harassment of lords lieutenant, see *Journal of the House of Lords*, 4:663. See also Fletcher, *Outbreak of the English Civil War*, pp. 334, 355.

130. See Mark Kishlansky, *The Rise of the New Model Army* (Cambridge, 1977).

131. Commission of Lieutenancy, first earl of Exeter, 1603, in Wake and Longden, eds., *Montagu Musters Book*, p. 217.

132. See Hutton, *Royalist War Effort*, and Joyce Malcolm, *Caesar's Due: Loyalty and King Charles I*, Royal Historical Society Studies in History, vol. 38 (1983), esp. chaps. 2 and 3.

3. Restoration, 1660–1663

1. For example, the Derbyshire lieutenancy created a very complex assessment routine involving a detailed survey of the entire county, hundred by hundred. See DRO, Constable's Accounts, 1648–77, D63, pp. 44–60.

2. Norwich Lieutenancy Letter Book, July 18, 1664, NNRO. This book has been published, with an informative introduction by R. S. Dunn, by the Norfolk Record Society, Publications, vol. 45 (1977).

3. Ibid., July 19, 1664.

4. Kishlansky, *Rise of the New Model Army*, esp. chap. 2; Everitt, *Community of Kent*, pp. 128–30. For two important studies of the civil war and interregnum in the provinces, see Hughes, *Politics, Society, and Civil War*, and Roberts, *Recovery and Restoration*.

5. David Underdown, *Pride's Purge: Politics in the Puritan Revolution* (Oxford, 1971), p. 302. For a brief discussion of the expedients devised to administer the militia during the interregnum, see Western, *English Militia*, pp. 3–8. The Lords were abolished on February 6 by a vote of forty-four to twenty-nine. (S. R. Gardiner, *History of the Commonwealth and Protectorate*, 4 vols. [London, 1903], 1:3).

6. Oliver Cromwell's regime has received attention from several recent scholars. See Austin Woolrych, *Commonwealth to Protectorate* (Oxford, 1987); J. S. Morrill, ed., *Oliver Cromwell and the English Revolution* (London, 1990); and Barry Coward's useful synthesis of recent scholarship, *Cromwell*.

7. Gardiner, *History of the Commonwealth and Protectorate*, 4:29.

8. Rannie, "Cromwell's Major Generals," pp. 491, 490.

9. Ibid., pp. 500–501. Of course, Edmund Ludlow, as a victim of this persecution, was biased—but he had good reason to know all about the power of the major generals.

10. See, for example, Ann Hughes's tabulation of gentle justices of the peace in interregnum Warwickshire (*Politics, Society, and Civil War*, appendix 1, pp. 353–

56). She notes that despite the gentlemen on the bench, overall the Warwickshire magistracy was of "significantly lower status" (p. 272). Roberts describes the same process in *Recovery and Restoration*, chap. 2.

11. See Austin Woolrych, "The Cromwellian Protectorate: A Military Dictatorship?," *History* 75 (1990): 207–31.

12. As the foremost historian of the conspirators has said, they waited for the republic to "die of its own contradictions" (David Underdown, *Royalist Conspiracy in England* [New Haven, 1960], p. 286). For a detailed discussion of Royalist activity in England in late 1659 and early 1660, see ibid., esp. chaps. 13 and 14.

13. See Jones, *Charles II*, chap. 2, and Hutton, *Charles II*, esp. chaps. 6 and 7, for an account of the general political situation in early 1660. See also Paul Seaward's brief but useful *Restoration*.

14. These included Sir Horatio Townshend in Norfolk, Sir John Grenville in Cornwall and Devon, and Lord Falkland in Oxfordshire. See Underdown, *Royalist Conspiracy*, p. 297; O. Ogle, W. H. Bliss, and W. D. Macray, eds., *Calendar of the Clarendon State Papers*, 4 vols. (Oxford, 1872–1938), 3:676.

15. Thomas Slaughter, ed., *Ideology and Politics on the Eve of Restoration: Newcastle's Advice to Charles II* (Philadelphia, 1984), quotations on pp. 7–8. Newcastle's "letter" was eighty-eight pages long.

16. The decision not to wait on Parliament was a wise one in the event because definitive militia acts were not passed until 1662 and 1663, in spite of considerable effort on the part of the crown to promote the legislation. In any case, the acts had no effect on the traditional procedure for the appointment of the lieutenants themselves. See Smith, "Militia Rates."

17. See E. B. Fryde, D. E. Greenway, S. Porter, and Ian Roy, eds., *The Handbook of British Chronology*, 3d ed. (London, 1986), and Joseph Haydn and Horace Ocherby, eds., *The Book of Dignities* (London, 1894), esp. pt. 6.

18. Hutton, *Restoration*, pp. 129–30. For the speed with which the lieutenancy was reestablished in one county, see Roberts, *Recovery and Restoration*, p. 151. For more on the reconstruction of the national administration, see Howard Tomlinson, "Financial and Administrative Developments in England, 1660–88," and Jennifer Carter, "Law, Courts, and Constitution," in J. R. Jones, ed., *The Restored Monarchy* (London, 1979), pp. 94–117; 71–93.

19. Sainty, ed., *Lieutenants of Counties*. The first to be appointed were the marquess of Hertford for Somerset and Wiltshire and the earl of Winchilsea for Kent, on July 10.

20. John Cecil, fourth earl of Exeter (lieutenant of Northamptonshire), was the scion of a parliamentarian family, but he did not come of age until the 1650s. For the role of Presbyterians in the Restoration, see George Abernathy, *The English Presbyterians and the Stuart Restoration, 1648–1663*, Transactions of the American Philosophical Society n.s., 55 (1965).

21. For Suffolk, see *DNB*, s.v. "James Howard." Carlisle was captain of Cromwell's bodyguard and was ennobled by the Protector. Fauconberg was Cromwell's son-in-law. See *DNB*, s.v. "Charles Howard" and "Thomas Belasyse."

22. See GEC, s.v. "Brooke" for further biographical details about the fourth lord.

23. Paul Seaward has also noticed the government's tendency to stick with Royalists in its appointment (*Restoration,* p. 37).

24. The Restoration created a few new grandees, Albemarle and Sandwich, for example. One of the most interesting, James Butler, first duke of Ormond (later lord lieutenant of Somerset), was the head of an Old English family who had led the king's cause in Ireland and who after 1660 became more closely involved with English politics. See Thomas Carte, *The Life of James Duke of Ormond,* new ed., 4 vols. (Oxford, 1858).

25. Lieutenants of Cornwall and Devon, Norfolk, and Cumberland and Westmorland, respectively. All were subsequently ennobled: Grenville as the earl of Bath, Townshend as Baron Townshend, and Howard as the earl of Carlisle. Howard had been granted a peerage by Cromwell, but of course this was not recognized by the crown. See Sainty, ed., *Lieutenants of Counties.* For the continuing anomaly of the bishop-lieutenants of Durham, see Gladys Scott Thomson, "The Bishops of Durham and the Office of Lord Lieutenant in the Seventeenth Century," *EHR* 40 (1925): 351–74.

26. Sainty, ed., *Lieutenants of Counties.* Maynard's tenure was limited to the minority of the second duke of Buckingham. This figure excludes six lieutenants appointed from 1640 to 1642, as well as those lieutenants, heirs to earldoms, who were joined with their fathers during their lifetime.

27. See *DNB,* s.v. "Marmaduke Langdale." The only biography of Langdale is F. H. Sunderland, *Marmaduke Lord Langdale and Some Events of His Time* (London, 1926). Some of his letters are calendared in HMC, *Various Collections,* vol. 2 (Harford MSS).

28. For the Act of Indemnity, see Hutton, *Restoration,* pp. 132–38, and Jones, *Charles II,* pp. 57, 60, 65–66; for the church, R. S. Bosher, *The Making of the Restoration Settlement* (London, 1957), Ian M. Green's revision of that work, *The Reestablishment of the Church of England* (Cambridge, 1978), and John Spurr, "Latitudinarianism and the Restoration Church," *HJ* 31 (1988): 21–52, "Schism and the Restoration Church," *Journal of Ecclesiastical History* 41 (1990): 408–24, and his forthcoming monograph, *The Restoration Church of England, 1646–89.*

29. Ogle, Bliss, and Macray, eds., *Calendar of the Clarendon State Papers,* 3:381.

30. Ibid., p. 676.

31. PRO, SP29/4/38, 135.

32. See *DNB,* s.v. "Thomas Wentworth."

33. For Warwick's estate, see GEC, s.v. "Robert Rich, earl of Warwick." For Albemarle, see T. R. Jamison, *George Monck and the Restoration* (Fort Worth, Texas, 1975).

34. There is evidence of friction in the Northamptonshire Lieutenancy Book covering the period from 1660 to 1666, BL, Add. MSS 34222; Exeter's response was generally to withdraw from lieutenancy business.

35. Bodl., Clarendon State Papers 73, f. 63v.

36. BL, Egerton MSS 2537 f. 231. On Royalist attitudes toward the king's tolerant leanings, see Mark Goldie, "Danby, the Bishops, and the Whigs," in Tim Harris, Paul Seaward, and Mark Goldie, eds., *The Politics of Religion in Restoration England* (Oxford, 1990), pp. 75–105.

37. Gladys Scott Thomson, ed., *The Twysden Lieutenancy Papers, 1583–1688,* Kent Archaeological Society Records, vol. 10 (1926), pp. 15–16.

38. PRO, SP29/65/25. Legh's nefarious dealings were apparently never uncovered, for he remained a deputy on good terms with his lieutenant until Derby's death in 1672. See his biography in Basil D. Henning, ed., *History of Parliament, 1660–1690,* 3 vols. (London, 1983).

39. Anthony Hamilton claimed that in the early 1660s the duke of York attempted to get the lieutenancy of Cornwall for Lord Robarts to remove the crotchety old man from London so the duke could consummate an affair with Lady Robarts. (*Memoirs of the Count de Grammont,* trans. Horace Walpole [New York, 1928], p. 117).

40. Henry Townshend, *The Diary of Henry Townshend of Elmley Lovett, 1640–1663,* ed. J. W. Willis Bund, 2 vols. (London, 1920), 2:47.

41. See, for example, Roberts's account of the new commission in *Recovery and Restoration,* p. 152.

42. My own research leads me to believe that the government was far less evenhanded in its dispensation of deputy lieutenancies from 1660 to 1662 than is indicated by Hutton, *Restoration,* p. 129, though as P. J. Norrey has shown, it was not impossible for individuals of questionable antecedents to gain a place on the commission. See Norrey, "Central Government," p. 3.

43. For biographical details of all of these men, see Henning, ed., *History of Parliament.* For their nominations, see PRO, SP29/11/146, 150, SP29/4/31.

44. See D. P. Carter, "The Lancashire Militia, 1660–88," *THSLC* 132 (1983): 155–82.

45. A similar preference for the old ways was displayed by the duke of Somerset's nominations for deputy lieutenants in Wiltshire, all of whom were chosen for their social standing and wealth (Norrey, "Central Government," p. 3).

46. In August 1662, for example, the earl complained that the king was acting too slowly on his nominations (PRO, SP29/58/63).

47. In fact, by early 1663, a number of those who opposed the seventh earl's occupation of Man had been sentenced to death for bearing arms against Derby, who was lord of the isle. One correspondent was pleased by the development but noted that it went unreported in the official newspapers "for fear the brethren should grumble" (BL, Add. MSS 32324 f. 165 [Seymour Correspondence]).

48. The bill was designed to force purchasers of his father's lands, sold when the seventh earl was executed, to compound with the earl. See Barry Coward, *The Stanleys Lords Stanley and Earls of Derby,* Chetham Society, 3d ser. vol. 30 (1983), esp. chaps. 6 and 11.

49. See their biographical articles in Henning, ed., *History of Parliament.*

50. PRO, SP29/61/85.

51. PRO, SP44/1/70.

52. Quoted by Coward in *The Stanleys,* pp. 179–80.

53. Rigby apparently never conformed to the Church of England, though he was made a deputy by Lord Gerard in 1689. See his biography in Henning, ed., *History of Parliament.*

54. PRO, SP29/61/85.

55. PRO, SP29/61/85I.

56. Sir John Bramston, *Autobiography,* Camden Society, vol. 32 (1845), p. 117.

57. LAO, Monson MSS 7/12/3. For a general discussion of Restoration Lincoln-shire, see Holmes, *Seventeenth Century Lincolnshire.*

58. P. J. Challinor, "Restoration and Exclusion in the County of Cheshire," *Bulletin of the John Rylands University Library* 64 (1982): 361.

59. PRO, SP29/14/92.

60. Thomson, ed., *Twysden Lieutenancy Papers,* p. 24.

61. For Lincolnshire, LAO, Yarborough MSS 8/2/3 (1629), 8/2/5 (1662); for Staffordshire, William Salt Library, HM Chetwynd 114 (1627); SRO, s/7/3 (1677); s/7/7 (1689) (Leveson Gower, deputy lieutenant, MSS). For a parallel instance of this inflation in the west, see Norrey, "Central Government," p. 12, n. 44, p. 44, n. 106.

62. PRO, SP29/87.

63. For a closer look at the politicization of the lieutenancy, see below, Chapter 5.

64. See the accounts of the Restoration militia given by J. R. Western, *English Militia,* chaps. 1 and 2, and Fletcher, *Reform in the Provinces.*

65. Bagot to Lord Brooke, ca. August 1661, SRO, Bagot MSS 3/231B.

66. PRO, SP29/63/19; other letters from Colepepper can be found in SP29/62/30, 80, 110, 63/60. Colepepper was heavily involved in the farcical search for Edmund Ludlow which convulsed the south of England in late 1662 (see below, Chapter 4).

67. PRO, SP44/1/62, SP29/61/85.

68. For Bedfordshire, PRO, SP29/8/78, and Staffordshire, SRO MS. 100/1. This document has been published as "The Gentry of Staffordshire" in *Collections for a History of Staffordshire,* Staffordshire Record Society, 4th ser., vol. 2 (1958). The numbers for Staffordshire are probably minimum figures because they appear to be estimates of income derived only from Staffordshire estates; some (if not all) of the deputies had interests outside of the county. For the Wiltshire deputies, see Norrey, "Central Government," p. 37, n. 12.

69. Rye, ed., *State Papers,* p. 6. HMC, *Lothian Manuscripts,* p. 125, for a 1677 list of twenty-two Norfolk deputies, excluding those commissioned for Norwich. Other lists are in Basil Cozens-Hardy, ed., *Norfolk Lieutenancy Journal, 1676–1701,* Norfolk Record Society, vol. 30 (1961).

70. Wake and Longden, eds., *Montagu Musters Book,* p. 224 (1607); PRO, SP29/7/24, for 1660; and House of Lords Record Office, Main Papers, November 20, 1680, f. 287(3), for 1680.

71. PRO, SP29/8/78.

72. "Gentry of Staffordshire," pp. 22, 27.

73. See Henning, ed., *History of Parliament.* By 1712 his son the second baronet was described as a professional beggar.

74. For a detailed account of the Restoration militia (as distinct from the lieutenancy), see Western, *English Militia,* esp. pt. 1, and Fletcher, *Reform in the Provinces.*

75. Hutton, *Restoration,* p. 286. Other accounts of the militia on the local

level are Carter, "Lancashire Militia"; introductions to Cozens-Hardy, ed., *Norfolk Lieutenancy Journal*, and Richard M. Dunn, ed., *Norfolk Lieutenancy Journal, 1660–1676*, Norfolk Record Society, vol. 45 (1977); and M. A. Faraday, ed., *Herefordshire Militia Assessments of 1663*, Camden Society, 4th ser., vol. 10 (1972). See also John Childs, *The Army of Charles II* (London, 1976), chaps. 1 and 2. The army was viewed with considerable suspicion in a society whose recent experience with armies had been very unhappy. See Lois Schwoerer, *No Standing Armies!* (Baltimore, 1974).

76. PRO, SP29/18/1, 50. The duke of Albemarle was appointing militia colonels as early as September 1660 (HMC, *Fifteenth Report, Appendix 7—Duke of Somerset Manuscripts; Ailesbury Manuscripts* (London, 1898), pt. 8, p. 92).

77. PRO, SP29/18/1. Companies of foot during Charles I's reign were almost always at least one hundred strong and in some counties had up to two hundred men. See Boynton, *English Militia*, chap. 4.

78. SRO, Bagot MSS, 3/321B, Brooke to deputy lieutenants, November 18, 1660.

79. LAO, Monson MSS 7/11/23, 7/12/11, 7/14/9.

80. BL, Egerton MSS 2537 f. 266 (Nicholas MSS).

81. Western, *English Militia*, p. 11.

82. SP29/26/102 (for Monmouthshire), and ChRO, DLT/B11, pp. 92–93 (Leicester de Tabley MSS; Papers of Sir Peter Leicester, deputy lieutenant). The deputies in Wiltshire had similar problems (BL, Add. MSS 32324 ff. 98, 119 [Seymour Correspondence]).

83. 13 and 14 Car. II, cap. 3. A supplemental act, 15 Car. II cap. 4, was passed in 1663, which enabled the government to maintain a small proportion of each county's militia (generally fewer than one hundred men) on rotating duty to guard against disorder.

84. A complete and detailed account of the provisions of the act of 1662 are given in Western, *English Militia*, pp. 16–29. See also Smith, "Militia Rates."

85. Western, *English Militia*, p. 20. For the weight of post-Restoration taxation, which was much greater than that of the prewar period, see C. D. Chandaman, *The English Public Revenue, 1660–1688.* (Oxford, 1975).

86. Dunn, ed., *Norfolk Lieutenancy Journal*, p. 89.

87. Chandaman, *English Public Revenue*, p. 144. Needless to say, the government declared that a state of apparent danger existed in each of the years of the grant. Because only £2,000 of the money was paid into the exchequer, the rest bypassing it, it is unclear exactly how much was eventually collected. See ibid., table of receipts, p. 348 (under "militia money").

88. Western, *English Militia*, p. 17. Obligations rose with income; £500 in land required an additional horseman, for example.

89. Richard Gough, *History of Myddle* (Harmondsworth, 1981), p. 36. An exception was the volunteer companies that were formed in many places immediately following the Restoration and were generally composed of the gentry. These units gradually died out as the 1660s drew on and the reorganized militia seemed able to perform its security tasks.

90. PRO, SP29/83/55 (Westmorland); BL, Add. MSS 32324 f. 176 (Wilt-

shire) (from the Seymour Correspondence); SP29/81/56 (Sussex). For a detailed account of the situation in Wiltshire, Somerset, and Dorset, see Norrey, "Central Government," pp. 2–35.

91. PRO, SP29/57/74. For the lieutenancy as guarantor of local security, see below, Chapter 4.

92. PRO, SP29/57/70, 57/85, 62/97, 63/110.

93. Bodl., Carte MSS 46 f. 80v.

94. SRO, Brooke to deputy lieutenants, Bagot MSS 3/231B. Orders for Cheshire are in ChRO, DLT/B11, p. 91 (Leicester de Tabley MSS); and for Norfolk, Dunn, ed., *Norfolk Lieutenancy Journal*, p. 23.

95. Dunn, *Norfolk Lieutenancy Journal*, p. 14 and passim; Cozens-Hardy, ed., *Norfolk Lieutenancy Journal*, passim.

96. *Hertford County Records, Sessions Rolls*, 9 vols. (Hertford, 1905–39), 1:211–15.

97. For the lieutenancy's role in the suppression of dissent and defense of the country in wartime, see below, Chapter 4.

98. Dunn, ed., *Norfolk Lieutenancy Journal*, p. 88.

99. Ibid., p. 140.

100. Ibid., p. 141. Considering the treatment meted out to Quakers, it is interesting that they were serving in the militia at all. For more on Quakers, see Reay, *The Quakers and the English Revolution;* Watts, *Dissenters,* esp. chaps. 2 and 3, and William C. Braithwaite, *The Second Period of Quakerism,* 2d ed., ed. Henry Cadbury (Cambridge, 1961).

101. Dunn, ed., *Norfolk Lieutenancy Journal*, pp. 17, 119.

102. BL, Add. MSS 39246 (Suffolk) (from the Wodehouse Lieutenancy Book, 1664–76); LRO, DDBa, Lieutenancy Book (Bankes MSS). Regular meetings are also noted in the Northamptonshire Lieutenancy Book, BL, Add. MSS 34222, passim.

103. LRO, DDBa, Lieutenancy Book, f. 65 and passim.

104. Western, *English Militia*, chap. 2. See Norrey, "Central Government," chap. 1. Despite the lieutenancy's disorganization, the militia effectively deterred resistance to the government.

105. BL, Add. MSS 34306 f. 49.

106. Bodl., Clarendon State Papers, 92 f. 143.

107. PRO, SP29/160/119.

108. PRO, SP29/160/121, 161/41, 75, 126.

4. Internal Security, 1660–1674

1. John Miller, *Popery and Politics in England, 1660–88* (Cambridge, 1973), p. 91. Unfortunately, few works deal explicitly with the ideology of the Cavaliers, but for some aspects of this question, see Keith Feiling, *A History of the Tory Party, 1640–1714* (Oxford, 1924); Corinne Weston and Janelle Greenberg, *Subjects and Sovereigns: The Grand Controversy over Legal Sovereignty in Stuart England* (Cambridge, 1981), esp. chap. 6; Clayton Roberts, *The Growth of Responsible Government in Stuart England* (Cambridge, 1966); Richard Ollard, *The Image of the King: Charles I and*

Charles II (New York, 1979); Goldie, "John Locke and Anglican Royalism"; and Hutton, *Restoration* and *Charles II*.

2. A crisis such as that following the Gunpowder Plot in 1605 usually underlay such activity. See John Bossy, *The English Catholic Community, 1570–1850* (Oxford, 1976), and Martin Havran, *The Catholics in Caroline England* (Stanford, 1962). See also B. W. Quintrell, "The Practice and Problems of Recusant Disarming," *Recusant History* 17 (1984): 208–22; and J. N. N. McGurk, "Lieutenancy and Catholic Recusants in Elizabethan Kent," *Recusant History* 12 (1973–74): 157–70.

3. For the crucial importance of religion and religious tensions in the Restoration, see Tim Harris, Paul Seaward, and Mark Goldie, eds., *The Politics of Religion in Restoration England* (Oxford, 1990). For an interesting view of the metamorphosis of 1640s-style Presbyterians to political radicals (at least in the minds of Royalist gentlemen), see Jonathan Barry, "The Politics of Religion in Restoration Bristol," ibid., pp. 163–89.

4. Greaves, *Deliver Us from Evil*, p. 8. "Former republican" refers to officers in arms in 1659. For the Fifth Monarchists, see Capp, *Fifth Monarchy Men,* and P. G. Rogers, *The Fifth Monarchy Men* (London, 1966), esp. chaps. 7–10.

5. Greaves, *Deliver Us from Evil*, p. 10.

6. PRO, SP29/58/73. For former republicans in a Welsh county, see Philip Jenkins, "The 'Old Leaven': The Welsh Roundheads After 1660," *HJ* 24 (1981): 807–24.

7. Sir John Reresby, *Memoirs,* ed. Andrew Browning (Glasgow, 1936), p. 48.

8. See Greaves, *Deliver Us from Evil* and *Enemies Under His Feet,* and Wilbur C. Abbott, "English Conspiracy and Dissent, 1660–1674," *American Historical Review* 14 (1908–9): 503–28. For the more local level, see Judith Hurwich, "Dissent and Catholicism in English Society: A Study of Warwickshire, 1660–1720," *JBS* 16 (1976): 24–58; Margaret Spufford, "Dissenting Churches in Cambridgeshire from 1660–1700," *Proceedings of the Cambridgeshire Antiquarian Society* 61 (1908): 67–95; and D. G. Hey, "The Pattern of Nonconformity in South Yorkshire, 1660–1851," *NH* 8 (1973): 86–118. For the impact of persecution on several individual dissenters, see Richard L. Greaves, *Saints and Rebels: Seven Nonconformists in Stuart England* (Macon, Ga., 1985).

9. Creed was still in jail ten years later, held prisoner in Guernsey, and complimented by his jailor for his "modest civil behaviour" (BL, Add. MSS 29552, f. 392 [Hatton Papers]).

10. BL, Add. MSS 34306, Milward Lieutenancy Book, f. 12.

11. PRO, SP29/44/34.

12. DRO, Constables' Accounts, D 156/168, deputy lieutenants to high constables.

13. BL, Add. MSS 34306 f. 7v (Milward Lieutenancy Book).

14. ChRO, DLT/B11 p. 97 (Leicester Papers).

15. Rogers, *Fifth Monarchy Men,* pp. 110–11. See also Greaves, *Deliver Us from Evil,* esp. chap. 2, and Champlin Burrage, "The Fifth Monarchy Insurrections," *EHR* 25 (1910): 722–47.

16. Rogers, *Fifth Monarchy Men,* pp. 112–13; Greaves, *Deliver Us from Evil,* pp. 50–51.

17. Rogers, *Fifth Monarchy Men*, p. 113.

18. Ibid., pp. 114–20. Several were spared execution, and four were acquitted of bearing arms against the king.

19. Pepys, *Diary*, 2:7.

20. BL, Add. MSS 29597 f. 21 (Carew MSS).

21. BL, Add. MSS 34306 ff. 8v-9 (Milward Lieutenancy Book).

22. Greaves, *Deliver Us from Evil*, p. 54.

23. Watts, *Dissenters*, p. 223.

24. Lord Brooke to deputy lieutenants, September 21, 1661, SRO, D(W) 1721/3/231B.

25. BL, Add. MSS 32324 f. 82 (Seymour Correspondence).

26. Greaves, *Deliver Us from Evil*, pp. 54–55.

27. Hutton, *Restoration*, p. 151. For the position of Quakers at this time, see Braithwaite, *Second Period of Quakerism*, and Barry Reay, "The Authorities and Early Restoration Quakerism," *Journal of Ecclesiastical History* 34 (1983): 69–84. ChRO, DLT/B11, pp. 102–3, for a copy of the proclamation (Leicester Papers).

28. ChRO, DLT/B11, pp. 98, 104–5 (Leicester Papers).

29. Watts, *Dissenters*, p. 222. A typical example of the vigor of a single deputy lieutenant can be seen in an examination of the papers of Sir Daniel Fleming of Westmorland, calendared in HMC, *Twelfth Report, Appendix 7—Le Fleming Manuscripts* (London, 1890). They are full of references to Quakers and other dissenting sects, whom Fleming pursued unmercifully. For the work of another Restoration justice of the peace see James Rosenheim, "Robert Doughty of Hanworth: A Restoration Magistrate," *Norfolk Archaeology* 38 (1983): 296–312, and his edition of *The Notebook of Robert Doughty, 1662–65*, Norfolk Record Society, vol. 54 (1989).

30. Quoted in Greaves, *Deliver Us from Evil*, p. 111.

31. BL, Add. MSS 32324 ff. 135, 91 (Milward Lieutenancy Book).

32. BL, Loan MSS 29, vol. 236, f. 282 (Portland Papers; Vere/Cavendish Papers, 1661–95).

33. Bodl., Clarendon State Papers, 82 f. 44.

34. PRO, SP29/81/56, 21/58, 62/18, 68/35.

35. NRO, IC 537 (Isham Correspondence). For Isham, see Henning, ed., *History of Parliament*.

36. See Spurr, "Schism and the Restoration Church."

37. PRO, SP29/83/111.

38. Reresby, *Memoirs*, p. 54.

39. Lord Townshend's Letter Book, Raynham Hall, Norfolk. The lieutenancy spent £49/10/0 on pay for the men engaged in this exercise. My special thanks to the current Marquis Townshend for making this document available to me. For an excellent account of Townshend and the Townshend family, using all of the relevant family papers, see Rosenheim, *Townshends of Raynham*.

40. SP29/62/110, 92/42, 83/57.

41. HMC, *Twelfth Report, Appendixes 4 and 5*, 4:548.

42. This was the so-called Yarrington Plot, which was a hoax. See Greaves, *Deliver Us from Evil*, pp. 72–81.

43. BL, Add. MSS 32324 ff. 107–8, 93 (Milward Lieutenancy Book).

44. Ibid., f. 141.

45. Lord Townshend's Letter Book December 16, 1668, Raynham Hall, Norfolk.

46. BL, Add. MSS 34222 f. 166 (Earl of Westmorland's Northamptonshire Lieutenancy Book, 1660–65).

47. Watts, *Dissenters*, p. 246.

48. DRO, Constables' Accounts, D258, Box 29/35, deputy lieutenants to high constables.

49. Watts, *Dissenters*, pp. 230–31.

50. Bodl., Clarendon State Papers, 92 f. 143.

51. Unfortunately, the opinions of most people below the gentry remain obscure, but it certainly is true that they were often willing to inform on dissenters or serve as common soldiers in raids against their meetings. For a recent examination of "ale-bench Anglicanism" during this period, see David Underdown, *Revel, Riot, and Rebellion: Popular Politics and Culture in England, 1603–1660* (Oxford, 1985). Alan Macfarlane also provides an interesting look at the lower orders and the law in this period in his *Justice and the Mare's Ale: Law and Disorder in Seventeenth Century England* (Oxford, 1981).

52. Macfarlane discusses the importance of rumor in *Justice and the Mare's Ale*, esp. chap. 1.

53. One of his agents told him about the sudden appearance of one Bayly, a former republican captain, in the county. Bayly was accompanied by another man, Packe, "suspected to be very ill-affected to king and church, who had travelled about of late night and day to effect some great work." "I pray you consider of it," Bagot's informant said, "and believe from such an egg a cockatrice may proceed" (SRO, D[W] 1721/3/231B [Bagot MSS]).

54. Greaves, *Deliver Us from Evil*, pp. 181–83.

55. Henry Gee, "The Derwentdale Plot, 1663," *TRHS* 3d ser., 11 (1917): 125–42, and James Walker, "The Yorkshire Plot, 1663," *Yorkshire Archaeological Journal* 31 (1934): 348–59.

56. For the lieutenancy's role in the campaign against borough charters, see below, Chapter 5. For more on the government's relations with municipal corporations generally, see J. H. Sacret, "The Restoration Government and Municipal Corporations," *EHR* 45 (1930): 232–59, and John Miller, "The Crown and the Borough Charters in the Reign of Charles II," *EHR* 100 (1985): 53–84.

57. Bodl., Clarendon State Papers, 77 f. 236.

58. BL, Add. MSS 34222 ff. 22v–27, 34; Bodl., Westmorland's Lieutenancy Book, Clarendon State Papers, 77 f. 66a; PRO, SP29/57/79, 107.

59. See Bodl., Carte MSS 32 f. 9v, for one expression of this sentiment: it refers to "the Presbyterians that would deal with the sectaries, as the ape did with the cat." Cavalier distrust for Presbyterians was widespread (see, for example, Northampton's comments on Coventry Presbyterians, above), PRO, SP29/83/54.

60. SP29/63/56.

61. Norfolk magistrates, to take one typically far-flung example, arrested one man on suspicion of dealing with the conspirators. The charges—as in many other like cases—proved to be ill-founded. See Rosenheim, ed., *Notebook of Robert*

Doughty, p. 38. For a detailed discussion of the Derwentdale Plot, see Greaves, *Deliver Us from Evil,* chap. 6, and Gee, "Derwentdale Plot."

62. Greaves, *Deliver Us from Evil,* p. 191; PRO, SP29/81/17, 44.

63. Greaves, *Deliver Us from Evil,* p. 190.

64. Faraday, in his introduction to *Herefordshire Militia Assessments of 1662,* p. 1, notes the success of the lieutenancy when dealing with treason.

65. Miller, *Popery and Politics,* p. 95. For the revival of antipopery as a powerful force in English society in the 1670s, see below, Chapter 5.

66. The existence of a Roman Catholic plot at court was a very different matter. See Caroline Hibbard, *Charles I and the Popish Plot* (Chapel Hill, 1983).

67. Quoted by Greaves, *Deliver Us from Evil,* p. 174.

68. The lieutenant of Cheshire, for example, was ordered in January 1664 to release all but two of the prisoners held in Chester Castle, and the deputy lieutenants of Cumberland were outraged by the king's pardon of one of that plot's chief conspirators. Lord Lovelace, lieutenant of Berkshire, was also instructed to release all prisoners "as are not notorious" (PRO, SP29/137/121).

69. Bodl., Clarendon State Papers, 77, f. 340.

70. For the strength of antipopery as an ideology, see P. G. Lake, "Anti-Popery: The Structure of a Prejudice," in Richard Cust and Ann Hughes, eds., *Conflict in Early Stuart England* (London, 1989), pp. 72–106. I would like to thank Professor Lake for allowing me to read this article prior to publication. See also Miller, *Popery and Politics.*

71. For a detailed discussion of the rise and progress of anti-Catholic sentiment from the late 1660s on, see Miller, *Popery and Politics,* esp. chaps. 6–14.

72. See W. G. Bell, *The Great Fire of London* (London, 1951).

73. PRO, SP29/170/152.

74. PRO, SP29/171/29, 37, 173/35.

75. PRO, SP29/171/56.

76. The duke of Newcastle had warned of such a combination as early as 1665. Newcastle to duke of York, August 10, 1665, (BL, Loan MSS 29, vol. 236 unf. [Portland Papers]). Indeed, the monument erected on the site of the fire's origin specifically blamed papists for the deed.

77. Miller, *Popery and Politics,* p. 105. There is little evidence that the lieutenancy engaged in any widespread disarming of papists as a result of this proclamation.

78. PRO, SP29/171/112.

79. Ibid.

80. Ibid.

81. PRO, SP29/171/128.

82. PRO, SP29/173/83.

83. For the general political situation at this time, see Hutton, *Restoration* and *Charles II.* To cite one contemporary example, Samuel Pepys's diary for 1666–67 becomes increasingly pessimistic about the state of the kingdom.

84. Hutton, *Restoration,* pp. 236, 263, and Watts, *Dissenters,* chap. 3.

85. PRO, SP29/276/173, 203, 277/206; BL, Loan MSS 29 vol. 236, f. 395 (Portland MSS).

86. For a discussion of the Anglo-Dutch Wars, see Charles Wilson, *Profit and Power: A Study of England and the Anglo-Dutch Wars* (London, 1957). For British foreign policy during the period, see Keith Feiling, *British Foreign Policy, 1660–72* (Oxford, 1930), and Jeremy Black, *A System of Ambition? British Foreign Policy, 1660–1793* (London, 1991), esp. chaps. 2 and 9. For a brief account of Dutch foreign policy, M. A. A. Franken, "The General Tendencies and Structural Aspects of the Foreign Policy and Diplomacy of the Dutch Republic in the Latter Half of the Seventeenth Century," *Acta Historiae Neerlandica* 3 (1968): 1–42. Another recent study of Anglo-Dutch diplomacy is K. H. D. Haley, *An English Diplomat in the Low Countries: Sir William Temple and John de Witt, 1665–1672* (Oxford, 1986). See also Pincus, "Popery, Trade, and Universal Monarchy."

87. The MP who proposed this colossal sum, Sir Robert Paston, was rewarded with a peerage and later was to become lord lieutenant of Norfolk. See below, Chapter 5. Hutton, *Restoration,* p. 218, and Bodl., Carte MSS 34 f. 427.

88. Pepys's *Diary* gives the reader a good idea of the Navy Office's side of the war. See also Bryant, *Pepys,* esp. vol. 1, and J. R. Tanner, *Samuel Pepys and the Royal Navy* (Cambridge, 1928).

89. PRO, SP44/20/89; BL, Add. MSS 39246 f. 12 (Wodehouse MSS; Suffolk Lieutenancy Book, 1664–76); Bodl., Carte MSS 34 f. 440. See also J. R. Bruijn, "Dutch Privateering During the Second and Third Anglo-Dutch Wars," *Low Countries Historical Yearbook* 11 (1978): 79–93.

90. Discussions of the Restoration navy—as opposed to Pepys—are meager. See Arthur W. Tedder, *The Navy of the Restoration* (Cambridge, 1916).

91. PRO, SP29/159/112; BL, Add. MSS 37820 f. 151v (Nicholas MSS; Minutes of the Privy Council).

92. PRO, SP29/163/11.

93. Anthony Fletcher discusses this in the context of local administration in his *Reform in the Provinces.* For a view of the process at work on the local level, see Norrey, "Central Government," pp. 29–31.

94. Hutton, *Restoration,* p. 221.

95. The king to Newcastle, May 29, 1666, BL, Loan MSS 29/236 unf. (Portland MSS).

96. Brooke to deputy lieutenants, March 24, 1666, SRO, D(W) 3/231B (Bagot MSS).

97. PRO, SP29/161/95.

98. Hutton, *Restoration,* p. 258.

99. Brooke to deputy lieutenants, July 1, 1667, SRO, D(W) 3/231B (Bagot MSS); HMC, *Twelfth Report, Appendix 5,* p. 10.

100. PRO, SP29/167/133, accounts of money held in the Tower. In August 1666 these totaled some £20,000.

101. PRO, SP29/146/24.

102. BL, Add. MSS 39246 f. 15v (Wodehouse MSS; Suffolk Lieutenancy Book).

103. PRO, SP44/20/112.

104. Bodl., Carte MSS 46 f. 327.

105. Pepys, for example, noted the departure of Lord Bellasis for Yorkshire on July 4 (*Diary,* 7:193).

106. SP29/160/119, 121, 161/136, 141, 162/78.

107. PRO, SP29/162/136; *London Gazette* 71 (July 14, 1666); and Brooke to deputies, July 1, 1666, SRO, D(W) 231B (Bagot MSS).

108. PRO, SP29/164/49, 159/112.

109. PRO, SP29/160/119, 121, 162/91.

110. *Oxford Gazette* 28 (February 8, 1666).

111. PRO, SP29/163/64.

112. PRO, SP29/163/126.

113. PRO, SP29/160/25, 65.

114. Hutton, *Restoration,* pp. 242–44.

115. PRO, SP29/170/37, 17.

116. Brooke to deputies, October 27, 1666, SRO, D(W) 231B (Bagot MSS).

117. PRO, SP29/170/65, 126. Militiamen sent to London were ordered to carry tools and food for two days and were to be employed in tearing down buildings to stop the spread of the flames.

118. PRO, SP44/20/145.

119. Reresby, *Memoirs,* pp. 73–74; PRO, SP29/207/2, 29, 43.

120. PRO, SP29/204/24. For a detailed discussion of the Dutch raid on the Royal Navy in the Medway, see P. G. Rogers, *The Dutch in the Medway* (London, 1970); see also A. D. Coox, "The Dutch Invasion of England: 1667," *Military Affairs* 13 (1949): 223–33.

121. Pepys, *Diary,* 8:260.

122. Frank Hussey, *Suffolk Invasion: The Dutch Attack on Landguard Fort, 1667* (Lavenham, Suffolk, 1983), p. 49.

123. Rogers, *Dutch in the Medway.* The ship was broken up and its timber sold for scrap. The city of Amsterdam kept the elaborate royal coat of arms on the *Royal Charles*'s stern as a trophy, which may still be seen in the Rijksmuseum.

124. Quoted in Rogers, *Dutch in the Medway,* p. 111.

125. PRO, SP29/205/119, 206/13, 63, for some examples of the lieutenancy's activity in raising the militia in Yorkshire, Cornwall, and Cheshire; BL, Add. MSS 28052 f. 59 (Godolphin Correspondence, 1663–1783).

126. PRO, SP44/20/158; SP29/205/66, 212/23; Hussey, *Suffolk Invasion.*

127. Rogers, *Dutch in the Medway,* pp. 66–67.

128. *London Gazette* 170 (July 4, 1667).

129. PRO, SP29/209/20I, 80.

130. PRO, SP29/209/79.

131. PRO, SP29/214/8.

132. PRO, SP29/209/84.

133. Quoted in Hussey, *Suffolk Invasion,* p. 110.

134. PRO, SP29/160/25.

135. David Ogg, *England in the Reign of Charles II* (Oxford, 1956), p. 386.

5. *Politics and Rebellion, 1660–1685*

1. Though the Colledge trial was a cause célèbre at the time, no detailed analysis of it has been published since the seventeenth century. A number of contemporary

accounts were produced, however; this retelling relies especially on *An Impartial Account of the Arraignment, Trial and Condemnation of Stephen Colledge* (London, 1682); *The Speech and Carriage of Stephen Colledge* (London, 1681); and John Hawles, *Remarks upon the Tryals of Edward Fitzharris, Stephen Colledge, Count Conigsmark . . .* (London, 1689).

2. For an excellent account of the Exclusion crisis in London, see Tim Harris, *London Crowds in the Reign of Charles II* (Cambridge, 1987), and David Allen, "The Role of the London Trained Bands in the Exclusion Crisis," *EHR* 87 (1972): 287–303. See also Max Beloff, *Public Order and Popular Disturbances, 1660–1714* (London, 1938), and J. R. Jones, *The First Whigs: The Politics of the Exclusion Crisis, 1678–1683* (Oxford, 1961). For London politics later in the century, see de Krey, *Fractured Society.* For the social and political role of the London coffee house, see Ellis Ayton, *The Penny Universities: A History of the Coffee Houses* (London, 1956).

3. *Speech and Carriage,* p. 1.

4. *Impartial Account,* pp. 9, 5; *A True Copy of the Dying Words of Stephen Colledge* (London, 1681).

5. PRO, SP44/62/198.

6. *A Letter from the Grand Jury of Oxford* (Oxford, 1681).

7. *Impartial Account,* passim.

8. *Speech and Carriage; True Copy,* p. 2. The "unfairness" complained of was in fact standard procedure in such cases. For an excellent account of the criminal law and its procedures, see J. M. Beattie, *Crime and the Courts in England, 1660–1800* (Princeton, 1986), esp. pt. 2.

9. PRO, SP44/62/226.

10. For the view minimizing Exclusion, see Scott, *Algernon Sidney and the Restoration Crisis,* "England's Troubles," and "Radicalism and Restoration." Another recent statement of the centrality of Exclusion from a different perspective may be found in Paul Hammond, "The King's Two Bodies: Representations of Charles II," in Jeremy Black and Jeremy Gregory, eds., *Culture, Politics, and Society in Britain, 1660–1800* (Manchester, 1991), pp. 41–42.

11. For the prewar period, see Clive Holmes, "The County Community in Stuart Historiography," *JBS* 19 (1979): 54–73.

12. For parliamentary elections, see Kishlansky, *Parliamentary Selection,* and John Miller, "Faction in Later Stuart England, 1660–1714," *History Today* 33 (1983): 5–11.

13. For the role of the first earl of Yarmouth, see my "Continuity and Change in English Provincial Politics: Robert Paston in Norfolk, 1676–1682," *Albion* 25 (1993): 194–216.

14. Sacret, "Restoration Government," pp. 246–54.

15. Ibid., pp. 239–40; PRO, SP29/33/51.

16. Norrey, "Central Government," pp. 120–21 and n. 14. Chapman was subsequently dismissed for his action.

17. CRO, Assembly Book 2, ff. 135–36v.

18. Sacret, "Restoration Government," p. 252; *CSPD,* 1661–62, p. 517.

19. Bodl., Carte MSS 77 f. 380a.

20. LRO, DDBa acc. 1263 ff. 3–4 (Bankes MSS; Lancashire Lieutenancy Book).

See also M. A. Mullett, "Conflict, Politics, and Elections in Lancaster, 1660–1688," *NH* 19 (1983): 65.

21. For the Stanleys, see Coward, *The Stanleys,* and "The Social and Political Position of the Earls of Derby in Later Seventeenth Century Lancashire," *THSLC* 132 (1983): 127–54.

22. BL, Egerton MSS 2538 f. 168 (Nicholas MSS); Sacret, "Restoration Government," pp. 252–54.

23. Norrey, "Central Government," pp. 122–27.

24. S. A. H. Burne, ed., "Chetwynd Papers," *Collections of the Staffordshire Record Society* (Stafford, 1941), pp. 101–2; Brooke to Sir Edward Bagot, October 22, 1662, SRO, D(W) 1721 (Bagot MSS); Forster, "Government in Provincial England," p. 30.

25. BL, Add. MSS 34306 ff. 10v; 11 (Milward Lieutenancy Book).

26. See Henning, ed., *History of Parliament,* s.v. "Derbyshire."

28. See Stater, "Continuity and Change," for a closer look at this process at work in Norfolk.

29. Feiling, *History of the Tory Party,* p. 122. See also Seaward, *Cavalier Parliament,* and Harris, *Clarendon and the English Revolution.*

30. Kishlansky, *Parliamentary Selection,* p. 162. There are several accounts of this election, the winner of which was Sir William Bucknall. See M. A. Mullett, "The Politics of Liverpool, 1660–1688," *THSLC* 124 (1973): 31–56; E. B. Saxton, "Fresh Light on the Liverpool Election of 1670," *THSLC* 93 (1941): 54–68; Kishlansky, *Parliamentary Selection,* pp. 158–62; and Henning, ed., *History of Parliament,* s.v. "Liverpool."

31. For the role of Thomas Osborne, who became the earl of Danby in 1674, in Yorkshire boroughs, see Roy Carroll, "Yorkshire Parliamentary Boroughs in the Seventeenth Century," *NH* 3 (1968): 70–104.

32. BL, Add. MSS 28051 f. 26 (Leeds MSS).

33. Andrew Browning, *Thomas Osborne, Earl of Danby,* 3 vols. (Glasgow, 1944–51), 1:29; Henning, ed., *History of Parliament,* s.v. "York." The corporation argued that Danby's son was underage and so ineligible.

34. PRO, SP29/368/65; Henning, ed., *History of Parliament,* s.v. "King's Lynn." For more on Townshend's role in this election, see Rosenheim, *Townshends of Raynham,* pp. 40–46.

35. Browning, *Thomas Osborne,* 1:344; Glassey, *Politics and the Appointment of Justices of the Peace,* pp. 32–37.

36. Quoted in Holmes, *Seventeenth Century Lincolnshire,* p. 241.

37. Quoted in Feiling, *History of the Tory Party,* p. 155.

38. Landau, *Justices of the Peace,* p. 73.

39. Townshend, perhaps because of his intervention at King's Lynn, was the only lord lieutenant—except for Lord St. John in Hampshire—to have been sacked for what appear to have been political reasons during this period. For Townshend, see Rosenheim, *Townshends of Raynham,* pp. 40–42; for St. John, see Coleby, *Central Government and the Localities,* p. 99.

40. BL, Egerton MSS 3329 f. 111 (Leeds MSS; Correspondence, 1674–76).

41. Glassey, *Politics and the Appointment of Justices of the Peace,* pp. 34–35.

42. PRO, SP29/378/14, 379/52, 383/100, 101. See also Howard Reinmuth, "A Mysterious Dispute Demystified: Sir George Fletcher vs. the Howards," *HJ* 27 (1984): 289–308.

43. See Henning, ed., *History of Parliament*, s.v. "Philip Musgrave."

44. Andrew Browning, "Parties and Parliamentary Organization in the Reign of King Charles II," *TRHS* 4th ser., 30 (1948): 33.

45. HMC, *Twelfth Report, Appendixes 4 and 5*, vol. 2, 33, 35.

46. BL, Egerton MSS 3329 f. 113 (Leeds MSS). See Henning, ed., *History of Parliament*, s.v. "John Manners."

47. For Carr, see Henning, ed., *History of Parliament;* for more detail on the Bertie/Carr feud, see Holmes, *Seventeenth Century Lincolnshire*, chap. 14.

48. HMC, *Ormonde Manuscripts*, 8 vols. (London, 1902–20), 4; 429.

49. HMC, *Twelfth Report, Appendixes 4 and 5*, vol. 2, 44, 48; Henning, ed., *History of Parliament*, s.v. "Grantham"; Holmes, *Seventeenth Century Lincolnshire*, pp. 240–42. See also Geoffrey Davies, "The By-election at Grantham, 1678," *Huntington Library Quarterly* 7 (1943–44): 179–82.

50. HMC, *Twelfth Report, Appendixes 4 and 5*, vol. 2, 48.

51. Henning, ed., *History of Parliament*, s.v. "Sir Robert Carr"; Holmes, *Seventeenth Century Lincolnshire*, p. 242.

52. For the Popish Plot in general, by far the best account is J. P. Kenyon, *The Popish Plot* (London, 1972). Oates's narrative, along with several others relevant to the plot, has been published with a modern introduction by Douglas Greene, ed., *Diaries of the Popish Plot* (Delmar, N.Y., 1977).

53. HMC, *Ormonde Manuscripts* 4:245.

54. Several works offer an account of the events of this period: Jones, *First Whigs;* K. H. D. Haley, *Shaftesbury* (Oxford, 1968); and Browning, *Thomas Osborne.* See also Hutton, *Charles II,* and John Miller, *James II: A Study in Kingship* (London, 1977). But see also Scott, *Algernon Sidney and the Restoration Crisis,* which challenges the received view of Shaftesbury's importance. Clayton Roberts deals with Shaftesbury's brief period in office in *Schemes and Undertakings: A Study of English Politics in the Seventeenth Century* (Columbus, Ohio, 1985), chap. 4.

55. BL, Loan MSS 29, vol. 236, f. 397 (Portland Papers).

56. BL, Add. MSS 36988 f. 135 (Paston MSS).

57. In a comment of masterful ambiguity (hinging on the definition of the term "free election"), Yarmouth claimed that "I acknowledge that all elections ought to be free, and I do hope this will appear to be so" (ibid., f. 138). For the meaning and significance of a "free election," see Kishlansky, *Parliamentary Selection,* chap. 1.

58. Jones, *First Whigs,* pp. 40–41; Henning, ed., *History of Parliament*, s.v. "Oxfordshire."

59. Jones, *First Whigs,* pp. 43–44; Henning, ed., *History of Parliament*, s.v. "Leicestershire."

60. PRO, SP29/401/35.

61. Jones, *First Whigs,* p. 61; Haley, *Shaftesbury,* chap. 24.

62. BL, Loan MSS 29, vol. 236, ff. 407–9 (Portland Papers).

63. Glassey, *Politics and the Appointment of Justices of the Peace,* pp. 41–44.

64. BL, Egerton MSS 3331 f. 126 (Leeds MSS; Correspondence, 1677–80).

65. Glassey, *Politics and the Appointment of Justices of the Peace,* pp. 42–43.

66. Jones, *First Whigs,* p. 93.

67. Ibid., pp. 97–98; Henning, ed., *History of Parliament,* s.v. "Essex."

68. Jones, *First Whigs,* pp. 96–97; Henning, ed., *History of Parliament,* s.v. "Norfolk."

69. Glassey, *Politics and the Appointment of Justices of the Peace,* pp. 45–52; Jones, *First Whigs,* p. 120.

70. HMC, *Fifteenth Report, Appendix 7,* p. 107 (Duke of Somerset MSS).

71. HMC, *Twelfth Report, Appendixes 4 and 5,* vol. 2, 54.

72. PRO, SP44/56/25.

73. Bodl., Carte MSS 39 f. 129v.

74. Landau, *Justices of the Peace,* p. 74.

75. Hutton, *Restoration,* p. 129 and n. 25.

76. PRO, SP44/62/140, 151. Pembroke was a very difficult man to deal with; possibly a homicidal maniac, he was known to have committed several murders and violent assaults. See also Norrey, "Central Government," pp. 189–90.

77. For the crown's role in the regulation of corporations in the 1680s, see Sacret, "Restoration Government," and Miller, "The Crown and the Borough Charters."

78. Cozens-Hardy, ed., *Norfolk Lieutenancy Journal,* pp. 30–31.

79. CRO, Great Letter Book, no. 512, dated May 17, 1680.

80. PRO, SP29/413/136. A new charter was eventually issued in 1683; Albemarle was named recorder in the new document. See Henning, ed., *History of Parliament,* s.v. "Devon."

81. For a detailed narrative of these months, see Ogg, *England in the Reign of Charles II.*

82. BL, Add. MSS 29573 f. 317; Add. MSS 29558 f. 142 (Hatton Papers).

83. PRO, SP29/416/2, 2I.

84. PRO, SP44/56/49. For biographical information, see Henning, ed., *History of Parliament,* s.v. "Grimston" and "Titus."

85. PRO, SP44/62/155; Henning, ed., *History of Parliament,* s.v. "Luttrell."

86. PRO, SP44/62/211; SP29/416/16.

87. PRO, SP44/56/56.

88. The lieutenants were sometimes at a loss to monitor every officeholder. The earl of Peterborough had to confess that despite his zealous toryism he could not recall the names of all the militia officers under his command in Northamptonshire: "I cannot charge my memory with the names of all inferior officers." But he nevertheless assured the crown that "there is none but such as are qualified from their principles and practices to serve the king and kingdom" (House of Lords Record Office, Main Papers, November 20, 1680).

89. Quoted in Lee, " 'Fanatic Magistrates,' " p. 51.

90. PRO, SP29/416/16.

91. PRO, SP44/62/136; HMC, *Twelfth Report, Appendixes 4 and 5,* vol. 2, 75.

92. For examples, see PRO, SP44/44/160, 56/52, 164/5, 58.

93. PRO, SP29/413/136.

94. PRO, SP29/413/136I, attorney general's report. In the event, Tiverton did not receive a new charter until 1684.

95. PRO, SP44/62/352.

96. PRO, SP29/423/109, 129.

97. PRO, SP29/419/139.

98. BL, Add. MSS 29910 f. 172 (Swynfen MSS); Jones, *First Whigs*, p. 162; Henning, ed., *History of Parliament*, s.v. "Worcestershire."

99. ChRO, DDX 384, p. 233 (Thomas Mainwaring Diary), and see Challinor, "Restoration and Exclusion in the County of Cheshire"; Jones, *First Whigs*, p. 163. For more on Lord Winchilsea's intervention in Kent, see Maurice Bond, ed., *The Diaries and Papers of Sir Edward Dering, Second Baronet, 1644–84* (London, 1976), pp. 130–31.

100. PRO, SP29/415/44; Jones, *First Whigs*, pp. 163–64.

101. For an interesting account of the impact of the Exclusion Crisis on provincial society, see Daniel Beaver, "Conscience and Context: The Popish Plot and the Politics of Ritual, 1678–1682," *HJ* 34 (1991): 297–327.

102. Quoted in Ogg, *England in the Reign of Charles II*, pp. 618–19. The king was also quoted by the marquis of Worcester as saying, "By the grace of God I will stick to that that is law [i.e., the legal succession]" in reply to Shaftesbury's suggestion of the duke of Monmouth as a successor (HMC, *Twelfth Report, Appendix 9*, p. 84 [Beaufort MSS]).

103. For the shape of Charles's political system, see Clayton Roberts, "Party and Patronage in Later Stuart England," in S. B. Baxter, ed., *England's Rise to Greatness,* (Berkeley, 1983). Jonathan Barry has described the lieutenancy as the "storm troopers of the Tory reaction" in "The Politics of Religion in Restoration Bristol," p. 51.

104. Jones, *First Whigs*, p. 117.

105. BL, Add. MSS 29573 f. 222 (Hatton Papers).

106. BL, Egerton MSS 2985 f. 240 (Paston MSS); Cozens-Hardy, ed., *Norfolk Lieutenancy Journal*, p. 33.

107. Cozens-Hardy, ed., *Norfolk Lieutenancy Journal*, p. 33.

108. For the duke of Beaufort's role in promoting a loyal address in Bristol, see Barry, "Politics of Religion in Restoration Bristol," p. 178. Sir Richard Temple, an ambitious deputy lieutenant in Buckinghamshire, also promoted an address from Buckingham in August 1683. See Godfrey Davies, "The Political Career of Sir Richard Temple (1634–97) and Buckingham Politics," *HLQ* 4 (1940): 70.

109. PRO, SP29/419/81.

110. Jones, *First Whigs*, pp. 117–19.

111. For orders for publication, see PRO, SP44/68/332, 344; SP29/429/9; W. M. Wigfield, *Recusancy and Nonconformity in Bedfordshire,* Publications of the Bedfordshire Record Society, vol. 20 (Bedford, 1938), p. 185.

112. PRO, SP29/431/8.

113. SP44/68/337. J. R. Jones believes that the king deliberately discouraged addresses in an attempt to reduce political activity in the countryside. See Jones, *Charles II,* esp. chap. 7.

114. PRO, SP29/419/81.

115. PRO, SP29/415/7. For Kent, see Lee, "'Fanatic Magistrates,'" p. 52; Norrey, "Central Government," p. 280. Norrey also noted a dramatic increase in persecution in the west; see ibid., esp. chap. 2.

116. Ogg, *England in the Reign of Charles II*, p. 685; HMC, *Twelfth Report, Appendixes 4 and 5*, vol. 2, 116.

117. PRO, SP44/69/39. A more detailed account of the conspiracy may be found in Ogg, *England in the Reign of Charles II*, pp. 647–56. See also Maurice Ashley, *John Wildman* (New Haven, 1947).

118. PRO, SP29/425/81, 112, 113.

119. PRO, SP29/425/80, 93, 112, 113, 427/2.

120. PRO, SP29/428/147.

121. Cozens-Hardy, ed., *Norfolk Lieutenancy Journal*, p. 43; BL, Add. MSS 29560 f. 54 (Hatton Papers); and ChRD, DDX 384, p. 315 (Mainwaring Diary).

122. PRO, SP29/425/114.

123. PRO, SP29/430/134.

124. LAO, MM6/10/11, nos. 1–4 (Massingberd MSS).

125. ChRO, DDX 384, p. 315 (Mainwaring Diary). For Bridgwater, see Norrey, "Central Government," p. 280.

126. HMC, *Twelfth Report, Appendixes 4 and 5*, vol. 2, 82.

127. PRO, SP29/427/120.

128. BL, Add. MSS 41803 f. 52 (Middleton MSS).

129. PRO, SP29/429/97, 135.

130. Bodl., Tanner MSS 34 ff. 36, 109.

131. Miller, "The Crown and the Borough Charters," pp. 54–59, and Sacret, "Restoration Government."

132. PRO, SP29/428/90, 438/42.

133. PRO, SP44/68/135, 139, 142, 206; SP29/438/83. For Norwich, see John T. Evans, *Seventeenth Century Norwich: Politics, Religion, and Government, 1620–90* (Oxford, 1979). See also R. G. Pickavance, "The English Boroughs and the King's Government" (D. Phil. dissertation, Oxford University, 1976), p. 176.

134. Miller, "The Crown and the Borough Charters," p. 79, n. 3.

135. Pickavance, "English Boroughs," pp. 266–69.

136. See ibid., esp. chap. 6.

137. PRO, SP29/438/83, 438/89.

138. SP29/423/47, 432/92. See also Barry, "Politics of Religion in Restoration Bristol," pp. 171–72.

139. M. A. Mullett, "'Deprived of Our Former Place': The Internal Politics of Bedford, 1660–1688," *Publications of the Bedfordshire Historical Record Society*, vol. 59 (1980): 20.

140. Quoted ibid., p. 21.

141. Pickavance, "English Boroughs," p. 247.

142. PRO, SP44/68/142.

143. Davies, "Political Career of Sir Richard Temple," p. 72.

144. For the offices held by Newcastle and Peterborough, see GEC; for Norwich, Evans, *Seventeenth Century Norwich*.

145. Quoted in Mullett, " 'Deprived of Our Former Place,' " p. 22.

146. In at least one case, a lieutenant evidently protected a borough in which he already had influence from a quo warranto—the earl of Derby in Clitheroe, Lancs. See M. A. Mullett, " 'Men of Knowne Loyalty': The Politics of the Lancashire Borough of Clitheroe, 1660–89," *NH* 21 (1985): 132–33.

147. For some of the lieutenancy's letters concerning the days of the king's final illness and death, see BL, Add. MSS 41803 ff. 122–54 (Middleton MSS), and Hutton, *Charles II*, pp. 442–45.

148. HMC, *Twelfth Report, Appendixes 4 and 5*, vol. 2, 86–87.

149. SRO, DW 1721/3/291, March 10, 19, and 21, 1685 (Bagot MSS); Bramston, *Autobiography*, pp. 164, 169.

150. Gilbert Burnet, *History of His Own Time*, 6 vols., ed. M. J. Routh (Oxford, 1833), 3:16.

151. HMC, *Twelfth Report, Appendixes 4 and 5*, vol. 2, 86. The king also ordered Lindsey to support another candidate in Grantham, St. Leger Scrope, who evidently never stood (PRO, SP44/56/187).

152. PRO, SP44/56/182.

153. Henning, ed., *History of Parliament*, s.v. "Harwich."

154. PRO, SP44/56/198, 212. For a detailed account of the Monmouth Rising, see Peter Earle, *Monmouth's Rebels* (New York, 1977).

155. PRO, SP44/56/217–28.

156. BL, Add. MSS 41803 ff. 303, 305, 333 (Middleton MSS).

157. Western, *English Militia*, pp. 54–55. Norrey's view of the militia's utility is more pessimistic. See "Central Government," pp. 416–23.

158. Western, *English Militia*, p. 55.

159. Cozens-Hardy, ed., *Norfolk Lieutenancy Journal*, p. 212.

160. LAO, MM 6/10/11, no. 4 (Massingberd MSS).

161. BL, Add. MSS 41804 f. 7 (Middleton MSS).

6. Revolution: The Deposition of James II

1. See Miller's very convincing account of the king's motives in *Popery and Politics*, pp. 196–202. J. R. Jones, largely agrees with Miller's assessment in his essay "James II's Revolution: Royal Policies, 1686–1692," in Jonathan Israel, ed., *The Anglo-Dutch Moment* (Cambridge, 1991), p. 70. Other narratives of the period are David Ogg, *England in the Reigns of James II and William III*, rev. ed. (Oxford, 1955), and J. R. Jones, *The Revolution of 1688 in England* (London, 1972). For more recent analyses of the revolution, see W. A. Speck, *Reluctant Revolutionaries: Englishmen and the Revolution of 1688* (Oxford, 1989), and George Hilton Jones, *Convergent Forces: Immediate Causes of the Revolution of 1688 in England* (Ames, Iowa, 1990).

2. Thus, for example, his refusal to convert to Catholicism until his deathbed.

3. Robin Clifton, *The Last Popular Rebellion* (London, 1987), pp. 292–93. Clifton's assessment of the militia's performance should be contrasted with Western's, however, in *English Militia*, pp. 54–57.

4. J. S. Clarke, *Life of James II*, 2 vols. (London, 1816), 2:48.

5. Ogg, *England in the Reigns of James II and William III*, p. 160. For antiarmy

sentiment in general, see Schwoerer, *No Standing Armies!* See also John Childs, *The Army, James II, and the Glorious Revolution* (Manchester, 1980).

6. Anchitell Grey, ed., *Debates of the House of Commons*, 10 vols. (London, 1763), 8:355.

7. Grey, ed., *Debates*, 8:355, 357–58. Other deputies speaking in behalf of the militia were William Ashburnham (Sussex), Sir Richard Temple (Buckingham-shire), Thomas Meres (Lincolnshire), and Sir William Trumbull (Buckingham-shire).

8. Ibid., p. 359.

9. Ibid., p. 360; Clarke, *James II*, 2:55; *Journal of the House of Commons*, 9:757–60. The king was offered £700,000. The militia bill was never reported out of committee; Parliament was prorogued before the members finished their work. See Reresby, *Memoirs*, p. 397.

10. Clarke, *James II*, 2:49.

11. Reresby, *Memoirs*, p. 359.

12. Ogg, *England in the Reigns of James II and William III*, pp. 167–68. For James's relations with his judges, see A. F. Havighurst, "James II and the Twelve Men in Scarlet," *Law Quarterly Review* 69 (1953): 522–46.

13. Glassey, *Politics and the Appointment of Justices of the Peace*, p. 70; Miller, *Popery and Politics*, p. 209, Appendix 3, pp. 269–72.

14. For the Catholic influence in James's council, see Jones, *Revolution*, esp. chaps. 5–6.

15. See Jones, *Revolution*, chap. 5. For the Declaration of Indulgence, see R. E. Boyer, "The English Declarations of Indulgence of 1687 and 1688," *Catholic Historical Review* 1 (1964): 322–71.

16. HMC, *Twelfth Report, Appendix* 9, pp. 89–90 (Beaufort MSS).

17. For biographical information, see Henning, ed., *History of Parliament*, s.v. "Thomas Tufton."

18. John Kenyon, *Robert Spencer, Earl of Sunderland, 1641–1702* (London, 1958), pp. 88n, 188n. For Jeffreys, see G. W. Keeton, *Lord Chancellor Jeffreys* (London, 1965).

19. See Norrey, "Central Government," p. 346.

20. Jones, *Revolution*, pp. 136–37.

21. Bramston, *Autobiography*, pp. 306–7.

22. BL, Add. MSS 29578 f. 89 (Hatton Papers, 1684–97); HMC, *Twelfth Report, Appendix* 9, pp. 89–90 (Beaufort MSS).

23. Jones, *Revolution*, pp. 132–37; Glassey, *Politics and the Appointment of Justices of the Peace*, pp. 78–82.

24. From the king's instructions to Beaufort, October 26, 1687, HMC, *Twelfth Report, Appendix* 9, p. 91 (Beaufort MSS).

25. BL, Add. MSS 29578 f. 134 (Lyttleton/Hatton Correspondence).

26. Burnet, *History*, 3:193 and n.

27. Secretary of state to the earl of Derby, BL, Add. MSS 41804 f. 308 (Middleton MSS).

28. Thomas Bruce, second earl of Ailesbury, *Memoirs*, 2 vols. (London, 1890), 1:162.

29. Bodl., Tanner MSS 243 f. 55v.

30. For a compilation of the answers of many deputies and justices of the peace, see Sir George Duckett, *Penal Laws and Test Act* (London, 1883).

31. Thomas Bruce, second earl of Ailesbury, *Memoirs,* 2 vols. (London, 1890), 1:164.

32. BL, Add. MSS 52924 f. 2 (Sir John Knatchbull Diary, 1688–89. There is another copy of this manuscript in BL, Add MSS 33923).

33. Duckett, *Penal Laws,* p. 48.

34. Wigfield, *Recusancy and Nonconformity in Bedfordshire,* pp. 187–98; Bruce, *Memoirs,* p. 163.

35. Bodl., Tanner MSS 243 ff. 52–54; Duckett, *Penal Laws,* pp. 12–14. See also Norrey, "Central Government," p. 346.

36. Duckett, *Penal Laws,* pp. 11, 205–6. The only other deputy who agreed to the questions was Lord Fitzharding, who qualified his acceptance by saying, "provided that the Church of England be by anyway secured." Fitzharding went on to lead the resistance in Somerset to the king's policies (ibid., pp. 19–26).

37. Some of the names may have come from the Privy Council committee, the "Board of Regulators" set up in November 1687, which included Sunderland, Jeffreys, and a number of Catholics, including Father Petre (Glassey, *Politics and the Appointment of Justices of the Peace,* p. 82).

38. Bruce, *Memoirs,* 1:162.

39. Duckett, *Penal Laws,* pp. 296, 196, 276. CRO, Earwaker MSS 63/2/691 f. 49.

40. Duckett, *Penal Laws,* pp. 260, 151.

41. Whether James recognized the irony in relying on former Exclusionists to implement his policies seems doubtful. Titus's service on the council was brief, July to December 1688. In later life he became a Whig Speaker of the House of Commons. See Henning, ed., *History of Parliament,* s.v. "Silius Titus."

42. For the peculiar dependence of the kings of England on their subjects' cooperation for their success, see John Miller's article on Britain in his volume of essays, *Absolutism in Seventeenth Century Europe* (New York, 1990), esp. pp. 201–4.

43. See Jones, *Revolution,* chap. 6.

44. Bruce, *Memoirs,* 1:176, 132.

45. Duckett, *Penal Laws,* pp. 22, 25.

46. Wigfield, *Recusancy and Nonconformity in Bedfordshire,* pp. 199–200.

47. Bruce, *Memoirs,* 1:173–75.

48. BL, Egerton MSS 3344 f. 41 (West Riding) Leeds MSS); *CSPD, James II,* 3:284.

49. See Bodl., Tanner MSS 27/116 for Cambridgeshire; SRO DW 1721/3/291 (Bagot MSS); NNRO, microfilm reel 81/3 (Norfolk Lieutenancy Order Book), f. 91.

50. *CSPD, James II,* 3:287.

51. Jones, *Revolution,* p. 135.

52. S. B. Baxter, *William III* (London, 1966); John Carswell, *The Descent on England: A Study of the English Revolution of 1688 and Its Background* (New York, 1972), esp. pt. 3. For a firsthand account of William's preparations, see Burnet, *History.*

53. Carswell, *Descent on England,* pp. 164–70.

54. BL, Add. MSS 29563 f. 268 (Hatton MSS, 1688–89).

55. BL, Add. MSS 52924 f. 8 (Knatchbull Diary).

56. BL, Add. MSS 34173 ff. 37–39 (Twysden Letters); Bramston, *Autobiography*, p. 326.

57. Cozens-Hardy, ed., *Norfolk Lieutenancy Journal*, p. 88.

58. BL, Add. MSS 29563 f. 303 (Hatton MSS, 1688–89).

59. BL, Add. MSS 40746 f. 137 (Bowes Papers). Evidence on this point is sketchy, but Durham certainly wholeheartedly supported William after his landing. See D. H. Hosford, *Nottingham, the Nobles, and the North* (Hamden, Conn., 1976), p. 31.

60. See Clive Jones, "Journal of the Voyage of William of Orange from Holland to Torbay, 1688," *Journal of Army Historical Research* 51 (1973): 15–18, Jones, and "The Protestant Wind of 1688: Myth and Reality," *European Studies Review* 3 (1973): 201–20.

61. See Childs, *The Army, James II, and the Glorious Revolution*, chaps. 6–7.

62. BL, Add. MSS 41805 ff. 72, 91, 129 (Middleton MSS).

63. Ibid., ff. 85, 109.

64. BL, Add. MSS 29563 f. 303 (Hatton Papers).

65. Cozens-Hardy, ed., *Norfolk Lieutenancy Journal*, pp. 89–94.

66. BL, Add. MSS 29573 f. 217 (Hatton Papers).

67. BL, Add. MSS 41805 f. 63 (Middleton MSS).

68. Carswell, *Descent on England*, p. 146 and n.

69. BL, Add. MSS 41805 f. 129 (Middleton MSS).

70. Carswell, *Descent on England*, p. 194; Jones, *Revolution*, p. 296.

71. BL, Add. MSS 41805 f. 293 (Middleton MSS).

72. BL, Add. MSS 29563 f. 342 (Hatton Papers); Egerton MSS 3336 ff. 18, 50 (Leeds MSS).

73. The most detailed discussion of the events in the north at this period is Hosford, *Nottingham, the Nobles, and the North*. Sir John Reresby's *Memoirs* also provide much detail.

74. This account of the coup in York is based on Reresby's *Memoirs*, pp. 410–20; see also A. M. Evans, "Yorkshire and the Revolution of 1688," *Yorkshire Archaeological Journal* 29 (1929): 258–85.

75. See Henning, ed., *History of Parliament*, s.v. "Henry Goodricke."

76. Reresby, *Memoirs*, p. 414; BL, Egerton MSS 3335 f. 80 (Leeds MSS).

77. Reresby, *Memoirs*, p. 415.

78. Ibid., p. 418.

79. For the names of the new lieutenants, see J. C. Sainty, ed., *List of Lieutenants of Counties, 1660–1974*, List and Index Society, special ser., vol. 12 (1979).

BIBLIOGRAPHY

Manuscript Sources

Public Record Office

PC2	Privy Council Registers, Charles I
E401	Declared Accounts, Exchequer, Charles I
SP14	State Papers, James I
SP16	State Papers, Charles I
SP29	State Papers, Charles II
SP44	Domestic Entry Books, Charles II
SP46	State Papers, Supplementary

British Library

ADDITIONAL MSS

10609	Breconshire Lieutenancy Papers
11050–52	Herefordshire Military Affairs
11601	Norfolk Lieutenancy Book, 1661–75
15048	Suffolk Lieutenancy Book, 1693–1740
18979	Fairfax Letters
21048	Suffolk Lieutenancy Book, 1661–63
21922	Norton Letter Book, 1625–40
22959	Rous Diary
23006	Norfolk Lieutenancy Book
26781	Dering Papers
27447–48	Paston Correspondence
28000	Oxenden MSS
28051	Leeds MSS
28052	Godolphin Correspondence
29552–78	Hatton Papers
29597	Carew MSS

29910	Swynfen MSS
32093	Malet Papers, ca. 1625–60
32324	Seymour Correspondence
34173	Twysden Letters
34222	Northamptonshire Lieutenancy Book, 1660–66
34306	Milward Lieutenancy Book, 1660–66
34729	West Papers
36922	Aston Papers, 1663–96
36924	Norris Papers
36988	Paston MSS
37820	Nicholas MSS
39245–46	Wodehouse MSS; Official Letter Books, 1608–40, 1664–76
39978	Baigent Collection
40746	Bowes Papers
41254	North Riding MSS
41654, 56	Townshend Papers
41803–5; 23	Middleton MSS
42592, 96–97	Brockman MSS; Political and Official Papers, ca. 1598–1800
52924	Sir John Knatchbull Diary
62081	Benet Letters
63082, 63101–9	Blakeney/Townshend MSS

ADDITIONAL CHARTERS

2146

EGERTON MSS

860	Duke of Buckingham's Lieutenancy Letter Book
1626	Farnborough MSS; Militia Papers, William III
2537–41	Nicholas MSS
2643–51	Barrington MSS
2716	Gawdy MSS
2985	Paston MSS
3329–36	Leeds MSS

HARLEIAN MSS

305	Libri Pacis, James I
382–83	Dewes Papers
389	Stuteville Newsletters
703	Sussex Lieutenancy Book, James I–Charles I
1622	Libri Pacis, Charles I
3783–90	Sancroft Letters, ca. 1600–1690
4014	Cambridgeshire Lieutenancy Book, 1628–40
6988	Duke of Buckingham's Letter Book
7000	Puckering Papers

KING'S MSS

265   Norfolk Lieutenancy Book, 1588–1615

LANSDOWNE MSS

89   Hicks MSS
153, 65   Caesar MSS; Official and Political Papers, James I

LOAN MSS

29   Portland (Harley) Papers
Althorp MSS.

STOWE MSS

200–216   Capel MSS

House of Lords Record Office

Lieutenancy commissions, 1640–42
Main Papers

Bedfordshire Record Office

St. John MSS

Bodleian Library, Oxford

Carte MSS
Clarendon State Papers
Essex Lieutenancy Book, t. James I–Charles I (Firth MSS c4)
Fleming Letters (MS Donc 37)
Lothian MSS
Oxfordshire Lieutenancy Book, t. Charles II (MS Eng. Hist b. 212)
Rawlinson MSS (Reresby Letters)
Tanner MSS (Norfolk Lieutenancy Papers)

Cheshire Record Office

Arderne MSS
Cholmondeley MSS
Leicester de Tabley MSS
Thomas Mainwaring Diary

City of Chester Record Office

Chetwode MSS
Earwaker MSS
Corporation Great Letter Books
Corporation Assembly Books

Derbyshire Record Office

Burdett of Foremark MSS
Constables' Accounts, 1648–77
Gell MSS
Gresley MSS

Huntington Library, San Marino, California

Temple MSS

Lancashire Record Office

Bankes MSS
Kenyon MSS
Molyneux MSS
Sir Alexander Rigby's Lieutenancy Book

Lincolnshire Archive Office

Lindsey Deposit
Massingberd MSS
Monson MSS
Society of Friends MSS
Yarborough MSS

Norwich and Norfolk Record Office

Aylsham MSS
Bradfer-Lawrence MSS
Hare MSS
Lestrange MSS
Norfolk Lieutenancy Letter Book, 1660–76
Norwich City Lieutenancy Letter Book
Walsingham (Merton) MSS

Northampton Central Library

John Conant's Letters, ca. 1646–93

Northamptonshire Record Office

Brudenell MSS
Cokayne MSS
Finch-Hatton Papers
Fitzwilliam MSS
Isham Correspondence
Isham of Lamport MSS
St. John MSS
Stopford-Sackville MSS

Raynham Hall, Norfolk

Townshend Letters, 1660–80
Lieutenancy Book, 1660–76

William Salt Library, Stafford

Aston MSS
Chetwynd MSS
William Salt MSS
Tixall MSS

Staffordshire Record Office

Bagot MSS
Leveson Gower MSS
Paget MSS
Sutherland MSS

Printed Primary Sources

Acts of the Privy Council of England, 1613–32, 32 vols. London, 1929–64.

Agar-Ellis, G. W. *The Ellis Correspondence.* 2 vols. London, 1829.

Axon, Ernest, ed. *Manchester Quarter Sessions.* Vol. 1, 1616–22/23. Record Society of Lancashire and Cheshire, vol. 42 (1901).

Baker, W. T., ed. *Records of the Borough of Nottingham.* Vol. 5, 1625–1702. London, 1902.

Besse, Joseph, ed. *A Collection of the Sufferings of the People Called Quakers.* London, 1753.

Bigland, R., ed. *Historical Collections Relative to the City of Gloucester.* 2 vols. Gloucester, 1786–92.

Birch, Thomas. *The Court and Times of Charles I.* 2 vols. London, 1848.

Bond, Maurice, ed. *The Diaries and Papers of Sir Edward Dering, Second Baronet, 1644–84.* London, 1976.

Bradney, J. A. *Diary of Walter Powell.* Bristol, 1907.

Bramston, Sir John. *Autobiography.* Camden Society, vol. 32. 1845.

Browne, A. L., ed. "King James II's Proposed Repeal of the Penal Laws and Test Act in 1688." *Transactions of the Cumberland and Westmorland Antiquarian and Archaeological Society* n.s., 38 (1938): 180–93.

Browning, Andrew. *English Historical Documents, 1660–1714.* London, 1953.

Bruce, John, ed. *Letters and Papers of the Verney Family.* London, 1853.

Bruce, Thomas, second earl of Ailesbury. *Memoirs.* 2 vols. London, 1890.

Burne, S. A. H., ed. "Chetwynd Papers." *Collections of the Staffordshire Record Society,* pp. 83–124. Stafford, 1941.

Burnet, Gilbert. *History of His Own Time.* 6 vols., ed. M. J. Routh. Oxford, 1833.

Calendar of State Papers, Domestic. 81 vols. London, 1857– .

Calendar of Treasury Books, 1660–89. 32 vols. London, 1904–62.

Camden, William. *Britannia.* London, 1722.

Carte, Thomas. *A Collection of Original Letters and Papers Concerning the Affairs of England from the Years 1641–1660*. London, 1739.

Cavendish, Margaret, Duchess of Newcastle. *Life of William Cavendish, Duke of Newcastle*. London, 1667.

Christie, W. D., ed. *Letters Addressed from London to Sir Joseph Williamson, 1673–74*. 2 vols. Camden Society n.s., 8 (1874).

Coate, Mary, ed. *The Letter Book of John, Viscount Mordaunt, 1658–60*. Camden Society, 3d ser., vol. 69 (1945).

Coate, W. H., ed. *The Journal of Sir Symonds D'Ewes*. New Haven, 1942.

Cozens-Hardy, Basil, ed. *Norfolk Lieutenancy Journal, 1676–1701*. Norfolk Record Society, vol. 30 (1961).

Dalton, Michael. *The Countrey Justice*. London, 1661.

Duckett, Sir George. *Penal Laws and Test Act*. London, 1883.

————, ed. "King James II's Proposed Repeal of the Penal Laws and Test Act in 1688." *Yorkshire Archaeological Journal* 5 (1877–78): 433–73.

Dugdale, William. *The Antiquities of Warwickshire*. London, 1656.

Dunn, Richard M., ed. *Norfolk Lieutenancy Journal, 1660–1676*. Norfolk Record Society, vol. 45 (1977).

Evelyn, John. *Diary,* ed. E. S. deBeer. 6 vols. Oxford, 1955.

Elyot, Thomas. *The Book Named the Governor*. London, 1906.

Faraday, M. A., ed. *Herefordshire Militia Assessments of 1663*. Camden Society, 4th ser., vol. 10 (1972).

Fiennes, Celia. *Journies,* ed. Christopher Morris. London, 1947.

Fox, George. *Journals*. 2 vols. Cambridge, 1911.

Fuller, Thomas. *History of the Worthies of England*. London, 1662.

Gardiner, S. R., ed. *The Constitutional Documents of the Puritan Revolution, 1625–1660*. 3d ed. Oxford, 1906.

Goring, Jeremy, and Joan Wake, eds. *Northamptonshire Lieutenancy Papers, 1580–1614*. Northamptonshire Record Society, vol. 27 (1975).

Gough, Richard. *History of Myddle*. Harmondsworth, 1981.

Greene, Douglas, ed. *Diaries of the Popish Plot*. Delmar, N.Y., 1977.

Grey, Anchitell, ed. *Debates of the House of Commons*. 10 vols. London, 1763.

Guilding, J. M., ed. *Reading Records: Diary of the Corporation*. 4 vols. London, 1895.

Hamilton, Anthony. *Memoirs of the Count de Grammont,* trans. Horace Walpole. New York, 1928.

Harland, John, ed. *The Lancashire Lieutenancy Under the Tudors and Stuarts*. Chetham Society, vols. 49–50 (1859).

Hawles, John. *Remarks upon the Tryals of Edward Fitzharris, Stephen Colledge, Count Coningsmark. . . .* London, 1689.

Hertford County Records: Sessions Rolls. 9 vols. Hertford, 1905–39.

Historical Manuscripts Commission. *Buccleuch and Queensbury Manuscripts*. 3 vols. London 1899–1926.

————. *Eighth Report, Appendix 2—Duke of Manchester's Manuscripts*. London, 1881.

————. *Eleventh Report, Appendix 2—House of Lords Manuscripts*. London, 1898.

————. *Fifteenth Report, Appendix 7—Duke of Somerset Manuscripts; Ailesbury Manuscripts*. London, 1898.

————. *Fourth Report—House of Lords Manuscripts*. London, 1874.

————. *Hastings Manuscripts*. 4 vols. London, 1928–47.

————. *Lindsey Manuscripts*. London, 1895.

————. *Lothian Manuscripts*. London, 1905.

————. *Ninth Report, Appendix 2—Woodforde Manuscripts*. London, 1883–84.

————. *Ormonde Manuscripts*. 8 vols. London, 1902–20.

————. *Report on the Manuscripts in Various Collections*. 8 vols. London, 1901–1914.

————. *Tenth Report, Appendix 6*. London, 1887.

————. *Twelfth Report, Appendixes 4 and 5—Rutland Manuscripts*. 4 vols. London, 1888–1903.

————. *Twelfth Report, Appendix 7—LeFleming Manuscripts*. London, 1890.

————. *Twelfth Report, Appendix 9—Ketton Manuscripts; Beaufort Manuscripts*. London, 1891.

Howell, T. B., ed. *State Trials*. 33 vols. London, 1809–26.

Hunter, Joseph, ed. *Ralph Thoresby's Diary*. 4 vols. London, 1830–32.

Hyde, Edward, first earl of Clarendon. *The History of the Rebellion and Civil Wars in England,* ed. W. D. Macray. 6 vols. Oxford, 1888.

————. *Life*. 2 vols. Oxford, 1857.

An Impartial Account of the Arraignment, Trial and Condemnation of Stephen Colledge. London, 1682.

Jeayes, I. H., ed. *Letters of Philip Gawdy*. London, 1906.

Jenkinson, H. A., and D. L. Powell, eds. *Surrey Quarter Sessions Records, 1659–66*. 3 vols. London, 1934–38.

Johnson, Robert, et al., eds. *Commons Debates, 1628*. 6 vols. New Haven, 1977–83.

Jones, David. *The Secret History of White-Hall from the Restoration of Charles II down to the Abdication of the Late King James*. London, 1697.

Journal of the House of Commons.

Journal of the House of Lords.

LeHardy, William, ed. *Calendar to the Sessions Books, Sessions Minute Books, and Other Session Records*. Vol. 6. Hereford, 1930.

A Letter from the Grand Jury of Oxford. Oxford, 1681.

London Gazette.

Lord, George, ed. *Poems on Affairs of State*. 7 vols. New Haven, 1963–75.

McIlwain, C. W., ed. *The Political Works of James I*. Cambridge, Mass., 1918.

Mares, F. H. *Memoirs of the First Earl of Monmouth*. Oxford, 1972.

Markham, C. A., and J. C. Cox, eds. *The Records of the Borough of Northampton*. 2 vols. Northampton, 1897.

Markham, Gervase. *The Muster Master,* ed. C. L. Hamilton. Camden Miscellany, 4th ser., vol. 14 (1975).

Milward, John. *Diary,* ed. Caroline Robbins. Cambridge, 1938.

Miscellanies Relating to Lancashire and Cheshire. Vol. 1. Record Society of Lancashire and Cheshire, vol. 12 (1885).

Murphy, W. P., ed. *The Earl of Hertford's Lieutenancy Papers.* Wiltshire Record Society, vol. 23 (1969).

Nalson, John. *An Impartial Account of the Great Affairs of State.* 2 vols. London, 1682–83.

Oglander, Sir John. *A Royalist's Notebook,* ed. Francis Bamford. New York, 1971.

Ogle, O., ed. *Calendar of the Clarendon State Papers.* 4 vols. Oxford, 1872–1938.

Oxford Gazette. Oxford, 1681.

Peck, Francis. *Desiderata Curiosa.* 2 vols. London, 1779.

Pepys, Samuel. *Diary,* ed. Robert Latham and William Matthews. 10 vols. Berkeley, 1970–83.

Raines, F. R., ed. *Nicholas Assheton's Journal.* Chetham Society, vol. 14 (1848).

Reresby, Sir John. *Memoirs,* ed. Andrew Browning. Glasgow, 1936.

Rosenheim, James, ed. *The Notebook of Robert Doughty, 1662–65.* Norfolk Record Society, vol. 54 (1989).

Rous, John. *Diary of John Rous, Incumbent of Santon Downham, Suffolk,* ed. Mary Greene. Camden Society, vol. 66 (1856).

The Royalist Composition Papers. Vol. 6. Record Society for the Publication of Original Documents Relating to Lancashire and Cheshire, vol. 95 (1941).

Rushworth, John. *Historical Collections.* 7 vols. London, 1659–1701.

Rye, William, ed. *State Papers Relating to Musters, Beacons, and Subsidies in Norfolk.* Norwich, 1907.

Sainty, J. C., ed. *Lieutenants of Counties, 1585–1642.* Bulletin of the Institute of Historical Research, Special Supplement 8. London, 1970.

——— , ed. *List of Lieutenants of Counties, 1660–1974.* List and Index Society, Special Ser., vol. 12 (1979).

Slaughter, Thomas, ed., *Ideology and Politics on the Eve of the Restoration: Newcastle's Advice to Charles II.* Philadelphia, 1984.

The Speech and Carriage of Stephen Colledge. London, 1681.

State Papers Collected by Edward Earl of Clarendon. 3 vols. Oxford, 1786.

Statutes of the Realm, Car. II.

Stevenson, W. H., et al., eds. *Records of the Borough of Nottingham.* 9 vols. London and Nottingham, 1882–1956.

Stocks, Helen, and W. H. Stevenson, eds. *Records of the Borough of Leicester.* Cambridge, 1923.

Tait, James, ed. *Taxation in Salford Hundred, 1524–1802.* Chetham Society, n.s., vol. 83 (1924).

Thomson, Gladys Scott, ed. *The Twysden Lieutenancy Papers, 1583–1668.* Kent Archaeological Society Records, vol. 10 (1926).

Townshend, Henry. *The Diary of Henry Townshend of Elmley Lovett, 1640–1663,* ed. J. W. Willis Bund. 2 vols. London, 1920.

A True Copy of the Dying Words of Stephen Colledge. London, 1681.

Turner, G. Lyon, ed. *Original Records of Early Nonconformity.* 3 vols. London, 1911–14.

Wake, Joan, ed. *A Copy of Papers Relating to Musters, Beacons, Subsidies, et cetera, in the County of Northampton.* Northamptonshire Record Society, vol. 3 (1925).

Wake, Joan, and H. I. Longden, eds. *The Montagu Musters Book*. Northampton-shire Record Society Publications, vol. 7 (1932–33).

Wigfield, W. M., ed. *Recusancy and Nonconformity in Bedfordshire*. Bedfordshire Historical Record Society, vol. 20 (1938).

Yonge, Walter. *Diary*, ed. George Roberts. Camden Society, vol. 41 (1847).

Published Secondary Sources

Abbott, Wilbur C. "English Conspiracy and Dissent, 1660–1674." *American Historical Review* 14 (1908–9): 503–28.

Abernathy, George. *The English Presbyterians and the Stuart Restoration, 1648–1663*. Transactions of the American Philosophical Society n.s., 55 (1965).

Acheson, Eric. *A Gentry Community: Leicestershire in the Fifteenth Century*. Cambridge, 1992.

Adamson, J. S. A. "Politics and Nobility in Civil War England." *HJ* 34 (1991): 231–55.

Allen, David. "The Role of the London Trained Bands in the Exclusion Crisis." *EHR* 87 (1972): 287–303.

Ashley, Maurice. *John Wildman*. New Haven, 1947.

Ashton, Robert. *Reformation and Revolution: England, 1558–1660*. London, 1984.

Axon, W. E. A. *Echoes of Old Lancashire*. London, 1899.

Aylmer, Gerald. *The King's Servants*. London, 1961.

―――. "St. Patrick's Day, 1628, in Witham Essex." *Past and Present* 61 (1973): 139–48.

Ayton, Ellis. *The Penny Universities: A History of the Coffee Houses*. London, 1956.

Baines, Edward. *History of the County Palatine and Duchy of Lancashire*, ed. James Croston. New ed. London, 1888.

Barnes. T. G. "Deputies Not Principals, Lieutenants Not Captains: The Institutional Failure of the Lieutenancy in the 1620s." In Mark Charles Fissel, ed., *War and Government in Britain, 1598–1650*, pp. 58–86. Manchester, 1991.

―――. *Somerset, 1625–1640: A County's Government During the Personal Rule*. Cambridge, Mass., 1961.

Barry, Jonathan. "The Politics of Religion in Restoration Bristol." In Tim Harris, Paul Seaward, and Mark Goldie, eds., *The Politics of Religion in Restoration England*, pp. 163–89. Oxford, 1990.

Baxter, S. B. *William III*. London, 1966.

―――, ed. *England's Rise to Greatness*. Berkeley, 1983.

Beattie, J. M. *Crime and the Courts in England, 1660–1800*. Princeton, 1986.

Beaver, Daniel. "Conscience and Context: The Popish Plot and the Politics of Ritual, 1678–1682." *HJ* 34 (1991): 297–327.

Beckett, J. V. *The Aristocracy in England, 1660–1914*. Oxford, 1986.

Beddard, Robert, ed. *The Revolutions of 1688*. Oxford, 1991.

Beier, A. L. *Masterless Men: The Vagrancy Problem in England, 1560–1640*. New York, 1985.

Bell, W. G. *The Great Fire of London*. London, 1951.

Beloff, Max. *Public Order and Popular Disturbances, 1660–1714.* London, 1938.

Black, Jeremy. *A System of Ambition? British Foreign Policy, 1660–1793.* London, 1991.

Black, Jeremy, and Jeremy Gregory, eds. *Culture, Politics, and Society in Britain, 1660–1800.* Manchester, 1991.

Blomefield, Francis. *History of Norfolk.* 2d ed., 11 vols. London, 1806.

Bosher, R. S. *The Making of the Restoration Settlement.* London, 1957.

Bossy, John. *The English Catholic Community, 1570–1850.* Oxford, 1976.

Bowle, John. *John Evelyn and His World.* London, 1981.

Boyer, R. E. "The English Declarations of Indulgence of 1687 and 1688." *Catholic Historical Review* 1 (1964): 322–71.

Boynton, Lindsay. "Billeting: The Example of the Isle of Wight." *EHR* 74 (1959): 24–40.

———. *The Elizabethan Militia, 1558–1638.* London, 1967.

———. "Martial Law and the Petition of Right." *EHR* 79 (1964): 255–84.

———. "The Tudor Provost Marshal." *EHR* 77 (1962): 437–55.

Braithwaite, William C. *The Second Period of Quakerism.* 2d ed., ed. Henry J. Cadbury. Cambridge, 1961.

Browning, Andrew. "Parties and Parliamentary Organization in the Reign of Charles II." *TRHS* 4th ser., 30 (1948): 21–36.

———. *Thomas Osborne, Earl of Danby.* 3 vols. Glasgow, 1944–51.

Bruijn, J. R. "Dutch Privateering During the Second and Third Anglo-Dutch Wars." *Low Countries Historical Yearbook* 11 (1978): 79–93.

Bryant, Sir Arthur. *Samuel Pepys.* 3 vols. Cambridge, 1933–38.

Burrage, Champlin. "The Fifth Monarchy Insurrections." *EHR* 25 (1910): 722–47.

Cannadine, David. *The Decline and Fall of the British Aristocracy.* New Haven, 1990.

Capp, Bernard S. *The Fifth Monarchy Men: A Study in Seventeenth Century English Millenarianism.* London, 1972.

Carlton, Charles. *Going to the Wars: The Experience of the British Civil Wars, 1638–51.* London, 1992.

Carroll, Roy. "Yorkshire Parliamentary Boroughs in the Seventeenth Century." *NH* 3 (1968): 70–104.

Carruthers, S. W. "Norfolk Presbyterians in the Seventeenth Century." *Norfolk Archaeology* 30 (1952): 89–100.

Carswell, John. *The Descent on England: A Study of the English Revolution of 1688 and Its Background.* New York, 1972.

Carte, Thomas. *The Life of James Duke of Ormond.* 4 vols. New ed. Oxford, 1858.

Carter, D. P. "The Exact Militia in Lancashire, 1625–1640." *NH* 11 (1975): 87–106.

———. "The Lancashire Militia, 1660–88." *THSLC* 132 (1983): 155–82.

Carter, Jennifer. "Law, Courts, and Constitution." In J. R. Jones, ed., *The Restored Monarchy, 1660–1688,* pp. 71–93. London, 1979.

Challinor, P. J. "Restoration and Exclusion in the County of Cheshire." *Bulletin of the John Rylands University Library* 64 (1982): 360–85.

Chandaman, C. D. *The English Public Revenue, 1660–1688.* Oxford, 1975.

Charlesworth, Andrew, ed. *An Atlas of Rural Protest in England, 1548–1900*. London, 1983.

Childs, John. *The Army, James II, and the Glorious Revolution*. Manchester, 1980.

———. *The Army of Charles II*. London, 1976.

Christianson, Paul. "The Peers, the People, and Party Management in the First Six Months of the Long Parliament." *Journal of Modern History* 49 (1977): 575–99.

Clark, J. C. D. *English Society, 1688–1832*. Cambridge, 1985.

———. *Revolution and Rebellion: State and Society in England in the Seventeenth and Eighteenth Centuries*. Cambridge, 1986.

Clark, Peter, A. G. R. Smith, and Nicholas Tyacke, eds. *The English Commonwealth, 1547–1640: Essays in Politics and Society*. New York, 1979.

Clarke, J. S. *Life of James II*. 2 vols. London, 1816.

Clifton, Robin. *The Last Popular Rebellion*. London, 1987.

Coate, Mary. *Cornwall During the Great Civil War*. Oxford, 1933.

Cogswell, Thomas. *The Blessed Revolution: English Politics and the Coming of War, 1621–24*. Cambridge, 1990.

Cokayne, G. E. *The Complete Peerage*. 14 vols. London, 1910–59.

Coleby, Andrew. *Central Government and the Localities: Hampshire, 1649–1689*. Cambridge, 1987.

Colvin, Howard, ed. *History of the King's Works*, vol. 4. London, 1982.

Coox, A. D. "The Dutch Invasion of England: 1667." *Military Affairs* 13 (1949): 223–33.

Cope, Esther. "The Debate over Muster Masters." *Huntington Library Quarterly* 45 (1982): 271–84.

———. *The Life of a Public Man: Edward, First Baron Montagu of Boughton, 1562–1644*. Philadelphia, 1981.

———. *Politics Without Parliaments*. London, 1986.

Coward, Barry. *Cromwell*. London, 1991.

———. "The Lieutenancy of Lancashire and Chesire in the Sixteenth and Early Seventeenth Centuries." *THSLC* 119 (1967): 39–64.

———. "The Social and Political Position of the Earls of Derby in Later Seventeenth Century Lancashire." *THSLC* 132 (1983): 127–54.

———. *The Stanleys Lords Stanley and Earls of Derby*. Chetham Society, 3d ser., vol. 30 (1983).

Cross, Claire. *The Puritan Earl: Henry Hastings, Third Earl of Huntingdon*. New York, 1966.

Cruickshank, C. G. *Elizabeth's Army*. Oxford, 1946.

Cunliffe, Edward. "Booke Concerning the Deputy Lieutenantshipp." *Sussex Archaeological Society* 40 (1896): 1–37.

Cust, Richard. "Charles I, the Privy Council, and the Forced Loan." *JBS* 24 (1985): 208–35.

———. *The Forced Loan and English Politics*. Oxford, 1988.

———. "News and Politics in Early Seventeenth Century England." *Past and Present* 112 (1986): 60–90.

Cust, Richard, and Ann Hughes, eds. *Conflict in Early Stuart England*. London, 1989.

Daly, James. "The Idea of Absolute Monarchy in Seventeenth Century England." *HJ* 21 (1978): 227–50.

——— . *Sir Robert Filmer and English Political Thought.* Toronto, 1979.

Davies, Godfrey. "The By-Election at Grantham, 1678." *Huntington Library Quarterly* 7 (1943–44): 179–82.

——— . "The Political Career of Sir Richard Temple (1634–97) and Buckingham Politics." *HLQ* 4 (1940): 47–83.

——— . *The Restoration of Charles II.* London, 1955.

Dean, David. "Parliament, Privy Council, and Local Politics in Elizabethan England. The Yarmouth-Lowestoft Fishing Dispute." *Albion* 22 (1990): 39–64.

DeKrey, Gary. *A Fractured Society: The Politics of London in the First Age of Party.* Oxford, 1987.

Dictionary of National Biography. 21 vols. 1885–1900. Reprint. Oxford, 1921.

Donagan, Barbara. "A Courtier's Progress: Greed and Consistency in the Life of the Earl of Holland." *HJ* 19 (1976): 317–53.

Donald, Peter. *An Uncounselled King: Charles I and the Scottish Troubles.* Cambridge, 1990.

Duncomb, John, W. H. Cooke, et al. *Collections Towards the History and Antiquities of the County of Hereford.* 6 vols. Hereford, 1804–12.

Earle, Peter. *Monmouth's Rebels.* New York, 1977.

Edwards, P. W. *The Horse Trade in Tudor and Stuart England.* Cambridge, 1988.

Eisenstadt, S. N., and Louis Roniger. "Patron-Client Relationships as a Model of Structuring Social Exchange." *Comparative Studies in Society and History* 22 (1980): 42–77.

Elliott, J. H. "Revolution and Continuity in Early Modern Europe." *Past and Present* 42 (1969): 35–56.

Elrington, C. R., and B. E. Harris, eds. *Victoria County History of Cheshire.* 3 vols. London, 1880–87.

Elton, Sir Geoffrey. *Studies in Tudor and Stuart Politics and Government.* 3 vols. Cambridge, 1974–83.

Evans, A. M. "Yorkshire and the Revolution of 1688." *Yorkshire Archaeological Journal* 29 (1929): 258–85.

Evans, John T. *Seventeenth Century Norwich: Politics, Religion, and Government, 1620–90.* Oxford, 1979.

Everitt, Alan. *The Community of Kent and the Great Rebellion, 1640–1660.* Leicester, 1966.

Feiling, Keith. *British Foreign Policy, 1660–72.* Oxford, 1930.

——— . *A History of the Tory Party, 1640–1714.* Oxford, 1924.

Fielding, John. "Opposition to the Personal Rule of Charles I: The Diary of Robert Woodford, 1637–41." *HJ* 31 (1988): 769–88.

Fisher, Thomas. *Collections Historical, Genealogical, and Topographical for Bedfordshire.* 1812–36.

Fissel, Mark, ed. *War and Government in Britain, 1528–1650.* Manchester, 1991.

Fletcher, Anthony. *A County Community in Peace and War: Sussex, 1600–1660.* London, 1975.

——— . *The Outbreak of the English Civil War.* New York, 1981.

————. *Reform in the Provinces: The Governance of Stuart England.* New Haven, 1985.

Fletcher, Anthony, and John Stevenson, eds. *Order and Disorder in Early Modern England.* Cambridge, 1985.

Forster, G. C. F. "Government in Provincial England Under the Later Stuarts." *TRHS* 5th ser., 33 (1983): 29–48.

Franken, M. A. A. "The General Tendencies and Structural Aspects of the Foreign Policy and Diplomacy of the Dutch Republic in the Latter Half of the Seventeenth Century." *Acta Historiae Neerlandica* 3 (1968): 1–42.

Fryde, E. B., D. E. Greenway, S. Porter, and Ian Roy, eds. *The Handbook of British Chronology.* 3d ed. London, 1986.

Gardiner, S. R. *A History of England from the Accession of James I to the Outbreak of the English Civil War.* 10 vols. London, 1884–1909.

————. *History of the Commonwealth and Protectorate.* 4 vols. London, 1903.

Gee, Henry. "The Derwentdale Plot, 1663." *TRHS* 3d ser., 11 (1917): 125–42.

Geyl, Peter. *Orange and Stuart.* London, 1969.

Glassey, Lionel K. *Politics and the Appointment of Justices of the Peace, 1675–1720.* Oxford, 1979.

Goldie, Mark. "Danby, the Bishops, and the Whigs," in Tim Harris, Paul Seaward, and Mark Goldie, eds., *The Politics of Religion in Restoration England,* pp. 75–105. Oxford, 1990.

————. "John Locke and Anglican Royalism." *Political Studies* 31 (1983): 86–102.

————. "The Political Thought of the Anglican Revolution." In Robert Beddard, ed., *The Revolutions of 1688* (Oxford, 1991), pp. 102–36.

Goring, J. J. "Social Change and Military Decline in Mid-Tudor England." *History* 60 (1975): 192–97.

Gough, Richard. *History of Myddle.* Harmondsworth, 1981.

Greaves, Richard. *Deliver Us from Evil.* Oxford, 1986.

————. *Enemies Under His Feet.* Stanford, 1990.

————. *Saints and Rebels: Seven Nonconformists in Stuart England.* Macon, Ga., 1985.

Green, Ian M. *The Reestablishment of the Church of England.* Cambridge, 1978.

Gruenfelder, J. K. *Influence in Early Stuart Elections.* Columbus, Ohio, 1981.

Guy, John. "The Petition of Right Reconsidered." *HJ* 25 (1982): 289–312.

Hale, J. R. *War and Society in Renaissance Europe.* Baltimore, 1985.

Haley, K. H. D. *An English Diplomat in the Low Countries: Sir William Temple and John de Witt, 1665–1672.* Oxford, 1986.

————. *Shaftesbury.* Oxford, 1968.

Hammond, Paul. "The King's Two Bodies: Representations of Charles II." In Jeremy Black and Jeremy Gregory, eds., *Culture, Politics, and Society in Britain, 1660–1800,* pp. 13–48. Manchester, 1991.

Harding, Robert R. *Anatomy of a Power Elite: Provincial Governors in Early Modern France.* New Haven, 1978.

Harris, R. W. *Clarendon and the English Revolution.* Stanford, 1983.

Harris, Tim. *London Crowds in the Reign of Charles II.* Cambridge, 1987.

————. "Radicalism and Restoration: The Shape of the Stuart Experience." *HJ* 31 (1988): 453–68.

Harris, Tim, Paul Seaward, and Mark Goldie, eds. *The Politics of Religion in Restoration England.* Oxford, 1990.

Harriss, G. L. "Aids and Benevolences." *HJ* 6 (1963): 1–19.

——— . "Medieval Doctrines in the Debates on Supply, 1610–29." In Kevin Sharpe, ed., *Faction and Parliament*, pp. 73–104. Oxford, 1978.

Havighurst, Arthur. "James II and the Twelve Men in Scarlet." *Law Quarterly Review* 69 (1953): 522–46.

Havran, Martin. *The Catholics in Caroline England.* Stanford, 1962.

Haydn, Joseph, and Horace Ocherby, eds. *The Book of Dignities.* London, 1894.

Henning, Basil D., ed. *History of Parliament, 1660–1690.* 3 vols. London, 1983.

Hey, D. G. "The Pattern of Nonconformity in South Yorkshire, 1660–1851." *NH* 8 (1973): 86–118.

Heyd, Michael. "The Reaction to Enthusiasm in the Seventeenth Century: Towards an Integrative Approach." *JMH* 53 (1981): 258–80.

Hibbard, Caroline. *Charles I and the Popish Plot.* Chapel Hill, 1983.

Higgins, G. P. "The Government of Early Stuart Cheshire." *NH* 12 (1976): 32–52.

Hill, Christopher. *The Experience of Defeat: Milton and Some Contemporaries.* London, 1984.

——— . *The World Turned Upside Down.* Harmondsworth, 1972.

Hirst, Derek. "Court, Country, and Politics Before 1629." In Kevin Sharpe, ed., *Faction and Parliament*, pp. 105–38. Oxford, 1978.

——— . "Local Affairs in Seventeenth Century England." *HJ* 32 (1989). 437–48.

——— . "The Privy Council and the Problem of Enforcement in the 1620s." *JBS* 18 (1978): 46–66.

——— . *The Representative of the People?* Cambridge, 1975.

Holmes, Clive. "The County Community in Stuart Historiography." *JBS* 19 (1980): 54–73.

——— . *Seventeenth Century Lincolnshire.* Lincoln, Eng., 1980.

Hopkinson, R. "The Electorate of Cumberland and Westmorland in the Late Seventeenth and Early Eighteenth Centuries." *NH* 15 (1979): 96–116.

Hosford, D. H. *Nottingham, the Nobles, and the North.* Hamden, Conn., 1976.

Hughes, Ann. *The Causes of the English Civil War.* London, 1991.

——— . "Thomas Dugard and His Circle in the 1630s: A Parliamentary-Puritan Connection?" *HJ* 29 (1986): 771–93.

——— . *Politics, Society, and Civil War in Warwickshire, 1620–1660.* Cambridge, 1987.

Hulme, Harold. *The Life of Sir John Eliot.* London, 1957.

Hurwich, Judith. "Dissent and Catholicism in English Society: A Study of Warwickshire, 1660–1720." *JBS* 16 (1976): 24–58.

Hussey, Frank. *Suffolk Invasion: The Dutch Attack on Landguard Fort, 1667.* Lavenham, Suffolk, 1983.

Hutton, Ronald. *Charles II.* Oxford, 1989.

——— . *The Restoration.* Oxford, 1985.

——— . *The Royalist War Effort.* London, 1982.

Israel, Jonathan, ed. *The Anglo-Dutch Moment.* Cambridge, 1991.

James, Mervyn. *Society, Politics, and Culture: Studies in Early Modern England.* Cambridge, 1986.

Jamison, T. R. *George Monck and the Restoration*. Fort Worth, Texas, 1975.

Jenkins, Philip. *The Making of a Ruling Class: The Glamorgan Gentry, 1640–1790*. Cambridge, 1983.

———. "The 'Old Leaven': The Welsh Roundheads After 1660." *HJ* 24 (1981): 807–24.

Johnson, Paul. *The National Trust Book of Castles*. New York, 1979.

Jones, Clive. "Journal of the Voyage of William of Orange from Holland to Torbay, 1688." *Journal of Army Historical Research* 51 (1973): 15–18.

———. "The Protestant Wind of 1688: Myth and Reality." *European Studies Review* 3 (1973): 201–20.

———, ed. *Britain in the First Age of Party*. London, 1987.

Jones, George Hilton. *Convergent Forces: Immediate Causes of the Revolution of 1688 in England*. Ames, Iowa, 1990.

Jones, J. R. *Charles II: Royal Politician*. London, 1987.

———. *The First Whigs: The Politics of the Exclusion Crisis, 1678–1683*. Oxford, 1961.

———. "James II's Revolution: Royal Policies, 1686–1692." In Israel, Jonathan ed., *The Anglo-Dutch Moment*, pp. 47–72. Cambridge, 1991.

———. *The Revolution of 1688 in England*. London, 1972.

———, ed. *The Restored Monarchy, 1660–1688*. London, 1979.

Keeton, G. W. *Lord Chancellor Jeffreys*. London, 1965.

Kent, Joan. *The English Village Constable, 1580–1642*. Oxford, 1986.

———. "The English Village Constable, 1580–1642: The Nature and Dilemmas of the Office." *JBS* 20 (1981): 26–49.

Kenyon, John. *The Civil Wars of England*. New York, 1988.

———. *The Popish Plot*. London, 1972.

———. *Revolution Principles: The Politics of Party, 1689–1720*. Cambridge, 1977.

———. *Robert Spencer, Earl of Sunderland, 1641–1702*. London, 1958.

Ketton-Cremer, R. W. *Norfolk in the Civil War*. Hamden, Conn., 1970.

———. *Norfolk Portraits*. London, 1944.

Key, Newton. "Comprehension and the Breakdown of Consensus in Restoration Hertfordshire." In Tim Harris, Paul Seaward, and Mark Goldie, eds., *The Politics of Religion in Restoration England*, pp. 191–215. Oxford, 1990.

Kishlansky, Mark. "The Emergence of Adversary Politics in the Long Parliament." *JMH* 49 (1977): 617–40.

———. *Parliamentary Selection: Social and Political Choice in Early Modern England*. Cambridge, 1986.

———. *The Rise of the New Model Army*. Cambridge, 1977.

———. "Saye No More." *JBS* 30 (1991): 397–448.

———. "Saye What?" *HJ* 33 (1990): 817–37.

Lake, Peter. "Anti-Popery: The Structure of a Prejudice." In Richard Cust and Ann Hughes, eds., *Conflict in Early Stuart England*, pp. 72–106. London, 1989.

Lake, Peter, and Kenneth Fincham. "Sir Richard Grosvenor and the Rhetoric of Magistracy." *BIHR* 54 (1981): 40–53.

———. "Constitutional Consensus and Puritan Opposition in the 1620s." *HJ* 25 (1982): 805–25.

Landau, Norma. *The Justices of the Peace, 1679–1760*. Berkeley, 1984.

Lee, Colin. "'Fanatic Magistrates': Religious and Political Conflict in Three Kent Boroughs, 1680–1684." *HJ* 35 (1992): 45–61.

Lee, Maurice. *The Road to Revolution: Scotland Under Charles I, 1625–37.* Urbana, 1985.

Levy, F. J. "How Information Spread Among the Gentry, 1550–1640." *JBS* 21 (1982): 11–34.

Lindley, K. J. "Riot Prevention and Control in Early Stuart London." *TRHS* 5th ser., 33 (1983): 109–26.

Lodge, Edmund. *Portraits of Illustrious Personages.* 8 vols. London, 1825.

Macfarlane, Alan. *The Justice and the Mare's Ale: Law and Disorder in Seventeenth Century England.* Oxford, 1981.

McGurk, J. N. N. "The Clergy and the Militia, 1580–1610." *History* n.s., 50 (1975): 198–210.

———. "Lieutenancy and Catholic Recusants in Elizabethan Kent." *Recusant History* 12 (1973–74): 157–70.

McNeill, William. *The Pursuit of Power.* Chicago, 1982.

Malcolm, Joyce. *Caesar's Due: Loyalty and King Charles I.* Royal Historical Society Studies in History, vol. 38 (1983).

———. "A King in Search of Soldiers: Charles I in 1642." *HJ* 21 (1978): 251–74.

Miller, John. *Charles II.* London, 1991.

———. "Charles II and His Parliaments." *TRHS* 5th ser., 32 (1982): 1–23.

———. "The Crown and the Borough Charters in the Reign of Charles II." *EHR* 100 (1985): 53–84.

———. "Faction in Later Stuart England, 1660–1714." *History Today* 33 (1983): 5–11.

———. *James II: A Study in Kingship.* London, 1977.

———. "The Militia and the Army in the Reign of James II." *HJ* 16 (1973): 659–80.

———. *Popery and Politics in England, 1660–1688.* Cambridge, 1973.

———. "The Potential for 'Absolutism' in Later Stuart England." *History* 69 (1984): 187–207.

———, ed. *Absolutism in Seventeenth Century Europe.* New York, 1990.

Morrill, John S. *Cheshire, 1630–60: County Government and Society.* Oxford, 1974.

———. *The Revolt of the Provinces.* London, 1976.

———. "The Sensible Revolution." In Jonathan Israel, ed., *The Anglo-Dutch Moment,* pp. 73–104. Cambridge, 1991.

———, ed. *Oliver Cromwell and the English Revolution.* London, 1990.

Mullett, M. A. "Conflict, Politics, and Elections in Lancaster, 1660–1688." *NH* 19 (1983): 61–86.

———. "'Deprived of Our Former Place': The Internal Politics of Bedford, 1660–1688." *Publications of the Bedfordshire Historical Record Society* 59 (1980): 1–42.

———. "'Men of Knowne Loyalty': The Politics of the Lancashire Borough of Clitheroe, 1660–89." *NH* 21 (1985): 108–36.

———. "The Politics of Liverpool, 1660–1688." *THSLC* 124 (1973): 31–56.

Norrey, P. J. "The Restoration Regime in Action: The Relationship Between Central and Local Government in Dorset, Somerset, and Wiltshire." *HJ* 31 (1988): 799–812.

Ogg, David. *England in the Reign of Charles II.* Oxford, 1956.

——— . *England in the Reigns of James II and William III.* Rev. ed. Oxford, 1955.

Ollard, Richard. *The Image of the King: Charles I and Charles II.* New York, 1979.

Packett, C. Neville. *A History and "A to Z" of Her Majesty's Lieutenancy of Counties.* N.p., 1972.

Page, William, and R. B. Pugh, eds. *Victoria County History of Leicestershire.* 5 vols. London, 1907–54.

Parker, Geoffrey. *The Military Revolution: Military Innovation and the Rise of the West, 1500–1800.* Cambridge, 1988.

Peck, Linda. *Court Patronage and Corruption in Early Stuart England.* Boston, 1990.

——— . " 'For a King Not to Be Bountiful Were a Fault': Perspectives on Court Patronage in Early Stuart England." *JBS* 25 (1986): 31–61.

Pincus, S. C. A. "Popery, Trade, and Universal Monarchy: The Ideological Context of the Outbreak of the Second Anglo-Dutch War." *EHR* 105 (1992): 1–29.

Powicke, Michael. *Military Obligation in Medieval England.* Oxford, 1962.

Quintrell, B. W. "The Making of Charles I's Book of Orders." *EHR* 95 (1980): 553–72.

——— . "The Practice and Problems of Recusant Disarming." *Recusant History* 17 (1984): 208–22.

Rannie, David. "Cromwell's Major Generals." *EHR* 10 (1895): 471–506.

Reay, Barry. "The Authorities and Early Restoration Quakerism." *Journal of Ecclesiastical History* 34 (1983): 69–84.

——— . *The Quakers and the English Revolution.* New York, 1985.

——— . "The Quakers, 1659, and the Restoration of the Monarchy." *History* 63 (1978): 193–213.

Reeve, L. J. *Charles I and the Road to Personal Rule.* Cambridge, 1989.

Reinmuth, Howard. "A Mysterious Dispute Demystified: Sir George Fletcher vs. the Howards." *HJ* 27 (1984): 289–308.

Richards, Judith. " 'His Nowe Majestie' and the English Monarchy: The Kingship of Charles I Before 1640." *Past and Present* 113 (1986): 70–96.

Roberts, Clayton. *The Growth of Responsible Government in Stuart England.* Cambridge, 1966.

——— . "Party and Patronage in Later Stuart England." In S. B. Baxter, ed., *England's Rise to Greatness,* pp. 185–212. Berkeley, 1983.

——— . *Schemes and Undertakings: A Study of English Politics in the Seventeenth Century.* Columbus, Ohio, 1985.

Roberts, Michael. *Essays in Swedish History.* Oxford, 1967.

Roberts, S. K. *Recovery and Restoration in an English County: Devon Local Administration 1642–1670.* Exeter, 1985.

Rogers, P. G. *The Dutch in the Medway.* London, 1970.

——— . *The Fifth Monarchy Men.* London, 1966.

Rosenheim, James. "Robert Doughty of Hanworth: A Restoration Magistrate." *Norfolk Archaeology* 38 (1983): 296–312.

——— . *The Townshends of Raynham.* Middletown, Conn., 1989.

Rowe, V. A. "The Influence of the Earls of Pembroke on Parliamentary Elections, 1625–1641." *EHR* 50 (1935): 242–56.

Russell, C. S. R. *The Causes of the English Civil War*. Oxford, 1990.

——— . *The Fall of the British Monarchies, 1637–42*. Oxford, 1991.

——— . "Monarchies, Wars, and Estates in England, France, and Spain, c. 1580–1640." *Legislative Studies Quarterly* 7 (1982): 205–19.

——— . *Parliaments and English Politics, 1621–29*. Oxford, 1979.

——— . "The Scottish Party in English Parliaments, 1640–42." *Historical Research* 66 (1993): 35–52.

——— , ed. *The Origins of the English Civil War*. London, 1973.

Sacks, David Harris. "The Corporate Towns and the English State: Bristol's 'Little Businesses,' 1625–41." *Past and Present* 110 (1986): 69–105.

Sacret, J. H. "The Restoration Government and Municipal Corporations." *EHR* 45 (1930): 232–59.

Saxton, E. B. "Fresh Light on the Liverpool Election of 1670." *THSLC* 93 (1941): 54–68.

Schochet, Gordon. *Patriarchalism in English Political Thought*. Oxford, 1975.

Schwoerer, Lois. "The Fittest Subject for a King's Quarrel: The Militia Controversy, 1641–42." *JBS* 11 (1971): 45–76.

——— . *No Standing Armies!* Baltimore, 1974.

Scott, Jonathan. *Algernon Sidney and the English Republic, 1623–77*. Cambridge, 1989.

——— . *Algernon Sidney and the Restoration Crisis, 1677–1683*. Cambridge, 1991.

——— . "England's Troubles: Exhuming the Popish Plot." In Tim Harris, Paul Seaward, and Mark Goldie, eds., *The Politics of Religion in Restoration England*, pp. 107–31. Oxford, 1990.

Seaver, Paul. *Wallington's World: A Puritan Artisan in Seventeenth Century London*. Stanford, 1985.

Seaward, Paul. *The Cavalier Parliament and the Reconstruction of the Old Regime, 1661–67*. Cambridge, 1988.

——— . *The Restoration, 1660–88*. New York, 1991.

Sharpe, Kevin. "Crown, Parliament, and Locality: Government and Communication in Early Stuart England." *EHR* 101 (1986): 321–50.

——— . *The Personal Rule of Charles I*. New Haven, 1992.

——— , ed. *Faction and Parliament*. Oxford, 1978.

Slack, Paul. "Books of Orders: The Making of English Social Policy, 1577–1631." *TRHS* 5th ser., 30 (1980): 1–22.

——— . *The Impact of the Plague in Early Modern England*. London, 1985.

Smith, A. Hassell. *County and Court: Government and Politics in Norfolk, 1558–1603*. Oxford, 1974.

——— . "Militia Rates and Militia Statutes, 1558–1663." In Peter Clark, A. G. R. Smith, and Nicholas Tyacke, eds., *The English Commonwealth, 1547–1640: Essays in Politics and Society*, pp. 93–110. New York, 1979.

Sommerville, J. P. *Politics and Ideology in England, 1603–1640*. London, 1986.

Speck, W. A. *Reluctant Revolutionaries: Englishmen and the Revolution of 1688*. Oxford, 1989.

Spufford, Margaret. "Dissenting Churches in Cambridgeshire from 1660–1705." *Proceedings of the Cambridgeshire Antiquarian Society* 61 (1908): 67–95.

Spurr, John. "Latitudinarianism and the Restoration Church." *HJ* 31 (1988): 21–52.

———. "Schism and the Restoration Church." *Journal of Ecclesiastical History* 41 (1990): 408–24.

Stater, Victor. "Continuity and Change in English Provincial Politics: Robert Paston in Norfolk, 1676–1682." *Albion* 25 (1993): 194–216.

———. "The Lord Lieutenancy on the Eve of the Civil Wars: The Impressment of George Plowright." *HJ* 29 (1986): 279–96.

———. "Reconstructing the Restoration." *JBS* 29 (1990): 393–401.

———. "War and the Structure of Politics: Lieutenancy and the Campaign of 1628." in Mark Fissel, ed., *War and Government in Britain, 1598–1650*, pp. 87–109. Manchester, 1991.

Stearns, S. J. "Conscription and English Society in the 1620s." *JBS* 11 (1972): 1–23.

Stewart, Richard. "Arms Accountability in the Early Stuart Militia." *BIHR* 57 (1984): 113–17.

Stone, Lawrence. *The Crisis of the Aristocracy*. Oxford, 1965.

———. "The Electoral Influence of the Second Earl of Salisbury, 1614–68." *EHR* 71 (1956): 384–400.

———. *Family and Fortune: Studies in Aristocratic Finance in the Sixteenth and Seventeenth Centuries*. Oxford, 1973.

Sunderland, F. H. *Marmaduke Lord Langdale and Some Events of His Time*. London, 1926.

Swinton, Henry. *The History and Antiquities of Yarmouth*. Norwich, 1772.

Tanner, J. R. *Samuel Pepys and the Royal Navy*. Cambridge, 1928.

Tedder, Arthur W. *The Navy of the Restoration*. Cambridge, 1916.

Thirsk, Joan, ed. *Chapters from the Agrarian History of England and Wales, 1500–1750*. 5 vols. Cambridge, 1990.

Thompson, I. A. A. *War and Government in Hapsburg Spain*. London, 1976.

Thomson, Gladys Scott. "The Bishops of Durham and the Office of Lord Lieutenant in the Seventeenth Century." *EHR* 40 (1925): 351–74.

———. *The Lords Lieutenants in the Sixteenth Century*. London, 1923.

———. "The Origins and Growth of the Office of Deputy Lieutenant." *TRHS* 4th ser., 5 (1922): 150–66.

Tomlinson, Howard. "Financial and Administrative Developments in England, 1660–88." In J. R. Jones, *The Restored Monarchy*, pp. 94–117. London, 1979.

Underdown, David. *Pride's Purge: Politics in the Puritan Revolution*. Oxford, 1971.

———. *Revel, Riot, and Rebellion: Popular Politics and Culture in England, 1603–1660*. Oxford, 1985.

———. *Royalist Conspiracy in England*. New Haven, 1960.

Watts, Michael. *The Dissenters: From the Restoration to the French Revolution*. Oxford, 1978.

Walker, James. "The Yorkshire Plot, 1663." *Yorkshire Archaeological Journal* 31 (1934): 348–59.

Walter, John. "Grain Riots and Popular Attitudes to the Law: Maldon and the Crisis of 1629." In John Brewer and John Styles, eds., *An Ungovernable People: The English and Their Law in the Seventeenth and Eighteenth Centuries*, pp. 47–84. New Brunswick, N.J., 1980.

Western, J. R. *The English Militia in the Eighteenth Century*. London, 1965.

————. *Monarchy and Revolution: The English State in the 1680s*. London, 1972.

Weston, Corinne, and Janelle Greenberg. *Subjects and Sovereigns: The Grand Controversy over Legal Sovereignty in Stuart England*. Cambridge, 1981.

Wigfield, W. M. *Recusancy and Nonconformity in Bedfordshire*. Publications of the Bedfordshire Record Society 20 (Bedford, 1938).

Wilkinson, D. J. "The Commission of the Peace in Lancashire, 1603–1642." *THSLC* 132 (1983): 41–66.

Wilson, Charles. *Profit and Power: A Study of England and the Anglo-Dutch Wars*. London, 1957.

Wolf, Erich R. "Kinship, Friendship, and Patron-Client Relationships in Complex Societies." In Michael Banton, ed., *The Social Anthropology of Complex Societies*, pp. 1–22. New York, 1966.

Woolrych, Austin. *Commonwealth to Protectorate*. Oxford, 1987.

————. "The Cromwellian Protectorate: A Military Dictatorship?" *History* 75 (1990): 207–31.

Zagorin, Perez. *The Court and the Country*. New York, 1970.

Theses and Dissertations

Beats, L. "Government and Politics in Derbyshire, 1640–60." Ph.D. dissertation, Sheffield University, 1978.

Carter, D. P. "The Lancashire Lieutenancy, 1660–88." M.Litt. thesis, Oxford University, 1981.

Challinor, P. J. "The Structure of Politics in Cheshire, 1660–1715." Ph.D. dissertation, Wolverhampton Polytechnic, 1983.

Cust, Richard. "The Forced Loan and English Politics, 1626–28." Ph.D. dissertation, University of London, 1983.

Durston, C. G. "Berkshire and Its County Gentry, 1625–49." Ph.D. dissertation, Reading University, 1970.

Fielding, A. J. "Conformists, Puritans, and the Church Courts: The Diocese of Peterborough, 1603–42." Ph.D. dissertation, Birmingham University, 1989.

Fulkerson, Stephen V. "The English Landed Gentry, 1660–1700." Ph.D. dissertation, University of Chicago, 1952.

Goring, J. J. "The Military Obligations of the English People." Ph.D. dissertation, University of London, 1955.

Hebb, David. "The English Government and the Problem of Piracy, 1616–1642." Ph.D. dissertation, University of London, 1985.

Hodges, Vivienne. "The Electoral Influence of the English Aristocracy, 1604–41." Ph.D. dissertation, Columbia University, 1977.

Hughes, Ann. "Politics, Society, and Civil War in Warwickshire, 1628–50." Ph.D. dissertation, Liverpool University, 1980.

Johnson, W. G. "Postrestoration Nonconformity and Plotting, 1660–75." M. A. thesis, Manchester University, 1967.

Norrey, P. J. "The Relationship Between Central Government and Local Government in Dorset, Somerset, and Wiltshire, 1660–1688." Ph.D. dissertation, Bristol University, 1988.

O'Farrell, Brian. "Politician, Patron, Poet: William Herbert, Third Earl of Pembroke, 1580–1630." Ph.D. dissertation, University of California at Los Angeles, 1966.

Phillips, C. B. "The Gentry of Cumberland and Westmorland, 1600–65." Ph.D. dissertation, University of Lancaster, 1974.

Pickavance, R. G. "The English Boroughs and the King's Government." D.Phil. dissertation, Oxford University, 1976.

Quintrell, B. W. "The Government of the County of Essex, 1603–42." Ph.D. dissertation, London University, 1965.

Reay, B. G. "Early Quaker Activity and Reactions To It, 1652–1664." D.Phil. dissertation, Oxford University, 1979.

Silcock, R. H. "County Government in Worcestershire, 1603–60." Ph.D. dissertation, University of London, 1974.

Stater, Victor. "The Lord Lieutenancy in Stuart England." Ph.D. dissertation, University of Chicago, 1988.

INDEX

Acland, Hugh, 116
Act of Uniformity, 101, 105, 107
Albemarle, duke of (Christopher Monck),
    140–42, 144, 146–47, 157–58
Anderson, Steven, 84–85
Arundel, earl of (Thomas Howard), 13, 17,
    19, 26, 28, 48, 84
Arundel, Sussex, 129
Arundell of Wardour family, 14–15
Astley, Sir Jacob, 67
Aston, Walter, third lord, 174

Bagot, Sir Edward, 83–84, 105
Bakewell, Derbyshire, 93
Bankes, John, 62
Barnham, Robert, 79
Bath, 127, 159
Batten, Sir William, 120
Bedford, 154–56
Bedford, earl of (William Russell), 76
Bedfordshire, 12, 13, 75, 104, 168, 169–
    70, 173; press in, 43–44; deputy
    lieutenants of, 84
Belasyse, Lord (Thomas Fauconberg),
    73–74, 90–91, 107, 120
Bentham, John, 114
Berkshire, 12, 16, 113, 170–71
Berry, James, 69
Bertie, James, Lord Norreys, first lord
    Abingdon, 122–24, 137, 146, 150, 167
Berwick, 154
Berwick, duke of (James Fitzjames), 167
Bigg, John, 170

Billeting, 44–45, 56–57, 112
Bishop's Wars, 48–60
Blundell, Sir George, 41, 44
Bradshaigh, Sir Roger, 80–81
Bramston, Sir John, 81, 167–68, 175
Brereton, William, second lord, 128
Bridgewater, earl of (John Egerton), 143
Bristol, 146, 154, 159, 178
Brooke, Lord (Fulke Greville), 36
Brooke, Lord (Robert Greville), 73, 86–
    87, 90–91, 100, 114–15, 117,
    129–30
Browne, Sir Richard, 99, 103–4
Bruce, Thomas, first earl of Ailesbury, 79,
    91, 143–44, 149, 154–56, 168–73
Buckingham, 155
Buckingham, first duke of (George
    Villiers), 14
Buckingham, second duke of (George
    Villiers), 107, 132
Buckinghamshire, 62, 104, 143, 172, 179
Burlington, first earl of (Richard
    Boyle), 118
Butler, Sir Nicholas, 173

Calthorpe, Sir Christopher, 137
Cambridgeshire, 59, 119, 143
Campden, Viscount (Baptist Noel), 74
Canterbury, 144, 149
Canvey Island, Essex, 118
Capel, Arthur, earl of Essex, 72, 75,
    91, 143

Carlisle, earl of (Charles Howard), 73, 109, 125, 134, 145

Carr, Sir Robert, 135–36

Catelyn, Sir Neville, 137, 170

Cavendish family, 13, 15

Cecil, John, fourth earl of Exeter, 76

Cecil, Thomas, first earl of Exeter, 24, 85

Cecil family, earls of Exeter, 76

Cecil family, earls of Salisbury, 14

Channel Islands, 118

Chapman, Henry, 127

Charles II: and dissenters, 100, 108, 187; and Second Dutch War, 115; and persecution, 124–26; and Exclusion, 138–39; and loyal addresses, 148; and Royalist Anglicans, 161–62, 164–65, 187–88

Cheshire, 13, 77, 87, 90, 98–101, 107, 109, 128–29, 146, 151–52, 176; deputy lieutenants in, 20–21, trained bands in, 24; Bishop's Wars in, 50, 58–59

Chester, 26, 82, 100, 128, 142

Cholmondeley, Sir Hugh, 162

Clarges, Sir Thomas, 162

Cleveland, earl of (Thomas Wentworth), 12, 75, 84

Coat and conduct money, 43–44, 53–54, 56–57

Coke, Robert, 132

Colepepper, Thomas, 83–84, 102

Colledge, Stephen, 122–24

Commissions of Array, 59–60, 63–64, 68

Compton, William, first earl of Northhampton, 16

Conventicle Act, 101, 105–6, 111

Conway, Edward, viscount, 12, 15–16, 24, 74

Cooper, Sir Anthony Ashley, earl of Shaftesbury, 6, 77, 136, 138–41

Cornwall, 97, 115–16, 118, 120, 126, 153, 157

Corporation Act, 106, 127–29, 130, 142

Coventry, 105–6, 152

Cowell, William, 103

Craven family, 14–15

Cromwell, Oliver, 69, 98

Cullen, Stephen, 92

Cumberland, 51, 102, 109, 115, 132–34, 145, 166–67, 169, 179

Cumberland, earl of (Henry Clifford), 62

Curwen, Sir Patricius, 51

Curzon, Sir John, 130

Deputy lieutenants: origins of office, 19; appointment, 19, 21–22, 78–86, 141–45, 171–72, 175–76, 184; wealth, 20, 84–85; growing numbers of, 21, 82–83, 117. *See also* Lieutenancy; Lords lieutenant

Derby, earl of (Charles Stanley), 77–81, 87, 91, 100, 107, 115–16, 125–29, 131–32

Derby, ninth earl of (William Stanley), 142, 146, 151–52, 175–76

Derby, sixth earl of (William Stanley), 26, 50

Derbyshire, 13, 50, 93, 98–99, 104

De Ruyter, Michael, 117–19

Derwentdale Plot, 107–8

de Vere, Aubrey, earl of Oxford, 76, 115, 118, 166, 175

Devonshire, 23, 35, 45–46, 55, 83, 115, 126, 133, 141–42, 153, 158, 175, 177

Devonshire, third earl of (William Cavendish), 129

Dissenters, 93, 96–111, 149, 158–60, 167, 172–73, 175, 187

Dolman, Thomas, 119–20

Dorset, 36, 42–44, 57, 115, 129, 150, 158, 176

Dorset, earl of (Richard Sackville), 73, 150, 154

Dover Castle, 118

Duncombe, Sir John, 84–85

Durham, 35, 62

Durham, bishops of, 13, 105, 107, 175

Ellis, Sir William, 135–36

Elmes, William, 55–56

Essex, 12–13, 29, 38–39, 100, 115, 118, 168, 175; billets in, 45; Bishop's War in, 57; Exclusion in, 139–40, 146–47

Exact militia, 33, 48

Exclusion, 3–4, 111, 122–25, 136–56, 188–89

Exeter, 178

Exeter, second earl of (William Cecil), 26–27, 35, 55, 85

Falkland, Viscount (Henry Carey), 77, 82, 91, 100

Falmouth, Cornwall, 120
Fane, Mildmay, earl of Westmorland, 76, 84, 106
Fane, Sir George, 127–28
Fauconberg, Thomas. *See* Belasyse, Lord
Feversham, earl of (Louis de Duras), 175
Fifth Monarchists, 96, 98–100
Finch, Heneage, 135
Fitzharding, third viscount (Maurice Berkeley), 173
Five Mile Act, 101, 111
Fletcher, Sir George, 134, 145
Flintshire, 99
Foley, Thomas, 145–46
Forced loan, 16–17, 37–38
Fox, George, 100
Friend, John, 56

Gainsborough, earl of (Edward Noel), 167
Glamorganshire, 75
Gleane, Sir Peter, 133
Gloucester, 103–6
Gloucestershire, 93, 100–101, 115–16, 146, 159
Goodricke, Sir Henry, 180
Gostwick, Sir William, 170
Gough, Richard, 89
Gower, Sir Thomas, 105, 107
Grantham, Lincolnshire, 135–36
Granville, John, earl of Bath, 73, 97, 118, 126, 133, 153, 157, 168, 176–78, 181
Grey, John, 134–35
Grey family, 13, 15
Grey of Groby, Lord, 21–22
Grimston, Sir Harbottle, 143

Hampshire, 12, 74, 101, 108, 115, 120, 157, 167; trained bands in, 24; press in, 41–42; billets in, 45; Bishop's War in, 57
Harbord, William, 151
Hare, Sir John, 26
Hare, Sir Ralph, 67
Harley, Sir Edward, 145
Hartopp, Sir John, 137
Harvey, Sir Eliah, 140
Harwich, Essex, 38, 119–20, 157
Haselrig, Sir Arthur, 61
Hastings, Henry, fifth earl of Huntington, 8–11, 21–22

Hatton, Charles, 177–78
Herbert, Edward, 97–98
Herbert, John, 93, 116
Herbert, Lord, marquis Worcester, duke of Beaufort (Henry Somerset), 75, 133, 143–44, 146, 153–54, 166–68, 178
Herefordshire, 21, 166
Hertford, Marquis, duke of Somerset (William Seymour), 14, 62, 72–73, 76
Hertfordshire, 58, 75, 91, 117, 143
Hobart, Sir John, 133, 137, 150
Holland, earl of (Henry Rich), 16, 44, 62
Holland, Sir John, 67, 133, 170
Hope, Ralph, 110
Hope, Robert, 97
Hotham, Sir John, 56
Houghton, Sir Richard, 80
Howard, Theophilus, earl of Suffolk, 16, 59
Howard, Thomas, earl of Berkshire, 73
Howard family, 15
Hubbard, Samuel, 41
Huntingdonshire, 22, 168, 172
Hyde, Edward, earl of Clarendon, 74–78, 108, 118, 131

Impressment, 39–43, 48–58, 112–13
Irby, Sir Anthony, 53
Ireland, Sir Gilbert, 80
Isham, Sir Justinian, 101–2
Isle of Wight, 118

James I: on nobility, 12; appointment of deputy lieutenants, 19
James II: and Roman Catholics, 127, 161–91 passim; and Exclusion, 136–46 passim; and Monmouth's rebellion, 159; and Royalist Anglicans, 162, 172, 190–91; and militia, 162–63; and the bench, 164–65; and the three questions, 168
Jeffreys, George, lord, 164, 172
Jenkins, Sir Leoline, 124
Jermyn, Sir Thomas, 14–15

Kemp, Sir Robert, 133
Kent, 58, 63, 77, 101–2, 107, 115, 118, 143, 146–47, 149, 170; deputy lieutenants in, 82–83
Kidderminster, 129
King, William, 103

Kirkby, Colonel Richard, 80–81
Knatchbull, Sir John, 170

Lancashire, 13, 77, 79, 80–81, 90, 93,
    115–16, 120, 128, 175; deputy
    lieutenants in, 20, 84; Bishop's Wars in,
    49–50
Lancaster, 128
Landguard Fort, 39, 112, 118–20
Lane, John, 85
Langdale, Marmaduke, lord, 74, 77
Leicester, 41
Leicestershire, 8–11, 13, 99, 100, 114,
    134–35, 137, 144, 151, 157, 166
Leigh, Sir Thomas, 130
Lestrange, Hamon, 19
Lichfield, 91, 114
Lichfield, earl of (Edward Henry Lee), 167
Lieutenancy: origins of, 2, 11–12;
    patronage, 18–19, 22–24, 86–87, 152–
    53; and elections, 22, 45–47, 55–56,
    68–69, 125–26, 129–37, 139–40, 156–
    57, 165–66, 169; and JPs, 22, 72,
    133–34, 138–41, 163–64; and
    procurement, 24; and grain trade, 28;
    and Privy Council, 27, 30, 42, 59; and
    local defense, 38–39, 93, 112–21; and
    royal prerogative, 46–48, 56, 59, 72;
    authority of, 59; militia defaulters, 67–
    68, 88, 92–94; and corporate boroughs,
    80, 142, 153–56; and taxes, 89, 92–93,
    113–14; and dissent, 98–111 passim; and
    spies, 103, 107; and loyal addresses,
    146–49; and arms market, 152–53; and
    Monmouth's Rising, 158–60; and purges
    of 1687, 169–73. See also Deputy
    lieutenants; Lords lieutenant
Lincolnshire, 52–53, 57, 76, 83, 87, 93,
    99, 104, 135–36, 141, 151–52, 168,
    171, 174
Lindsey, first earl of (Robert Bertie),
    16–18, 52, 57
Lindsey, second earl of (Montagu Bertie),
    76, 133, 135–36, 139, 151, 152–53, 159,
    168, 176, 181
Littleton, Sir Edward, 130
Liverpool, 131–32
Lloyd, Sir Evan, 82
London, Great Fire of, 109–11, 117
Lords lieutenant: appointment of, 12–13,
    16–17, 60–64, 71–78, 141–42, 166–
    68, 175, 182, 184; and court office, 15;
    military service of, 15–16, 72–73; as
    mediators, 26–28. See also Lieutenancy
Loughborough, Lord (Henry Hastings), 74
Lovelace, John, lord, 74, 79, 113, 129
Ludlow, Edmund, 70, 107
Luke, Sir Samuel, 79
Luttrell, Francis, 143
Lynn, Norfolk, 113

Major Generals, 69–70
Malden, Essex, 28
Malmesbury, 153
Manchester, earl of (Edward Montagu), 73
Manchester, earl of (Robert Montagu), 140,
    142–43
Manners, Francis, sixth earl of Rutland,
    17–18
Markham, Sir Robert, 136
Martindale, Adam, 100
Mason, Sir Robert, 98
Massingberd, Sir Drayner, 151, 159
Maynard, William, lord, 59, 73
Middlesex, 16, 24, 41, 24, 58, 73,
    99–100, 103, 123–24
Middleton, Sir Thomas, 140
Militia. See Deputy lieutenants;
    Lieutenancy; Musters; Second
    Dutch War
Militia Acts, 45–47, 71–72, 78, 80,
    86–93, 117
Militia Ordinance, 61–63
Milward, John, 93, 129–30
Molyneux, Caryll, viscount, 131, 167, 175
Monck, George, duke of Albemarle, 73,
    76, 86
Monmouth, duke of (James Scott), 6, 123,
    131, 140, 149–50, 152, 158–60. See also
    Monmouth's Rising
Monmouthshire, 75, 87
Monmouth's Rising, 158–60, 162–63
Montagu, fourth viscount (Francis
    Browne), 167, 172
Mordaunt, John, viscount, 74
Morley, Benjamin, 101–2
Musgrave, Sir Christopher, 90
Musgrave, Sir Philip, 102, 133–34
Musters, 10–12, 25, 68, 117, 174–76. See

also Deputy lieutenants; Lieutenancy;
Militia Acts; Second Dutch War

Nanfan, Bridges, 145–46
Newcastle, first duke of (William
Cavendish), 16–17, 24, 71–73, 99, 101,
114, 129
Newcastle, second duke of (Henry
Cavendish), 136–37, 141, 149, 153–55,
175, 179–81
Newport, Francis, lord, 74, 87, 166
Norfolk, 89, 91–93, 102, 109, 115, 117,
142, 150, 159, 170, 174–78; deputy
lieutenants in, 20–21, 66–68, 84;
trained bands in, 23; Exclusion in, 126,
146–48; elections in, 132–34, 137–38,
140, 146. *See also* Norwich
Norfolk, duke of (Henry Howard),
168–70, 181
Northampton, 105–6, 115–16, 144, 155
Northampton, fourth earl of (George
Compton), 169
Northampton, third earl of (James
Compton), 106, 110–11
Northamptonshire, 26–28, 76, 90, 99,
101–2, 104, 106, 144, 150–51, 171;
privy seal loan in, 35–36; election of
1640 in, 55–56; deputy lieutenants of,
84–85
Northhampton, first earl of. *See* Compton,
William
Northumberland, 99, 109, 136–37,
148–49, 153
Northumberland, earl of (Algernon Percy),
58, 62, 72–73, 129
Norton, Thomas, 110
Norwich, 48, 66–68, 92, 103, 109, 153,
155, 176–77; elections in, 138, 140,
142. *See also* Norfolk
Norwich, Sir Roger, 151
Nottingham, 129, 155
Nottinghamshire, 69, 73, 114, 136,
148–49, 153

Oldham, Hampshire, 44
Ormond, first duke of (James Butler),
90–91, 113, 115, 131, 136, 141
Osborne, Sir Thomas, earl of Danby, duke
of Leeds, 132–38, 179–81, 183–84, 191
Oxfordshire, 12, 29, 76–77, 82, 91, 100,

108, 113, 150, 167; Exclusion in,
122–24, 137, 146, 179

Packering, Sir Henry, 110–11
Paget, William, lord, 62–63
Parliament: of 1628, 45–47, 185; Short,
55–56; Long, 59–65; Commons
committee on lieutenancy, 1640, 60;
Convention, 95, 129; Cavalier, 129–33;
Exclusion, 138–39, 140–42; of 1685,
161–63, 165; proposed Parliament of
1688, 172–74. *See also* Militia Acts;
Militia Ordinance
Pembroke, earl of (Philip Herbert),
141–42, 154, 159, 166
Pendennis, Cornwall, 116
Penn, William, 172
Pepys, Samuel, 2, 99, 117–18, 120, 157
Peterborough, earl of (Henry Mordaunt),
140, 144, 155, 167, 173
Petre, Thomas, lord, 167, 175
Phelips, Sir Robert, 45–47
Popish Plot, 122–25, 136. *See also* Roman
Catholics
Portsmouth, Hampshire, 120
Powis, marquis of (William Herbert), 167
Presbyterians, 74–75, 79–82, 86, 100,
104–7, 181. *See also* Conventicle Act;
Dissenters
Preston, Lancashire, 81, 115, 128
Preston, Viscount (Richard Graham),
166–67, 169
Prettyman, Sir John, 85, 134
Privy Council: and militia defaulters, 48,
88. *See also* Lieutenancy; Militia Act
Privy Seal loan, 34–37
Pym, John, 56

Quakers, 92, 96, 100–101, 103–4, 106,
149, 163. *See also* Conventicle Act;
Dissenters

Reading, Berkshire, 129, 158
Reresby, Sir John, 97, 163, 179–80
Reynolds, John, 128
Richardson, Thomas, lord, 67
Rich family, 15
Richmond, duke of (Charles Stuart), 120
Rigby, Alexander, 80
Riot, 9–10, 28

Rochester, earl of (Laurence Hyde), 168
Roman Catholics, 96, 108–11, 122–23, 133, 145, 161–75. *See also* Dissenters; Popish Plot
Roos, Lord, earl of Rutland (John Manners), 103, 135, 137, 141, 144, 150–51, 157, 166
Royalist Anglicanism, 4–6, 111, 125–26, 161–64, 172, 174, 177, 187–91
Rutland, 55, 167
Rutland, earl of (John Manners), 114, 134–35
Rye House Plot, 111, 142, 150–52. *See also* Dissenters; Presbyterians

Salisbury, second earl of (William Cecil), 58
Sandwich, earl of (Edward Montagu), 73, 86
Savile, Thomas, viscount, 13–14, 17
Say, Viscount (William Fiennes), 62
Scarborough, Yorkshire, 120
Scott, Robert, 58
Scrope, Emmanuel, lord, earl of Sunderland, 35
Second Dutch War, 112–21. *See also* Militia
Seymour, Edward, 162
Ship money, 33
Shropshire, 21, 74, 166
Somerset, 17, 90–91, 102–3, 129, 143, 149, 152, 158, 166–67, 170, 173; deputy lieutenants in, 21; trained bands in, 22–23
Sondes, Sir George, 79
Spencer, Sir John, 21–22
Stafford, 91
Staffordshire, 73, 86, 96, 99–100, 105, 114–15, 140, 171, 174; deputy lieutenants in, 83–85
Stamford, Lincolnshire, 135
Stanley, William, 131–32
Stanley family, 13
Stonehouse, Sir John, 170
Strafford, earl of (Thomas Wentworth), 7
Strange, Lord (James Stanley), 57, 62
Strode, Edward, 173
Suffolk, 13–14, 28, 93, 101, 112–13, 115, 117, 119–20, 143; impressment in, 42; Bishop's War in, 58–59
Suffolk, earl of (James Howard), 73, 119, 143

Sunderland, earl of (Robert Spencer), 164, 166, 169
Surrey, 28, 99–100, 117
Sussex, 28, 39, 50, 73, 90, 101, 107, 150, 153–54, 171
Sussex, earl of (Henry Radcliffe), 13, 29

Tamworth, Staffordshire, 129
Taylor, Simon, 132
Temple, Sir Richard, 163
Test Act, 163, 168–71. *See also* Roman Catholics
Teynham, Lord (Christopher Roper), 170, 175
Thanet, earl of (Thomas Tufton), 166
Thelwall, Anthony, 50
Thetford, Norfolk, 92, 153
Thirty Years War, 16, 30. *See also* Exact militia; Musters
Thynne, Thomas, 141, 143
Titus, Silius, 143, 172
Tiverton, 142–43
Townshend, Henry, 78
Townshend, Horatio, lord, 66–68, 73, 91, 109, 113, 117, 132
Trafford, Sir Cecil, 20–21

Vane, Henry, 62
Venner, Thomas, 98–100. *See also* Dissenters; Fifth Monarchists
Verney, Sir Ralph, 79

Waldegrave, Henry, lord, 167
Wallingford, Berkshire, 127
Wallingford, Lord, earl of Banbury (William Knollys), 12, 14, 29
Wallington, Nehemiah, 58
Warwick, 109–10
Warwick, earl of (Robert Rich), 12, 28, 38–39, 62, 119
Warwickshire, 20, 58, 106, 109–10, 150
Westmorland, 90, 109, 134, 166–67, 169
Whalley, Edward, 69
Whitby, Yorkshire, 120
White, John, 178
William of Orange, 174–82
Wiltshire, 54, 76–77, 87, 90, 97–98, 100, 103, 129, 149, 133–34, 166
Wimbledon, Viscount (Edward Cecil), 16, 73

Winchester, 157

Winchilsea, earl of (Heneage Finch), 77, 79, 115, 118, 142–44, 146–47

Windsor, Thomas, 74, 145–46, 166

Wingfield, John, 91

Woodbridge, Suffolk, 28

Woodford, Robert, 53

Worcester, earl of (Edward Somerset), 12, 17

Worcestershire, 20, 74, 145–46

Wrottesley, Sir Walter, 85

Wymondham, Norfolk, 102

Yarmouth, earl of (Sir Robert Paston), 126, 134, 137–38, 142, 147–48, 153, 155

Yarmouth, Norfolk, 104, 117, 150

York, 132, 179–81

Yorkshire, 13, 17, 74, 90–91, 100, 105, 107, 109, 115, 118–19, 120, 138, 162, 174–75, 179–81